Contents

As you work toward achieving that **5** on your AP United States History exam, here are five essentials that you **MUST** know above everything else:

1 **Major periods in American history.** You will *not* be asked the dates of specific events in the American history. But you should know the defining features, key events, and years of the major periods—such as the Critical Period, Jacksonian Era, the Progressive Era, and the Cold War. If you can grasp the sequence and significance of the major periods in American history and can identify key events in each, you will have a firm grasp of the chronological unfolding of American history.

2 **Reading documents.** Documents are the building blocks of history and are central to the AP exam. The document-based question (DBQ) is a hugely important indicator of your success on the exam. In the weeks leading up to the test, practice at least a few complete DBQ responses. Focus on how the documents relate to the question and on how the documents often relate to one another. Your score on the DBQ will be based on the thoroughness of your response. Remember that historical documents contain a point of view. You should be able to read a diary entry, a newspaper article, or a speech, and ascertain the point of view and intent of the author.

3 **Growth and conflict in American history.** The rapid growth of the United States—territorially, economically, and demographically—is unprecedented in world history. On the one hand, this growth decimated Native American cultures; on the other, the nation has provided a haven for immigrants. The territorial growth of the country—inspired by the spirit of "manifest destiny"—intensified the debate over slavery in the antebellum period. The series of compromises over expansion eventually unraveled and helped bring about the Civil War. The economic and territorial growth of the United States continued in the period following the Spanish-American War, as the United States joined the other imperialist powers of the world. Be familiar with the causes of American expansion as well as its profound impact.

4 **The changing nature of the American experiment in democracy.** The United States had made major contributions to modern representative government. However, recognize that democracy did not emerge fully formed with the birth of the nation. Americans have struggled over its meaning throughout history. Abigail Adams encouraged her husband, John, to "remember the ladies" at the time of the creation of the United States. The civil rights movement struggled to fully include African Americans in the democratic system. These conflicts over the meaning of democracy are crucial to understanding the evolution of the United States.

5 **The dynamic nature of history.** Traditional historians saw history as unidirectional—emanating from the minds and priorities of the elites in society. More recently, historians have seen events as part of a more dynamic process. Social and cultural historians have explored "history from below." As you study, look for such connections and interactions. For instance, while it is important to remember that President Lyndon Johnson endorsed and pushed for passage of the 1964 Civil Rights Act, you should be able to connect that with the growth of the grassroots civil rights movement, with the violent backlash against the movement, with shifts within the major political parties, and with the dynamics of the Cold War. Historical events do not occur in isolation of one another. Therefore memorizing discreet events in American history is not sufficient for success on the AP exam.

Preface: The Basics

Mastering the AP United States History exam requires more than merely memorizing facts. You have to think through problems, engage in debates, organize your thinking, develop your communication skills, and take thoughtful stands on important issues.

USING THIS BOOK TO HELP YOU PREPARE FOR THE EXAM

Your textbook has, hopefully, given you a detailed understanding of American history. In the pages that follow, by contrast, we have distilled that unwieldy narrative down to those elements of American history that appear repeatedly on the AP exam. As you take practice exams, you will get a sense of the topics that the College Board often references in both multiple-choice and free-response questions. This book focuses on topics that are most likely to appear on an actual AP exam. In addition, it is designed to help you make connections over time and to think through complex historical problems.

The first two chapters describe the multiple-choice section and the free-response (or essay) section of the exam. These chapters offer strategies and approaches for achieving high scores on the exam. The book then provides a chronological summary of American history. Each chapter roughly corresponds to the breakdown of chapters in most Advanced Placement American history textbooks. Each chapter contains a timeline of important events and practice multiple-choice and free-response questions.

Each of the content chapters concludes with a "Subject to Debate" section. These sections are designed to call your attention to important debates in regard to historical interpretation. Often, essays can be strengthened by a discussion of how historians have addressed a question. For example, the exam might ask, "To what degree was Reconstruction successful in improving conditions for African Americans?" Although you should discuss your view of the period, you should also discuss the nature of the historical debate over interpretations of the period. You might write, "Historians have held dramatically different views of the period. Many Southern historians in the late nineteenth and early twentieth century looked at the Reconstruction period as a bitter failure. They were dismissive of any attempts to extend basic rights to African Americans. However, since the Civil Rights era of the 1950s and 1960s, historians have reexamined the record of the period and acknowledged its successes as well as shortcomings." In this way, you're recognizing the contentious nature of historical interpretation. You should be prepared not only to recognize these ongoing debates about the past but also to participate in them.

Finally, the book contains two practice exams. You should time yourself as you take these exams so that you'll get used to the pacing required for the actual Advanced Placement exam. The exams are followed by explanations to the multiple-choice questions. Please consult these explanations if the material in the question is not clear to you.

TAKING THE EXAM

As the test date approaches, review, review, and review some more. Get a good night's rest before you take the exam, because it is truly an endurance test. Time would be better spent getting a good rest than cramming. You need to be sharp for the exam. When the exam begins, remain calm and focused. Pace yourself and read each question carefully and calmly. Think clearly as you move through the questions. Then wait for an e-mail from the College Board with your score.

The Multiple-Choice Section

CHAPTER 1

The first part of the exam consists of 80 multiple-choice questions. You will have 55 minutes to complete this part of the exam. About 20 percent of the exam will deal with the period up to the ratification of the Constitution (1789). This includes exploration, the colonial period, the American Revolution, and the Articles of Confederation period. These questions tend to be weighted more heavily toward the latter part of the period. There could be a couple of questions on non-English exploration and colonization, but expect more questions on the English phase of colonization and on the formation of the United States. Approximately 65 percent of the questions cover the period 1790 to 1914, and the remaining 35 percent cover the period from 1915 to the present. A couple of multiple-choice questions could be on the period since 1980. It takes several years for questions to be written, reviewed, and approved, so do not expect questions on current events to appear on the May exam.

About 40 percent of the questions deal with cultural and social developments in United States. These topics can range from the "Lowell girls" to the Harlem Renaissance, from immigration patterns in colonial America to the Chinese Exclusion Act, from literature of the "American Renaissance" to "white flight" in the 1960s and 1970s. Note that this reflects a change both in the AP exam and in the field of history. Both have put more emphasis on social and cultural history in recent decades. The historical field used to focus on political and diplomatic developments; social history was not taken seriously. However, since the 1960s, historians have devoted more energy to social and cultural history, and this is reflected in the AP exam.

In the rest of the exam, 35 percent of the questions cover political behavior and institutions as well as issues of public policy, 15 percent cover diplomacy and international relations, and 10 percent cover economic development. Questions on political history can be on government programs, laws, actions and initiatives, political parties, and voter behavior. These topics can include a wide array of topics, such as Alexander Hamilton's move to create a national bank, the differences between the Whigs and the Democrats in the 1840s, shifts in voting patterns among African Americans in the 1930s, and the rise of Senator Joseph McCarthy in the 1950s. Questions on diplomacy and international relations include relations with the British during the colonial period and the American Revolution, the various wars and treaties America has participated in, and changes in American foreign policy. The final 10 percent are on economic developments. Topics covered in these questions can include the role of the various national banks, the causes of the Great Depression, or "stagflation" in the 1970s.

Of course, many multiple-choice questions cover more than one area. Slavery, for instance, is both an economic institution as well as a social system. Further, the debates about slavery become political question. So likewise, a question on the populists in the 1890s touches on three areas: social developments, political history, and economic development.

It would be unlikely to find questions on the exam of a purely military nature. You will probably not be asked, for example, about specific battlefield strategies. This is not to say to you can ignore America's wars when studying for the exam. Certainly the causes and impacts of wars are crucial, as are home front issues. Comparative strengths and weaknesses are certainly fair game. You should also be familiar with turning points in wars—moments when the fortunes of the two sides changed (such as the Battle of Saratoga in the American Revolution). The test can also include broad strategies of combatants (the "Anaconda strategy" in the Civil War or "island hopping" in World War II). However, you will probably not find a question on Lee's strategy at the Battle of Gettysburg or on troop movements during the Spanish-American War.

The questions are not designed to trick you, nor do they ask obscure details. The questions are usually well written and logical. If you find yourself genuinely unfamiliar with a topic, try to eliminate choices and then guess (see below).

Pacing

Bring a watch with you, and try to work at a steady pace. You have less than a minute for each multiple-choice question—41.25 seconds per question to be exact. This means that you cannot get hung up on difficult questions. If the answer doesn't immediately come to you, make a notation in the test book and come back to it if you have time. Make sure you leave yourself time to get to all the questions.

Guessing

In the past, the College Board deducted a quarter of a point for each incorrect answer to prevent guessing. Now there is no deduction for incorrect responses. So guess away, even if you are completely unfamiliar with the topic of a question. DO NOT LEAVE ANY BLANK RESPONSES on your answer sheet.

Arrangement of Questions

For the most part, the College Board no longer presents questions in chronological order. Previously, questions were presented in groups of 10 to 12 in chronological order. Now expect the questions to be scrambled. You can expect questions to get more difficult as you proceed through the test. The last 20 questions are of a higher degree of difficulty than the first 20 questions.

How Many Questions Do You Need to Answer Correctly?

The College Board does not expect you to get every multiple-choice question correct. You can receive a top score of 5 on the exam while answering 70 percent of the multiple-choice questions correctly (and doing a decent job on the essays). Remember, do not leave any blank responses on your answer sheet.

TYPES OF MULTIPLE-CHOICE QUESTIONS

The College Board will present you with a variety of types of multiple-choice questions when you take the Advanced Placement exam. It is rare for the exam to include a simple recall or identification question. Virtually all the questions require you to analyze historical information. You might be asked to make connections, discern a point of view, determine cause or effect, or assess significance or impact.

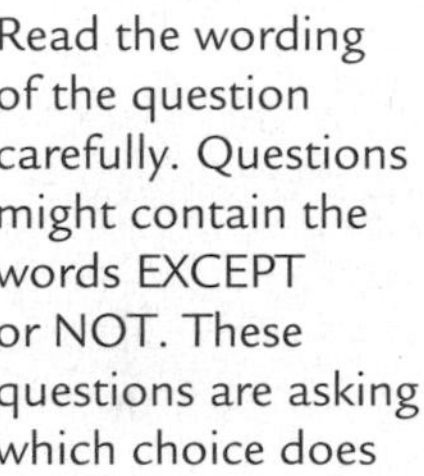

TIP

Read the wording of the question carefully. Questions might contain the words EXCEPT or NOT. These questions are asking which choice does *not* belong.

"Cause" Questions

Many questions ask you to determine the most important cause of a historical event or phenomena. The following question asks you to determine which of the choices describes a cause of the "Great Migration."

1. Which of the following would be considered a cause of the Great Migration of African Americans?

   (A) The relaxation of interstate travel restrictions for African Americans.
   (B) Booker T. Washington's call to "cast down your bucket."
   (C) The economic dislocation cause by the "dust bowl."
   (D) The increase in industrial production for World War I.
   (E) The mechanization of the textile industry in New England.

   (D) The question requires an understanding of what the Great Migration was and why it occurred. It was the large migration of African Americans from the rural South to the urban North during the 1910s and 1920s. The causes were many: discrimination in the South, lynching, the failure of the cotton crop due to the boll weevil infestation of the 1910s, and an increase in industrial production in the North, especially during World War I. Booker T. Washington urged African Americans to stay put (B). The "dust bowl" led to a migration of mostly white farmers from the Great Plains to the West coast during the 1930s, but this is not the Great Migration (C). The mechanization of the textile industry in New England occurred in the 1820s and 1830s—much too early for the Great Migration. In fact, slavery existed in the 1820s and 1830s, precluding any sort of voluntary migration.

Here is another example of a "cause" question. The wording is slightly different. The phrase "in the aftermath of" is another way of saying "was caused by."

2. Richard Nixon's "Checkers speech" was made in the aftermath of
   (A) accusations of financial improprieties in relation to his campaign for Senate.
   (B) the verdict in the Alger Hiss spy case.
   (C) his disappointing performance in a televised debate with John F. Kennedy.
   (D) the killing of four students at Kent State College.
   (E) revelations about his involvement in the Watergate cover-up.

   (A) This question is asking you to identify the cause of an event. The event is a famous speech that Nixon gave when he was running for vice president with Dwight D. Eisenhower in 1952. Nixon had been accused of financial improprieties in an early Senate campaign. He denied any improper behavior. He said that his family did receive a pet dog as a gift, Checkers, and that he would not take that dog away from his daughter. All the other events occurred during Richard Nixon's political career, but they are not the reason he made the "Checkers speech."

The following question requires you to be familiar with multiple causes of a phenomenon and to identify the choice that was *not* a cause.

3. Which of the following was <u>not</u> a factor in the destruction of independent Native-American groups in the West?
   (A) The United States army had greater firepower than Native Americans.
   (B) The bison (American buffalo) herds that Native Americans depended on were decimated.
   (C) Railroads brought increased pressure on development and led to Native Americans being pushed off their land.
   (D) Native Americans abandoned traditional religious practices and no longer believed they had the protection of the Great Spirit.
   (E) Discoveries of gold and silver on Native-American lands led the government to go back on earlier treaties.

   (D) This question asks about the causes of the defeat of Native Americans in the West. The context of the question is the brutal "Indian wars" of the post–Civil War period. All the choices contain important factors in this defeat except D. During this violent period, Native Americans saw a resurgence of traditional religious beliefs. The Ghost Dance movement inspired many Native Americans as they went into battle. Also, even if some Native Americans were less religious that their ancestors, that was not a factor in their military defeat.

Map Questions

Map questions require you to read the information on a map successfully and to provide outside knowledge. Take, for example, the following question:

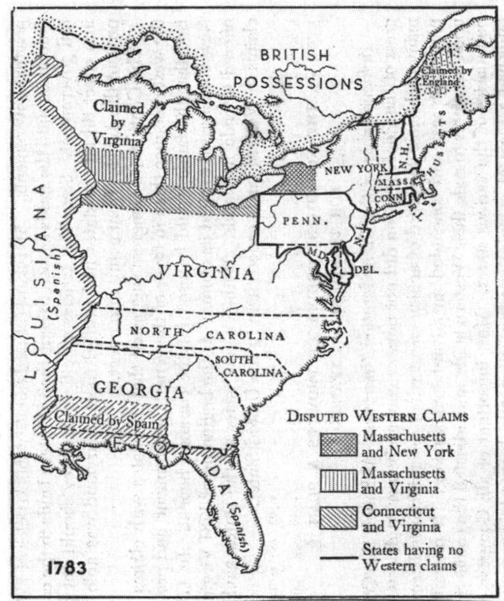

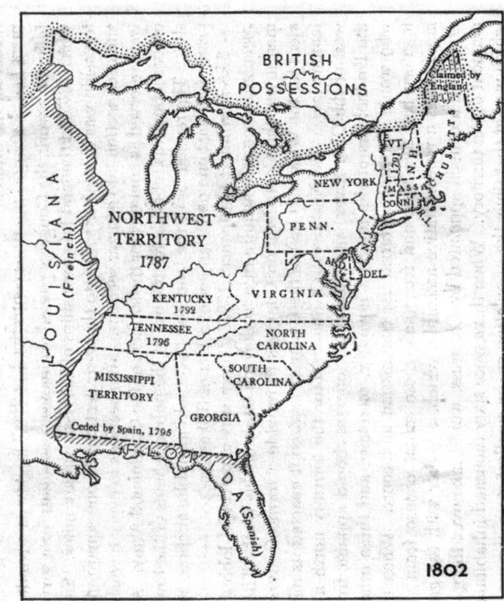

4. The differences in the two maps shown above illustrate which of the following?
   (A) The result of the Articles of Confederation government successfully handling the question of western lands.
   (B) Territorial transfers that were brought about by the treaty ending the French and Indian War.
   (C) The evolving status of slavery in the newly acquired territories of the United States.
   (D) The impact of the "quasi-war" with France on competing land claims in the American West.
   (E) The changing electoral fortunes of the Democratic-Republicans and the Federalists in presidential elections.

(A) The key to answering the question is noting that the western land claims of the various states that are evident in the 1783 map are absent from the 1802 map. The map legend notes "Disputed Western Claims." Those claims were settled by 1802. In addition, it is helpful to know that the Articles of Confederation government successfully dealt with this question. This constituted one of the few successes for the Articles of Confederation government. It persuaded the various states to give up their land claims in the region. Then it passed two significant pieces of legislation. The Land Ordinance provided for an orderly system of development of the Northwest Territory. The Northwest Ordinance spelled out the steps that these areas would have to go through in order to become states. In addition, the Northwest Ordinance banned slavery in the Northwest Territory. The maps come well after the French and Indian War (1754–1763) (B). There is no allusion to slavery on either map (C). The "quasi-war" occurred during this period (1798–1799), but it did not result in property being transferred (D). Political power did change hands by the time of the second map (1802), but that is not alluded to in either map (E).

Illustration, Photo, and Cartoon Questions

Expect to encounter questions that test both your interpretive abilities as well as your knowledge of history. Political cartoons are a staple of the AP exam. Look at the one below:

The New-York Historical Society, N. Y. C.

"This Is a White Man's Government."

5. The political cartoon shown on page 6 makes the point that
   (A) northern capitalists benefit as much from the institution of slavery as southern plantation owners do.
   (B) Reconstruction was brought to an unfortunate end by a coalition of forces in the North and South.
   (C) Jim Crow segregation laws are inherently unfair.
   (D) Africans Americans were incapable of effectively participating in the political process.
   (E) nativist politicians were unfairly presenting Irish Americans as ignorant and brutish.

(B) This wonderfully rich political cartoon requires you to read a whole host of clues before you can understand its meaning. The man on the left is an Irish immigrant; the "5 Points" on his hat refers to the Irish neighborhood in New York City. Note his almost apelike face. This was typical of representations of Irish immigrants as drawn by nativist cartoonists. The man in the middle has "C.S.A." on his belt buckle—Confederate States of America. His knife says "Lost Cause"—an allusion to the southern nostalgia for the noble fight the South put up in the Civil War. The man on the right has "Capital" written on the object he is holding; he is a northern capitalist. These three sinister forces are working together to deny African Americans the right to vote. Note the ballot box strewn on the ground in the lower right-hand corner of the cartoon. These changes represent the end of Reconstruction, as evidenced by the title "This Is a White Man's Government." The cartoon does not allude to the slave system or cotton production (A). The cartoonist would probably agree that Jim Crow laws are unfair, but that is not the subject of the cartoon (C). The cartoon is drawn sympathetically toward African Americans; there is no allusion that the man on the ground is ignorant or debased (D). It is true that Irish immigrants were presented as brutish and ignorant, but the cartoonist is not critiquing that. In fact, he himself is presenting an Irish immigrant in an unflattering manner (E).

Charts, Graphs, and Tables

You will probably encounter one or more questions that involve tables, graphs, or charts. You are asked to understand and interpret information. The question will almost certainly require additional historical knowledge. Here is a question involving a table of figures.

Wholesale Price Index of Farm Products (Based on 1910–1914 = 100)	
1866	140
1870	112
1876	89
1880	80
1882	99
1886	68
1890	71
1896	56
1900	71

6. Which of the following was a demand that the populist movement made in the 1880s and 1890s to address the situation reflected in the figures in the table above?

(A) A national sales tax
(B) Government funding for the purchase of agricultural machinery
(C) "Internal improvements" in the West, including railroads and canals
(D) An end to the gold standard and a shift to currency backed by silver as well as gold
(E) Government-run farm collectives

(D) The numbers in the table illustrate a major problem for farmers in the post–Civil War period. Commodity prices for agricultural products were falling. In other words, farmers were earning less and less for their produce. It reached a point where it was hardly worth growing crops. The costs of production were almost more than the price farmers received for their goods. A primary culprit in this situation was the money supply. During the post–Civil War era, the United States was on a gold standard, meaning that currency could not exceed the government's amount of gold. This led to a tight money supply. In response to this situation, farmers took action. The populist movement was a reaction to the dire straits that farmers found themselves in. An important demand of the movement was to base currency on silver as well as on gold. This would lead to inflation and higher prices for agricultural goods. A national sales tax would not have helped (A); farmers wanted more money in circulation, not less. The populists did not demand federal subsidies for farm equipment. Increased mechanization was part of the problem. It led to a glut of crops on the market, which also pushed down prices (B). Farmers were angry at the railroads. They demanded government regulation of the railroads, not additional lines (C). Government-run farm collectives were a characteristic of the Soviet Union, not the United States (E).

Answers:

1. **(D)** 3. **(D)** 5. **(B)**
2. **(A)** 4. **(A)** 6. **(D)**

The Free-Response Section

CHAPTER 2

The free-response, or essay, section of the exam, is 50 percent of your grade. In the free-response portion of the exam, you are required to write three essays—a document-based question (DBQ) and two standard essays. One DBQ is offered in the exam; you have no choice here. The DBQ is labeled "Section II, Part A" (following the multiple-choice section, which is labeled "Section I"). For the standard free-response questions, you have some choice. There are two sets of two questions, labeled "Section II, Part B" and "Section II, Part C." In each part, you must pick one question to answer. Section II, Part B consists of two questions from the first half of American history, up to and including the Civil War. Section II, Part C consists of two questions from the second half of American history since the Civil War. For parts B and C, pick the question you think you know the most about. Also, pick a question that you think you can construct an interesting and thoughtful response to.

Once again, the free-response section accounts for 50 percent of your overall grade. Within the free-response section, the DBQ has a weight of 45 percent. The standard free-response questions together have a weight of 55 percent—27.5 percent for each question. To put it in the context of the entire exam, your score on the DBQ comprises 22.5 percent of your overall score. Your score on the two standard free-response essays comprises 27.5 of your overall score—13.75 for each one.

The free-response portion of the exam is labeled as such because you are free to respond to the questions as you see fit. Here, your sense of history, your interpretative skills, your critical-thinking capabilities, and your point of view can come to the fore in constructing your response. The term "free-response" is in juxtaposition to the multiple-choice section, where there is only one correct answer.

The free-response portion of the exam consists of a 15-minute planning period and 115 minutes of writing time. During the 15-minute planning period, you open the question booklet. However, you are not permitted to write in the essay booklet. You should take this time to look at the questions and think about your responses. You are allowed to write in the exam booklet, and you should absolutely do so. For the documents, underline important points, jot down notes to yourself, and think about how you will use each document. For the standard free-response questions, think about which ones you'd like to do and begin jotting down pieces of information you think you will be able to use. Finally, in this 15-minute period, create a rough outline of each of your responses (more on creating an outline follows) and plan your DBQ.

Once you are allowed to open your essay booklet, you will have 115 minutes to write (just under two hours). The College Board suggests you spend 45 minutes writing your response to the DBQ. The College Board also recommends that you spend 35 minutes on each of the standard essays—5 minutes for preparation and 30 minutes for writing. However, you will not be told to move on after 45 minutes. You must keep your own pace as you write. Do not depend on the proctor to keep time. Be very careful not to get so engrossed in writing the DBQ that you don't have time for the standard free-response questions.

Grades for essays range from 0 to 9 on the AP rubric. Earning a 9 is extremely rare at AP grading tables; even an 8 is a rarity. Excellent essays get scores in the range of 6 to 7. Very good essays can expect to receive a grade in the 4 to 5 range.

TYPES OF FREE-RESPONSE QUESTIONS

Free-response questions, both in the DBQ section and in the standard essay section, are phrased in a variety of ways. However, no matter what the phrasing, all free-response questions are basically asking you to do the same thing: to look at a historical problem and try to understand it using historical evidence. Implicit in all essay questions is an invitation to judge "to what extent." The question might use the words "assess," "evaluate," or "analyze," but the intent is similar. They almost always ask you determine "to what extent . . . ." Here are two essay questions, phrased slightly differently.

> Assess the factors that explain the development of the modern civil rights movement (1910–1955).

> Analyze the social, political, and economic factors that contributed to the thirteen British colonies declaring independence in 1776.

Both of these questions are asking you to look at factors that help explain a historical phenomenon. In both cases, you must ultimately weigh the factors and evaluate to what extent one factor was more important than other ones. Both questions also invite you to enter into the debate. Historians try to understand causation. Their work is more than a list of factors; it seeks to understand the workings of society—to evaluate and to interpret. You are to do the same. To receive high grades on the free-response section, you must enter the debate—you must evaluate, interpret, offer a perspective.

WRITING RESPONSES

Developing a Thesis

The thesis is the most important and most difficult element of your essay. After evaluating the period under discussion and looking at the historical evidence, you need to develop an answer to the question. Very rarely are things black and white in history. Look for nuance and subtlety in history. Good theses are often complex, rather than simple, assertions. Suppose an essay question asks about the level of success of the anti–Vietnam War movement of the 1960s. Here are two possible thesis statements:

> The antiwar movement failed in its goal to stop the war in Vietnam. The war continued until President Nixon decided to pull out of Vietnam in 1973.

> The antiwar movement failed in its ultimate goal of quickly ending hostilities in Southeast Asia, but it succeeded in limiting President Nixon's options. The movement created a situation in which Nixon knew that the domestic costs of escalating the conflict would be so high that an escalation would not be worthwhile. This left Nixon with only one option—to withdraw.

The second thesis reflects a sophisticated understanding of the period and a nuanced approach to the topic. Note that it takes somewhat of a middle ground, but it is still making a bold assertion. Some students, by contrast, evade the responsibility of taking a stand by making a bland statement with no real point of view. For example, "The antiwar movement was somewhat unsuccessful but also somewhat successful." This takes a middle ground, but it says absolutely nothing. The successful thesis above makes a bold assertion within a nuanced approach to the problem.

The Opening Paragraph

The opening paragraph of each essay should clearly state your approach and strategy. You should define terms, state your thesis, and mention the topics your essay will address. Be sure to define or explain basic terms in the question itself. Don't assume the reader will know what these terms mean. Let him or her see that *you* know what they mean. If the essay makes a reference to the Gilded Age of the Critical Period, briefly explain the defining features of the period. The Gilded Age, for example, could be described as "the period from the end of the Civil War to the turn of the twentieth century in which the United States experienced rapid industrial growth." Terms like "progressive," "conservative," "militant," and "radical" must be explained as well. Also, be sure to explain words like "effective," "successful," and "consistent." Although these words seem self-evident, they might not be in the context of the question.

In addition, briefly mention the main factors you will discuss in your response. Let the reader know what to look for as he or she reads your essay. Finally, include your thesis in the opening paragraph. Don't try to set up a suspense story in which the reader has to wait until the final paragraph to know what your position is. Put it out there right in the opening paragraph

Organize Evidence

Graphically organizing information and evidence before you begin writing is useful. During the 15-minute reading period before you are allowed to write, you can jot down an outline at the back of the question booklet. For the question,

"Did President Lyndon Johnson effectively address the problems of poverty in the United States?," the topics for an outline could be pretty straightforward: effective and ineffective. The topics could more sophisticated, as well. You could create an outline under the headings initiatives and constraints. Many essay questions lend themselves to the classic outline structure of political, economic, and social. Take advantage of the 15 minutes and create at least an outline for the DBQ. If you have time, make an outline for the standard essays as well.

Concession or Counterargument Paragraph

Strong essays have a point a view but also acknowledge that opposing views have legitimacy. The idea of your essay should not be to dismiss or belittle other points of view. Accept that other views are reasonable. It shows a real lack of sophistication to convey an attitude that says, "Those who disagree with my argument have clearly misread the evidence." Perhaps they have simply read the evidence differently. This acknowledgment of opposing viewpoints can be conveyed throughout your essay or can be the focus of a concession paragraph in which you acknowledge the legitimacy of other views.

Let us again look at the Lyndon Johnson question to illustrate the idea of a concession paragraph.

> Did President Lyndon Johnson effectively address the problems of poverty in the United States?

A reasonable response might be built around the thesis, "Johnson failed to address the problem of poverty in the United States effectively, because the war in Vietnam drained resources and energy from domestic problems. The urban rioting in the later 1960s is testament to his ineffectiveness."

A concession paragraph would acknowledge the legitimacy of other points of view. You might craft your concession this way, "Certainly Johnson implemented some important programs, such as Medicare and Medicaid. These programs brought healthcare to millions of Americans." You might go on in this vein and conclude the paragraph with, "However, these programs were underfunded and did not lead to real, long-term change." There will almost always be more than one reasonable way to look at a historical question. If there weren't, posing the question in the first place probably would not be worthwhile.

Agency

Many free-response questions will deal with social issues and problems. A sophisticated approach to such an essay should account for the agency of ordinary people. When writing about history, you should acknowledge that people are not the helpless victims of historical forces. People have hopes, fears, dreams, animosities, prejudices, and anxieties. People often act on these. The sense of being an active participant in history is called "agency," as in being an active agent in history. Not looking at agency can lead to an incomplete understanding of the past. For years, historians looked at the period of Reconstruction by examining whether the freed men and women of the South benefited from government programs. Was Reconstruction good for them, or was it bad for them? It took a long time for historians, other than the African-American historian W.E.B. Du Bois, who wrote in the first part of the twentieth century,[1] to examine what African Americans were actually doing in the South. More recently, historians have begun to examine meetings held by African American, and have tried to figure how they shaped the outcome of Reconstruction.

THE DBQ

The above suggestions for structuring and writing your essay apply to both the standard essay as well as the DBQ. However, the DBQ requires a few additional specific suggestions. The document-based question accounts for 22.5 percent of your grade for the entire AP exam. Writing a strong DBQ is central to getting a high grade on the exam.

Integrate the Documents Into Your Response

Make sure the documents are integrated into your overall response. You know you are on the wrong track when paragraphs begin as: "According to Document A . . . " or "As Document C indicates . . ." This is the making of a very low-scoring essay. You must begin the paragraphs with your ideas. Within each paragraph, you should mention the appropriate document that illustrates that paragraph's idea. For example, in an essay about the reasons for the success of the prohibition movement, you might have a paragraph that leads with the following sentence. "The prohibition movement was successful because it was able to tap into antiforeign sentiment in the United States." Then within that paragraph, you might use a cartoon showing a drunk, impoverished Irish immigrant. Again, avoid leading a paragraph with the sentence: "Document A shows a poor drunk, Irishman. This cartoon made people want to pass prohibition . . . ."

Notice Connections Between Documents

Often in DBQs, two or more of the documents talk to one another. That is, one responds to something in another one. One document might amplify an earlier one or, more likely, offer a different perspective. In a DBQ on the North during the Civil War, one document might defend the New York City draft riot as a justified response to the "$300 rule" in the draft law. The next document might condemn the rioters as misguided and racist. Your job is to let the documents communicate with one another. Bring out the tensions implicit in these two documents. Begin a paragraph with these tensions, "New Yorkers had markedly different reactions to the draft riot . . . ." Do your best to make sense of the tensions between documents. Don't simply avoid the documents that don't immediately conform to your thesis.

[1]W.E.B. Du Bois, "Black Reconstruction" (New York: Harcourt Brace, 1935).

Avoid Mentioning the Word "Document" in Your Text

When you make reference to a document, avoid using the word "document" in the text of your essay. If you are referencing a speech, refer to it as such. "Roosevelt's internationalism was evident in a speech he gave in Chicago in 1937" will be taken more seriously than "Document A demonstrates Roosevelt's internationalism." The first sounds far more sophisticated than the second.

For the sake of clarity, you should indicate, by letter, which documents you use. You can do this by referencing the document in parentheses. For example, "Document A," or simply "A". So the Roosevelt sentence would read as follows: "Roosevelt's internationalism was evident in a speech he gave in Chicago in 1937 (Document A)." Please remember to do this for each document you use.

Take Into Consideration the Source

Do not take every document at face value. Note the origins and dates of particular documents before you use them, and take that knowledge into consideration. A report about the corruption and inefficiencies of Reconstruction governments in the South should be questioned if it was written by a former Confederate official. He has a particular ax to grind.

Outside Information

A strong response must have significant outside information. You cannot get a high grade by simply discussing the documents themselves. You must introduce relevant additional information. Often, the documents themselves will suggest to you outside information that can be introduced. If a New Deal–era document discusses Supreme Court opposition to New Deal programs, you might be expected to discuss President Franklin D. Roosevelt's "court packing" scheme. If a civil rights era document mentions police brutality during the 1963 Birmingham, Alabama, campaign, you should mention Public Safety Commissioner "Bull" Connor or Martin Luther King's "Letter from Birmingham Jail." These pieces of outside information are hinted at by the documents themselves. The exact outside information you introduce into a DBQ response is, of course, contingent upon the nature of the question and the nature of your response. We shall revisit the question of outside information in the discussion of the DBQ that follows.

Sample DBQ:

Look at the DBQ below for 15 minutes, and then take 45 minutes and construct a response. Following the DBQ, we will discuss strategies for drafting a response.

Directions: Write a coherent essay that incorporates your analysis of Documents A–I *and* your knowledge of the period in the question. To earn a high score, cite key information from the documents and use your knowledge of the period.

1. To what degree was President Woodrow Wilson successful in addressing home front concerns during World War I?

   Use the documents and your knowledge of the years 1914–1921 in your answer.

DOCUMENT A

Source: Poster, Central States Paper Trade Association, R. Fayerweather Babcock (artist), 1917.

DOCUMENT B

Source: Announcement, The War Industries Board, June 6, 1918, reprinted in *The New York Times*, June 7, 1918.

Be it Resolved, by the War Industries Board, That the following agreement reached as a result of several conferences between a committee of the board and the American Iron and Steel Institute, be and the same is hereby ratified, confirmed, and approved, to become effective at once:

Whereas, A careful study of the sources of supply in connection with the present and rapidly increasing direct and indirect war requirements for iron and steel products has convinced the War Industries Board of the necessity for (1) a strict conservation of the available supply of iron and steel products, on the one hand, and (2) the expansion of existing sources and the development of new sources of supply of iron and steel products, on the other hand; and

Whereas, the producers iron and of iron and steel products in the main concur in this conclusion reached by the said board, and have expressed their to cooperate wholeheartedly with the said board . . ."

DOCUMENT C

Source: Poster, United States Food Administration, L.N. Britton (artist), 1917.

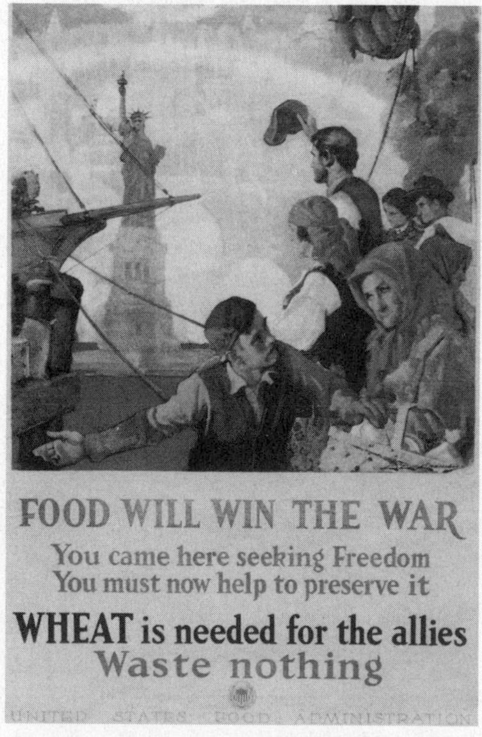

DOCUMENT D

Source: Letter, John J. Pershing, Commander-In-Chief, France, American Expeditionary Forces To Carl Vrooman, Assistant Secretary Of Agriculture, October 16, 1918.

> DEAR MR. VROOMAN: Will you please convey to farmers of America our profound appreciation of their patriotic services to the country and to the allied armies in the field. They have furnished their full quota of fighting men; they have bought largely of Liberty Bonds; and they have increased their production of food crops both last year and this by over a thousand million bushels above normal production. Food is of vital military necessity for us and for our Allies, and from the day of our entry into the war America's armies of food producers have rendered invaluable service to the Allied cause by supporting the soldiers at the front through their devoted and splendidly successful work in the fields and furrows at home.
>
> Very sincerely,
> JOHN J. PERSHING

DOCUMENT E

Source: Poster, Milwaukee Country (Wisconsin) Council of Defense, 1917.

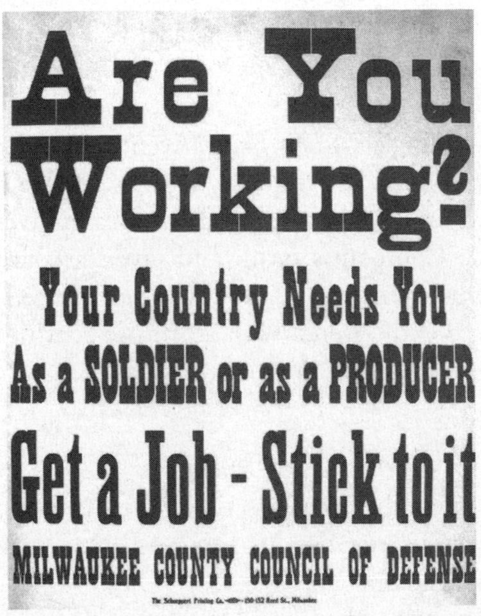

DOCUMENT F

Source: "Exponent of Violence Not a Four Minute Man" Committee on Public Information, *Four Minute Men Bulletin*, May 22, 1917.

A newspaper in Pennsylvania recently ran an item concerning an alleged Four Minute Man who said in a speech at a moving-picture house that the people of his town were "determined to wipe out seditious talk among pro-Germans here even if it requires tar and feathers and a stout rope in the hands of a necktie party." The speaker then went on to mention the names of several citizens of the town whom he accused of being "slackers in the purchase of war stamps and also disloyal to their adopted country in uttering seditious remarks." An investigation was immediately instigated by headquarters, and we were glad to find the speaker was not a Four Minute Man but had been so styled simply through the ignorance of a newspaper reporter who had not inquired concerning the speaker's credentials. This disclosure rendered it unnecessary to demand the immediate dismissal of this individual from our ranks; but his inflammatory statements did not go entirely unpunished. Our chairman for that community informs us that one result of his speech was that he was soundly trounced by two sons of one of the men whose name he mentioned, which may have had a subduing effect.

DOCUMENT G

Source: "Another Tar and Feather Party is Stager," *Ashland Daily Press*, April 11, 1918.

Adolph Anton, residing at 1100 Sixth Avenue West, was taken from his home at about nine o'clock last night by a party of five or six who came to the house in an auto, carried to a spot on the Beaser Avenue road known as the Chequamego Ice Company's farm, and given a coat of tar and feathers for alleged pro-German sentiments. He was then released and told to beat it for home. Stark naked and covered with a profuse coat of tar and feathers, he walked the distance to his home, about a mile.

DOCUMENT H

Source: Portion of the amendment to Section 3 of the Espionage Act of June 15, 1917, United States, *Statutes at Large*, Washington, D.C., 1918.

SECTION 3. Whoever, when the United States is at war, shall willfully make or convey false reports or false statements with intent to interfere with the operation or success of the military or naval forces of the United States, or to promote the success of its enemies, or shall willfully make or convey false reports, or false statements, . . . or incite insubordination, disloyalty, mutiny, or refusal of duty, in the military or naval forces of the United States, or shall willfully obstruct . . . the recruiting or enlistment service of the United States, or . . . shall willfully utter, print, write, or publish any disloyal, profane, scurrilous, or abusive language about the form of government of the United States, or the Constitution of the United States, or the military or naval forces of the United States . . . or shall willfully display the flag of any foreign enemy, or shall willfully . . . urge, incite, or advocate any curtailment of production . . . or advocate, teach, defend, or suggest the doing of any of the acts or things in this section enumerated and whoever shall by word or act support or favor the cause of any country with which the United States is at war or by word or act oppose the cause of the United States therein, shall be punished by a fine of not more than $10,000 or imprisonment for not more than twenty years, or both . . . .

DOCUMENT I

Source: Eugene V. Debs, Speech (excerpt), Canton, Ohio, June 16, 1918.

I realize that, in speaking to you this afternoon, there are certain limitations placed upon the right of free speech. I must be exceedingly careful, prudent, as to what I say, and even more careful and prudent as to how I say it. I may not be able to say all I think; but I am not going to say anything that I do not think. I would rather a thousand times be a free soul in jail than to be a sycophant and coward in the streets. They may put those boys in jail—and some of the rest of us in jail . . . but their souls are here this afternoon. They are simply paying the penalty that all men have paid in all the ages of history for standing erect, and for seeking to pave the way to better conditions for mankind.

Answering the DBQ:

The first task in answering this question is setting the stage. In the introductory paragraph, let the reader see your familiarity with the period. Mention the beginnings of the war in 1914, the initial reluctance of Wilson to get involved in the war ("He kept us out of war," his campaign literature boasted in 1916). Mention his eventual decision to get involved.

Next, we have to define terms. The main operative phrase in this question is "home front concerns." What concerns must a president address during times of war? What specific concerns did President Wilson face during World War I? Home front concerns, in any war, would include staffing the army, funding the war effort, producing sufficient amounts of war materials, and controlling inflation. As we look at the documents, some specific World War I era concerns will also become apparent. The other key word is "successful." As you develop a thesis, keep in mind there are different criteria for judging success in this case. One criterion might be simply winning the war. Another criterion might be keeping the country united. Another criterion might be keeping the progressive reform spirit of the prewars years alive. Finally, another criterion might be maintaining important American traditions, such as respect for civil liberties and tolerance for a diversity of people and ideas. As you formulate our response, you must sort out these various criteria.

With these questions in mind, let's look at the documents. An examination of the documents should indicate that they touch on six home front issues. Documents A and B address the efforts by the War Industry Board to organize production for war. Documents C and D allude to the Food Administration and the efforts to provide sufficient quantities of food to the soldiers in the war as well as to society at large. Document E addresses the question of employment during the war. Documents F and G address two issues at once. First we have a discussion of wartime propaganda—the Committee on Public Information and its Four Minute Men program. The documents also address the other side of the propaganda coin—intolerance, prejudice, and violence. Finally, documents H and I address the issue of civil liberties during times of war. Once we can identify issues, we can begin to structure our response. The six issues mentioned could serve as the basis for six paragraphs.

The first paragraph after the introduction addresses the effort by the War Industries Board (WIB). Document A is a poster that urges conservation. We see here voluntary cooperation from the paper industry as well as efforts to engage the entire society in the war effort. Document B discusses an agreement between the WIB and the steel and iron industries. Both documents seem to point toward success in meeting the industrial needs of the war. If we want to argue that the government did not go far enough—it could have mandated compliance instead of seeking voluntary compliance—we could find fault. However, the two documents point toward success. We could also bring in outside information here. For instance, we could put this voluntary board in the context of the progressive era. It is exactly the type of government oversight the movement was calling for.

Next we move on to food. Document C is another poster. It is urging a change in diet to prevent shortages of certain commodities (meat, sugar, and fat) for the war effort. The effort seems to have been effective. Document D is a letter from Gen. Pershing, Commander-In-Chief of American forces in France. He is letting the secretary of agriculture know that he is quite pleased with the effort to provide food to the war effort. We seem to have another success. A key piece of outside information here might be Herbert Hoover—he headed the Food Administration and did an exemplary job.

Document E stands alone; it highlights the effort to get sufficient numbers of workers into war-related factories. The document is another poster. This one is local in origin. It was issued by the Milwaukee County Council on Defense. In addition to highlighting the issue of employment, this document also shows that the war effort was carried out on the local level as well as on the national level. Here, we can bring in important outside information—the Great Migration of African Americans to the North. African Americans were key to the war effort. We might also note tensions that developed between the white residents of northern cities (such as Milwaukee); a major race riot occurred in Chicago in 1919.

Documents F and G address the difficult issue of propaganda. On the one hand, we can discuss the Committee on Public Information, George Creel (outside information), Four Minute men, and propaganda posters (such as the ones in Documents A and C). Here we might note the success in gaining support for the war effort. After all, in 1914, isolationist sentiment was strong. Even in 1917, Americans were decidedly mixed. We can also discuss the Americanizing aspect of all the wartime propaganda. America was a nation of immigrants on the eve of the war. We can discuss here the "new immigration" of the late 1800s and early 1900s. Wartime propaganda is asking not only for support of the war; it is also asking for a united effort, despite one's background.

We must also discuss the ugly side of wartime propaganda. Both documents F and G allude to violence against German Americans. In document F, we see the Committee on Public Information warning against acts of violence. However, these warnings were not so successful. Document G shows the tarring and feathering of a man for "alleged pro-German sentiments." Here we can bring in additional outside information. We can mention the tarring and feathering during the American Revolution. We can expand upon the incident in document G to discuss a rash of violent incidents during the war, as well as an almost irrational dislike of anything German. The word "frankfurter" become suspect. Here we can fault the government's war effort for unleashing irrational and violent impulses.

Finally, we come to the issue of civil liberties. Document H contains the text of the Espionage Act. Document I is a speech by Socialist leader Eugene V. Debs decrying the arrest of his comrades. He himself would soon be arrested. Here, we can bring in pertinent outside information—Charles Schenck, his arrest, and the Supreme Court case *Schenk* v. *U.S.* From this case we get the phrase "clear and present danger" and the idea that shouting "Fire!" in a crowded theater is not protected speech. We can see the government effort as successful for getting thousands of opponents of the war in jail. However, is this success? Was Debs presenting a clear and present danger? These are the questions that add nuance to our essay.

Finally, let's write a thesis. This, of course, is up to you. Here are a couple of approaches. First, "President Woodrow Wilson was successful in addressing home front concerns. He won the war and kept the nation united." This thesis is weak. It doesn't show much engagement with the documents, nor does it show a working understanding of the period. "Keeping the country united," is excessively vague. Here is a stronger attempt at a thesis. "Wilson's record on addressing home front concerns is mixed. On the one hand, it cannot be denied that he successfully expanded the power of the federal government to guarantee that the material needs of the war were met—from meat and wheat to steel and iron. On the other hand, the government's insistence on ideological conformity created an atmosphere of intolerance, narrowness and violence. Wilson unleashed forces that ultimately did in his own progressive agenda and paved the way for the horrors of the Red Scare and a revived Ku Klux Klan." That is a solid thesis that would set up a high-scoring response.

Practice Standard Free-Response Question and Sample Response:

Now let us take a stab at a standard essay question. Below is a standard free-response question followed by a sample response. Take 35 minutes to construct a response and then compare it to the sample response below. After the response are some brief comments on the sample.

1. "The New Deal of the 1930s should be considered a failure because it did not resolve the economic crisis of the decade." Assess the validity of this statement.

Sample Response:

The New Deal, Franklin Delano Roosevelt's set of programs designed to deal with the Great Depression of the 1930s, had mixed results. The programs, from short-term relief efforts to long-term attempts at restructuring the American economy, did not bring prosperity and stability to the United States. As late as 1938, five years into the New Deal, unemployment was still over 15 percent. It is true that Roosevelt's personality did give the public a sense of hope and confidence and many New Deal programs provided needed assistance to people. But ultimately, Roosevelt lacked political discipline and direction to implement policies that would stabilize the economy. For this reason, the success of the New Deal was limited.

Roosevelt's personality gave people a sense of hope. As he ran for president in 1932, he was able to connect with voters in ways that Herbert Hoover could not. As president he urged people not to give up hope. He told them, "We have nothing to fear but fear itself." He talked directly to the American people through his "fireside chats" that were broadcast on the radio. The American people believed that the president was on their side. He was perceived as a maverick in Washington, who would shake things up, like the hero in Frank Capra's depression-era movie, *Mr. Smith Goes to Washington.*

Roosevelt turned this perception of empathy into an ambitious set of programs known as the New Deal. Roosevelt tried out a variety of approaches and ideas. He was, by nature, a pragmatic man—more interested in seeing what works than in sticking to a rigid ideology. In this regard, he was very different from Herbert Hoover, who stuck doggedly to the idea of laissez-faire, or nonintervention in the economy. Roosevelt created an alphabet soup of government programs designed to provide economic relief to the poor and to resuscitate the economy. These included the Civilian Conservation Corps, which provided outdoor jobs to young men; the Glass-Steagall Act, which provided insurance to people's bank deposits; and the Agricultural Adjustment Act, which urged farmers to grow fewer crops in order to boost commodity prices. Later New Deal Programs included the Works Progress Administration, which provided jobs for millions of Americans, and the Wagner Act, which gave government support to workers' attempts at unionization. The Social Security Act created the system of payments to senior citizens that is still in effect today. Overall, the New Deal attempted to lessen cutthroat competition in the business community so that firms could cooperate in setting fair wages and prices. Roosevelt also tried to increase the amount of money people had in their pockets so that they could increase their purchasing power.

The wide array of New Deal programs had some definite positive effects. Millions of people found jobs through public works programs, and poor people were able to get access to relief money. Yet, Roosevelt's penchant for experimentation ultimately did in the New Deal. He was leery about increasing the federal deficit too much. Just as the New Deal began to have an effect, Roosevelt cut back on government spending. He listened to the more conservative members of his cabinet and did go full speed forward with his program for social and economic change. The economist John Maynard Keynes urged Roosevelt to go further in government spending programs. Keynes developed a set of ideas that challenged laissez-faire notions. He wanted the government to intervene in economic activity in order to stabilize the economy. Roosevelt was unwilling to stick with a Keynesian approach.

This tentativeness prevented the New Deal from fully achieving its goals. Only when the government put its full set of resources behind production for World War II did the economy revive. If Roosevelt had put the same amount of money into the New Deal that the government put into World War II production, the Depression would have ended quickly and Roosevelt would have achieved the success he sought.

This essay would probably be in the range of a 5 or 6. The thesis is fairly sophisticated. Rather than simply agreeing or disagreeing with the statement in the question, it takes a middle position. It asserts that the New Deal was somewhat successful. However, a good essay must do more than give a middle-of-the-road response. It must give specific reasons for why the New Deal was only somewhat successful. The paragraph structure is very good. Each paragraph conveys an idea that is developed within the paragraph. Ample factual information is provided. All in all, this is a fairly strong essay.

Practice your essay writing. In each of the subsequent chapters are practice free-response questions for you to address. Think about complex, nuanced thesis statements for each one and how you would develop that thesis into a strong essay.

CHAPTER 3

The Meeting of Three Peoples, Prehistory–1600

TIMELINE

1488	Bartolomeu Dias (Portugal) sails around the Cape of Good Hope
1492	Christopher Columbus (Italian, sailing for Spain) arrives in the New World, beginning the era of European colonization of the Americas
1498	Vasco da Gama (Portugal) sails to India
1517	Martin Luther challenges Roman Catholic beliefs and practices; initiated Protestant Reformation
1521	Spanish forces, led by Hernan Cortes, defeat the Mexica people, led by Montezuma
1530	John Calvin breaks with the Catholic Church
1532	Spanish forces, led by Francisco Pizarro, defeat the Inca people
1549	The *repartimiento* reforms begin to replace the *encomienda* system
1587	Founding of the "lost" British colony of Roanoke
1588	British defeat of the Spanish Armada

A remarkable series of events between the 1200s to the 1500s led to a broad transformation of much of the world, bringing peoples together from far-flung corners of the globe. The local and regional systems of an early era gave way to a global system. This reordering of the world created great wealth for some and utter destruction for others as peoples from three regions—the Americas, Europe, and Africa—encountered one another. Out of these encounters developed new settlements and colonies in the New World, including the thirteen British colonies that would eventually become the United States.

THE AMERICAS BEFORE CONTACT WITH EUROPEANS

Homo sapiens are relatively new to the Americas. Historians and archaeologists believe the first people migrated to the new world many millennia ago—as recently as 15,000 years ago and as far back as 30,000 years ago. Current theories hold that people from Asia crossed into North America across a land mass called Beringia. North America was experiencing an Ice Age, locking up enormous quantities of water and lowering sea levels. Thus, the area that today is beneath the Bering Straits was then a land bridge connecting Asia and North America.

Continental Expansion

Once in North America, these early migrants quickly—within 1,000 to 2,000 years—spread throughout the Americas. The first Americans initially displayed striking cultural similarities. Archaeologists have found similarly shaped arrowheads, labeled "Clovis points," throughout the Americas. The ubiquity of these arrowheads, which have often been found in proximity to the remains of mammoths, indicates a similar nomadic hunting culture among these disparate Americans.

Adaption and Diversity

Between approximately 11,000 and 5,000 years ago, the uniformity of "Clovis culture" gave way to regional adaptation and variation. The reasons for this are varied. The mammoth—central to Clovis culture—became extinct. In addition, the Ice Age gave way to the vast variety of climates, rainfall levels, temperatures, and wind patterns that characterize the Americas of today. Over time, the peoples of the Americas adapted to the different regions of the Americas, developing a vast variety of cultural patterns.

Regional Variation on the Eve of Contact with Europeans

Several distinct regional groupings of native people developed in North and Central America. The people of the Great Plains, occupying the grassy areas east of the Rocky Mountains, depended on hunting the bison. The people of the Great Basin, between the Rocky Mountains and the Sierra Nevada Mountains in present-day California, depended on a variety of fish, game, and plants. Eastern woodlands peoples settled along rivers and depended on hunting small game such as deer. About 4,000 years ago, they developed agricultural practices and pottery. Southwestern peoples adapted to the dry climate, which is without abundant natural vegetation, by cultivating corn about 3,500 years ago.

Over time, these regional variations gave way to the specific tribal groupings that European settlers and explorers encountered. On the eve of Columbus's arrival in the Americas, these native peoples numbered anywhere from 4 to 20 million in North America—making for low population density throughout the vast continent.

EUROPE AND THE AGE OF EXPLORATION

Starting in the fifteenth century, Europeans embarked on an era of exploration and colonization unprecedented in human history. These journeys transformed life for large numbers of people in the Americas, in Europe, and in Africa. A variety of factors help to explain why these journeys took place when they did and why they led to such momentous changes.

The Crusades and the Revival of Trade

The series of religious wars known as the Crusades shook the stability of European feudal society and whet the appetites of European for foreign trade goods. The wars, with the goal of securing Christian control of the "Holy Land," occurred primarily in the twelfth and thirteenth centuries. The relatively self-sufficient manorial world of feudal Europe began its long demise during this period, as trade routes and both regional and international economic activity shifted power and priorities. Europeans became interested in circumventing the Italian city-states and finding new trade routes with the East.

The Black Death and the Decline of Feudalism

The Black Death, probably caused by a pandemic outbreak of bubonic plague in the fourteenth century, reduced the European population by anywhere from 30 to 60 percent. It also played a role in weakening the feudal system.

The Impact of the Renaissance

The Renaissance spirit of curiosity about the world inspired people to explore and map new areas. Universities and scholarly books—also infused with the spirit of renaissance humanism—spread these new discoveries.

The Protestant Reformation and the Catholic Counter-Reformation

Religious movements in the sixteenth century renewed many people's religious zeal and their desire to spread their gospels. The most important religious movement was the Protestant Reformation. Theologians Martin Luther and John Calvin both led breaks with Rome over church practices and beliefs. Both believed that the church had drifted from its spiritual mission. The Catholic Church's abuse of the practice of selling indulgences—or remissions of sin—was especially galling to Luther.

In England, King Henry VIII also led a break with Rome, but his break was more political than theological. The event that precipitated the break was the Pope's refusal to grant Henry a divorce. Some English Protestants, the Puritans, believed that the English Protestant Reformation did not go far enough. Motivated by Calvinist thinking, the Puritans argued for a complete reformation in England (see Chapter 4 for more on the Puritans).

The Catholic Church itself underwent a reform in the sixteenth century. The Counter-Reformation focused on a renewed sense of spirituality within the Catholic Church. Out of this movement came the Jesuits, a Catholic order devoted to spreading their gospel throughout the world.

Technological Advances and a Revolution in Navigation

A series of technological developments encouraged exploration. Johannes Gutenberg's printing press (developed in the 1440s) helped spread information and stimulated interest in new discoveries. The compass, the astrolabe, the quadrant, and the hourglass all aided navigation, helping sailors plot direction, determine speed, and assess latitude. *Portulanos*, which are detailed maps, also helped navigators. Portugal developed a quick, sturdy sailing ship called the caravel.

Portugal and Spain Lead the Way

Portugal, with the encouragement and guidance of Prince Henry the Navigator, embarked on a search for new trade routes to Asia that would bypass the Italian city-states that controlled Mediterranean trade. Portuguese explorers moved down the coast of Africa with the goal of rounding the Cape of Good Hope and crossing the Indian Ocean to arrive at India and China. Bartolomeu Dias sailed around the Cape of Good Hope (1488), and Vasca da Gama reached India by 1498.

Spain also sought new trade routes. The Italian sailor Christopher Columbus convinced the Spanish monarchs, Isabella and Ferdinand, to fund a venture west, across the Atlantic, to reach the East. Columbus argued that the diameter of Earth was smaller than cartographers believed and that a venture in a westerly direction was both possible and feasible. (Most educated Europeans, including Columbus, believed Earth was round.) Columbus's three ships, the *Nina*, the *Pinta*, and the *Santa Maria*, set sail in 1492 and reached a Caribbean island that he named San Salvador six weeks later. Columbus assumed that he had reached the East Indies and named the Taino people he encountered "Indians." The misnomer stuck. Columbus made two more voyages but never fully realized that he had encountered an entirely new continent. Others who followed in his footsteps made that realization, paving the way for a century of exploration, conquest, and riches.

AFRICA AND THE GLOBAL SLAVE TRADE

TIP 

Slavery in History
Slavery has existed since ancient times. However, be prepared to discuss the aspects of modern slavery that differentiate it from ancient slavery.

Even before forming settlements in the New World, Europeans began taking Africans from their villages and forcing them into slavery. Slavery has existed since ancient times, but the concept of slavery changed in the 1500s. Africans were thought of as slaves for life; it was not a temporary condition. Also, the children of slaves would now be considered slaves as well. This was also a break from tradition. African slaves were considered property, with no rights, as opposed to people who were enslaved for a period of time.

There are two main impacts of the slave trade on African people from the 1500s onward. First, entire generations of strong, young people were kidnapped and taken off the continent. They would never become the leaders of their tribe or village. Second, the introduction of European manufactured items undermined the traditional African economy.

NEW WORLD ENCOUNTERS

Within a generation of Columbus's first journey to the New World, Spanish forces wrested control of much of Central and South America from the native peoples. The Spanish transformed the economic and social structures of the region. They also decimated the native population.

The Conquistadores and the Defeat of Native Peoples

The sixteenth century saw brutal fighting in the Americas as Spain extended its hegemony over much of Central and South America. One of the more brutal episodes of violence between the Spanish conquistadores and native peoples was the defeat of the Mexica people (also known as the Aztecs) and their leader Montezuma by the Spaniard Hernan Cortes from 1518–1521. The Incas of South America were defeated by Spanish forces led by Francisco Pizarro (1532).

Gold and the *Encomienda* System

Once gaining control of much of the Americas, known as New Spain, the Spanish created a system to extract gold and silver and to ship it to Spain. Spain became the wealthiest country in Europe with the influx of New World precious metals. Initially, the Spanish system of colonization resembled Old World feudalism. Spaniards ruled over a given area, known as an *encomienda.* While acting as feudal lords, the *encomenderos* had a free hand to run their holdings as long as a percentage of gold and silver was sent back to the monarchy. The *encomienda* system led to brutal exploitation. Spurred by Spanish critics such as Bartolome de Las Casas, the crown issued a series of reforms to the governance of New Spain known as the *repartimiento* (1549). Treatment of native peoples did not improve appreciably, but control of New Spain came to be exercised more directly by the crown.

The "Columbian Exchange"

Historians refer to the introduction of new products on each side of the Atlantic as the "Columbian exchange." This exchange had a major impact on transforming the ecology of the New World. The Europeans introduced to the new world horses, goats, cows, chickens, coffee, lettuce, wheat, and many other products. A list of items brought by Europeans back to the Old World included turkeys, corn, sweet potatoes, and tomatoes.

TIP

The Impact of Disease
Remember that the main cause of the massive die-off of Native Americans in the 1600s was disease, not warfare. Warfare was brutal, but it could not have affected as many people as did diseases.

Disease and Death

By far, the most important organisms brought from Europe to the New World were germs. The peoples of the New World, having evolved and adapted away from the peoples of the Old World, had no immunities to many of these germs and the infectious diseases they caused. These diseases included bubonic plague, cholera, scarlet fever, and, most importantly, smallpox. It is estimated that between 50 and 90 percent of the native peoples of the Americas died between 1500 and 1650.

Spanish and Portuguese Ambitions

Spain was able to secure a dominant role in the New World following the Treaty of Tordesillas (1494) between Spain and Portugal. The treaty settled the competing claims of the two countries to the newly explored lands outside of Europe. The treaty drew a longitudinal line through the Atlantic Ocean and South America. Portugal was granted lands to the east of the line, including Brazil in the Western Hemisphere and Africa. Spain was granted the rest of the lands of the Americas. Spanish explorers made those claims real by establishing settlements throughout Central and South America. Spanish explorers even made it as far as California and New Mexico, the area around the Mississippi River, and Florida. Ponce de Leon reached Florida in 1513. Spaniards later established the first permanent European settlement in what would become the United States at St. Augustine, Florida (1585).

Parallels
The Spanish and English colonial systems have many parallels. In both cases, the crown initially gave local governors a free hand in the New World. Subsequently in both cases, the crown exercised direct control over its New World holdings. In New Spain, look at the *repartimiento*. In New England, look at the creation of the Dominion of New England.

French and English Exploration

France and England salivated at the great riches brought back to Europe by Spanish vessels. Both countries sought to duplicate Spain's successes in the New World, but neither country found mineral wealth comparable with New Spain's. By the close of the sixteenth century, neither country had even established a successful settlement in the New World.

Early failures did not deter England. Domestic economic factors pushed the drive for New World colonization forward. Population was rising in England in the 1500s, just as England was devoting more land to wool production and less to food production. The wool industry enriched merchants, but it put many English peasants in a vulnerable position.

A last obstacle to English colonization in the New World—concerns about a potential clash with the powerful Spanish navy—were largely overcome in 1588. In that year, the Spanish Armada was roundly defeated by a smaller but more mobile British fleet.

Subject to Debate

Most American history textbooks provide vivid accounts of the brutality of the Spanish conquistadores toward Native Americans. That the Spaniards were often cruel to the native peoples of the Americas is not in question. However, recently historians have begun to question the extent of Spanish brutality. Many of the early accounts of Spanish brutality are from British sources. Although these sources from the 1500s onward should not be discounted, it would be prudent for you to take into account their origin. British writers might have been trying to demonize Spanish behavior in order to portray British behavior in the New World in a more favorable light. The British portrayed themselves as altruistic, bringing God and civilization to the inhabitants of the New World, while the Spanish were portrayed as greedy and cruel. Of course, the historical record demonstrates that the British committed their share of atrocities in the New World, probably comparable to those committed in New Spain. The controversy provides us with a cautionary lesson. Look carefully at the source of documents as you use them to write about the past. The documents in the document-based question on the Advanced Placement exam clearly indicate their source. Do not ignore this information.

Practice Multiple-Choice Questions:

Directions: Pick the letter that best answers the following questions.

1. When historians refer to the "Columbian exchange," they are referring to
   (A) a series of letters between Columbus and King Ferdinand of Spain in which Columbus reports on his finds in the New World.
   (B) a prisoner exchange between Spain and the Mexica (Aztec) people in the aftermath of the Spanish conquest of Mexico.
   (C) a sharing of ideas and technology among the intelligentsia of Columbus's era.
   (D) the diffusion of cultural traits that the Europeans and the Native Americans shared with one another.
   (E) the animals, plants, and diseases that were exchanged between the Eastern and Western Hemispheres in the century after Columbus's journeys.

2. In 1513, Ponce de Leon led explorations into modern-day
   (A) California.
   (B) New Mexico.
   (C) Texas.
   (D) Florida.
   (E) Mississippi.

3. The fact that Venice, Genoa, Byzantium, and Turkey controlled Mediterranean trade routes led Spain and Portugal in the fifteenth century to
   (A) declare war throughout Europe.
   (B) begin the Crusades to recapture these routes.
   (C) search for alternative trade routes.
   (D) create self-sufficient economies.
   (E) trade with each other.

4. The *encomienda* system in New Spain most resembled
   (A) feudalism.
   (B) communism.
   (C) capitalism.
   (D) a hunter and gatherer society.
   (E) the factory system.

Practice Free-Response Questions:

1. Assess the ways in which European colonization transformed the Americas in the sixteenth century.

2. Why did Columbus's journeys to the New World generate a wave of exploration and colonization when journeys to the New World by Viking sailors five centuries earlier did not?

Answers and Explanations to Multiple-Choice Questions:

1. **(E)** The "Columbian exchange" transformed both the Old World and the New World. The most significant organisms to go from the Old World to the New World were germs. The inhabitants of the New World had not developed immunity to European diseases. Disease was, by far, the largest cause of death among Native-American peoples in the 1500s.

2. **(D)** Ponce de Leon made it as far north as Florida. He was in search of the fabled "fountain of youth." Later, Spaniards established the first permanent European settlement in what would become the United States at St. Augustine, Florida (1565). The United States acquired Florida from Spain in 1819 with the Adams-Onis Treaty.

3. **(C)** Spain and Portugal were looking for a new way to get to Asia without having to pay excessive fees to the Italian city-states that controlled Mediterranean trade routes. Portugal focused on getting to Asia by going around the tip of Africa. Spain, upon the urging of Columbus, focused on going west to get to the East.
4. **(A)** The *encomienda* system allowed local Spanish governors to act as feudal lords. They governed their area as if it were a medieval manor. The crown insisted that the *encomenderos* send a portion of the profits back to Spain. Other than that, the local rulers had a relatively free hand.

Establishment of the Thirteen Colonies, 1607–1711

TIMELINE

1607	Jamestown Colony founded
1609	Henry Hudson explores the area that will become New York
1609–1610	"Starving time" in Virginia
1619	House of Burgesses established
1620	Founding of the Plymouth Colony
	Mayflower Compact signed
1622	Attack on Jamestown by local Algonquian Indians
1624	New Amsterdam founded by the Dutch
1630	Founding of the Massachusetts Bay Colony
1630–1640	"Great Migration" of Puritans from England to Massachusetts
1632	Founding of the Georgia Colony
1636	Founding of the Rhode Island Colony
1638	Anne Hutchinson banned from Massachusetts
1639	The Fundamental Orders of Connecticut are adopted
1649	Act of Religious Toleration passed in Maryland
1663	Founding of the Carolina Colony
1679	The New Hampshire Colony separated from Massachusetts
1681	Founding of the Pennsylvania Colony
1711	Founding of the North Carolina Colony

England was eager to duplicate the stunning success of the Spanish in the New World. England emerged as the most powerful nation on the global stage after defeating the Spanish Armada in 1588. England then set its sights on North America. British colonization of the New World differed from the Spanish model. The early Spanish ventures were primarily funded directly by the crown. The early English colonies, however, were privately funded by joint-stock companies. Joint-stock companies were formed by a group of investors who hope to gain a profit from a successful venture. These joint-stock companies were granted charters to establish colonies in the New World. The plan was that the profits from the ventures would ultimately enrich Britain. Later, the British crown granted charters to proprietors, who the crown expected to be more compliant to royal prerogatives. Ultimately, almost all the colonies—charter colonies and proprietary colonies—were taken over directly by the crown and became royal colonies.

MERCANTILISM

Mercantilism Versus Capitalism
Be prepared to distinguish the economic ideas that shaped mercantilism from those that shaped capitalism. Mercantilism involved extensive government regulation of trade and economic activities; modern capitalism puts much more emphasis on free trade.

England's ambitions in the New World were shaped by mercantilism—a set of economic and political ideas that shaped colonial policy for the major powers in the early modern world. Mercantilism holds that only a limited amount of wealth exists in the world. Nations increase their power by increasing their share of the world's wealth. Nations therefore try to maximize the amount of precious metals they hold. One way of acquiring precious metals is to maintain a favorable balance of trade, with the value of exports exceeding the value of imports. Mercantilist theory suggests that governments should advance these goals by maintaining colonies so as to have a steady and inexpensive source for raw materials. The theory also holds that the colonies should not develop manufacturing but should purchase manufactured goods from the ruling country. England imposed several navigation laws on the American colonies to make sure the colonies fulfilled their role. However, some of these laws were difficult to enforce. The thirteen colonies began to develop an economy independent of England.

THE SOUTHERN COLONIES

Jamestown, Virginia

The earliest permanent English settlement in what would become the United States was Jamestown. It was founded in 1607. Investors in England formed a joint-stock company, the Virginia Company, to fund the expedition. King James I chartered the company and territory in the new world.

INITIAL DIFFICULTIES

The Jamestown colony nearly collapsed during its first few years of existence. The colonists were not prepared to establish a community, grow crops, and sustain themselves. They were mostly gentlemen, unaccustomed to working with their hands. These early settlers hoped to find gold and silver and to duplicate the Spanish successes in Central and South America quickly. They neither found precious metals nor planted crops. Their store of food diminished quickly. By 1608, only 38 of the original 144 colonists were still alive. By 1610, things hadn't improved. Only 60 settlers, out of 500 who had come over, were still alive. Many had perished during the "starving time" winter of 1609–1610.

TIP

Geography and Society
The "starving time" for the Virginia colony illustrates that geography and biology cannot always determine the outcomes of human events. One would have expected the Puritans in bitter-cold New England to die off in large numbers and the Virginians in a mild climate to thrive. The opposite occurred, showing that planning and organization trump geography and biology.

Jamestown and Its Native-American Neighbors

Relations with local Native Americans also deteriorated rapidly during the early years of the Jamestown colony. The local Algonquian people were led by their chief Powhatan, who was the father of Pocahontas. Powhatan's people traded corn with the settlers at first. When the Algonquians could not supply a sufficient amount of corn for their English neighbors, the English initiated raids on Powhatan's people. These skirmishes occurred for years until the Native Americans organized an assault on Jamestown in 1622. The raid did not dislodge the Jamestown settlement, but it turned the local Native Americans into bitter enemies of the English settlers. In many ways, the incidents in Jamestown foretell the history of relations between the Native-Americans of North America and the white settlers from Europe. Whites consistently encroached on Native American lands and consistently defeated the native peoples in the violent encounters that ensued.

Representative Government in Virginia: The House of Burgesses

Virginians organized the first representative legislative body in British North America, the House of Burgesses, in 1619. The company saw the need for some sort of body to govern the inhabitants of the colony and created this representative assembly. All free adult men could vote for representatives. The body continued to exist after King James revoked the Virginia Company's charter in 1624. Over time, the House of Burgesses became less powerful and more exclusive, as smaller planters were excluded from voting.

FROM CHARTER COLONY TO ROYAL COLONY

King James I revoked the charter of the Virginia Company in 1624 and made Virginia a royal colony under the control of a governor appointed by the king. King James was alarmed at the level of violence with the Native Americans, the high mortality rate, and the general level of mismanagement in the colony.

"BROWN GOLD": THE CULTIVATION OF TOBACCO

TIP

Agriculture, North Versus South
From the beginning, the northern and southern colonies developed different patterns of agriculture. The southern colonies focused on a few staple crops, grown for export. The northern colonies focused on smaller-scale agriculture and a variety of crops.

Eventually, the Virginia settlers figured out a way to survive and even thrive. Although the region did not contain vast deposits of gold or silver, it did contain the soil and weather conditions to grow vast amounts of tobacco. Tobacco had been introduced by the Spanish to Europe in the 1500s, but it remained a scarce luxury there. John Rolfe first planted tobacco in Virginia in 1612, and the first shipments of it were sent to England in 1617. With its addictive properties, tobacco soon became hugely popular in Europe and hugely profitable in the Chesapeake Bay region. By 1700, the American colonies were exporting more than 35 million pounds of tobacco a year.

THE PROBLEM OF LABOR IN VIRGINIA

The persistent problem of the wealthy Virginia planters was attracting enough settlers to do the difficult work of tobacco cultivation and processing. New immigrants were enticed to come to the New World with the offer of 50 acres, called a headright, upon arrival. However, this still required a potential settler to scrape together the fare for passage to the New World—approximately a year's income for an agrarian worker in England. After failing to enslave the native population, wealthy Virginians settled on indentured servitude as a means of bringing laborers to the New World. Under this system, a potential immigrant in England would agree to sign a contract to work as an indentured servant for a certain number of years in the New World (usually four to seven) in exchange for free passage. An agent would then sell this contract to a planter in the New World. The system accomplished its goal, allowing for tens of thousands of impoverished English men and women to migrate to the New World. However, the system also created an entire underclass of mistreated workers.

Maryland

Maryland was the first proprietary colony established by England in North America. The crown was moving away from the model of granting charters to joint-stock companies. It hoped that the proprietor (owner) of a colony would be more accountable to the monarch. The proprietor of Maryland was to be George Calvert, Lord Baltimore. Calvert was Catholic and hoped to create a refuge for Catholics in the New World. He was granted a charter by King Charles I but died weeks before the colony was to be established. His son, Cecelius Calvert, became the actual proprietor of Maryland. Almost immediately, Protestants outnumbered Catholics, but Catholicism continued to be tolerated in Maryland. In 1649, Maryland passed the Act of Religious Toleration, guaranteeing rights to Christians of all denominations.

The Carolinas

The colony of Carolina was established in 1663 by King Charles II. He was restored to the throne in 1660 and sought to reward eight noblemen who helped him regain the throne by granting them a charter for the lands south of Virginia. The proprietors of Carolina successfully recruited wealthy slave-owning English settlers in Barbados to resettle in Carolina. These early Carolinians looked to reproduce the export-oriented plantation economy of Barbados, but they could not find a crop nearly as profitable as sugar to grow in the Carolinas. By the late 1600s, they began making money growing and exporting rice. In 1711, the northern part of Carolina separated and formed North Carolina. The economy of North Carolina more closely resembled that of the Chesapeake colonies. South Carolina, which was made a royal colony in 1719, continued to replicate the economic conditions of Barbados, with thousands of slaves controlled by a relatively small number of elite planters.

Georgia

The last of the original thirteen colonies to be established was Georgia. Britain became increasingly concerned about competition from other European nations in regard to New World land claims. Britain wanted to establish a buffer between South Carolina and Spanish-held Florida. Toward this end, Britain granted a charter to James Oglethorpe to establish the colony of Georgia in 1732. Oglethorpe was a philanthropist and hoped to establish a paternalistic colony for England's "deserving poor," including imprisoned debtors. Oglethorpe did not grant his charges any element of representative government. He did mandate military service for all males. The royal plan seems to have been to have the poor of Georgia protect the wealthy planters of South Carolina from Spanish encroachment. Oglethorpe's plans did not come to fruition. Few "deserving poor" met Oglethorpe's requirements. Instead, Carolinians in search of new land moved into Georgia and brought slavery with them. In 1752, Oglethorpe gave up on his project and ceded control of the colony to the crown.

THE NEW ENGLAND COLONIES

The first colonists of the New England region were driven more by religious reasons than economic gain. The first New England settlers were devout Puritans. This religious motivation helps explain the unique patterns of development in New England.

Origins of Puritanism

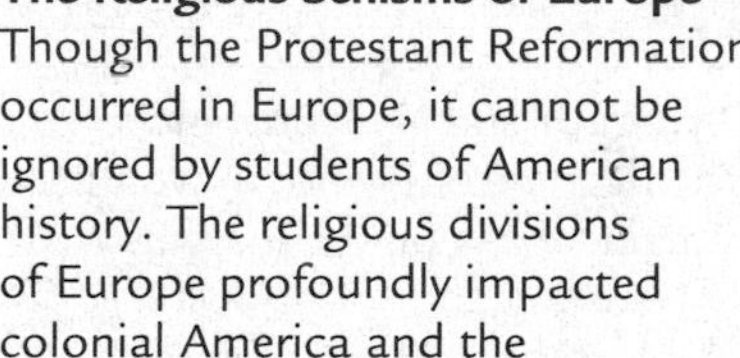

TIP

The Religious Schisms of Europe
Though the Protestant Reformation occurred in Europe, it cannot be ignored by students of American history. The religious divisions of Europe profoundly impacted colonial America and the United States.

The roots of Puritanism can be found in the Protestant Reformation of the first half of the sixteenth century. Martin Luther and John Calvin both broke with the Catholic Church over theological reasons. Both argued that the Catholic Church had strayed from its spiritual mission. The Protestant Reformation took hold in much of Northern Europe but not initially in England. In the 1530s, King Henry VIII of England initiated his own break with the Catholic Church. His break, however, was not over theological differences with Rome but over political control. Henry wanted control of the vast holdings of the church in England, the power to appoint members of the church hierarchy, and the power to annul his marriage. Because Henry's break with Rome was not theological in nature, he did not question, nor did he change, the traditional Roman Catholic religious practices. This "halfway reformation" upset many true Protestants in England. Those who sought a full reformation in England, who wanted the Church of England to be "purified" of Catholic practices, came to be known as Puritans. Some Puritans went even further and argued for a complete separation from the Church of England.

Puritan Beliefs and Practices

The Puritans took their inspiration from Calvinism. Calvinist doctrine taught that individual salvation was subject to a divine plan rather than to the actions of individuals. This doctrine of predestination left true believers in a state of anxiety since it was impossible to know God's will. To lessen this sense of anxiety, Puritans lived lives of strict piety, framed by prayer, righteous living, and hard work. Calvinism held that everyone had a "calling"—work on Earth that God intended the individual to do. Being diligent at one's calling, therefore, was central to Puritanism.

The Puritans also put a great value on community. Puritans believed it was God's wish that members of the community take care of one another and watch that members don't go astray. Individual malfeasance could result in divine punishment for the entire community.

TIP

The "City Upon a Hill"
The phrase is from Winthrop's sermon "A Model of Christian Charity." The sermon is very important and gives an excellent description of the Puritan mission in the New World.

Finally, the Puritan approach to humanity and to God was markedly dour, even dark. The Puritans put a great deal of emphasis on "original sin" (stemming from Eve and then Adam violating God's injunction not to eat the forbidden fruit in the Garden of Eden). They saw humanity as tainted with this inheritance. Further, the Puritans' vision of God was closer to the vengeful, jealous God that is in much of the Old Testament, rather than the loving God found in many of the New Testament books.

Plymouth and the Mayflower Compact

A group of English separatists, known to history as the "Pilgrims," fled England in 1608 to find a more hospitable religious climate in Holland. By this time, Holland was tolerant of different beliefs and had a strong Calvinist presence. It seemed like the ideal location for this group of English Calvinists. Although the Pilgrims did not suffer religious persecution in Holland, Pilgrim leaders became concerned about the material temptations of Holland. These leaders came to believe that the challenges of establishing a settlement in the New World would steel the congregants for the rigors of religious piety. William Bradford and the leadership of the Separatist community received permission from the king to settle in the land granted to the Virginia Company. They formed a joint-stock company to fund the expedition. Slightly over one hundred Separatists set sail on the *Mayflower* in 1620, arriving on Cape Cod eleven weeks later. They quickly realized that they were well north of their targeted area and did not have legal authority to settle. To provide a sense of legitimacy, they drew up and signed the Mayflower Compact, calling for orderly government based on the consent of the governed. The colony of Plymouth struggled the first year. By 1630, it achieved a small degree of success. However, it failed to attract large numbers of mainline Puritans.

TIP

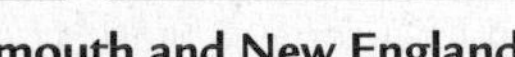

Plymouth and New England
The Pilgrims of Plymouth would remain largely on the margins of New England society. The Massachusetts Bay Colony founded a decade later than Plymouth would prove to be far more successful. One reason for the centrality of Plymouth in historical accounts is that it was the first New England colony.

Massachusetts Bay Colony—A City Upon a Hill

In 1629 King Charles I granted a charter to the Massachusetts Bay Company to establish a colony in the northern part of British North America. The charter did not specify the exact location of the company's headquarters, allowing the governance of the Massachusetts Bay Company to be located in the colony instead of in

England. This gave the colony a high degree of autonomy. The leader of the Massachusetts Bay Colony was John Winthrop. Before their ship, the *Arbella*, landed in present-day Salem in 1630, Winthrop gave a sermon that has become one of the more important sermons in American history. He stressed the importance of the mission that he and his fellow congregants were on. They should think of themselves as being "a city upon a hill," he insisted, for "the eyes of all people are upon us."

TIP 

Church and State
Students of American history often make a profound mistake about church and state in colonial Massachusetts. They hear in history class, "The Puritans came to America to practice their religion freely." From this they conclude that the origins of religious freedom can be found in Massachusetts. This is absolutely incorrect. The Puritans (with the exception of Roger Williams) established theocratic governments.

THE "GREAT MIGRATION" AND THE GROWTH OF NEW ENGLAND

Like their fellow New Englanders in Plymouth, the Massachusetts Bay Colony, centered in present-day Boston, had a difficult first year. However, unlike the Pilgrims in Plymouth, Winthrop's colony quickly thrived. By 1640, a "great migration" of more than 20,000 Puritan settlers came to the Massachusetts Bay Colony. The settlers arriving in Massachusetts Bay were "middling sorts"—farmers, carpenters, textile workers—not the noblemen of Jamestown. While the Jamestown settlers were primarily men, families came to the Massachusetts Bay Colony. The settlers in Massachusetts were eager to build permanent, cohesive communities, and they were willing to engage in strenuous labors. They were not looking for quick riches. The Massachusetts Bay Colony spun off ten new towns in the first decade after 1630 and over 130 by the end of the century.

Great Migrations
Avoid confusing the seventeenth-century Great Migration of the Puritans to New England with the twentieth-century Great Migration of African Americans from the rural South to the urban North and West.

New Hampshire

Some Puritans moved north to the area that would become New Hampshire. These Puritans were predated by some small fishing villages that were founded by Englishmen in the 1620s. Massachusetts claimed the region of New Hampshire, and a 1641 agreement gave it jurisdiction over New Hampshire. A royal decree separated the two colonies in 1679.

Roger Williams and the Founding of Rhode Island

Puritan society encouraged intensive studying and understanding of scripture. At the same time, the Puritan hierarchy enforced a rigid conformity to religious doctrine. This combination of learning and conformity led to inevitable conflicts in New England. Roger Williams was a devout Puritan minister who became an important dissenter in Massachusetts. Williams was increasingly concerned about the mistreatment of Native Americans by the Puritans. He was also critical of the involvement of the church in matters of civil governance. He was worried that the concerns of civil government would distract ministers from godly matters. He fled to the Narragansett Bay area in 1636 and founded the colony of Rhode Island. One of the distinguishing characteristics of Rhode Island was the separation of church and state.

The Banishment of Anne Hutchinson

Another important theological dispute in Puritan New England involved Anne Hutchinson. Hutchinson was a deeply religious thinker and had the temerity to hold meetings in her house to discuss theological matters with both men and women. In many ways, she took Puritan thought to its logical extreme, arguing that ministers were not needed to interpret and convey the teachings of the Bible. Rather God could communicate directly to true believers. Further, she accused Puritan leaders of backsliding on the idea that salvation was determined solely by God's divine plan, not by the actions of individuals. In 1638, John Winthrop and other Puritan leaders tried, excommunicated, and banished Hutchinson and her family.

The Founding of Connecticut

Some settlers to the growing Massachusetts Bay Colony sought to rid themselves of the heavy-handed rule of the colony's governor, John Winthrop. The Reverend Thomas Hooker argued with Winthrop over who should be admitted to church membership. Hooker argued for the less rigorous requirement of basing membership on living a godly life. Winthrop, however, insisted that new members be able to demonstrate to church leaders that they had had a conversion experience. Hooker led a group to the Connecticut River valley in 1636, where they founded the town of Hartford, well away from the reach of Winthrop. Other towns formed along the Connecticut River, combining with Hartford to form the colony of Connecticut. The Fundamental Orders of Connecticut were adopted in 1639. In 1662, the town of New Haven merged into the Connecticut Colony.

Puritanism and the Native Americans

The Puritan project of building an ideal community did not preclude them from forcing Native-American populations off land they hoped to expand to eventually. The interactions between the English settlers and native populations mirrored the violent clashes that occurred in Virginia. The most violent episode in the first years of settlement was the Pequot War of 1634–1638. The colonies of Massachusetts Bay and Plymouth worked in alliance with each other and with the Narragansett and the Mohegan peoples to defeat the Pequots. Later, additional warfare would virtually eliminate a cohesive native presence from New England.

THE MIDDLE COLONIES

The Dutch Presence in North America: New Amsterdam

The colony that would eventually become New York was founded by the Dutch as New Amsterdam. The Dutch West India Company sent Henry Hudson to explore the area in 1609. The company set out to establish a colony in the 1620s. Peter Minuit was an early director of the colony. Legend has it, he purchased the island of Manhattan for goods estimated to be worth $24. Almost all aspects of this transaction are in doubt—the value of the goods, the intentions of the Native Americans, and even the legitimacy of the Manhate people to "sell" the island. However, the myth of the "$24 Deal" has persisted.

From New Amsterdam to New York

Like the English companies that funded moneymaking ventures to the New World, the Dutch West India Company did not see immediate profits. The colony floundered. Few Dutch settlers came. The company tried to induce immigrants with generous land grants along the Hudson River. Slowly, settlers began to arrive—an amalgam of Europeans of diverse national and religious backgrounds. The colony even attracted some Jewish settlers. The Dutch also brought African slaves to New Amsterdam. The colony began to thrive under the leadership of the heavy-handed Peter Stuyvesant, who was hired by the company in 1647. Soon the restored English King Charles II set his sight on the "Dutch wedge," which divided England's holdings in North America. The king sent a fleet of warships to New Amsterdam. Stuyvesant surrendered in 1664 without a fight. Charles II granted the colony to his brother James, the Duke of York, who rechristened it New York.

TIP 

New Amsterdam and New York
There are commonalities between colonial New Amsterdam and modern New York City. In both, commerce plays a more important role than religion. Both are also incredibly diverse ethnically and racially.

New Jersey

The Duke of York gave the land adjacent to New York, between the Hudson and Delaware Rivers, to two friends who established the colony of New Jersey.

Delaware

Delaware was first settled by the Dutch in 1631, but all the initial settlers were soon killed in a dispute with Native Americans. In 1638, Sweden established a trading post and colony in Delaware at Fort Christina (present-day Wilmington). In 1651, the Dutch established a fort in the Swedish colony. Holland took over the colony and incorporated it into its North American holdings, New Netherlands, in 1655. When the Dutch were ousted by the British in 1664, the Duke of York granted Delaware to his friend William Penn, who incorporated it into his Pennsylvania land grant. In 1704, Pennsylvania's Lower Counties, as Delaware was referred to, developed their own representative body and effectively became independent of Pennsylvania.

Pennsylvania

In 1681, King Charles II granted an enormous piece of land (25,000 square miles) to William Penn to settle a debt that the king had owed to Penn's father. William Penn and the king were on friendly terms, despite the fact that Penn had become a devout Quaker and was often at odds with the official Church of England. Charles was no doubt pleased to see the establishment of a colony to draw the dissenting Quakers out of England. The king named the colony after William Penn's father, much to the embarrassment of the younger Penn.

QUAKERISM AND THE "HOLY EXPERIMENT"

TIP

Deference and Egalitarianism
Deference—the ritualistic display of submission by common people toward those of a "superior" class—was standard social practice in the European and colonial American world of the seventeenth and eighteenth centuries. The egalitarian spirit of Quakerism would come to shape social norms in the early United States.

Quakerism developed in the religious ferment of seventeenth-century England. Its approach to religion, and indeed to life, was radically nonhierarchical. In a society characterized by social titles and rules of deference, Quakers saw one another as equals in the eyes of God. They addressed one another as "friend" (hence their formal name, "the Religious Society of Friends"). They avoided the practice of the "lower sorts" bowing or removing their hat to their "betters;" Quakers shook hands with one another. Quakers did not have sermons; they attended "meetings" in which each congregant could speak if moved. Penn wanted to establish a "holy experiment" in the New World to put Quakerism's egalitarian values into practice. Penn initiated friendly relations with local native groups. Pennsylvania's Quakers practiced religious tolerance and frowned upon slavery (although it did exist in colonial Pennsylvania). Pennsylvania thrived in the seventeenth century. Its largest city, Philadelphia, surpassed New York as a commercial center.

Subject to Debate

Several important historiographical questions surround the English settlement of North America. Historians have questioned traditional accounts contrasting English colonization with Spanish colonization. In such accounts, the Spanish are portrayed as brutal, almost to point of sadistic, in their treatment of the native populations of Central and South America. Traditional accounts of the English settlement of North America have de-emphasized warfare with Native Americans and focused more on theological issues among Puritans and economic development. More recently, historians have questioned the veracity of some of the more graphic descriptions of Spanish actions in the Americas and have shed new light on the history of violence by Englishmen against native peoples.

Another question that has engaged historians is the comparisons between the New England and the Chesapeake colonies in the seventeenth century. Historical accounts have looked for differences between the northern and southern regions almost from the first day of settlement. To some degree, historians can be faulted for reading the more recent past (the Civil War) into the more distant past (the colonies in the 1600s) and concluding that the bloodshed of the 1860s was rooted in seventeenth-century patterns of development. It is open to interpretation whether the differences between the regions are more important than the commonalities.

Practice Multiple-Choice Questions:

Directions: Pick the letter that best answers the following questions.

1. The Puritans in colonial Massachusetts
   (A) believed in the concept of religious toleration.
   (B) coexisted peacefully with Native Americans and compensated the native peoples fairly for their land.
   (C) carried on the traditions of the Church of England.
   (D) encouraged debate about the fundamental beliefs of Puritanism.
   (E) set up theocratic governments.

2. Which of the following is *not* part of the Quaker tradition?
   (A) Quakers believed that God's "inner light" burned inside everyone.
   (B) Quakers held services without formal ministers, allowing anyone to speak as he or she pleased.
   (C) Quakers maintained a strict code of deference, where the "lowly" were to treat their "betters" with respect.
   (D) Quakers believed in treating the Native Americans in their presence with dignity and respect.
   (E) Quakers were critical of the institution of slavery (although slavery did exist in Pennsylvania).

3. The colony of Connecticut was established in 1636 when Thomas Hooker
   (A) attempted to expand the Dutch West India Company's holdings in the New World.
   (B) broke with Massachusetts governor John Winthrop over theological issues.
   (C) was given a gift of land by King Charles I to settle a debt the King owed to Hooker's family.
   (D) established a colony for British convicts.
   (E) created a series of tobacco plantations along the Connecticut River.

4. The "$24 deal" refers to
   (A) the amount of money, expressed in contemporary currency, needed to fund one's passage to the New World.
   (B) the transaction that the Dutch believed gave them title to the island of Manhattan.
   (C) the average price of a slave at auction in colonial Virginia.
   (D) a bribery attempt made by colonial merchants of British customs officials.
   (E) the purchase of a "letter of indulgence" from Catholic officials in Maryland in order to be forgiven of one's sins.

Practice Free-Response Questions:

1. To what extent did religion help shape the initial settlement of the New England colonies in the years 1620–1650?

2. How successful were the colonies of the Chesapeake in the years from 1607 to 1670? Analyze the factors that contributed to the level of success achieved.

Answers and Explanations to Multiple-Choice Questions:

1. **(E)** The Puritans set up theocratic governments. They did not believe in religious toleration. They demanded adherence to Puritan dictates. Anne Hutchinson was banned from the community for questioning these dictates.
2. **(C)** The Quaker tradition includes all the choices except choice C. The Quakers were against deference. They believed that we were all created by God, and there no "betters" or "lowly." That is why they shake hands instead of bow and why they refer to one another as "friend" rather than "sir."
3. **(B)** Thomas Hooker was a Puritan who believed in the doctrines of the faith. However, he found John Winthrop excessively rigid and overbearing. Hooker's inability to live side by side with Winthrop led Hooker to move to Connecticut with his followers.
4. **(B)** Many Americans are familiar with the story of the origins of New Amsterdam (New York). Wise Europeans bought it from the naive Native Americans for $24 in trinkets. The story is mainly myth, but it has persisted in the popular memory.

The Evolution of Colonial Society, 1620–1755

TIMELINE

1662	The Half-Way Covenant
1675	King Philip's War
1676	Bacon's Rebellion
1680	Pueblo Revolt (Pope's Rebellion)
1686	Creation of the Dominion of New England
1688	The Glorious Revolution
1689	New Englanders Topple the Dominion of New England
1692	Salem Witch Trials
1733	Molasses Act
1735	Zenger Trial
1739	Stono Rebellion
1741	Arrests and executions in the supposed "Negro Plot" in New York City
	Jonathan Edwards' sermon, "Sinners in the Hands of an Angry God"

Once established, the thirteen British colonies developed along different but parallel paths. We see distinct patterns of development in the three regions of colonial America. The southern colonies—Virginia, South Carolina, North Carolina, and Georgia—all moved toward an economy dominated by the institution of slavery. The New England colonies of Massachusetts, Rhode Island, Connecticut, and New Hampshire all experienced economic transformations that cast into doubt the ideal pious communities of the founding generation of Puritan settlers. The middle colonies of New York, New Jersey, Pennsylvania, and Delaware saw the development of economic and ethnic diversity as immigrants from Europe began to fill up these colonies. However, the thirteen colonies were united by shared experiences as much as they were separated by different patterns of development. All lived under the British crown and practiced some form of Protestantism. All maneuvered within mercantilist trade rules. All pushed back and fought with Native Americans. All were exposed to new philosophical and religious ideas. We begin to see in the eighteenth century a pattern of development in North America distinct from Great Britain. These distinctions begin to lay the groundwork for the political break that followed the intellectual break from the British.

DEVELOPMENT OF THE SLAVE SYSTEM IN THE SOUTHERN COLONIES

Slavery was part of English colonial North America from the earliest years. In 1619, twenty Africans arrived in Virginia, probably as slaves. However, slavery did not become central to the southern economy until later in the seventeenth century.

Bacon's Rebellion and the Development of Slavery in Virginia

TIP 

The Shift to Slavery
Remember, historians view Bacon's Rebellion as a key event in the shift from indentured servitude to slavery as the main form of labor in the South.

In the latter half of the seventeenth century, Virginia planters began to experience problems with the system of indentured servitude. Upon the end of their indenture, these men and women were generally not integrated into Virginia society. Many moved from the fertile tidewater region of Virginia into the hilly piedmont region. This inland region was also where many Native Americans had settled after being dislocated by the initial wave of English settlers. The former indentured servants grew resentful at the taxes they were required to pay the Virginia government and at their lack of representation in the House of Burgesses. Things grew worse for them as violence intensified on the frontier between these hardscrabble farmers and the nearby Native Americans.

In 1676, these frontier tensions erupted into a full-scale rebellion, known as Bacon's Rebellion. Nathaniel Bacon, a lower-level planter, championed the cause of the frontier farmers and became their leader. Governor William Berkeley refused to offer help in fighting the Native Americans. Many of the wealthy grandees engaged in a profitable trade with Native Americans and, therefore, did not want war waged against them. When colonial authorities refused to aid the frontier farmers, Bacon led a group of them into Jamestown, burning the homes of the elite planters and even the capital building. During the rebellion, Bacon himself died of disease. The rebellion was soon put down.

The rebellion proved to be an important turning point in colonial history as the elite planters turned increasingly to African slaves as their primary labor force. African slavery allowed the elite planters to emphasize a commonality of interests between themselves and the frontier farmers. Although the position of these frontier farmers did not appreciably improve, they could at least take solace in the fact that they were among the free Virginians and a member of the race they believed was superior.

Slavery in the Eighteenth-Century South

Slavery existed in all the British colonies of North America but grew most dramatically in the southern colonies in the last quarter of the seventeenth century and in the eighteenth century. The five southern colonies of Virginia, Maryland, South Carolina, North Carolina, and Georgia became the most populous region of the thirteen colonies—far surpassing both the New England colonies and the middle colonies. The main factor in this dramatic increase was the increase in the number of slaves in the South.

The upper South—consisting of the Chesapeake Bay colonies of Virginia and Maryland—was the most populous part of the South, containing 90 percent of the white population and 80 percent of the black population of the South. The main crop of the upper South was tobacco.

The population of the lower South—South Carolina, North Carolina, and Georgia—was considerably less than the upper South's, but the ratio of blacks to whites was significantly different. Blacks were the majority in the lower South, while they were in the minority in the upper South. In South Carolina by the mid-eighteenth century, there were approximately twice as many black slaves as there were whites. The primary crops of the lower South during the eighteenth century were rice and indigo.

The African Slave Trade

The African slave trade became a thriving business in the eighteenth century. European traders set up operations in coastal towns and encouraged Africans to venture into the interior to kidnap members of other ethnic groups. The slave trade not only resulted in the kidnapping of individuals, it also exacerbated ethnic tensions and served to destabilize the region. The victims of the slave trade were from a variety of cultural and linguistic groups. These Africans—mostly young and mostly male, with men outnumbering women two to one—were brought to coastal ports where they were sold to European slave traders. They were next transported to the New World in horrid conditions. This grueling, and often deadly, part of the journey is known as the middle passage. The most famous account of the middle passage by an African is contained in the narrative of Olaudah Equiano. This African slave trade is one of the legs of the Atlantic trade (also known as the triangle trade) that evolved during the colonial period.

Resistance to Slavery

Slaves resisted the brutality, humiliations, and grueling work of slavery in a number of ways. The main fear of slave owners was violent, open rebellion by their slaves. However, outright rebellion was not common. Since slave owners and white authorities had a monopoly on weaponry as well as the law behind them, outright rebellion was tantamount to suicide. Yet, attempts at rebellion did occur. The most famous slave rebellion of the colonial period was the Stono, South Carolina, rebellion in 1739. The rebellion, initiated by 20 slaves who obtained weapons by attacking a country store, led to the death of 20 slave owners and the plundering of half a dozen plantations. However, the rebellion was quickly put down. The heads of the participants were put on mileposts along the road. Lesser forms of resistance occurred on a daily basis, from working slowly to breaking tools. Also, slaves resisted by retaining cultural connections to Africa, maintaining traditional names and practices.

THE EVOLUTION OF PURITAN NEW ENGLAND

Puritan New England in the sixteenth and seventeenth centuries could be considered a successful failure. It was a success in that the economy of New England thrived during the colonial period. New England towns developed a diversified economy that generated wealth and contributed to a growing population. However, Puritan leaders expressed consternation at the decline of piety in New England. The Congregational Church (as the Puritan church was called) experienced a series of challenges and a decline in membership as time went on. By the mid-seventeenth century, it did seem as if the fire that animated the first generation of Puritan settlers had been greatly diminished.

Decline in Membership and the Half-Way Covenant

By the 1650s, Puritan leaders were noting a decline in church membership. The first generation of settlers were dying off or migrating to other towns. The second and third generations of New Englanders did not possess the level of piety of their parents and grandparents. In addition, after the initial creation of the New England congregations, potential new members—either children of original members or new immigrants to New England—had to demonstrate to church elders that they had had a conversion experience. The candidate for church membership had to convince church elders that they had experienced the workings of God in their soul. Demonstrating a conversion experience was exceedingly difficult. Therefore the idea of partial membership evolved. The Half-Way Covenant (1662) was an initiative in the Congregationalist Church to allow for partial church membership for children of church members. Even if they could not demonstrate a conversion experience, they could be baptized and become partial, nonvoting members of the church.

King Philip's War

Another challenge to the Puritan community was a brutal war with Native Americans. Relations with Native Americans, including with the powerful Wampanoags, were relatively peaceful after the Pequot War (1634–1638) (see Chapter 4). New Englanders had steadily been pushing into the interior of New England until 1675. In that year, the Wampanoags launched an attack on settlements in western Massachusetts. The New Englanders called the chief of the Wampanoags, King Philip. The counterattack by the New Englanders was fierce, targeting several New England Native-American groups. By spring 1676, over a thousand colonists were killed in King Philip's War and thousands of Native Americans were killed.

The Dominion of New England

King Philip's War was highly destructive to Puritan New England, but it led to even more challenges to the underpinnings of the Puritan experiment. In the aftermath of the fighting, King Charles II sent an agent to New England to investigate the practices of the New Englanders. Charles II became increasingly resentful of the New Englanders, especially in light of the fact that Puritans had pronounced a death sentence on his father, Charles I, during the English Civil War. The agent found ample evidence of New Englanders not living in conformity with English law. In 1686, royal officials revoked the charters of all the colonies north of Maryland and formed one massive colony called the Dominion of New England. This new colony was ruled directly by a royal appointee, Sir Edmund Andros. The governance of New England was no longer based on Puritan beliefs and values. It was a devastating blow to the Puritan movement.

The Glorious Revolution and the Restoration of Colonial Charters

The Dominion of New England did not last long. Events in England again had a major impact on events in British North America. A crisis developed involving religion and succession to the throne. After King Charles II died, his brother James II became king (1685). James had previously converted to Catholicism. Many Protestants in England were troubled by this but were calmed by the fact that James's daughter Mary, the heir apparent, was Protestant, having married William of Orange. However, in 1688, James's wife bore a male child—a new heir apparent and a Catholic. If James's son assumed the throne, England could expect a long line of Catholic monarchs. Protestant parliamentarians would not stand for this. They rose up in the Glorious Revolution (1688), inviting the Dutch William of Orange and his wife Mary to become England's monarchs. King James was deposed in this bloodless revolution. The Glorious Revolution empowered Parliament and ended absolute monarchy in England. It also led to the establishment of the English Bill of Rights. The turmoil in England inspired New Englanders to arrest Andros and to topple the Dominion of New England in 1689. Soon, individual royal charters were issued by the crown to the New England colonies.

Salem Witch Trials

In a global sense, the Salem witch trials are a mere footnote to the centuries of witch hunts in Europe that led to perhaps a hundred thousand people being executed. By the end of the seventeenth century, the fervor of witch hunts had subsided. Events in Salem in 1692 came at the tail end of this chapter in history. Historians have debated the reasons for the panic over witchcraft in Salem, but there is consensus that the trials reflect serious divisions in the once-cohesive Puritan world.

The first to be accused were teenage girls. To be accused of witchcraft meant that the accused was thought to be working in consort with Satan. In Puritan thinking, every event had some cosmic explanation. Misfortune in one's life (from a stillborn child to a bad harvest) could be divine punishment for sinful behavior. However, it could also be the work of an enemy who was channeling the power of Satan. This second explanation of misfortune pushes blame onto someone else—a witch. The epidemic of accusations in Salem tells us much about the Puritan community, three generations after John Winthrop urged his fellow Puritans onboard the *Arbella* to "be knit together in this work as one man." The fact that over a hundred members of the Salem community were accused of consorting with Satan speaks to the perceived lack of godly piety in New England. Also, the fact that neighbors were so ready to turn on neighbors, that men were ready to turn on women (the majority of the accused were women), and that the poorer members were ready to turn on the wealthy members all reflect a fractured community.

Democratic Participation in New England

The New England colonies encouraged a high degree of democratic participation in decision making. New England town meetings were face-to-face decision-making assemblies that were open to all free male residents of a town.

TIP 

Democracy in Colonial America
It is tempting to argue in an essay that American democracy can be found in the history of the colonial period. Be cautious. One can easily find as many undemocratic features of colonial life, from theocracy in New England to slavery throughout the colonies.

THE GROWTH OF THE MIDDLE COLONIES

The middle colonies—Pennsylvania, New York, New Jersey, and Delaware—experienced remarkable growth in the eighteenth century. German, Scots-Irish, and other immigrants contributed to the growth of the colonies. The largest immigrant group in the eighteenth century were the Scots-Irish, which was a label created in America to describe the Protestant immigrants from Scotland, northern Ireland, and northern England. Difficult economic conditions in those regions propelled the migration. Immigrants from the southwestern German states were the second-biggest group. These immigrants tended to be "middling sorts"—farmers, artisans, and laborers.

Economic Opportunity in Pennsylvania

The primary destination of these immigrants was Pennsylvania. The availability of land and the need for workers brought immigrants to Pennsylvania, especially to Philadelphia. Farther south, slavery was the dominant form of labor. Farther north, the legacy of Puritanism still enforced a cultural homogeneity. New York City attracted immigrants, but farmers found the best land along the Hudson River taken up by large estates. By the 1720s, some farmers were settling beyond the crest of the Appalachian Mountains, in the "backcountry" of Pennsylvania, Virginia (the area that would later become West Virginia), and North Carolina. Small-scale farmers in Pennsylvania specialized in growing wheat and experienced a higher standard of living than their counterparts in Europe. These backcountry Scots-Irish farmers carried with them resentments toward British rule. A rowdy march on Philadelphia by the Paxton Boys in 1764 challenged the colony's lenient policy toward Native Americans.

Slavery in New York

Slavery existed in all the colonies of British North America, but it did not become a central part of the economy in most of the northern colonies. The smaller-scale farms in the North and the shorter growing season did not lend themselves to the use of slave labor. Also, some of the religious sects that settled in the North, such as the Quakers in Pennsylvania, looked unfavorably on slavery. The one northern colony to have a strong slave presence in the eighteenth century was New York. By mid-century, New York had a larger slave population than North Carolina (but less than the other southern colonies). On the eve of the American Revolution, New York City's 3,000 slaves accounted for 14 percent of the population.

TIP 

Slavery in the North
In an essay that addresses slavery in the colonial period, do not ignore slavery in the northern colonies. Slavery was legal in all thirteen colonies at one time. Northern slaves worked as sailors, domestic servants, longshoremen, and artisans' assistants. New York had an especially large slave population. Slavery in the North was never as strong as it was in the South, but it did exist.

The "Negro Plot of 1741"

The tensions in New York between whites and enslaved African Americans came to the surface in a series of events in 1741. A series of unexplained fires in the city led authorities to believe that a slave conspiracy was afoot. Over 150 African Americans were arrested, along with 20 whites. At least 20 people were executed, more than those executed in the Salem witch trials. Historians have debated the extent of the plot or whether there even was a plot.

COMMONALITIES AMONG THE THIRTEEN COLONIES

The thirteen colonies had different origins and histories. However, they all had certain broad commonalities.

Navigation Acts and Mercantilism

From the 1650s until the American Revolution, Great Britain passed a number of Navigation Acts. The goal of the acts, in conformity to mercantilist principles (see Chapter 3), was to define the colonies as suppliers of raw materials to Great Britain and as markets for British manufactured items. Toward this end, British policy developed a list of enumerated goods—goods from the colonies that could be shipped only to Great Britain. These included goods that were essential for shipping, such as tar, pitch, and masts. Also, Britain insisted that profitable staple crops from the southern slave colonies, such as rice, tobacco, sugar, and indigo, could be shipped only to Great Britain. These goods were sold within Great Britain and to other countries at a considerable profit. The remuneration of these goods was a double-edged sword. The colonies could not always get the highest price for their goods but had a consistent market for them. Several of the acts—such as the Wool Act (1699), the Hat Act (1732), and the Iron Act (1750)—prohibited the colonies from manufacturing items from raw materials produced in the colonies. Manufacturers in Great Britain benefited from this arrangement.

The Atlantic Trade (Triangle Trade)

A vibrant trade developed in the Atlantic in the seventeenth century. Traditionally labeled the "triangle trade," this complex trading network brought manufactured items from Great Britain to Africa and the Americas. These items included firearms, shoes, furniture, ceramicware, and many other items. From Africa, kidnapped Africans were forced into the international slave trade, usually by members of coastal African groups. Once brought to port towns, European traders exchanged manufactured items for human cargo. Then these Africans were forced to endure the brutal middle passage—the journey in cramped quarters to the New World. The colonies of the Americas produced a wide variety of raw materials. Caribbean sugar, for instance, was shipped both to New England and to Europe

Salutary Neglect and the Growth of Commerce

The Navigation Acts existed on paper but were difficult to enforce. The lax enforcement of parliamentary laws in regard to the North American colonies is often referred to as "salutary neglect." The policy is partly due to circumstances (the difficulty in enforcing laws in a sprawling empire, thousands of miles from the mother country) and partly due to intention. Prime Minister Robert Walpole (1721–1742) is often blamed because he urged the crown not to interfere excessively with the profitable trade generated by the North American colonies. However, the realities of distance in the age of sailing ships made enforcement of navigation acts difficult.

The Granting of Titles
The American tradition of not granting titles was made official when the framers of the Constitution prohibited the practice.

Social Mobility

Throughout the thirteen colonies, there was a far greater degree of social mobility than in Europe. A growing economy and the availability of land prevented the development of a permanent underclass. In addition, there was no landed aristocracy in the United States. The patroons who owned the large estates along the Hudson River and the grandees who owned large plantations in the South might have thought of themselves as old-world aristocrats, but no hereditary titles were given in America.

The Colonies Develop a Distinct Identity

Salutary neglect allowed the North American colonies to thrive economically. Merchants routinely smuggled banned goods into and out of the thirteen colonies. For example, the Molasses Act (1733) placed a prohibitive tax on sugar from non-British colonies imported into North America. Boston merchants routinely flouted this law, shipping illegal sugar to supply Massachusetts rum distilleries. However, salutary neglect allowed the colonies to develop a unique set of cultural and political practices that later made independence from Britain a viable option.

Self-Government in the Era of Salutary Neglect

One of the results of salutary neglect was the development of a high degree of self-government in colonial America. The British did not have the ability or the will to install a comprehensive bureaucracy in the colonies (as they later would in India). Rather, most of the thirteen colonies followed a different form of political development. Whether the colonies were first ruled by a corporation or a proprietor, they eventually all became royal colonies under the supervision of the crown. The king appointed a governor to rule over each colony (sometimes one governor ruler over two colonies). In all cases, some sort of colonial legislature existed. These legislatures dealt with local matters, including the power to tax the inhabitants of the colony. (Legislatures did not deal with trade regulations.) Governors came to depend on funding from this tax revenue to run the colony. So in many instances, the colonial legislatures were able to exercise a good deal of leverage over the royal governors. This "power of the purse" instilled in many colonists a sense of their ability to govern themselves.

The Zenger Trial and Freedom of the Press

The colonists also came to value a free press. By the time of the American Revolution, over 40 weekly newspapers existed in colonial America. An important precedent for freedom of the press in America occurred in 1735. A New York City newspaper publisher, John Peter Zenger, was arrested and charged with seditious libel for printing articles critical of the governor. His lawyer successfully argued that he had the right to print such articles because they were truthful. The jury acquitted Zenger. In the wake of the case, more newspaper printers were willing to print articles critical of royal authorities.

Deism and the Enlightenment

In the 1700s, many educated colonists moved away from the rigid doctrines of Puritanism and other faiths. They adopted a form of worship known as deism. In a deist cosmology, God exists but as a distant entity. Deists did not see God intervening in the day-to-day affairs of humanity. God had created the world at some point in the past and also created a series of natural laws that govern Earth. In this, deists share the Enlightenment ethos of trying to uncover and understand the natural laws that control life on Earth. Deists see God as a great clock maker. In this analogy,

Earth is like a clock. God created the clock. However, the mechanisms of the clock, rather than God's interventions, move the hour and the minute hands.

The Great Awakening

In the face of declining church membership, a decline in religious zeal, and the rise of Enlightenment philosophy and deism, pious Christian leaders sought to take action. By the 1730s, we see several charismatic ministers attempting to infuse a new passion into religious practice. These ministers and their followers were part of a religious resurgence known as the Great Awakening. The movement took a more emotional, and less cerebral, approach to religion. In Massachusetts, the Puritan minister Jonathan Edwards delivered his famous sermon, "Sinners in the Hands of an Angry God," to a mesmerized audience. The most well-known Great Awakening preacher was George Whitefield. He was an English minister who visited America seven times and held large revival meetings in various locales. He gave dozens of sermons in the 1740s, bringing huge audiences to a state of religious ecstasy. Other itinerant preachers brought this emotional message to thousands of Americans. The Great Awakening's core message was that anyone could be saved and that people could make choices in their lives that would affect their afterlife. In this, the movement was both egalitarian and democratic.

The Spanish Colonial Experience
Students often ignore developments in New Spain. Be familiar with Spanish colonization, especially in the areas that would eventually become the United States. Contrary to traditional accounts, the American West was not an empty region before the period of Manifest Destiny.

TENSIONS IN NEW SPAIN

In the seventeenth and eighteen centuries, the Spanish Empire continued to push northward into lands that would later become the United States. New Spain expanded its reach, establishing colonies in Florida (1565), New Mexico (1598), and California (1602). Spaniards settled in New Spain throughout the seventeenth and eighteenth centuries. However, these northern colonies did not attract large numbers of settlers.

Pueblo Revolt

By the second half of the seventeenth century, Pueblo Indians in New Mexico had grown increasingly resentful of Spanish rule. The Spanish *encomienda* system undermined the traditional economy of the Pueblos, forcing Pueblos to labor in mines and fields. In addition, the Spanish outlawed traditional Pueblo religious practices. In 1680, these grievances came to the surface in the Pueblo Revolt, also knows as Pope's Rebellion. The rebellion was centered in Santa Fe and resulted in attacks on Spanish Franciscan priests as well as ordinary Spaniards. Over 300 Spaniards were killed. Spanish residents fled but returned later in the decade. As a result of the uprising, Spanish authorities appointed a public defender to protect native rights and agreed to allow the Pueblo people to continue their cultural practices. Also, each Pueblo family was granted land. The outcome of this rebellion was markedly different from conflicts between English settlers and native peoples. Such conflicts usually resulted in removal or eradication of the native peoples.

Subject to Debate

Historians continue to debate several important issues in regard to the development of slavery. Historical work has examined the relationship between racism and slavery. Did African slavery develop because of preconceived notions of racial hierarchies? Instead, did these notions of superior and inferior races develop over time to justify the continued enslavement of hundreds of thousands, and finally, millions of black Americans?

In addition, historians have debated whether the thirteen colonies' ties to Great Britain were beneficial or not to the colonies. On the one hand, mercantilist rules restricted colonial economic activity. The economic activity that was permitted was designed to benefit Great Britain more than the colonies. To support the argument that mercantilist rules hampered colonial economic development, historians have cited many colonists themselves, complaining of being "oppressed" and reduced to the status of "slaves." Other historians note that many of the mercantilist rules were simply ignored by the colonists.

Practice Multiple-Choice Questions:

Directions: Pick the letter that best answers the following questions.

1. Why did plantation owners in the Chesapeake Bay region turn to African slaves as their primary source of labor?
   (A) African slaves knew more about farming than did indentured servants.
   (B) Plantation owners found African slaves easier to control than other sources of labor.
   (C) Indentured servitude was outlawed by the British government.
   (D) The head-right system was abolished.
   (E) The government of Virginia subsidized planters up to $100 for each slave they brought into the colony.

2. The Stono Rebellion of 1739 was

(A) a violent march through the streets of Boston by colonists protesting the stationing of British troops in Massachusetts.
(B) a response by rural farmers in western Pennsylvania against taxation policies.
(C) a violent uprising by slaves in South Carolina that was quickly put down by local authorities.
(D) an attack by the Pequot people of Connecticut in response to the continued encroachments on their tribal lands.
(E) a protest by yeoman farmers in the backcountry of Virginia that led to the formation of West Virginia.

3. A central message of the religious movement known as the Great Awakening was that

(A) anyone could be saved.
(B) slavery was sanctioned by the Bible.
(C) God is dead.
(D) reason is superior to faith.
(E) salvation was reserved for the elect.

4. The British policy of salutary neglect in the first half of the eighteenth century involved

(A) avoiding contact with the native peoples of North America in the hope of maintaining peaceful relations on the frontier.
(B) encouraging colonists to *not* focus on the religious practices of their neighbors but instead to live and let live.
(C) allowing for the North American colonies to develop economically without rigid enforcement of mercantilist trade laws
(D) cutting political ties with the North American colonies and redirecting attention to colonies in Africa and Asia.
(E) letting children play on their own, away from the watchful eyes of adults.

Practice Free-Response Questions:

1. Assess the impact of the British policy of salutary neglect on the thirteen North American colonies.

2. Analyze reasons for the decline of Puritanism in seventeenth- and eighteenth-century New England.

Answers and Explanations to Multiple-Choice Questions:

1. **(B)** This question alludes to Bacon's Rebellion. Before 1676, the primary source of labor for the Virginia plantation owners was indentured servants. However, Bacon's Rebellion led plantation owners to turn to African slavery. Many of the rebels were former indentured servants who grew resentful of the elite class. With the widespread use of slavery in Virginia, the slave-holding class could assure poor white folks that they, were part of the ruling class; both slaveholders and poor were white and free.

2. **(C)** The Stono Rebellion was carried out by slaves in South Carolina in 1739. The rebellion was quickly put down, and the heads of the participants were put on pikes along the road. The few slave rebellions that occurred in the United States all point to a lesson—open rebellion was tantamount to suicide. Slaves learned to resist in more subtle ways.

3. **(A)** Great Awakening ministers had a broader understanding of salvation. They moved away from the bleak Puritan view of original sin and predestination. The movement appealed more to the emotions than to the intellect.

4. **(C)** In the 1600s, Great Britain imposed several navigation laws on the American colonies to ensure that the colonies carried out their role within the mercantilist system. However, some of these laws were difficult to enforce. The thirteen colonies began to develop an economy independent of Great Britain.

The American Revolution, 1763–1783

TIMELINE

1763	Treaty of Paris ends French and Indian War
	Proclamation Act
1764	Sugar Act
1765	Stamp Act
	Stamp Act Congress
1766	Declaratory Act
1767	Townshend Revenue Acts
1770	Boston Massacre
1772	*Gaspee* Affair
1773	Tea Act and the Boston Tea Party
1774	Coercive (Intolerable) Acts
	First Continental Congress
1775	Fighting at Lexington and Concord
	Second Continental Congress
1776	Publication of *Common Sense* by Thomas Paine
	Declaration of Independence
1777	Articles of Confederation
1778	Battle of Saratoga
	France enters the war on the side of the colonists
1783	Treaty of Paris ends the American Revolution

The American Revolution was a monumental event in the history of the United States as well as in world history. The American Revolution brought to the surface tensions that existed between the thirteen American colonies and the government of Great Britain. It also brought into existence a democratic republic. The democratic spirit that imbued the founding of the United States inspired movements for change—both within the United States and abroad. The American Revolution did not immediately give birth to a perfect democracy. Americans have struggled with the meaning and extent of democracy for the intervening 230 years.

THE FRENCH AND INDIAN WAR AND ITS AFTERMATH

The French and Indian War (1754–1763) proved to be a turning point in the relationship between Great Britain and the thirteen colonies. Before the war, Britain's policy of salutary neglect allowed both Great Britain and the colonies to benefit under loosely enforced mercantilist rules (see Chapter 5). After the war, the British government enacted a series of measures that many colonists found objectionable.

Causes of the War

The French and Indian War had complex origins. In part, it was a continuation of decades of European conflict between Great Britain and France. However, the causes of the war can also be traced to the New World. Both Great Britain and France had extensive land claims in North America. France's land claims stretched from Quebec, Montreal, and Detroit in the North all the way to the mouth of the Mississippi River in New Orleans to the South and from the Appalachian Mountains all the way to the Rocky Mountains. France claimed more land, but Great Britain had far more actual colonists in the New World.

In the 1740s and 1750s, British colonists began to venture from Virginia to settle beyond the Appalachian Mountains in the Ohio River Valley, land claimed by France. France began building fortifications in the region, notably Fort Duquesne at present-day Pittsburgh. The British colonists built a makeshift fort of their own nearby, Fort Necessity. In 1754, skirmishes between the two groups led to the beginning of the war.

A Global War
The French and Indian War rivaled the world wars in its geographic scope. It was known as the Seven-Year's War in Europe. In the Americas, it was fought from Nova Scotia in the North to the Great Lakes region in the West to Cuba in the South.

Fighting During the War

There are three distinct phases of the French and Indian War. At first (1754–1756), the war was a local affair—a continuation of the skirmishes between British colonists and French forces. Most of the Native-American tribes sided with the French, who tended to be more accommodating to local peoples than the British were. The scattered colonists attempted, unsuccessfully, to work with one another during this period. Colonial leaders met in Albany, New York (1754), to organize some sort of intercolonial government. Benjamin Franklin's proposed Albany Plan was rejected by the delegates.

In the second phase (1756–1758), the British government under Prime Minister William Pitt took full charge of the war. Pitt alienated many British colonists with his heavy-handed tactics, including forcing colonists into the army and seizing supplies from colonists. The colonists resisted these moves, putting the entire British effort at risk.

In the final phase (1758–1761), Pitt tried to work with colonial assemblies and also reinforced the war effort with more British troops. These moves proved successful. In 1761, French forces surrendered at Montreal. Two years later, a formal peace treaty was signed.

The Treaty of Paris (1763)

In the Treaty of Paris, France surrendered virtually its entire North American empire. It ceded lands east of the Mississippi River and in Canada to Great Britain and ceded lands west of the Mississippi River to Spain. British North American colonists were pleased that the land beyond the Appalachians seemed ready for additional settlement.

The Reorganization of the British Empire

If British colonists celebrated the removal of the French from North America, their celebration was short-lived. Almost immediately, the British government attempted to confront an ongoing problem—the large debt that had accumulated during almost half a century of constant warfare. The British believed their victory in the French and Indian War had been especially beneficial to the colonists. In return, the British reasoned it was fair for the colonists to assume some of the costs of the war and of continued protection.

A Shift in Colonial Policy
Note the shift in British policy from the salutary neglect approach prior to the French and Indian War to close supervision in the postwar period.

The Proclamation Act (1763)

One of the first postwar British acts was not a revenue act. The Proclamation Act (1763) drew a line through the Appalachian Mountains. Great Britain ordered the colonists not to settle beyond the line. The British government did not want to provoke additional warfare with native peoples in the region. The land between the Appalachian Mountains and the Mississippi was set aside as an "Indian Reserve." Colonists were disgruntled. They felt like they had sacrificed for the war, and they were eager to settle in these newly claimed lands.

The Stamp Act

The Stamp Act (1765), which imposed a tax on the paper used for various documents in the colonies, provoked the most intense opposition. This tax was solely a revenue-raising measure as opposed to earlier taxes that were designed to regulate trade.

Quartering of British Troops

The British stationed troops in Boston, forcing local residents to house and feed British troops (1765). Often these troops were given part-time wages, forcing them to supplement their wages by finding work in Boston.

FROM PROTEST TO RESISTANCE

We tend to assume, erroneously, that the seeds of independence were planted in the minds of the British colonists from the moment of their arrival in the New World. Even in the decade before independence, most colonists considered themselves to be loyal subjects of the British monarch. Only through a wrenching process did colonists begin to resist British authority and finally break with Great Britain.

Purpose of Taxes
The distinction between taxation to regulate trade and taxation to raise revenue was important to many colonists.

The Stamp Act Congress

The first significant, coordinated protests against British policies occurred in response to the Stamp Act (see above). In October 1765, delegates from nine of the colonies met in New York and drew up a document listing grievances, which went beyond the Stamp Act. The Declarations of the Stamp Act Congress asserted that only representatives elected by them could enact taxes on the colonies. "No taxation without representation!" became a rallying cry of opponents of British policies. The declarations followed on the heels of a series of proposals, written by Patrick Henry, called the Virginia Resolves. Not all of the resolves were passed by the Virginia assembly. However, they were all written up and circulated throughout the colonies. The resolves, debated in June 1765, called for a degree of colonial self-government that went beyond more moderate proposals.

The British responded to the cry of "no taxation without representation!" with the theory of "virtual representation." The theory held that members of Parliament represented the entire British Empire. The colonists therefore were virtually represented by the members of Parliament.

Committees of Correspondence

In communities throughout the colonies, Committees of Correspondence were organized starting in 1764. These committees of opponents of British policies initially spread information and coordinated actions. By the 1770s, they had become virtual shadow governments in the colonies, assuming powers and challenging the legitimacy of the legislative assemblies and royal governors.

Mobs and Crowds
Be aware of the different implications of "mob actions" and "crowd actions." Mob actions imply random acts of violence committed by unthinking groups of people. Crowd actions imply acts taken with a particular goal in mind by groups of people with an articulated agenda. Social historians have, of late, tended to favor using the term crowd actions.

Crowd Actions

The Stamp Act generated a variety of crowd actions in the colonies. In cities and towns throughout the colonies, Sons of Liberty groups formed. They harassed and occasionally attacked Stamp Act agents. There were several incidents of stores ransacked if the proprietor did not comply with boycotts of British goods. In Boston, the home of the lieutenant governor, Thomas Hutchinson, was ransacked. Finally, the Stamp Act itself was rescinded (1766). However, a series of British moves and colonial responses in the coming years worsened the situation.

The Townshend Acts

The Townshend Acts (1767), passed in the wake of the Stamp Act fiasco, imposed additional taxes on the colonists. Chancellor of the Exchequer Charles Townshend made sure these new taxes—on paint, paper, lead, and tea—were external taxes on imports, not internal sales taxes on items.

TIP 

Standing Armies
During the eighteenth and nineteenth centuries, suspicion of standing armies was part of the British and American political tradition. In the contemporary world, most people accept standing armies, even in peacetime.

The Boston Massacre

During the winter of 1770, a deadly incident in Boston reverberated throughout the colonies. In March, a disagreement between a British officer and a young wigmaker's apprentice escalated into a scuffle. Angry colonists heckled and threw stones at British troops. Finally, the British troops opened fire on the colonists, resulting in five deaths, including the death of an African American named Crispus Attucks. The incident reflected colonial resentment of the standing army stationed in Boston. In years to come, the incident would be used repeatedly as colonial propaganda to illustrate the brutality of the British.

The *Gaspee* Affair

In 1772, the *Gaspee* affair represented a shift toward more militant tactics by colonial protestors. A British revenue schooner, the *Gaspee*, ran aground in shallow waters near Warwick, Rhode Island. Local men boarded the ship, looted its contents, and finally torched it.

The Tea Act and the Boston Tea Party

In 1773, the British passed the Tea Act, which eliminated British tariffs from tea sold in the colonies by the British East India Company. This act actually lowered tea prices in Boston, but it angered many colonists who accused the British of doing special favors for a large company. The colonists responded by dumping cases of tea into Boston harbor. The dumping of the tea into the water was more than a symbolic act. The tea's value, adjusted for inflation, would be over $1 million today.

The Coercive/Intolerable Acts

The British passed a series of acts in 1774 in the wake of the Boston Tea Party that were called the Coercive Acts, or Intolerable Acts.

- The Massachusetts Government Act brought the governance of Massachusetts under direct British control.
- The Administration of Justice Act allowed British authorities to move trials from Massachusetts to Great Britain.
- The Boston Port Act closed the port of Boston to trade until further notice.
- The Quartering Act required Boston residents to house British troops upon command of the troops.

- The Quebec Act was passed around the same time but was unrelated to the Boston Tea Party. The act let Catholics in Quebec freely practice their religion. Protestant Bostonians saw this as an attack on their faith.

Lexington and Concord

In April 1775, fighting began between colonists and British troops in the Massachusetts towns of Lexington and Concord. Americans often call this "the shot heard round the world." It symbolized a marked shift in the colonial situation from protest to rebellion.

DECLARING INDEPENDENCE

Even though fighting had begun between the colonists and the British, independence was not a forgone conclusion. Some colonists, known as patriots, wanted independence. Others, known as loyalists, wanted to retain ties to Great Britain. (Of course, many colonists did not choose either side in the conflict). Both sides had good reasons for their stance—economic as well as emotional reasons.

The Olive Branch Petition

Some members of the Continental Congress still hoped for reconciliation. Congress sent the Olive Branch Petition to the king of Great Britain in July 1775, affirming loyalty to the monarch and blaming the current problems on Parliament. King George III rejected the petition.

Common Sense

As the debate about independence ensued, Thomas Paine published a best-selling pamphlet in 1776 called *Common Sense.* He suggested that the American colonies declare independence from Great Britain. He wrote that he could not see a "single advantage" in "being connected with Great Britain." According to him, relations between Great Britain and the colonies were strained at the time. Paine argued against the logic of the Olive Branch petition, forcefully putting the blame on the king.

The Declaration of Independence

On July 4, 1776, the delegates to the Second Continental Congress formally ratified the Declaration of Independence. John Locke's theory of natural rights states that the power to govern belongs to the people. Locke was one of the main intellectual influences in the writing of the Declaration of Independence. He wrote *Two Treatises on Government* in the early 1690s to defend England's Glorious Revolution (1688). Locke's writings challenged Thomas Hobbes's defense of an absolutist monarchy and Sir Robert Filmer's assertion of the divine right of kings. The body of the Declaration of Independence is a list of grievances against the king of Great Britain, but the eloquent preamble contains key elements of Locke's natural rights theory. It states that "all men are created equal" and "endowed by their Creator with certain unalienable rights." The declaration goes on to assert that government gains its legitimacy from having "the consent of the governed." If a government violates people's natural rights, the people have the right "to alter or to abolish it." These ideas have shaped democratic practices in the United States and beyond.

Defensive Versus Offensive Wars
It is easier to defend one's territory than to conquer another's territory. This is seen in the American Revolution and was one of the advantages of the Confederacy in the Civil War.

THE WAR FOR INDEPENDENCE

By 1776, even before the Declaration of Independence was ratified, the patriots and the British were at war.

Advantages of Each Side

Both sides had important advantages and disadvantages. The British had a highly trained, professional army. They had the strongest navy in the world. They had substantial financial resources. The British could also count on the support of a percentage of the colonial population that remained loyal to Great Britain. Great Britain also offered freedom to slaves who joined the British side. The British also could count on a majority of Native-American tribes for support.

However, the British were fighting far from home. It was difficult to maintain supply lines throughout the course of a long war. Great Britain also had enemies, such as the French, that wanted it defeated. Finally, Britain's formal style of fighting was ill suited for the wild and vast North American countryside.

The patriot side had excellent leadership in General George Washington. In addition, he had support from excellent European generals: the Marquis de Lafayette (French), Baron von Steuben (German), and Thaddeus Kosciusko and Casimir Pulaski (Polish). The patriots had the advantage of simply having to defend their home territory; they did not have to attack Great Britain to emerge victorious. Finally, many patriot soldiers believed deeply in the cause of independence. Colonial disadvantages included financing and a lack of a central governing authority.

Later in American history, the United States came to realize that urban centers are easier to hold on to than rural areas. This lesson was shown in the Vietnam War.

Phases of the American Revolution

Historians point to three distinct phases of the American Revolution. **The first phase (1775–1776) took place primarily in New England.** In this phase, Great Britain did not quite grasp the depth of patriot sentiment among many colonists. The British thought that the conflict was essentially a few pockets of hotheads in New England. After the British were defeated at the Battle of Bunker Hill (March 1776), they abandoned Boston and reevaluated their strategy.

The second phase (1776–1778) occurred primarily in the middle colonies. The British thought that if they could maintain control of New York, they could isolate rebellious New England. A massive British force drove George Washington and his troops out of New York City in the summer of 1776. However, British forces coming south from Canada suffered a major blow at the Battle of Saratoga in October 1777. The battle made it evident that the British might be able to control urban centers, like New York City, but would have great difficulty controlling the vast wilderness of North America. The battle also showed France that the colonists were a formidable force. Early in 1778, France formally recognized the United States and agreed to supply it with military assistance. France's motivation was animosity toward Great Britain, not affinity with the ideas of the Declaration of Independence.

The third phase (1778–1781) took place mostly in the South. Great Britain hoped that it could rally loyalist sentiment in the South, where it was strongest, and hopefully tap into resentment among the slave population of the South. The southern strategy did not bear fruit. The British enjoyed major victories at Savannah, Georgia, and Charleston, South Carolina. In the North, fighting had reached a stalemate, despite the aid that turncoat Benedict Arnold supplied to the British (1780). By October 1781, a joint American-French campaign caught British General Cornwallis off guard. He surrendered at Yorktown, ending the hostilities of the American Revolution.

TIP

The Three Treaties of Paris
They follow the:
- French and Indian War (1763)
- American Revolution (1783)
- Spanish-American War (1898)

Look at contextual information to understand which treaty is being discussed in a document or a question.

The Treaty of Paris

It took another two years to work out the details of a peace treaty. Finally, the Treaty of Paris was signed in 1783. In the treaty, Great Britain recognized the United States and granted it all the land south of Canada and north of Florida, from the Atlantic Ocean in the East to the Mississippi River in the West.

Subject to Debate

Along with the Civil War, the American Revolution is one of the most hotly debated topics in history. The American Revolution gave birth to the United States, so the stakes in understanding and interpreting it seem especially high. A person's understanding of the revolution is shaped by and shapes understanding of the United States itself.

Historians for generations have debated the causes of the thirteen colonies declaring independence. Some historians have stressed economic grievances against the mother country. Colonists declared independence to be free of British mercantilist rules. These historians have emphasized the colonial cry of "no taxation without representation!" as central to the struggle. This theory assumes a basic continuity, in regard to social values, between the colonial period and the national period.

Opposing historians have argued that economic issues were only part of the equation. They see a real break with the past—socially, culturally, and ideologically. Bernard Bailyn's *The Ideological Origins of the American Revolution* (1967) points to the development of a new set of ideas about politics and democracy that are profoundly important.

Historians influenced by the "new left" look at class divisions within American society, not just divisions between the colonies and Great Britain. This approach sees a class conflict in colonial America. On one side of the conflict are the colonial elites who tried to prevent the American Revolution from becoming revolutionary. They wanted to maintain the colonial social structure but without the British overlords. On the other side were dockworkers, small-scale farmers, apprentices, slaves, free Blacks, and other "lower sorts" who pushed for a real break with the hierarchies of the past. Their radical agenda was largely derailed by the delegates at the Constitutional Convention, who put a lid on these revolutionary impulses.

Practice Multiple-Choice Questions:

Directions: Pick the letter that best answers the following questions.

1. The Boston Massacre (1770) occurred when
   (A) colonial authorities tried and executed 19 African-American slaves accused of fomenting a rebellion.
   (B) activists in the Sons of Liberty forced their way into the residence of British Governor Thomas Hutchinson and executed him and his family.
   (C) members of the Mohawk Nation killed eight colonists in the Boston suburb of Dorchester.
   (D) Protestant colonists and Irish-Catholic immigrants brawled at Faneuil Hall, resulting is 11 deaths.
   (E) British troops fired upon colonists following a violent standoff at the Custom House, leading to five deaths.

2. The Boston Tea Party (1773) was primarily a response to Great Britain's decision to
   (A) ban the sale, production, and consumption of tea in colonial America.
   (B) impose a steep import tax on tea, thus nearly doubling the price for a pound of tea.
   (C) enforce the Coercive (Intolerable) Acts on the Massachusetts Colony.
   (D) grant a monopoly on selling tea in colonial America to the British East India Company.
   (E) quarter British troops in the homes of Bostonians.

3. France agreed to aid the patriot side in the American Revolution in the immediate aftermath of the
   (A) outbreak of fighting at Lexington and Concord.
   (B) British declaration of war against France.
   (C) decision by the Continental Congress to abolish slavery.
   (D) patriot victory at the Battle of Saratoga.
   (E) resolution by the Continental Congress to support France in its revolution.

4. Which of the following is not a reason that the British lost the American Revolution?

   (A) The British had difficulty supplying an army so far from home.
   (B) The colonists had a long history of having a professional, regular army.
   (C) The British were unfamiliar with the terrain of the thirteen colonies.
   (D) The colonists had strong leadership in George Washington.
   (E) France supplied the Continental Army with much-needed military support in the hope of defeating its longtime nemesis, Great Britain.

TIP 

Historical Neutrality
Try to avoid using the words "us," "our," and "we" when discussing the United States. Refer to the United States in a neutral manner. Strong essays should be intellectually engaged but not emotionally invested in a particular outcome or position. Such personal investment tends to undermine one's argument.

Practice Free-Response Questions:

1. "The American Revolution was essentially a conflict over economics rather than ideas." Assess the validity of this statement.

2. Analyze motivations of the colonists to choose either the loyalist side or the patriot side in the American Revolution.

Answers and Explanations to Multiple-Choice Questions:

1. **(E)** The Boston Massacre highlighted the resentments between local residents and British troops. It was an important event in colonial history. It wasn't the most deadly massacre in world history (five people died). However, it was effectively used for propaganda purposes by colonists before the American Revolution.

2. **(D)** The Boston Tea Party was somewhat ironic. The price of tea actually came down as a result of the Tea Act. However, colonists smelled a conspiracy afoot to undermine their freedoms.

3. **(D)** The AP exam does not focus on military history. However, you must be familiar with certain turning points in American wars. The Battle of Saratoga was one of them. France's motivation in joining the patriot side in the American Revolution was animosity toward Great Britain, not support for democratic ideals.

4. **(B)** All of the reasons listed explain why the British lost the American Revolution except choice B. The colonists did not have a long tradition of a professional army. There was a real suspicion among colonists of professional, standing armies. Whipping this ragtag force into the Continental Army was one of General Washington's most difficult challenges.

The Critical Period, 1781–1789

CHAPTER 7

TIMELINE

1781	Articles of Confederation ratified by states
1783	Treaty of Paris signed
1784	First Land Ordinance
	Treaty of Fort Stanwix
1785	Second Land Ordinance
1786	Shays's Rebellion
	Annapolis meeting to revise Articles of Confederation
1787	Northwest Ordinance
	Constitutional Convention in Philadelphia
1787	Delaware becomes first state to ratify Constitution
1788	Constitution officially ratified (nine states were needed for ratification). The last of the original thirteen states (Rhode Island) ratified the Constitution later (in 1790).

The decade of the 1780s was a trying one for the new American nation. The newly born United States fought and won the final stages of the American Revolution. Then it was faced with a series of challenges from within and from abroad that threatened its very existence. By the end of the critical period, the nation had shifted directions in regard to its governing structure.

TIP

Critical Condition
When you see the label Critical Period used to describe the decade of the 1780s, think of a patient in critical condition. Just like the health of a patient in critical condition is uncertain, the existence of the United States was in question.

VISIONS OF REPUBLICANISM

When the United States declared and eventually won its independence from Great Britain, it was not immediately clear what type of government it would embrace.

Republicanism
The eighteenth-century ideology of republicanism is not synonymous with the ideas of the Democratic-Republicans (1790s–1820s) or with the ideas of the later Republican Party (1850s–present).

There was widespread agreement that America would become a republic—a country in which sovereignty, or power, ultimately rested with the people rather than with a monarch. This was a radical move for the time. There had been virtually no republics in the world since the Roman Republic two thousand years earlier.

There was, however, disagreement about what was expected of citizens in a republic. For many Americans, republicanism implied a particular moral stance in the world. Republican citizens in this formulation were independent people who embodied civic virtue, putting the interests of the community above their own self-interest. Republican citizens led industrious, simple lives. This vision of republicanism dated back to ancient Rome. In this understanding of republicanism, virtuous citizens had to be on the watch for decadent and corrupt leaders who pursued luxury and power at the expense of the common good.

At the same time, other Americans were developing a different set of ideas about republicanism. They argued that individuals pursuing their own self-interest were the ideal republican citizens. This understanding of republicanism drew inspiration from the economic ideas of Adam Smith. It put more of a focus on ambition and economic freedom, while the earlier understanding put more of an emphasis on public virtue and civic mindedness. These differing views emerged repeatedly throughout the first decades of the United States.

THE ARTICLES OF CONFEDERATION

The framers of the Articles of Confederation created a "firm league of friendship" among the states rather than a strong, centralized nation. Before 1776, they had lived under a powerful, distant authority and did not want to repeat that experience. Many of these early leaders were also fiercely loyal to their states and did not want to see states' power taken away.

The Articles of Confederation were written in 1776 just as the Declaration of Independence was being written and debated. The Articles, however, lack any of the philosophical grandeur of Thomas Jefferson's document. The Articles more or less put down on paper what had come to exist organically over the previous year as the First and Second Continental Congresses began to assume more powers and responsibilities. The main concern at the time was carrying out war against Great Britain. The document was edited and sent to the states for ratification in 1777. It took, however, an additional four years for all the states to ratify it. The issue of western land claims caused several states to reject the document initially.

Structure of Government Under the Articles

The Articles called for a one-house, or unicameral, legislature, continuing the practice of the Second Continental Congress. This Congress would have delegations from each state. States could send anywhere from two to seven delegates, but each state delegation would get one vote. Decision making in Congress was not easy. Routine decisions required just a simple majority or seven votes. Major decisions, however, required nine votes, allowing five states to block major legislation. Changes and amendments to the document required a unanimous vote in Congress and ratification by all the state legislatures. In retrospect, these decision-making requirements seem to be a recipe for dysfunction. At the time, however, many Americans were weary of distant authority and wanted to keep decision making close to home. They did not want to see a central government with a free hand to do as it pleased.

Raising Revenue

The central government's lack of broad powers was especially problematic in regard to raising revenue. This was an acute problem during wartime. The central government did not have the power to tax the people directly. The idea of being taxed only by local representatives carried over from the days of the Stamp Act. The central government depended on voluntary contributions from the states. Congress agreed that states would contribute revenue in proportion to their population, but states were often tardy or resistant.

DOMESTIC PROBLEMS

Like any emerging nation, the United States was beset by a host of domestic problems during its first decade.

Inflation, Debt, and Rejection of the Import Tax

The United States faced serious economic problems during the 1780s. The Confederation Government and the states printed millions of dollars worth of paper money, driving up inflation. In addition, the government borrowed millions of dollars during the war. After the war, the government had trouble paying off these debts.

Robert Morris, chosen by Congress to address these issues, proposed a 5 percent impost, or import tax, to raise revenues. Since this would require a change in the Articles themselves, all thirteen states had to be on board. Rhode Island and New York, which both had thriving ports, did not want to give up the revenue stream from state duties, so they rejected the proposal. This rejection demonstrated the difficulties the Congress faced in passing important reforms. Morris also got Congress to create a national bank. The bank, however, failed to calm the fluctuating economy.

Dealing with Western Lands

The Confederation Congress made important progress in incorporating the country's western lands. The Treaty of Paris set the boundary of the United States at the Mississippi River. There was debate about the status of the vast swath of land between the Appalachian Mountains and the Mississippi River. Some states insisted that western land claims from the colonial period should be honored. Virginia, for instance, claimed all of the land north of the Ohio River. New York claimed a huge portion of the West, including land that over-

TIP 

Success in the West
The most significant accomplishments of the Articles of Confederation government involved dealing with the complex problems associated with the lands to the west of the Appalachian Mountains.

lapped with Virginia's claim. Some states, such as New Jersey and Maryland, had no claims. Maryland insisted that it would not ratify the Articles until all states gave up their land claims and the western lands became part of a national domain. Congress persuaded the states with claims to do just that.

TIP

Lack of Progress in Foreign Relations
The United States failed to achieve important foreign-policy goals during the Articles of Confederation period. This can be attributed to the weaknesses of the Articles or to the precarious position of a newly created nation.

Land Ordinances and the Northwest Ordinance

Once the western lands came under the control of the national government, Congress set about passing a series of acts to clarify the status of these lands. The Land Ordinance of 1784 called for dividing the West into ten states, with the guarantee of self-government. The following year, Congress passed the Land Ordinance of 1785, reducing the number of states to three from five and calling for the area to be surveyed and divided into lots. A lot in every town was set aside for education; the rest were to be sold. In 1787, Congress passed the Northwest Ordinance, which set up a process by which areas could become territories and then states. Once the population of a territory reached 60,000, it could write a constitution and apply for statehood. These states would be on equal footing with the original thirteen states; they would not have a second-class, colonial status. The Northwest Ordinance also banned slavery in the territory north of the Ohio River. These acts encouraged the steady and orderly flow of settlers into the West. This, however, proved disastrous for Native Americans.

FOREIGN AFFAIRS POSE PROBLEMS

The Confederation Congress faced several foreign-policy challenges during the Critical Period. The United States did not, for the most part, resolve these problems in a satisfactory way. To some degree, the Articles of Confederation failed to unify the thirteen states and failed to allow the United States to speak with a strong, united voice. More significantly, the United States was a young, weak country. It would have been surprising if such a country could force world powers such as Great Britain or Spain to toe the line.

The British and Native Americans

Americans became increasingly frustrated that the British had not evacuated forts in the western part of the United States following the signing of the Treaty of Paris (1783). The British maintained a thriving fur trade with Native-American groups in the area of the West north of the Ohio River. Further, the British provided the Shawnees, the Miamis, and the Delawares with weapons. The British insisted that they would not abandon their western presence until the United States repaid their war debts and allowed loyalists to recover property that had been confiscated during the war. The United States's minister to Great Britain pressed for a resolution to these issues but to no avail. The United States did not do much better with the Native-American nations of the Ohio River Valley. The Confederation Government worked out the Treaty of Fort Stanwix (1784) that, in theory, opened the area to white settlement. However, the Native Americans who negotiated the treaty (members of the Iroquois League) were not the actual Native-American groups who occupied the region. Bloody conflict would continue in the region into the next decade and beyond.

Conflict with Spain

In 1763, Spain had gained control of the Louisiana Territory, the vast swath of land west of the Mississippi River as well as the river itself, as a result of the French and Indian War. Spain also controlled the city of New Orleans, where the Mississippi River empties into the Gulf of Mexico. Spain grew increasingly alarmed by the number of American settlers who were pouring into the West. It suspected that the growing American population would soon begin to cross into Louisiana Territory and that eventually the United States would challenge Spain's claims to the region. To discourage American settlement in the West, Spain closed the Mississippi River to American shipping. John Jay attempted to pressure the Spanish minister to the United States, Don Diego de Gardoqui, to open the river to American shipping but, again, to no avail. Jay perhaps did not push as hard as he might have; he was more interested in developing and expanding the Atlantic trade than western trade.

Toward a New Framework for Governance

By 1786, many Americans, especially elite property owners, began to raise concerns about the stature of the United States on the world stage and the competency of such a weak central government. With these concerns in mind, a group of reformers got approval from Congress to meet in Annapolis, Maryland, in 1786 to discuss possible changes in the Articles of Confederation. A follow-up meeting was scheduled for the following May (1787) in Philadelphia. Between these meetings, Shays's Rebellion erupted in Massachusetts (August 1787–February 1787). It was put down, but it added fuel to the impetus to reform the governing structure. By the time of the Philadelphia meeting, the delegates were ready to scrap the entire Articles of Confederation and write something new.

Shays's Rebellion
This incident is considered one of the catalysts for creating a completely new governing document rather than simply amending the Articles of Confederation.

Shays's Rebellion (1786–1787)

Several of the problems associated with the critical period were evident in a farmers' rebellion in Massachusetts called Shays's Rebellion (1786–1787). Struggling farmers in the western part of the state, many of whom were veterans of the American Revolution, were troubled by several government actions. Taxes in Massachusetts, unlike some states, were stiff and had to be paid in hard currency (backed by gold or silver), not cheap paper currency. Unable to pay these taxes, many farmers were losing their farms to banks. The farmers petitioned the legislature to pass stay laws, which would have suspended creditors' rights to foreclose on farms. This, along with petitions to lower taxes, was rejected by the Massachusetts legislature.

After being frustrated by the legislature, hundreds of Massachusetts farmers, led by Daniel Shays, protested and finally took up arms. They were responding to a perceived injustice as they had a decade earlier when under British rule. They closed down several courts and freed farmers from debtors' prison. Local militias did not try to stop the actions, which spread to more towns in Massachusetts. After several weeks, the governor and legislature took action, calling up nearly 4,000 armed men to suppress the rebellion. Concerns about the ability of the authorities to put down future uprisings were on the minds of the delegates to the Philadelphia convention, which convened just three months after Shays's Rebellion ended.

THE CONSTITUTION: A BUNDLE OF COMPROMISES

The delegates at the Philadelphia meeting quickly agreed to scrap the Articles altogether and to create a new framework for government. For four months, delegates met, argued, and wrote. These deliberations resulted in a series of compromises that formed the basis of the Constitution.

The Great Compromise

The delegates at the Constitutional Conventional agreed that a central government with far greater powers was needed, but several contentious issues occupied much of their attention. A major source of debate was how the various states should be represented in the new government. Larger states expressed dissatisfaction with the one vote per state system that existed under the Articles; they argued that larger states should have a larger voice in government. The delegates from the larger states rallied around the Virginia Plan, which would have created a bicameral legislature that pegged the number of representatives from each state to the population of the state. The small states feared that their voices would be drowned out in such a legislature. They countered with the New Jersey Plan, which called for a one-house legislature with each state getting one vote (similar to the existing congress under the Articles of Confederation). After much wrangling, the delegates agreed on the Great Compromise, which created the basic structure of the U.S. Congress as it now exists. The plan called for a House of Representatives in which representation would be determined by the population of each state and for a Senate in which each state would get two members.

The Three-Fifths Compromise

Once it was established that representation in the House would be based on population, the issue arose about who would be counted in determining a state's population. Would a southern state be able to count its slave population in the census? This was a major issue when one considered that for states such as South Carolina and Mississippi, the slave population comprised more than 50 percent of the population. To count slaves in the census would more than double the size of a state's delegation in the House. Northern states objected on the grounds that slaves could not vote. In fact, slaves were considered property, not human beings. After much debate, a compromise was reached in which southern states could count three-fifths of their slave populations in the census. This Three-Fifths Compromise defied common sense, but it got the delegates through an impasse.

Tacit Approval of Slavery

The Three-Fifths Compromise did not mention the word "slave." In fact, the word is not mentioned in the entire document. Slaves are often referred to as "other persons." The reluctance of the delegates to even use the word slave reflected their discomfort with the institution. Though it wasn't mentioned directly, slavery was dealt with in several instances in the Constitution. The delegates voted to protect the international slave trade for 20 years, guaranteeing the flow of slaves into the country from Africa and the Caribbean for another generation. (The international slave trade was ended by Congress in 1808, the earliest date that the Constitution allowed.) Finally, the Constitution provided for the return of fugitive slaves. (A mechanism for the return of fugitive slaves was contained in the Fugitive Slave Act of 1793. The process was strengthened with the Fugitive Slave Act of 1850.) Though slavery wasn't mentioned by name, the inclusion of regulations around slavery made clear that the Constitution recognized its existence.

The Three Branches of Government and Checks and Balances

The framers of the Constitution created three branches of government. The legislative branch creates laws, the executive branch carries out laws, and the judicial branch interprets laws. The Constitution spells out the powers of each branch. The powers of Congress are enumerated in Article I. These include the power to levy taxes, to regulate trade, to coin money, to establish post offices, to declare war, and to approve treaties. The framers of the Constitution wanted Congress to have the flexibility to deal with the needs of a changing society. Toward this goal, they included the elastic clause, which stretched the powers of Congress by allowing it to "make all laws necessary and proper . . . " However, the definition of "necessary and proper" soon became a matter of much debate. The powers of the president are included in Article II. These include the power to suggest legislation, to command the armed forces, and to nominate judges. The president is charged with carrying out the laws of the land. The powers of the judiciary, headed by the Supreme Court, are outlined in Article III.

TIP 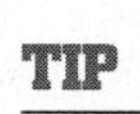

Madison and the Constitution

The basic structural elements of the Constitution—three branches of government with a system of checks and balances—are explained and defended in James Madison's *Federalist Number 51*.

The framers were very conscious of the problems of a government with limitless powers. After living under the British monarchy, they came to believe that a powerful government without checks was dangerous to liberty. Therefore, they created a governmental system with three branches, each with the ability to check the powers of the other two. The goal was to keep the three branches in balance. Examples of checks and balances include the president's ability to veto (or reject) bills passed by Congress and the Supreme Court's ability to strike down laws that it deems unconstitutional.

The Federal Government and the States

Under the Constitution, states would still hold onto certain powers (reserved powers), but an expanded national government would be given many new powers (delegated powers). The Constitution makes clear that the federal government is the "supreme law of the land."

DEBATE OVER RATIFICATION

TIP

Federalist Papers
Be familiar with the overall approach of the *Federalist Papers* and especially the arguments in *Federalist No. 10* and *No. 51*.

Once the Constitution was completed, it went to the states for ratification. Each state was to call a convention to vote on and ratify the document. Only nine states were needed for approval. This was still not an easy process. Large numbers of Americans opposed the creation of a powerful central government. Public opinion in Virginia, Massachusetts, and New York was clearly against ratification. North Carolina and Rhode Island did not even convene conventions.

The Federalists

The supporters of the Constitution labeled themselves Federalists. Three important Federalist theorists were Alexander Hamilton, John Jay, and James Madison. As the New York convention was debating ratification, the three wrote a series of articles that were late published in book form—*The Federalist* (see figure in multiple-choice question 2 in this section, below). This highly influential political tract outlined the failures of the Articles of Confederation and the benefits of a powerful government, with checks and balances. In *Federalist Number 10*, Madison argued that a complex government that governed a large and diverse population was the best guarantee of liberty. In such a scenario, no one group could gain control and dominate others. This argument challenged the traditional republican notion that republics must be small in order to function effectively. In *Federalist Number 51*, he argued for a separation of powers within the government and a system of checks and balances. In this essay, Madison asserted that "ambition must be made to counteract ambition."

TIP

The Antifederalists
The Antifederalists have been saddled with an unfortunate name. They sound like naysayers. However, you should take their ideas seriously. They had a comprehensive view of the world. Just because they lost the fight over ratification does not mean they should be dismissed. After all, their agitation led to the Bill of Rights.

Antifederalism

Opponents of the new Constitution, Antifederalists, as they were called by their Federalist adversaries, worried that the new government would be controlled by members of the elite. They saw the document as favoring the creation of a powerful, aristocratic ruling class. Leading Antifederalists were Patrick Henry and George Mason. They argued that government officials in the national government would be, almost by definition, removed from the concerns and the control of ordinary people. They were distrustful of distant authority. The thirteen colonies had just emerged from under the thumb of the British Empire, so many colonists were eager to see power exercised locally. One of the Antifederalists' primary concerns was that individual rights were not adequately protected by the Constitution. They noted that the document did not contain a bill of rights.

Ratification

Delaware ratified the Constitution almost immediately, in late 1787. By May of the following year, eight states had voted to ratify. New Hampshire provided the ninth and deciding vote in 1788. Since the Constitution itself does not devote much attention to individual rights, Antifederalists demanded a list of individual rights that the government would not be allowed to take away. Many Antifederalists in the various states refused to support ratification of the Constitution unless such a list was added. The Federalists promised to add such a list if the Antifederalists agreed to support ratification. This agreement led to the writing and ratification of the first 10 amendments to the Constitution, known as the Bill of Rights. By May 1790, the final four states— Virginia (1788) New York (1788), North Carolina (1789), and Rhode Island (1790)—voted for ratification and joined the new union.

Subject to Debate

You should be aware of several important questions in regard to the Critical Period. The first important question is the nature of the Articles of Confederation. Because it lasted less than a decade and because the Constitution has endured for over 230 years, there is a tendency to elevate the historical standing of the Constitution and to denigrate the Articles of Confederation. This is to be expected, but we should be careful not to go too far. To admit to the effectiveness of the Constitution does not require us to ignore anything positive about the Articles. The thirteen colonies won the American Revolution during the Articles of Confederation period. The Articles also did an excellent job dealing with the newly acquired western lands. It is true that the national government was weak under the Articles; but even this can be seen as a positive. The Articles, we can argue, effectively protected the traditional rights of the states. Historical debate should be fair to the much-maligned Articles.

Practice Multiple-Choice Questions:

Directions: Pick the letter that best answers the following questions.

1. In the Constitution, which of the following powers is a reserved, or state, power?
   (A) The power to ratify trade treaties with foreign nations
   (B) The power to print and issue currency
   (C) The power to establish uniform weights and measurements
   (D) The power to run an educational system
   (E) The power to run the postal service

THE

FEDERALIST:

ADDRESSED TO THE

PEOPLE OF THE STATE OF NEW YORK.

NUMBER I.

Introduction.

AFTER an unequivocal experience of the inefficacy of the ſubſiſting federal government, you are called upon to deliberate on a new conſtitution for the United States of America. The ſubject ſpeaks its own importance; comprehending in its conſequences, nothing leſs than the exiſtence of the UNION, the ſafety and welfare of the parts of which it is compoſed, the fate of an empire, in many reſpects, the moſt intereſting in the world. It has been frequently remarked, that it ſeems to have been reſerved to the people of this country, by their conduct and example, to decide the important queſtion, whether ſocieties of men are really capable or not, of eſtabliſhing good government from reflection and choice, or whether they are forever deſtined to depend, for their political conſtitutions, on accident and force. If there be any truth in the remark, the criſis, at which we are arrived, may with propriety be regarded as the æra in which

A that

2. The page shown above is from a collection of essays that was written in order to garner support for

   (A) declaring independence from Great Britain.
   (B) retaining the Articles of Confederation.
   (C) ratifying the Constitution.
   (D) electing George Washington as president.
   (E) chartering the National Bank.

3. The United States grew increasingly frustrated with Spain during the 1780s because Spain

   (A) closed the Mississippi River to American shipping.
   (B) intercepted American ships on the high seas and pressed American sailors into service.
   (C) sent agents into the American South to foment a slave rebellion.
   (D) refused to sell Cuba to the United States.
   (E) invoked the 1494 Treaty of Tordesillas to claim that the United States was actually Spanish territory.

4. Which of the following provisions is included in the Northwest Ordinance?

   (A) Slavery would be banned in future states in the northern portion of the Northwest Territory, but it would be permissible in the southern portion.
   (B) A territory could write a constitution and apply for statehood once it reached a population of 60,000.
   (C) Future states carved out of the Northwest Territory would have only one senator; only the original thirteen states would have the privilege of having two senators.
   (D) Families would be granted up to 160 acres by the federal government if they agreed to farm the land for at least seven years.
   (E) Settlers in the Northwest Territory would have to pay Native Americans at the rate of $50 per acre for land before they could set up a homestead.

Practice Free-Response Questions:

1. To what degree was the Articles of Confederation Government successful in addressing foreign-relations issues?

2. "The replacement of the Articles of Confederation with the Constitution amounts to an undemocratic coup." Assess the validity of this statement.

Answers and Explanations to Multiple-Choice Questions:

1. **(D)** Powers retained by the states were referred to as reserved; powers given to the federal government were called delegated powers.

2. **(C)** *The Federalist* is now available in bookstores as *The Federalist Papers.* Its authors (Alexander Hamilton, John Jay, and James Madison) set forth their reasons for a stronger federal government.

3. **(A)** In its early years, the United States was beset by a series of foreign-policy difficulties. Spain had gotten control of the Louisiana Territory after France lost the French and Indian War (1754). Spain was alarmed at the number of Americans who were coming into the Mississippi River Valley. It closed off the river to American shipping in the hope of discouraging migration to the region. France regained control of Louisiana in 1801, just before selling it to the United States in 1803.

4. **(B)** The Articles of Confederation did not have a lot of successes, but it was successful in dealing with western land holdings. The Northwest Territory is the vast stretch of land north of the Ohio River, between the western border of Pennsylvania and the Mississippi River. The Land Ordinance (1785) and the Northwest Ordinance (1787) both deal with this territory.

The Early National Period, 1789–1800

TIMELINE

1789	Inauguration of George Washington
	Judiciary Act
	Beginning of the French Revolution
1791	Ratification of the Bill of Rights
	Alexander Hamilton issues the *Report on Manufacturers*
	The Bank of the United States is approved
1793	War between Great Britain and France
	Washington Neutrality Proclamation
1794	Whiskey Rebellion
	Jay's Treaty
1795	Pinckney's Treaty
1796	Washington's Farewell Address
1798	XYZ Affair
	Quasi-War with France
	Alien and Sedition Acts
	Kentucky and Virginia Resolutions

The first dozen years after the ratification of the Constitution were key in the shaping of the United States political system. The government reformed in conformity with the Constitution. The Bill of Rights established important civil liberties. During this period, many of the American political system's traditions and precedents—collectively known as the "unwritten Constitution"—were established. We see the development of political parties and of the two-party system during these years.

WASHINGTON INAUGURATES THE GOVERNMENT

George Washington was the obvious choice to lead the nation following ratification of the Constitution. He was the hero of the American Revolution and the only figure of national prominence. Washington, however, was worried that assuming the office would seem like a power grab. He looked approvingly to the ancient Roman General Cincinnatus, who retired to his farm after achieving victory in battle. Washington saw himself as possessing similar republican qualities—simplicity and virtue. When the public clamor for Washington to assume the presidency was sufficiently loud, Washington agreed.

Washington and the Unwritten Constitution

Washington wisely chose capable and experienced men to run the new government's three departments—state, war, and treasury. Washington chose Thomas Jefferson for the Department of State, General Henry Knox for the Department of War, and Alexander Hamilton for the Treasury. He also chose Edmund Randolph as the nation's first attorney general and John Jay as chief justice of the Supreme Court. Washington began meeting regularly with these men, seeking their input on important decisions. This practice of meeting regularly with a presidential cabinet was subsequently practiced by all American presidents. The cabinet is one of several traditions and customs that Washington established and that have come to be known as the unwritten constitution. Washington's decision to run for no more than two terms was also part of the unwritten constitution until Congress and the states ratified the Twenty-second Amendment (1951), following Franklin D. Roosevelt's four electoral victories, making this tradition part of the actual Constitution.

THE BILL OF RIGHTS

During the debate over ratification of the Constitution, seven of the states that ratified the Constitution did so only under the condition that Congress would ratify a list of rights of the people. Antifederalists in these states feared that a sprawling, powerful government would step on individual liberties. As promised, one of the first acts of Congress was passage of the Bill of Rights—the first ten amendments to the Constitution. Much of the language in the Bill of Rights, written by James Madison, comes from the various states' Constitutions.

First, Second, Third, and Fourth Amendments: Basic Rights of the People

The First Amendment contains the establishment clause prohibiting the establishment of an official religion in the United States. The remainder of the First Amendment deals with various forms of freedom of expression. The Second Amendment guarantees the right to bear arms. Some have argued that the language of the Second Amendment seems to link the right to bear arms to participation in militias; others have argued that it an absolute individual right. The Third Amendment addressed a much-hated British practice—forcing colonial residents to house British soldiers. Americans would not be compelled to quarter soldiers. The Fourth Amendment guarantees a modicum of privacy from searches by government officials. People are protected in their "persons, houses, papers and effects" from "unreasonable searches and seizures." Authorities must first obtain a warrant issued by a judge if evidence has shown "probable cause."

Fifth, Sixth, Seventh, and Eighth Amendments: Rights of the Accused

Several amendments in the Bill of Rights address protections that people have when they are brought into the legal system. The logic of these amendments is that the legal system is powerful and well funded and should therefore have checks placed upon it to protect the individual. The Fifth Amendment calls for grand jury indictments, prohibits authorities from trying a suspect twice for the same crime (double jeopardy), and prohibits forcing a suspect to testify against himself or herself. The Fifth Amendment also prohibits the government from seizing someone's property unless it is for a "public use" and the owner receives "just compensation." This power of the government to seize private property, with these stipulations, is known as eminent domain. The Sixth Amendment guarantees suspects the right to a "speedy and public" trial, with a jury, conducted in the district in which the crime was committed. The suspect also has a right to be informed of the charges against him or her. The suspect has the right to question the witnesses against him or her. Finally, suspects have the right to call friendly witnesses to the stand and the right to a lawyer. The Seventh Amendment guarantees people the right to a trial by jury even in civil cases (conflicts between two parties over monetary damages). The Eighth Amendment prevents the government from inflicting "cruel and unusual" punishments and prevents the setting of "excessive bail."

Ninth and Tenth Amendments

The last two amendments of the Bill of Rights deal with the limits and parameters of rights and powers in the government. The Ninth Amendment guarantees that additional rights not mentioned in the Bill of Rights shall be protected from government infringement. The Tenth Amendment deals with governmental powers. It puts forth that powers not delegated to the federal government shall be retained by the states and by the people.

The Right to Vote

The right to vote is absent from the Bill of Rights. The federal government left it to the states to formulate rules for voting. Only later was voting seen as a fundamental right that needed the protection of constitutional amendments. The Fifteenth Amendment (1870) prohibited voting restrictions based on race. The Nineteenth Amendment (1920) prohibited venting restrictions based on sex. The Twenty-sixth Amendment (1971) lowered the voting age to 18.

HAMILTON'S ECONOMIC PROGRAM

TIP

Interpreting the Constitution
The debate over a national bank represents an ongoing debate in American history between those with a strict and a those with a loose interpretation of the Constitution.

Washington's secretary of the treasury, Alexander Hamilton, proposed a series of economic measures meant to put the United States on sound economic footing. Central to his plans was a national bank, which would hold the government's tax revenues and act as a stabilizing force on the economy. Hamilton proposed a national bank that would be 20 percent publicly controlled and 80 percent privately controlled. Hamilton thought it was important to have wealthy investors financially and psychologically invested in the new government. The proposal to create a national bank became a source of disagreement between Hamilton and Secretary of State Thomas Jefferson. Jefferson argued that the Constitution did not permit Congress to create a national bank. It was not among the powers listed in the Constitution. Hamilton countered that the elastic clause, which lets Congress do what it considered "necessary and proper," implicitly allowed for the creation of a national bank. President Washington agreed and signed the bank law in 1791.

Dealing with Debt

TIP

Funding and Assumption
Be familiar with these two terms in regard to Hamilton's approach to paying off war-related debt.

Hamilton's economic program included two other significant parts. He proposed an elaborate and controversial plan to deal with the new nation's substantial debt. He insisted that debts carried over from the war years be paid back, or funded, at full value. Many of the debt certificates had been sold by their holders. The original holders had little faith that the government would ever make good on the actual loans. The certificates were changing hands at a fraction of their original value. Full funding meant a financial windfall for speculators who bought up the certificates. In addition, Hamilton insisted that the government assume, or agree to pay back, state debts incurred during the war. The proposal met with strenuous opposition from states that either did not have a large debt or had already paid back their debts. To accomplish the goals of funding and assumption, Hamilton prodded the government to take out new loans by selling government bonds.

Encouragement to Manufacturing

The final piece of Hamilton's financial program was to encourage manufacturing by imposing tariffs on foreign-made goods and subsidizing American industry. (Congress adopted Hamilton's *Report on Manufactures*, except for his recommendation of subsidies to industry.) He believed industrial development would be the key to a balanced and self-reliant economy. The nation, however, was not yet ready for developing its manufacturing sector; the War of 1812 brought the importance of manufacturing to light.

The Excise Tax and the Whiskey Rebellion (1794)

TIP

Responses to Rebellions
Be prepared to contrast the ineffective response to Shays's Rebellion, which lasted for months in 1786 and 1787, with the massive force of troops sent to put down the Whiskey Rebellion.

To help raise revenues to pay for his ambitious plans, Hamilton proposed enacting new taxes. The most prominent and controversial of these taxes was an excise, or sales, tax on whiskey. This tax hit grain farmers especially hard. These hardscrabble farmers in remote rural areas were barely making ends meet. Distilling grain into whiskey allowed these farmers to increase their meager profits. Transporting bushels of grain over primitive roads to population centers was prohibitively expensive; distilling it down to whiskey made it easier to transport.

The grain farmers of western Pennsylvania felt that they could not shoulder this substantial tax. In 1794, farmers took action. Fifty men gathered and marched to the home of the local tax collector. From there, the gathering swelled to 7,000 men and marched to Pittsburgh. At this point, the federal government took action. Alexander Hamilton and George Washington had vivid memories of Shays's Rebellion, which occurred less than a decade later. Farmers in western Massachusetts had staged a violent rebellion for weeks before it was finally put down by local militias. Hamilton and Washington were determined that the current rebellion would not get out of control. Washington nationalized nearly 13,000 militiamen into the army. He marched them himself to Pennsylvania to suppress the rebellion and ensure that the laws of the land were followed. Washington's response to the rebellion had the desired effect. It established federal authority and made clear that a strong national government would not tolerate unlawful challenges to its authority.

CONFLICTS WITH NATIVE AMERICANS IN THE OLD NORTHWEST

Following the American Revolution, thousands of settlers pushed beyond the Appalachian Mountains into the lands along the Ohio River Valley. This was land that the British had tried to close to settlement by colonists following the French and Indian War. However, Great Britain had given up claims to all lands east of the Mississippi River in the Treaty of Paris (1783). Of course, Native-American residents of the old Northwest had not been consulted nor had they given up their claims to the lands north of the Ohio River in present-day Ohio and Indiana.

TIP

Ongoing Indian Wars
The Indian Wars of the 1790s are part of an ongoing pattern of the United States breaking treaties, expanding west, and engaging in military conflicts with Native Americans. The pattern stretches from the seventeenth century to the late-nineteenth century.

In 1784, the Articles of Confederation government tried to solve the problem of Native-American land claims north of the Ohio River by working out the Treaty of Fort Stanwix. However, this treaty was negotiated with members of the Iroquois Confederacy—a group of Native-American nations that did not, for the most, occupy the land in question. The main occupants of the region, the Shawnee, the Delaware, and the Miami, were not part of these negotiations and protested bitterly that their land had been ceded without their consent.

American Defeat at the Wabash River

The situation between Native-American and white settlers grew increasingly tense after 1790. White settlers were no longer content to settle in the area south of the Ohio River in present-day Kentucky. They were pushing north into territory that was fully claimed by its Native-American inhabitants. A series of military conflicts in the Ohio territory in the 1790s ensued. American troops led by General Arthur St. Clair suffered a massive defeat at the mouth of the Wabash River in 1791. More than 900 American troops were killed in this encounter, making it the single most costly battle, from an American point of view, in the entire history of wars with Native Americans.

The Battle of Fallen Timbers and the Treaty of Greenville

President Washington was determined to gain control of the region north of the Ohio River. He doubled the U.S. presence in Ohio and appointed General "Mad Anthony" Wayne to lead American forces. At the Battle of Fallen Timbers (1794), Native Americans were soundly defeated by superior American firepower. During the following year, 1795, Native Americans gave up their claim to most of Ohio in the Treaty of Greenville. The treaty brought only a temporary peace. Within a generation, settlers would push farther into Ohio and Indiana. These incursions would become connected with the United States' declaration of war against Britain in 1812.

CONFLICTS WITH EUROPEAN NATIONS

Despite America's intention to be independent of European affairs, events in Europe greatly impacted the newly formed United States. Just as Americans were ratifying the Constitution in 1789, the French Revolution was beginning. Americans were divided over France's revolution. The debates took on greater significance after France and Great Britain went to war in 1793. Many Americans felt that the United States had an obligation to help France because France had helped the United States in the Revolutionary War and because a 1778 treaty committed the United States to help France if it were under attack. Others argued that the United States should stay out. After all, the treaty was made with a French government that no longer existed. Additionally, the French Revolution had devolved from a democratic movement into a bloodbath. King Louis XVI and thousands of his countrymen were killed by the guillotine. Many of these neutrality-minded Americans also harbored warm feelings for the British system, despite the fact that the war with Great Britain had concluded a mere decade earlier. The two nations already had resumed commercial ties.

Washington and Neutrality

President Washington chose to remain neutral in the conflicts between Great Britain and France. He issued the 1793 Neutrality Act. In his Farewell Address in 1796, he urged the United States to avoid "permanent alliances" with foreign powers. He did not want the newly independent nation, which was on precarious footing, to be drawn into the seemingly endless conflicts of Europe. Washington's calls for neutrality have been invoked by isolationists throughout American history, including during debates about U.S entrance into both World Wars.

Conflicts with Great Britain and Jay's Treaty

The United States assumed that its proclaimed neutral status would allow it to carry on trade with both of the belligerent nations. In the early 1790s, United States' ships maintained a brisk trade with both the French West Indies and with France itself. Great Britain was none too pleased with this development and began intercepting American ships (almost 300) in or near the West Indies. This was one of several issues that the Washington administration had with Great Britain. Southern planters wanted reimbursement from the British for slaves that had fled to British lines during the American Revolution and were never returned. Also, western settlers were resentful of the continued presence of British forces in forts in the West. This last issue became significant in light of the increasingly bloody clashes between American forces and Native Americans. Americans accused the British of aiding Native Americans in order to maintain the profitable fur trade.

Washington sent John Jay, the chief justice of the Supreme Court, to Great Britain to seek redress of these grievances. Jay returned in 1795 with a treaty that was perceived as especially favorable to the British. The British did agree to withdraw from the West but only after 18 months. The British would not compensate American shippers for lost cargo nor American planters for lost slaves. In addition, American planters would be forced to repay debts to the British that dated from the colonial era. The one concession that Jay managed to wrest from the British was limited trading rights in the West Indies. Other issues would be addressed in the future by arbitration commissions.

Reactions to Jay's Treaty were decidedly mixed. Hamilton and his supporters saw the treaty as the best they could get at the moment. Supporters of Jefferson, especially from the South and the West, argued that their interests were sold out to the mercantile interests in New England. They saw the treaty as evidence of the pro-British sympathies of the Hamiltonians. An opponent of the treaty scrawled on a wall "Damn John Jay! Damn everyone who won't damn John Jay!"

Pinckney's Treaty

The United States was able to resolve ongoing issues with Spain, which controlled the land to the west and the south of the United States. Negotiations between American diplomat Thomas Pinckney and Don Manuel de Godoy of Spain resulted in Pinckney's Treaty (1795, ratified in 1796). Spain agreed to allow for American shipping on the Mississippi River. The treaty defined the border between the United States and Spanish-held territory in western Florida. Spain's willingness to negotiate with the United States was motivated, in part, by the apparent friendship between the United States and Great Britain following Jay's Treaty.

THE ADMINISTRATION OF JOHN ADAMS

President Washington was followed by his vice president, John Adams. Adams had represented the more conservative wing of the revolutionary movement. He served for one term as president.

The Election of 1796 and the Rise of Political Parties

Reactions to Hamilton's economic program, to the French Revolution, and to Jay's Treaty reflected a growing divide among the public. Around these divides coalesced two political groups, Federalists and Republicans. Federalists tended to be more pro-British, more critical of the French Revolution, more ready to use the power of the federal government to influence economic activity, and more friendly to urban, commercial interests. The leading theorist of the Federalists was Alexander Hamilton. The Republicans tended to be more critical of the British, more supportive of the French Revolution—at least in its early stages, more critical of centralized authority, and more favorable to agricultural interests. Jefferson was a leading theorist of the Republicans. In the years after the election of 1796, these groups coalesced into the first two political parties in American history.

TIP 

Parties and Foreign Policy
Note that during the administration of the Federalist John Adams, United States' relations with France were more strained. During the administrations of Democratic-Republican presidents in the early 1800s, the United States' relations with Great Britain were more strained.

In the election of 1796, the leading candidates were Washington's vice president, John Adams, who had the support of leading Federalists, and Thomas Jefferson, who had been Washington's Secretary of State until he resigned in 1793. Thomas Pinckney ran as Adams' vice presidential candidate, and Aaron Burr ran as Jefferson's. In the electoral process at the time, all four names were put on one ballot. The two candidates who won the electoral vote became president and vice president. This system allowed two rival candidates to win the presidency and the vice presidency. That is precisely what happened in 1796. Adams came in first in the electoral vote, and Jefferson came in second. During the next four years, however, Vice President Jefferson took a back seat in the administration and withdrew from debates as Adams surrounded himself with Federalist advisors. The problematic nature of the electoral system was rectified with the Twelfth Amendment (1804), which called for separate ballots for president and for vice president.

Conflict with France and the XYZ Affair

Adams's first international crisis grew from the ongoing conflicts between France and Great Britain. In 1797 in retaliation for America's favorable treaty with Great Britain (Jay's Treaty), France rescinded the 1778 alliance with the United States and allowed French privateers to interfere and seize American ships. After more than 300 ships were seized, Adams sent a delegation of negotiators to Paris to attempt a peaceful solution. The delegation was not initially allowed to discuss the matter with the French Foreign Affairs Minister Talleyrand. Rather, three agents approached the American delegation and informed them that they could begin negotiations if they paid $250,000 and promised a $12 million loan to France. The three French agents were never named. When word of this interchange made its way into American papers, the three agents were referred to simply as X, Y, and Z. The XYZ Affair incensed Americans. Congress allocated money for a military engagement against France. Warships were dispatched to the Caribbean and fought French ships in America's first undeclared war, labeled the Quasi-War (1798–1800) by historians. Americans were deeply divided by the military action.

The Alien and Sedition Acts (1798)

In an atmosphere of animosity and distrust between the Federalists and the Republicans, the Alien and Sedition Acts were passed by a Federalist-dominated Congress in order to limit criticism from the opposition Republican Party. There were actually four acts. The main two were the Alien Act, which made it more difficult for aliens to achieve American citizenship, and the Sedition Act, which made it a crime to defame the president or Congress. The broad wording of the Sedition Act was consistent with contemporary British sedition laws but seemed to challenge the free-speech guarantees of the recently ratified First Amendment. Jeffersonians were especially troubled by the expansion of federal power that the acts represented.

State Versus Federal Power
The Virginia and Kentucky Resolutions were part of an ongoing debate over the respective powers of the federal and the state governments. The issue was largely settled by the Civil War, but it continued to emerge in the post-war era.

The Kentucky and Virginia Resolutions (1798–1799)

Jefferson and James Madison were so opposed to the Alien and Sedition Acts that they proposed the idea of nullification in their Virginia and Kentucky Resolutions. In their proposals, Jefferson and Madison put forth the idea that a state had the right to nullify a law it found to be inconsistent with the Constitution. The idea of state nullification of a federal edict did not slow down the Alien and Sedition Acts. However, it raised the issue of the relationship between the federal government and the states. These issues emerged on several occasions in the first half of the nineteenth century and were part of the slavery debates that led to the Civil War.

Subject to Debate

The Constitutional Convention has been the subject of much debate in American history. Charles Beard, a progressive-era historian, asserted that the men who wrote the Constitution were all men of means who wrote the Constitution to protect their economic interests. This interpretation notes the undemocratic features of the Constitution (the electoral college and the method for selecting senators) and asserts that the document is essentially interested in protecting the economic interests of the propertied class at the expense of democracy. Some left-leaning historians see the ratification of the Constitution as a virtual coup d'état, checking the more revolutionary elements of the American Revolution. This view runs counter to mainstream thinking, which elevates the effectiveness of the Constitution, especially when contrasted with the ineffective Articles of Confederation.

Practice Multiple-Choice Questions:

Directions: Pick the letter that best answers the following questions.

1. The method of officially selecting a president and the procedure for selecting senators demonstrate that the writers of the Constitution
   (A) tried to take precautions to avoid the government turning into a tyrannical dictatorship.
   (B) feared that if the people had too much power, they might abuse it.
   (C) did not envision the territorial growth that occurred in the United States after the ratification of the document.
   (D) were intensely attached to their home states and cared little about the fate of the United States.
   (E) lacked a basic knowledge of constitutional theory.

2. After much debate, delegates at the Constitutional Convention in Philadelphia in 1787 agreed upon the Great Compromise, which
   (A) allowed for the continuation of slavery but began the process of gradual emancipation.
   (B) allowed the states to continue to exist as political entities but established the national government as supreme.
   (C) created a bicameral legislature, balancing the concerns of both big states and small states.
   (D) balanced the concerns of the agricultural and the industrial states in regard to trade and economic policies.
   (E) allowed for religious freedom in the United States but mandated that the words "In God We Trust" appear on all currency.

3. President Washington's forming a cabinet of advisors and the establishment of political parties both illustrate the principle of
   (A) judicial activism.
   (B) checks and balances.
   (C) one person, one vote.
   (D) *E pluribus unum.*
   (E) the unwritten Constitution.

4. In the 1790s, Republicans responded to the Alien and Sedition Acts by
    (A) welcoming them as needed reforms in immigration policy.
    (B) issuing the Virginia and Kentucky Resolutions.
    (C) organizing a boycott on paying taxes until the Federalists rescinded them.
    (D) impeaching President John Adams.
    (E) ordering the deportation of Alexander Hamilton to his native Nevis under the provisions of the Alien Act.

Practice Free-Response Questions:

1. Assess the impact of both Alexander Hamilton and Thomas Jefferson in shaping the direction of the United States (1786–1800).

2. Assess the impact of TWO of the following on American domestic politics:

    The French Revolution
    Jay's Treaty
    The XYZ Affair
    The Quasi-War with France

Answers and Explanations to Multiple-Choice Questions:

1. **(B)** The electoral college and the indirect election of senators reflect the fears of democracy that the framers of the Constitution had. The framers looked favorably on Great Britain's House of Lords as a check on the House of Commons. Over time, the electoral college has become a rubber stamp for the voters of each state. For years, state legislatures chose senators. In the early twentieth century, progressive reformers challenged this undemocratic aspect of the American political system and pushed for ratification of the seventeenth Amendment.

2. **(C)** The Great Compromise created the two-house legislature we still have. It created a House of Representatives, with each state's representation based on population, and a Senate, with each state being allocated two members.

3. **(E)** The unwritten constitution is the traditions and practices that have become part of the American political system but were not mentioned in the Constitution. Many of these practices date back to the administration of George Washington, such as the cabinet and the precedent of only serving for two terms (which is now in the actual Constitution).

4. **(B)** The Virginia and Kentucky resolutions written by Thomas Jefferson and James Madison set forth the theory of nullification. The theory was again put forward by John C. Calhoun and other opponents of the Tariff Act of 1828, labeled the Tariff of Abominations.

Jeffersonian Republicans in Power, 1800–1828

TIMELINE	
1800	Election of Thomas Jefferson
1803	Louisiana Purchase
	Marbury v. *Madison*
1804	Reelection of Jefferson
1807	*Chesapeake* Affair
	Embargo Act
1808	Election of James Madison
1810	*Fletcher* v. *Peck*
1811	Battle of Tippecanoe
1812	Beginning of War of 1812
	Reelection of Madison
1814	Hartford Convention
	Treaty of Ghent
1815	Battle of New Orleans
1816	Election of James Monroe
	Chartering of the Second Bank of the United States
1819	Panic of 1819
	Dartmouth College v. *Woodward*
	McCulloch v. *Maryland*
1820	Missouri Compromise
	Reelection of James Monroe
1821	*Cohens* v. *Virginia*
1824	*Gibbons* v. *Ogden*
	Election of John Quincy Adams

Despite fears of turmoil, power peacefully changed hands in 1800 from the Federalist Party to the Democratic-Republicans (known colloquially as the Republicans). Some of the political acrimony of the 1790s died down during the first decades of the nineteenth century, leading to an Era of Good Feelings—when only one major party existed in the country.

The first decades of the nineteenth century witnessed a paradox. The Federalist Party declined in popularity and, by the 1820s, effectively died. However, the agenda of the Federalists was largely implemented. The Supreme Court, not subject to the whims of the electorate, kept alive many of the ideas of the Federalists. The nation also began to adopt manufacturing, just as Alexander Hamilton had hoped. Henry Clay's American System also kept alive much of Hamilton's program.

THE JEFFERSON PRESIDENCY

Jefferson made clear in his inaugural address that he sought to break with the Federalist approach to governing. He had grown alarmed at the expansion of the size of the federal government. The Federalist use of government power to guide the economy and also to silence political opposition were anathema to Jefferson's ideals of republican simplicity. Jefferson later called his election as the "revolution of 1800," signifying a break with the monarchial tendencies of the Federalists.

The Election of 1800

The election of 1800 pitted Vice President Thomas Jefferson of the Democratic-Republicans against incumbent President John Adams of the Federalist Party. The electoral vote was tied—with Jefferson and his running mate, Aaron Burr, receiving an equal number of votes. At that point in history, electors each cast two votes. The man with the highest vote total became president, and the runner-up became vice president. The election was then thrown to the House of Representatives, as the Constitution requires. The House was bitterly divided. Many Federalist representatives voted for Burr. In the end, Alexander Hamilton lobbied vigorously for Jefferson. Hamilton opposed Jefferson politically but trusted his leadership more than Burr's. In 1804, Burr challenged Hamilton to a duel and killed him.

Jeffersonian Simplicity

At the heart of Jefferson's vision of republican simplicity was the independent yeoman farmer. He saw Hamilton's earlier financial plans as corrupt schemes designed to benefit speculators at the expense of the hardworking yeomanry.

Jefferson reduced the size of the federal government to a skeletal crew. Only 130 people were employed by the executive branch of the government in 1801. The hated Alien and Sedition Acts expired at the end of Adams's term, so Jefferson did not have to repeal them. He pardoned those arrested under the acts and affirmed his commitment to freedom of speech.

The Louisiana Purchase

Jefferson's commitment to reducing the scope of the federal government would soon be tested when the United States was given the opportunity to purchase the vast swath of land west of the Mississippi River known as the Louisiana Territory. The Louisiana Territory was long held by France until France ceded it to Spain in 1763 following the French and Indian War. France then regained the territory in 1801. The ambitious French leader Napoleon Bonaparte, in need of cash to fund his war with Great Britain, was ready to sell the Louisiana Territory at a reasonable price. American negotiators quickly agreed to a price of $15 million.

Jefferson was at first reluctant to approve the deal because the Constitution did not allow for the acquisition of additional lands. Jefferson had long held a strict constructionist view of the Constitution, asserting that the government's power was limited to what was explicitly allowed for in the Constitution. However, if Jefferson waited for a constitutional amendment specifically allowing Congress to acquire new lands, Napoleon could rescind his offer. So Jefferson violated his stated principle and quickly presented the offer to Congress, which assented and appropriated the money.

The purchase of the Louisiana Territory was arguably the most significant act of Jefferson's presidency. The purchase was important for two reasons. First, it doubled the size of the United States, adding the fertile Great Plains to the United States. This flat area west of the Mississippi would become the most important agricultural region in the United States. Second, the United States gained full control of the port of New Orleans. New Orleans is the outlet of the mighty Mississippi River, which stretches from Minnesota down the spine of the United States. The impact of the Louisiana Purchase on economic growth was remarkable. Between the 1810s and the 1850s, the value of produce from the interior of the United States received at the port of New Orleans went up over tenfold.

Challenges Abroad

Jefferson attempted to continue the policy of neutrality that President Washington had set forth.

THE BARBARY WARS, 1801–1805

Jefferson's first foreign policy crisis involved trade with the Middle East. Trade in the Mediterranean was controlled by four North African states—Morocco, Algiers, Tunis, and Tripoli—known as the Barbary States. These states demanded large payments from trading nations as tribute. Nations that did not comply found their shipping subject to seizure and plundering by Barbary pirates. Merchants during the colonial era enjoyed the protection of Great Britain. When the United States became independent, Presidents Washington and Adams agreed to the terms set by the Barbary States. In 1801, Tripoli demanded a steep increase in payment from the United States. When Jefferson refused, Tripoli declared war on the United States. Jefferson sent warships to the region to engage in fighting and to protect American shipping. The move proved popular. The slogan "millions for defense, but not a cent for tribute" became popular in America. In the end, the United States did not achieve a decisive victory. However, the fighting boosted America's profile on the world stage.

CONTINUED TROUBLES WITH EUROPEAN NATIONS

The conflicts between Great Britain and France that occupied the Washington and Adams Administrations reemerged during the Jefferson Administration. In 1803, Napoleon declared war on Britain. At first, the United States benefited from trading with both warring partners. Soon, both countries tried to block American trade with the other. Great Britain was more aggressive in its efforts to stop American ships. British ships routinely stopped and boarded American ships, often seizing cargo. More irritating still for the Americans was the practice of seizing American seamen and pressing them into service in the British navy. Britain claimed that these men were deserters from the British navy, but most were not. This practice of impressment affected 6,000 American seamen between 1803 and 1812. The situation between the United States and Britain reached a crisis in 1807 when the British ship *Leopard* fired on the American ship *Chesapeake*. Three Americans were killed and four were abducted in the *Chesapeake* Affair.

Economic Independence
The Embargo Act (1807), the Non-Intercourse Act (1809), and the War of 1812 (1812–1815) created demand for American-made goods. The acts proved to be a catalyst for American manufacturing and contributed to the United States becoming more economically self-sufficient.

THE EMBARGO ACT OF 1807

Jefferson chose "peaceful coercion" over war. He passed the Embargo Act (1807), which cut off all U.S. trade to all foreign ports. Jefferson thought that this would pressure the belligerent nations to agree to leave U.S. ships alone. However, the main effect of the embargo was to cripple America's mercantile sector. The embargo proved to be very unpopular, especially in New England, where trade was nearly at a standstill.

THE MADISON PRESIDENCY

Jefferson threw his support to James Madison in the election of 1808. Madison was the architect of the Constitution and the writer of the Bill of Rights. He was a trusted confidant of Jefferson in the 1790s and was secretary of state during his presidency. James Monroe also vied for the Republican nomination, but he would have to wait eight years. The Jeffersonian Republicans were able to hold on to the White House, despite a strong showing by the Federalist Party candidate Charles Pinckney. New England and New York Federalists were able to capitalize on anger over the Embargo Act of 1807. When the electoral votes were counted, the Republicans won 122 to 47.

Madison and Conflict with Great Britain

Madison inherited the foreign policy conflicts of the Jefferson years. The United States sought a free-trade policy in the face of belligerent powers.

THE NON-INTERCOURSE ACT OF 1809

Madison replaced the unpopular Embargo Act (1807) with the Non-Intercourse Act of 1809, opening trade with all nations except for Great Britain and France. However, this act proved to be almost as unpopular, as Great Britain and France had been two of America's biggest trading partners.

MACON'S BILL NO. 2 (1810)

In an attempt to revive trade, Congress passed Macon's Bill No. 2 in 1810. The bill stipulated that if either Great Britain or France agreed to respect America's rights as a neutral nation at sea, the United States would prohibit trade with that nation's enemy. Napoleon agreed to this arrangement. Consequently, the United States cut trade to Britain in 1811. However, Napoleon did not honor his commitment, and France continued to seize American ships. The cutting off of trade to Britain worsened relations and pushed the two nations to the edge of war.

Native Americans and the West

As diplomats were dealing with the trade issue in the Atlantic, settlers in the West were fighting Native Americans. Westward settlers were continuing in the footsteps of early colonists—pushing into the interior of the continent and antagonizing Native Americans in the process. In the early 1800s, white Americans were pouring into the Ohio River Valley, which included the state of Ohio (1803) and the Indiana Territory. Federal and state officials had extracted land agreements from Native Americans for years. It was never clear if the Native Americans who made the agreements had the authority to do so, nor was it clear that white settlers would live by these agreements. In 1809, the governor of the Indiana Territory, William Henry Harrison, negotiated the Treaty of Fort Wayne. Native Americans agreed to cede 3 million acres at a nominal fee. The most important regional Native-American leader at the time, Tecumseh, was not present for this agreement. He was on a trip recruiting Native Americans to resist encroachments by white settlers. He and his brother Tenskwatawa, the Prophet, had been organizing a spiritual and political front, attempting to unite all the Native-American nations east of the Mississippi River.

War Hawks
The War Hawks tended to hail from western and southern states.

BATTLE OF TIPPECANOE AND THE WAR HAWKS

Settlers in the Indiana territory persuaded Harrison to wage war against Tecumseh's confederation. The Battle of Tippecanoe (1811) ousted members of the confederacy and was perceived as an American victory. Western congressmen, who became known as the War Hawks, became convinced that Britain was encouraging and funding Tecumseh's confederation. Just as relations with Britain were deteriorating over the trade issue, these War Hawks, led by Henry Clay of Kentucky and John C. Calhoun from South Carolina, were pushing for military action against the British. Such action, it was thought, would allow the United States to eliminate the Native-American threat and perhaps allow the United States to move into Canada.

War of 1812

Trade conflicts and pressure from the War Hawk congressmen pushed Madison to declare war against Britain in 1812. The vote on the war in Congress was divided along sectional lines. New England and some Middle Atlantic states opposed it; the South and West voted for it. The declaration of war occurred just as Britain was making assurances that it would stop interfering with American shipping.

The war lasted two and a half years. Britain achieved several stunning early victories in the war, defeating Americans forces at Fort Dearborn and Detroit. Madison managed to win reelection in the midst of the war. The Federalists, though, who were critical of the war effort, made a strong showing. By 1813, the United States began to achieve some victories in battle. The United States burned the city of York (now Toronto) and won several battles at sea. At the Battle of Thames in Canada, American forces defeated British and Native-American forces and killed Tecumseh. In one of the stunning episodes of the war, British forces seized and burned Washington, D.C., in 1814. The United States achieved a major victory in New Orleans in early 1815, led by General Andrew Jackson. Jackson didn't realize that the United States had signed a peace treaty, formally ending the war weeks before in late 1814.

THE TREATY OF GHENT

The Treaty of Ghent (1814) ended the War of 1812. Britain had grown weary of war after fighting Napoleon for over a decade and the United States for two years. The United States realized that it could not achieve a decisive victory over Great Britain. The treaty ended the war where it had begun. The two sides agreed to stop fighting, give back any territory seized in the war, and recognize the boundary between the United States and Canada that had been established before the war. The treaty did not mention the specific grievances the United States had against Britain—aid to Native Americans, interfering with American shipping, or impressment of American seamen.

THE HARTFORD CONVENTION AND OPPOSITION TO THE WAR

TIP

Talk of Secession
The Hartford Convention demonstrated that talk of secession was not restricted to Southerners.

The war was unpopular among some Americans, especially among New England merchants, who saw their trade with Great Britain disappear. As diplomats were negotiating the Treaty of Ghent in December 1814, Federalists from New England convened in Hartford, Connecticut, to express their displeasure with the war. Some of the more radical delegates suggested that New England secede from the union. However, this proposal was rejected by the delegates at the convention. The Hartford Convention did pass a resolution calling for a two-thirds vote in Congress for future declarations of war.

AFTERMATH OF THE WAR

The war had several important repercussions for the United States. First, the war fueled a growing sense of nationalism. Americans took pride in the fact that they held their own against one of the world's preeminent powers. It was during the war that Frances Scott Key wrote the poem "Defence of Fort McHenry," which later was renamed "The Star-Spangled Banner" and set to music as the United States' national anthem. Also, Uncle Sam, the personification of the United States Government, was born during the war.

Politically, the war further damaged the reputation of the Federalist Party. In the aftermath of the war, the party was seen as unpatriotic for its vocal opposition to a popular war. It was never again a force to be reckoned with in American politics. For a decade, only one political party existed in the United States, the Republicans.

Native Americans lost an important ally in the British. In the coming decades, Native Americans would try to resist encroachment by white settlers and U.S troops but without the support of a major power.

The interruption of trade with Great Britain, from the Embargo Act of 1807 through the war, led American entrepreneurs to move toward developing the industrial capacity of the United States.

THE ERA OF GOOD FEELINGS (1815–1825)

With the Federalist Party in its death throes, the Republican Party candidate, James Monroe, easily won the election of 1816. Four years later, the Federalists made even less of a challenge to Monroe. Monroe was a throwback to the eighteenth-century presidents. He was the last president to wear the silk stockings, knee breeches, and powdered wigs of an earlier era consistently. He also adopted Washington's practice of bringing men of differing ideological bents into his administration. Many of Monroe's policies, such as promoting "internal improvements," seemed like pages out of the Federalist playbook.

TIP

Hamilton and Clay

Note the marked similarities between Hamilton's economic program and Clay's American System. Both support a tariff, a central bank, and government encouragement for manufacturing. Contemporary Republicans often are pro-business. However, now pro-business policies involve being for low tariffs and deregulating the economy—not supporting internal improvements.

Henry Clay's "American System"

Monroe embraced much of the economic agenda put forth by Henry Clay, a leading member of the House of Representatives. In the nationalist mood that followed the War of 1812, Clay proposed a series of proposals to promote economic growth that he later called the American System. First, Clay realized that America needed internal improvements in transportation in order to grow economically. At the beginning of the century, the transportation system in the United States was woefully lacking. At the time of the War of 1812, the military had difficulty moving materials and men because of the nation's inadequate transportation system. Second, Clay proposed putting high tariffs on imported goods. He believed that high tariffs on incoming manufactured goods would promote American manufacturing. High tariffs would make foreign goods more expensive to the consumer, and American made goods would seem cheaper by comparison. Third, Clay proposed chartering a Second Bank of the United States in order to stabilize the economy and to make credit more readily available. These proposals were important steps taken by the government to usher in the market revolution (see Chapter 11). By the end of the Monroe administration, Congress had rechartered the Bank of the United States and passed a protective tariff (both in 1816).

The Marshall Court

The nationalist impulses of the early nineteenth century are reflected in many of the significant decisions of the Supreme Court under Chief Justice John Marshall (1801–1835). Many of the decisions made by the Marshall Court led directly to an increase in the power of the federal government over the states. These decisions put into practice much of the agenda of the discredited Federalist Party.

MARBURY V. *MADISON* (1803)

The most important decision of the Marshall Court was in the case of *Marbury* v. *Madison.* The important outcome of the case was that the principle of judicial review was established. The details of the decision have to do with the seating of judges that had been appointed in the last days of the John Adams Administration. These judges had been appointed by Adams to fill slots created by an expended judiciary that grew out of the Judiciary Act of 1801. The act was passed in the final weeks of the Adams Administration. The president worked feverishly to fill these seats before his term expired, thereby solidifying Federalist power in the court system for years to come. When Jefferson assumed office, not all the commissions had been formally delivered. Jefferson, angered at the eleventh-hour appointments, ordered his secretary of state, James Madison, to not deliver them. In this way, Jefferson could appoint his own judges.

One potential judge, William Marbury, sued to have his commission delivered. The Supreme Court ruled that Marbury was not entitled to his seat because the law he was basing his argument on—the Judiciary Act of 1789—was unconstitutional. Marshall established the Supreme Court's power to review laws and determine if they are consistent with the Constitution. Laws declared unconstitutional by the Court are immediately struck down. This power of judicial review has been the main function of the Supreme Court since then and has been instrumental in maintaining balance between the three branches of the government.

OTHER MARSHAL COURT DECISIONS

The Marshall Court affirmed the right of the Supreme Court to take appeals from state courts in the case of *Cohens* v. *Virginia* (1821). The case, which originated in the Virginia state court system, involved the ability of the state to prohibit the Cohen brothers from selling lottery tickets in Virginia. The Court upheld Virginia's right to forbid the sale of tickets.

Two important decisions strengthened federal power over state power. *McCulloch* v. *Maryland* (1819) prohibited Maryland from taxing the Second Bank of the United States, a federal institution. *Gibbons* v. *Ogden* (1824) invalidated a monopoly on ferry transportation between New York and New Jersey that had been issued by New York and asserted that only the federal government could regulate interstate trade. In several Marshall Court cases, such as *Dartmouth* v. *Woodward* (1819) and *Fletcher* v. *Peck* (1810), the Supreme Court intervened in economic transactions to assert the validity of contracts. (More on these two decisions appears in Chapter 11).

Sectional Divisions and the Missouri Compromise (1820)

The Era of Good Feelings was not free of disagreements and sectional competition. The issue of slavery, which most politicians sought to avoid, emerged in 1819. Controversy arose between the slave-holding states and the free states in 1819 when Missouri applied for statehood as a slave state. At the time, there were 11 slave and 11 free states. The admission of Missouri would have upset that balance. A compromise was reached in 1820 to maintain the balance between free and slave states by allowing for the admission of two new states— Missouri as a slave state and Maine as a free state. The Missouri Compromise also divided the remaining area of the Louisiana Territory at 36°30' north latitude. North of that line, slavery was not permitted (except in Missouri); south of that line, it was permitted.

Nationalist Sentiment and the Monroe Doctrine (1823)

America's newfound confidence on the international stage was evident in President Monroe's foreign policy address to Congress in 1823. The major purpose of the Monroe Doctrine was to limit European influence in the Western Hemisphere. President Monroe was alarmed at threats by the Holy Alliance of Russia, Prussia, and Austria to restore Spain's lost American colonies. He also opposed a decree by the Russian Czar that claimed all the Pacific Northwest above the 51st parallel. Though both problems worked themselves out, Monroe issued a statement warning European nations to keep their hands off the Americas. The United States did not have the military might to enforce this pronouncement at the time, but it was an important statement of intent. The Monroe Doctrine and Washington's farewell address became cornerstones of America's isolationist foreign policy.

The "Corrupt Bargain" of 1824

The seemingly nonpartisan nature of politics in the Monroe years came to an end in the election of 1824. We begin to see the political divisions that would result in the second two-party system. Monroe did not select an heir apparent to follow him. Three candidates ran for president that year carrying the Democratic Republican banner: John Quincy Adams, Monroe's secretary of state; William Crawford, the secretary of the treasury; and latecomer to the process General Andrew Jackson of the War of 1812 fame. Henry Clay also ran under the Federalist Party banner. Jackson received the largest percentage of the popular vote and the most electoral votes, but none of the candidates had the required majority of the electoral votes to win the presidency. So for the second and last time in American history, the election was thrown to the House of Representatives. Clay, who was fourth in the electoral vote count, urged his allies in the House to throw their support to Adams. This move was enough to allow Adams to get enough House votes to win the presidency. Soon after, Adams announced that Clay would be chosen as secretary of state. Jackson and his supporters were furious. Some history books, following Jackson's lead, have labeled this series of events the "corrupt bargain" of 1824. Most historians today, however, do not see evidence of any corruption in the election.

Adams's Postpresidency
Most presidents have rather dull retirements. John Quincy Adams did not. He is the only former president to serve in the House of Representatives. He became an outspoken critic of slavery. William Taft became chief justice of the Supreme Court after his presidency. Jimmy Carter has been an activist in Habitat for Humanity and for world peace since his presidency ended.

THE JOHN QUINCY ADAMS ADMINISTRATION

Adams sought to portray himself as being above partisan squabbles. His opponents painted this quality as being aloof and elitist. Adams saw his policies as following in the footsteps of Jefferson and Madison. He wanted the government to promote scientific and technological progress. However, his programs for federally funded infrastructure went even further than Clay's American System proposals. Adams was branded by his fellow Democratic Republicans as a latter-day Federalist. His demeanor seemed out of step with a political system that was becoming increasingly democratic. He, like his father, was a one-term president.

Subject to Debate

Historians have debated the nature of the Era of Good Feelings. Consensus historians—ones who deemphasize divisions in American history and focus on national commonalities—look to the era as a golden age of cooperation and growth. Other historians have noted the beginnings of divisions over the issue of slavery. These divisions were evident in the debates over the Missouri Compromise. Other historians have focused on class divisions that began to emerge in the United States as the old master-apprentice system gave way to the wage labor system that came to dominate the economy by the post–Civil War period.

Practice Multiple-Choice Questions:

Directions: Pick the letter that best answers the following questions.

1. The 1816 Democratic-Republican election handbill shown above is specifically reminding voters of the Federalist Party's
   (A) suppression of the Whiskey Rebellion.
   (B) creation of a National Bank.
   (C) passage of the Alien and Sedition Acts.
   (D) opposition to the War of 1812.
   (E) enactment of high tariff rates.

2. In the case of *Gibbons* v. *Ogden*, the Supreme Court
   (A) established the power of judicial review.
   (B) invalidated a New York State act granting a monopoly to a ferry boat company operating between New York and New Jersey.
   (C) declared a contract between a college and a colonial assembly no longer valid.
   (D) asserted that Native Americans are not entitled to the same constitutional protections as white people.
   (E) upheld the validity of a Maryland law placing a tax on the Second Bank of the United States.

3. How did the Embargo Act of 1807 affect the United States?
   (A) It enriched many southern cotton plantation owners.
   (B) It led to an increase in trade with the Native-American groups of the Ohio River Valley.
   (C) It led to a diplomatic crisis and, eventually, war with France.
   (D) It led to an increase in American manufacturing.
   (E) It led to an end to hostilities between France and Great Britain.

4. Which of the following was most responsible for the ending of the Era of Good Feelings?
   (A) Abolitionists and southern defenders of slavery became bitterly divided over the future of slavery in the United States.
   (B) Bitter political divisions led to the formation of a new political party, the Whigs, and a new two-party system.
   (C) The Panic of 1819 led to tension and violence between the "haves" and the "have-nots."
   (D) The War of 1812 led to divisions between western War Hawks and the eastern opponents of the war.
   (E) The Second Great Awakening led to culture wars between Americans over issues such as drinking, gambling, and prayer in public schools.

Practice Free-Response Questions:

1. Assess the level of success of TWO of the following presidents in solving foreign-affairs problems:

   Thomas Jefferson
   James Madison
   James Monroe

2. Assess the legacy of the ideas of the Federalist Party in the early nineteenth century (1800–1830).

Answers and Explanations to Multiple-Choice Questions:

1. **(D)** All the choices are positions or acts carried out by the Federalist Party, but the handbill is specifically reminding voters of the Federalists' opposition to the War of 1812. The giveaway is the allusion to the Hartford Convention. This was the meeting in which the Federalists expressed their displeasure with the war. Some delegates even suggested that New England secede from the union. The Democratic-Republicans wanted to keep this fresh in the minds of the electorate.

2. **(B)** In this case, the Court upheld federal power over state power. This was consistent with the thinking of the Marshall Court. Choice A alludes to *Marbury* v. *Madison*; choice C alludes to *Dartmouth* v. *Woodward.*

3. **(D)** The embargo was a response to both Great Britain and France stopping American ships. Jefferson's act cut off all U.S. trade with *all* nations—a bold move. Jefferson thought that this would pressure Great Britain and France. However, the main effect of the embargo was to give a boost to American manufacturers, who, all of a sudden, did not have any foreign competition.

4. **(B)** The Era of Good Feelings was the only era in American history when there was only one main political party. The Federalists had disappeared as a viable force. A new two-party system developed when the Whigs formed to oppose Jacksonian policies. Tensions existed during the Era of Good Feelings, despite its name.

The Age of Jackson, 1828–1844

CHAPTER **10**

TIMELINE

1828	Passage of the Tariff of Abominations
	Election of Andrew Jackson
1830	Passage of the Indian Removal Act
1831	*Cherokee Nation* v. *Georgia*
1832	Beginning of the Nullification Crisis
	Jackson vetoes renewal of the Second Bank of the United States
	Worcester v. *Georgia*
1834	Whig Party organized
1836	Jackson issues Specie Circular
1838	Trail of Tears
1840	Election of William Henry Harrison of the Whig Party
1841	John Tyler assumes the presidency upon Harrison's death

President Andrew Jackson was a larger-than-life, influential figure. The years of his presidency (1829–1837), as well as the immediate aftermath, bear the name the Age of Jackson, or the Age of Jacksonian Democracy. President Jackson expanded presidential power in several ways. After South Carolina asserted its intent to nullify the Tariff Act of 1828, Jackson challenged and prevented the move. Later, when the Supreme Court in the case of *Worcester* v. *Georgia* (1832) ruled that the Cherokee people were not subject to the 1830 Indian Removal Act, Jackson and the state of Georgia began moving them to the West anyway. Finally, Jackson destroyed the Second Bank of the United States in the 1830s. His critics labeled him King Andrew in response to these heavy-handed measures.

THE PRESIDENCY OF ANDREW JACKSON

Jackson and his supporters were bitter at the results of the election of 1824. They held onto the accusations of a "corrupt bargain" made by President John Quincy Adams (see Chapter 9). In the election of 1828, Jackson's supporters painted John Quincy Adams as out of touch and elitist, while Adams's supporters portrayed Jackson as ill-tempered. Jackson's backwoods, populist appeal helped him win the election.

The election of 1828 is considered by many historians to be the first modern election. First, the electorate was much broader than in previous elections. In the 1820s, most states reduced or removed property qualifications for voting so that most free males had the right to vote. Consequently, candidates had to campaign more aggressively and tailor their appeal to reach a broader audience. Related to the democratization of the voting process was an increased focus on character and personality.

Spoils System/Rotation of Office

The spoils system was used before and after President Jackson, but it is often associated with his presidency. The idea of the spoils system is for elected officials to reward supporters with government jobs. Jackson exercised this system enthusiastically. He fired nearly 10 percent of federal government employees when he assumed power and then gave those jobs to loyalists.

Indian Removal Act (1830)

One of the defining issues of the presidency of Jackson was the presence of Native Americans living in various settled areas of the United States—specifically the South, the old Northwest, and to a lesser degree, New England and New York. Jackson asserted that it was necessary for these Native Americans to be removed to the areas of the United States west of the Mississippi River. He said, perhaps disingenuously, that this was in the best interests of the Native Americans themselves, who were being subsumed by the encroachment of white settlers. He pushed for the Indian Removal Act of 1830.

The Supreme Court and Native-American Rights

The Cherokee People in Georgia challenged the Indian Removal Act. In two court cases, *Cherokee Nation* v. *Georgia* (1831) and *Worcester* v. *Georgia* (1832), the Supreme Court recognized the Cherokee people as a nation within the state of Georgia and ruled that they should not be subject to the Indian Removal Act of 1830.

The Trail of Tears

The state of Georgia, with the support of President Jackson, began moving Native Americans to the West despite Supreme Court decisions allowing them to stay. President Jackson purportedly said, "John Marshall has made his decision. Now let him enforce it." The resulting expulsion, labeled the Trail of Tears (1838), resulted in thousands of Cherokee deaths. In this case, Jackson's position was consistent with a state's rights position.

The Tariff of Abominations

In regard to the issue of Indian removal, Jackson sided with Georgia and those who supported state's rights. In regard to a controversy around tariff rates, Jackson came out in favor of federal power over states' rights. The controversy originated with the Tariff of 1828, which revised tariff rates on a variety of imports. The act, known by its critics as the Tariff of Abominations, dramatically raised tariff rates on many items and led to a general reduction in trade between the United States and Europe. This decline in trade hit South Carolina, which depended on cotton exports, especially hard. Congress lowered tariff rates slightly with the Tariff of 1832, but this did not satisfy many southern political leaders.

TIP 

Jackson and States' Rights
Be careful about generalizing in regard to Jackson's attitude toward states' rights. He comes from a tradition of southern states' rights. He defended Georgia against the Supreme Court decision *Worcester v. Georgia*. When John Calhoun challenged federal tariff policy, though, President Jackson took the side of federal power. Read Jackson's Farewell Address for a good summary of his political thought.

John C. Calhoun and the Nullification Crisis

By 1832, South Carolina politicians led by Jackson's former vice president, John C. Calhoun, asserted the right of states to nullify federal legislation. Under this theory of nullification, a state could declare an objectionable law null and void within that state. In actuality, only the Supreme Court can strike down a law if it finds the law to be inconsistent with the Constitution. Jackson was alarmed at this flaunting of federal authority and challenged the move. He pushed through Congress a bill, called the Force Bill (quickly nullified by the South Carolina legislature), which authorized military force against South Carolina for committing treason. At the same time, Congress revised tariff rates, providing relief for South Carolina. The Force Bill and the new tariff rates, passed by Congress on the same day, amounted to a face-saving compromise. However, the issue of states' rights versus federal power would emerge again in the coming decades in regard to the issue of slavery.

Tariffs in the 1800s
Though tariff rates do not stir passionate debate today, they were one of the most divisive issues throughout the nineteenth century and into the twentieth century.

Destruction of the Second Bank of the United States

One of the fiercest battles of the Jackson presidency was over the Second Bank of the United States. Jackson revived the criticism of a national bank that had been part of the national discourse since Hamilton had first proposed such an institution in 1791. Despite the fact that the bank was performing its function admirably, Jackson insisted that it put too much power into the hands of a small elite. Jackson's political opponents thought that Jackson's animosity to the bank would hand them a political victory. These opponents brought the issue of rechartering the bank to Congress in 1832, four years before the bank's charter was to expire. They thought that a Jackson veto would weaken his chances for reelection. However, Jackson's opponents miscalculated. Jackson did veto the rechartering of the bank. However, the angry class-based rhetoric in his veto message played well with the voters and he won reelection. Jackson, encouraged by his electoral success, was not satisfied to let the bank die its natural death upon its charter running out in 1836. He took actions to kill the "monster" bank immediately. He moved federal deposits from the Bank of the United States to state banks in Democratic-leaning states.

The Specie Circular (1836)

Jackson's suspicion of bankers and credit led him to issue the Specie Circular (1836), mandating that government-held land be sold only for hard currency (gold or silver "specie"), not paper currency. The move resulted in a shortage of funds by the government. Both the destruction of the Second Bank of the United States and the Specie Circular contributed to the economic downturn known as the Panic of 1837.

A NEW TWO-PARTY SYSTEM

As Jackson's policies aroused more controversy, a new political alignment emerged. The tense unity of the one-party Era of Good Feelings broke apart as the Jacksonian branch of the Democratic-Republicans became known simply as the Democratic Party and Jackson's opponents organized the Whig Party (1833). These two parties formed the second two-party system in the nation's history, following the rivalry between the Democratic-Republicans and the Federalists (1790s–1810s).

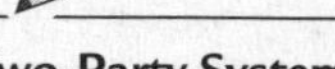

The Two-Party System
The United States has almost always had two principal political parties vying for power. During the Era of Good Feelings, though, there was only one viable party, the Democratic-Republicans.

It is difficult to generalize about the type of constituents in each party. Northerners and Southerners, for example, could be found in both parties. Many Whigs supported government programs aimed at economic modernization (based on the thinking of both Alexander Hamilton and Henry Clay). The language of the Democratic Party was more populist, arguing that high tariffs would fatten urban commercial interests. Issues, in general, tended to be less important in this period than they were in the formative years of the country or would again become during the lead-up to the Civil War. Both parties focused intently on winning elections and on holding power.

Martin Van Buren and the Election of 1836

The Whigs adopted an odd strategy in the election of 1836. They chose four candidates that they thought would carry particular regions of the country against the vice president, Democrat Martin Van Buren. They hoped that no one candidate would have a sufficient number of electoral votes and the election would be decided by the House of Representatives. The strategy backfired; Van Buren was able to win a majority of the electoral votes.

The Panic of 1837

Van Buren's presidency was mired in a serious economic downturn. The causes date back to Jackson's destruction of the Second Bank of the United States and his issuance of the Specie Circular. In addition, America was victim to a worldwide economic downturn. In 1837, 800 banks closed or suspended operations. This freezing of credit slowed down business activity. Unemployment quickly passed 10 percent nationally. As was customary in that era, the government did not take action to help the victims of the Panic of 1837. In response to the panic, Van Buren proposed creating an independent treasury and removing government assets from state banks. The proposal was implemented in 1846. The Panic of 1837 opened opportunities for the Whig Party.

TIP 

Federal Aid
The idea that the federal government should intervene to help the victims of economic downturns did not gain acceptance until the twentieth century. Politicians still debate the appropriate level of federal assistance.

William Henry "Tippecanoe" Harrison and the Election of 1840

In 1840, the Whigs nominated the hero of the Indian Wars, William Henry Harrison, nicknamed "Tippecanoe" after the site of Harrison's defeat of Tecumseh's forces. Harrison was presented as a man of humble origins despite being well off. In contrast, the Whigs portrayed Van Buren as distant and aristocratic. Ironically, Van Buren was from a humble background. These tactics along with the ongoing economic crisis paid off. Harrison won the election handily.

The Succession of Tyler

The Whig Party did not have long to savor their ascendency in the American political system. Harrison died of pneumonia after only a month in office. His replacement was his vice president, John Tyler. Tyler proved to be a Whig in name only. A former Democrat, he joined the Whigs more out of resentment toward Jackson than for ideological reasons. He consistently vetoed bills that the Whig-dominated Congress sent his way. These bills included the essential elements of Clay's American System—a new national bank, higher tariffs, and internal improvements. This was the Whig's moment in the sun, but it was squandered. They would win only one additional presidential election, in 1848.

Subject to Debate

The fortunes of the memory of Andrew Jackson have risen and fallen repeatedly in the nearly two centuries since his presidency. Jackson was a frequent topic of free-response questions on the AP exam—an understanding of how he has been remembered will be useful in discussions of the period. Early on, in the latter part of the nineteenth century, he was scoffed at in historical literature. Historians of the era were from the elite classes of New England. To them, Jackson seemed boorish, arrogant, ignorant, and authoritarian. By the early twentieth century, progressive-era historians influenced by Frederick Jackson Turner's frontier thesis looked more favorably upon Jackson. Turner saw the experience of the frontier as central to the shaping of the American character. The image of frontier pioneers became part of popular culture just as Americans were becoming more urban and more settled. Americans developed a sense of nostalgia for the pioneers, as is evident in the popularity of Laura Ingalls Wilder's *Little House on the Prairie* books. In this cultural moment, Jackson was rehabilitated. He was a man of the frontier and brought that democratic, pioneer spirit with him to the White House.

More recently, the historical memory of Jackson has again taken a turn for the worse. From the 1960s onward, younger historians have drawn unfavorable parallels between Jackson's expansionistic impulses and recent American foreign adventures abroad, from Vietnam to Iraq. Furthermore, since the 1970s many Americans have become more attuned to the historical suffering of Native Americans. In this context, the Indian Removal Act and the Trail of Tears began to loom large in the historical memory of Jackson.

Practice Multiple-Choice Questions:

Directions: Pick the letter that best answers the following questions.

1. Andrew Jackson was referred to as King Andrew by his critics primarily for
   (A) refusing to approve the removal of Native Americans to lands west of the Mississippi River.
   (B) his aristocratic family background and manner.
   (C) dismantling of the Second Bank of the United States.
   (D) vetoing the Tariff Act of 1828.
   (E) pushing for legislation that limited voting in federal elections to wealthy property owners.

2. The Supreme Court decision in the case of *Worcester* v. *Georgia* (1832) declared that
   (A) Native Americans were of an inferior order and not entitled to United States citizenship.
   (B) the Cherokee people were entitled to federal protection from state actions.
   (C) Navaho warriors can be tried in military courts for crimes against humanity.
   (D) the federal government had acted improperly in its dealings with the Shawnee people of the Great Lakes region.
   (E) southern Native-American tribes should be monetarily reimbursed for pain and suffering in the wake of the Trail of Tears.

3. President Jackson's decision not to recharter the Second Bank of the United States and his issuing of the Specie Circular had the effect of
   (A) making money available to develop the factory system.
   (B) forcing the United States to cancel loans to France and Great Britain.
   (C) centralizing financial power in the United States.
   (D) strengthening federal power over state power.
   (E) contributing to the Panic of 1837.

4. President John Tyler, who assumed the presidency upon the death of William Henry Harrison,
   (A) inherited Georgia's "Indian problem" and forced Native Americans on the Trail of Tears.
   (B) was a Whig in name only, consistently thwarting the Congressional Whig agenda.
   (C) pushed to extend slavery into the Kansas and Nebraska territories.
   (D) was the first Republican to win the presidency.
   (E) ushered in the Era of Good Feelings.

Practice Free-Response Questions:

1. Assess Andrew Jackson's position on federal power versus state power with reference to TWO of the following:

   The question of "Indian removal"
   The status of the Second Bank of the United States
   The "nullification crisis" of 1832

2. Assess similarities and differences between the first two-party system (Democratic-Republicans and Federalists) and the second two-party system (Democrats and Whigs).

Answers and Explanations to Multiple-Choice Questions:

1. **(C)** Jackson's most heavy-handed, kinglike act was destroying the Second Bank of the United States. Many politicians in a Hamiltonian mode saw the importance of the bank. These are the political leaders who founded the Whig Party to oppose King Andrew. None of the other choices reflect actual events.
2. **(B)** The case involved the Cherokee people of Georgia. The Court came to the aid of the Cherokee. However, the state of Georgia, with the support of President Jackson, enforced the Indian Removal Act and began moving the Cherokee to the West anyway.
3. **(E)** Jackson's actions had the effect of destabilizing the economy. The Panic of 1837 led to a five-year depression and high unemployment. It slowed down the growth of the economy.
4. **(B)** Tyler was an accidental president. He was not a natural Whig; he joined the party only out of resentment of President Jackson. When he came into office, he vetoed many of the internal improvements that were at the heart of Whig philosophy.

CHAPTER 11

Economic Transformations in Antebellum America: Market Revolution and Slavery, 1810–1850

TIMELINE

1810	*Fletcher* v. *Peck*
1817	Construction of Erie Canal begins
1819	*Dartmouth College* v. *Woodward*
1821	Opening of the Lowell factories
1825	Opening of the Erie Canal
1830	Opening of the Baltimore and Ohio Railroad
1834	First strike by the Lowell girls
1844	Samuel Morse invents the telegraph

Growth and expansion were defining features of the United States economy in the decades between the War of 1812 and the Civil War. The economy was rapidly changing and growing as an older subsistence economy was giving way to a market economy with a national and even an international reach. The market revolution affected different parts of the country differently. In the northern states, we begin to see the beginnings of industrialization while slavery grew dramatically in the South on the strength of the cultivation of cotton. In some ways, the regions of the United States became more interlinked as local economies were brought into national markets. At the same time, the issue of free versus slave labor pushed the country further apart.

THE MARKET REVOLUTION

America experienced a dramatic growth in economic activity following the War of 1812. Old patterns of economic activity gave way to new patterns of production, distribution, and consumption. The size of the money supply in the United States expanded, fueling investments in new enterprises.

TIP

The Development of a National Economy The market revolution linked cities and regions. The local economies of the eighteenth century gave way to a national and even an international economic system.

Advances in Transportation

Improvements in transportation made possible production for faraway markets. By 1850, the eastern half of the United States was crisscrossed by a series of roads, canals, and railroads that, along with navigable rivers, moved goods from city to city and from the interior to the coast. These projects were often encouraged by the government and at least partially funded by it. The cost of moving a ton of freight from Buffalo to New York City went from $100 to $5 with the development of the Erie Canal. The cost of moving a ton of wheat one mile went from about 30 to 70 cents by wagon in 1800 to about 1.2 cents by railroad in 1860.

Canals and Roads

The first set of improvements, which occurred in the years between the turn of the nineteenth century and about 1830, included the expansion and improvement of roads and canals and the development of the steamboat. The construction of canals and roads, called at the time *internal improvements,* did much to expand trade, especially between the Midwest (then known as the West) and eastern cities. Most significant was the Erie Canal (completed in 1825), which connected the Hudson River in upstate New York to the Great Lakes. Thus New York City was connected with the interior of the country. The most significant road project was the building of the National Road, also known as the Cumberland Road, stretching from Maryland into the Ohio River valley. Construction took place from 1811 to 1853. Soon, however, roads and canals were overshadowed by a quicker and more powerful means of transportation, the railroad.

Railroads

The first railroad tracks were laid in 1829 by the Baltimore and Ohio Railroad. By 1860, railroads connected the far reaches of the country east of the Mississippi River, and beyond. They sped up the movement of goods and expanded markets. The government encouraged this expansion of the railroad network by giving railroad companies wide swaths of land. The government gave railroad companies a total of 129 million acres in land grants. The railroad companies built rail lines and also sold land adjacent to the tracks. The price of land near railroad stops soared, bringing about $435 million into the pockets of the railroad companies. All of these transportation improvements dramatically increased the nation's economic activity.

Advances in Communication

The major advance in communications in the antebellum period was the telegraph. Samuel Morse developed and patented the telegraph, and sent the first message, "What hath God wrought?" in 1844. The first telegraph line was from Washington, D.C., to Baltimore. Telegraph messages were transmitted in a code of long and short electrical impulses called Morse code. By 1850, telegraph lines, usually built alongside railroad tracks, connected the country. The telegraph greatly facilitated the development of a national market of products and services. A clothing manufacturer in Massachusetts or even in Great Britain, could send their requirements to southern cotton growers in a matter of minutes. Previously, sending information across the sea could take weeks, and sending it across the country could take days. Orders could be placed, materials could be ordered, and information could be sent—all in minutes.

The Development of the Factory System

Before the Civil War, America began to move toward the industrial, mass production of goods. This trend continued with even greater energy after the Civil War. The first field to industrialize was the textile industry. As early as the 1790s, Samuel Slater built the first factory in the United States after smuggling plans out of Great Britain. This factory in Pawtucket, Rhode Island, and dozens that were built in the following years spun thread and yarn. The spinning machines in Slater's mill were powered by the fast-flowing Blackstone River. Water, human, and animal power characterized industry in the pre-Civil War era. Most of the workers were young women recruited from nearby farm families.

TIP 

An Industrial Revolution?
Most historians reserve the term "industrial revolution" for the post-Civil War expansion of American industry. Some label the prewar steps toward industrialization as "the first industrial revolution" and postwar developments as "the second industrial revolution."

The most famous factories of the era were built along the Merrimack River in Lowell, Massachusetts, starting in 1821. The owners continued the practice of recruiting young women from the New England countryside to operate the machines. It was thought that these women could be paid less and would be only temporary factory operatives. At some point, they would get married. Then new women would be recruited to replace them, earning only a starting wage. Also, the era of mass migration from Europe had not yet begun. So it was difficult to recruit male factory operatives, especially with farmland in the United States still reasonably priced. By 1830, eight mills in Lowell employed more than 6,000 women.

The fathers of these young women were told that their daughters would be working in a "factory in the garden"—a clean, bucolic setting, unlike the dirty and dangerous factory cities of Great Britain. The women tended to live in closely supervised boarding houses, and the work was also strictly monitored. Despite this scrutiny both on the job and even at the boarding houses, the Lowell girls experienced a degree of freedom and autonomy unheard of for young women at the time. Many participated in producing a periodical called the *Lowell Offering*. They demonstrated their sense of solidarity and assertiveness by going on strike in 1834 and again in 1836, following announced wage cuts. The 1836 strike restored their original wages. By the 1840s, the farm women were being replaced by Irish immigrants who were in dire straits and were ready to work for lower wages.

The Incorporation of America

Economic growth was facilitated by the changes in laws that made it much easier to create and expand a corporate entity. In the late 1700s and early 1800s, corporate charters were granted to groups of individuals. However, these charters were mainly temporary and mainly for a public-oriented purpose, such as building a bridge or a road. After 1810, states began rewriting corporate laws allowing for the chartering of businesses. Incorporation encouraged investment into the corporation and protected the individual investors from liability law. The Supreme Court in the decision of *Trustees of Dartmouth College* v. *Woodward* (1819) granted corporations several rights they had not previously had. The case revolved around New Hampshire's attempt to rescind the charter that Dartmouth College had received from the king during the colonial period. The state wanted to turn Dartmouth into a state college. This decision and the decision in *Fletcher* v. *Peck* also upheld the sanctity of contracts. In *Fletcher* v. *Peck* (1810), the Supreme Court upheld a corrupt land deal between the state of Georgia and private individuals. The Court ruled that the deal might not have been in the public interest, but a contract should be upheld. In the following decades, the number of corporations and investors grew dramatically.

The Expansion of Banking

Banking and credit began to play an increasingly important role in economic expansion, especially after the panic of 1819. The panic of 1819 demonstrated the volatility of this new market economy. However, the remarkable growth afterward demonstrated the vitality of the new economy. The Second Bank of the United State, chartered in 1816, extended credit, as did many newly chartered state banks. These banks issued bank notes, which were the only paper currency in circulation at the time. The system of banknotes as currency was imperfect—values of notes from one state might be less in another state—but the ability of banks to put currency into the economy fueled economic growth.

TIP 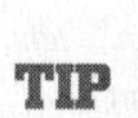

King Cotton, North and South
Cotton was not only king in the South. The increase in cotton production benefited many elements in the North as well. Cotton was bought and sold in New York City and processed into cloth in New England.

THE GROWTH OF SOUTHERN SLAVERY

Most of the cotton used in the mills in New England was grown by slave labor in the South. The invention of the cotton gin by Eli Whitney (1793) allowed for the rapid processing of cotton. That, combined with insatiable demand in the North and in Great Britain for cotton, led to more and more acres being put under cultivation. With an increase in cotton production came an increase in slavery.

Slavery become dominant in the South just as it was becoming unpopular in the eyes of the world. In 1807, Great Britain outlawed the international slave trade. The following year, the United States took the same step. (The international slave trade had been protected by the Constitution until 1808.) All of the northern states had voted to abolish slavery outright or gradually.

Some northerners and even some white southerners were critical of slavery. However, slavery and cotton were the main engines behind American economic growth in the first half of the nineteenth century. By 1860, 58 percent of American exports consisted of cotton. Cotton production increased from about 700,000 bales in 1830 to nearly 5 million bales on the eve of the Civil War. Cotton was justifiably called King Cotton. As cotton production increased, the number of slaves in the South also increased. In 1790, there were approximately 700,000 slaves in the United States. That figure climbed to 2 million by 1830 and to 4 million by 1860.

Both the North and South were growing economically in the first decades of the nineteenth century. In many ways, the growth of each region reinforced the growth of the other. However, this symbiotic relationship would not persist. Political and ideological differences would emerge as America moved toward the midway point in the century. These differences would come to overshadow commonalities and would lead to the Civil War.

Subject to Debate

The economic and social transformations of the antebellum period have become important topics in historical work recently. Social historians have become more interested in the lives of workers, women, Native Americans, frontier families, and slaves than in the policies and acts of presidents. These social historians, active in the field since the 1970s, have done much to topple the "great, white men" from their pedestal in the historical field. In place of laws, speeches, and treaties, social historians look at letter, diaries, census records, and court records to get a better sense of what life was like for ordinary Americans. Please note that this trend has shaped the writing of the AP exam. Recent free-response questions have involved industrial workers, women in antebellum America, and slaves during and after the Civil War. The Lowell girls are often mentioned in multiple-choice questions. This is not to say that political history is no longer relevant or important. It is both in the history field at large and on the AP exam. However, do not ignore the advances made in the field of social history. Be aware of the important social groups of each era and the impact they had on history.

Practice Multiple-Choice Questions:

Directions: Pick the letter that best answers the following questions.

1. The majority of workers at the Lowell textile mills, when they first opened in 1821, were

   (A) Irish immigrants.
   (B) free African Americans.
   (C) daughters of New England farmers.
   (D) veterans of the War of 1812.
   (E) French-Canadian immigrants.

2. The telegraph, the steamship, and the railroad had the effect of

   (A) strengthening the apprentice/master system.
   (B) isolating the United States from the rest of the world.
   (C) weakening the economic position of midwestern farmers.
   (D) raising transportation costs.
   (E) strengthening a national, market economy.

3. One effect of Eli Whitney's main contributions to the American economy was the

   (A) development of the factory system.
   (B) development of steam power.
   (C) development of the steel plow.
   (D) invention of the cotton gin.
   (E) invention of the mechanical reaper.

4. One characteristic of the factory system in the first half of the nineteenth century was that

   (A) mass-produced items were made at a higher quality and at higher prices than hand-crafted items.
   (B) work tended to be boring and repetitive.
   (C) the overall economic output of the United States declined as agricultural output dropped.
   (D) workers in factories enjoyed a great degree of freedom and control.
   (E) the Socialist movement enjoyed an upswing as disgruntled factory operatives began to question the logic of the factory system.

Practice Free-Response Questions:

1. Assess the relationship between the advent of Jacksonian democracy and the development of the market revolution.

2. Analyze the impact of the Supreme Court and of federal government policies on the economy of the United States (1800–1850).

Answers and Explanations to Multiple-Choice Questions:

1. **(C)** The first workers at the plants at Lowell, Massachusetts, were young farm women. These were the first real factory workers in the United States. When Irish immigration began in the 1840s, many of these women were replaced by Irish immigrants.
2. **(E)** The telegraph, the steamship, and the railroad all strengthened the nation and helped develop a market economy. Railroads allowed for the cheap transport of goods, and the telegraph allowed for instantaneous communication.
3. **(D)** Eli Whitney invented the cotton gin, a machine to separate the cotton seeds from strands. With Whitney's gin, the process became easy and cotton quickly became an important crop throughout the South. Cotton growers needed workers to plant, tend, and harvest the cotton crop. Thus, the institution of slavery saw a dramatic increase in the first half of the 1800s.
4. **(B)** Work in the textile mills of New England tended to be boring and repetitive. Factory work separated the parts of a process so that a worker would perform just one task again and again.

Antebellum American Culture, 1800–1855

CHAPTER 12

TIMELINE	
1827	Public school movement begins in Boston
1829	Publication of *David Walker's Appeal To the Coloured Citizens of the World*
1830	Founding of Mormonism
1831	William Lloyd Garrison begins publication of the *Liberator*
1833	Founding of the American Anti-slavery Society
1835	Publication of Alexis de Tocqueville's *Democracy in America*
1836	Congress passes the gag rule
1837	Elijah Lovejoy murdered by proslavery mob
1840	Formation of the Liberty Party
1841	Brook Farm founded
1843	Dorothea Dix organizes the movement for asylum reform
1848	Seneca Falls Convention
1851	Herman Melville writes *Moby Dick*

The aftermath of the War of 1812 saw not only an increase in nationalist sentiment but also the development of a uniquely American culture. To some degree, this was deliberate. Americans sought to differentiate themselves from the British. Noah Webster, for instance, sought to codify a specifically American dictionary, separate from British English, when he published his *American Dictionary of the English Language* in 1828. This American culture also developed without elite guidance. It was simply a result of the cultural practices of thousands of ordinary Americans an ocean away from Britain.

THE SECOND GREAT AWAKENING

In the first decades of the nineteenth century, American ministers sought to revive religious sentiment among the American people. The situation was similar to the first Great Awakening of a century earlier (see Chapter 5). At the turn of the century, many ministers worried that Americans seemed more captivated by politics—forming and building a new nation—than by God and salvation. Many ordinary Americans also felt a yearning to get in touch with a more immediate religious experience. The result was the Second Great Awakening. The movement of large camp meetings began in Kentucky early in the 1800s and soon spread to other states. It was especially strong in upstate New York and western Pennsylvania. The growing towns adjacent to the Erie Canal came to be known as the burned-over district because of the intensity of the religious revival there.

The movement spoke to many of the farmers, merchants, businessmen, and women who were brought into the larger society by the market revolution (see Chapter 11). The messages of the market and of the Great Second Awakening were similar. Market relations told the individual that success or failure was in his or her hands; hard work, dedication, and restraint would lead to economic success. The Second Great Awakening told the individual that salvation was also in his or her hands. Righteous living, self-control, and a strong moral compass would lead to salvation. This idea that one could determine his or her eternal life was very different from the old Puritan notion of predestination, which held that one's eternal life was planned out by God.

The Second Great Awakening not only encouraged individual redemption but also societal reformation. Not only could one become perfect in the eyes of God, but one could work to perfect society as well. In this respect, the Second Great Awakening acted as a springboard for a variety of reform movements.

Mormonism

The Church of the Latter-Day Saints, known as the Mormons, was founded in 1830 in upstate New York by Joseph Smith. It grew out of the Second Great Awakening. The group was met by hostility for its unorthodox teachings and practices. The most controversial practice was polygamy—allowing men to have multiple wives (long since renounced by the Mormon church). The group journeyed from New York to Ohio, then to Missouri, and finally to Illinois. In Illinois, Smith was killed by a mob (1844), and a new leader named Brigham Young led the majority of Mormons to Utah (see Chapter 13).

Periods of Reform
Be familiar with the three most prominent periods of reform in American history: the reform movements of the 1830s and 1840s, the progressive reform movement of the 1900s and 1910s, and the reform movements of the 1960s and 1970s that were inspired by the civil rights movement.

Reform Movements

Although reform movements have existed throughout most of American history, the antebellum period saw a dramatic upswing in reform activity. Reform movements have attempted to improve different aspects of American society but have had varying degrees of success.

Temperance

The goal of the temperance movement was to limit or even ban the production, sale, and consumption of alcoholic beverages. Many temperance activists focused on individual self-control; they encouraged people to take an oath to voluntarily abstain from alcohol. Others sought to use the power of government to limit or eliminate the consumption of alcoholic beverages. The temperance movement was the biggest reform movement of the first half of the nineteenth century.

The temperance movement attracted a large following in the antebellum period for several reasons. The temperance movement was especially popular among women. Many women were troubled by the large amount of alcohol their husbands drank. Alcohol was part of the fabric of daily life for many men. By 1830, the average man drank almost 10 gallons per year of hard liquor and about 30 gallons per year of beer, wine, and hard cider. In an era when pure water was difficult to come by, especially for urban working-class people, it made sense to drink alcoholic beverages. The alcohol killed dangerous bacteria. Women, who had the responsibility of putting food on the table, were troubled by the fact that their husbands often literally drank away their paychecks. Tavern owners were more than happy to cash men's paychecks on Friday evening, knowing that much of that money would stay in the tavern. Men not only came home with little money in their pockets; they came home drunk. Many men, in this drunken state, took out their frustrations on their wives and children. This acting out could take the form of verbal abuse and physical abuse. So it made sense for women to organize to stop liquor consumption.

TIP 

Reforming Self and Society
Many of the reform movements of the 1830s and 1840s were as much about reforming the self as about reforming society. Reformers urged individual self-restraint, whether in regard to alcohol or in regard to cruelty to slaves.

In the pre–Civil War period, the American Temperance Union had some success. Maine became a dry state in 1851, completely banning the sale or manufacture of all alcoholic beverages. However, alcohol consumption was on the rise throughout the 1800s, despite the efforts of the temperance movement.

Temperance and Nativism

The temperance movement went hand in hand with increased nativist, or anti-immigrant, sentiment. Nativism was both an emotional impulse as well as an organized movement. Many Americans thought that immigrants drank more than native-born Americans. They thought that the Irish Catholic immigrants lacked the self-control of "proper," middle-class Protestant Americans. Maybe these new immigrants didn't drink more than native-born Americans, but they probably drank more publicly. Middle-class people had their parlors in which to enjoy wine or scotch with their friends. Working-class immigrants drank at the local taverns—much more in the public eye.

The Asylum and Penitentiary Movement

In early America, the mentally ill were often treated as common criminals, spending years behind bars. In the 1840s, activists, including many women, spearheaded a movement to improve treatment for the mentally ill. One of the main organizers was Dorothea Dix. Her efforts led to the creation of the first generation of mental asylums in the United States.

Public Education

The campaign for free public education gained a large following in the 1840s. Horace Mann was among the most vocal advocates during this period. Mann was Secretary of Education in Massachusetts in the 1840s and 1850s and also served in the U.S. House of Representatives. The movement believed education is essential to democratic participation.

TRANSCENDENTALISM

TIP

The Impact of Thoreau
Thoreau's book *Walden*, or *Life in the Woods* (1854) was influential in the back-to-the-land movement of the 1960s and 1970s.

Transcendentalism was a spiritual and intellectual movement critical of the materialist direction the United States was taking. The movement put more stock in intuition than in empirical observation. Henry David Thoreau wrote about the importance of nature in finding meaning. He lived in relative isolation at Walden Pond for two years (1845–1847). In 1849, he wrote a famous essay called *Resistance to Civil Government* (commonly known as *Civil Disobedience*), urging individuals not to acquiesce to unfair and unjust government dictates. The other important figure in the movement was Ralph Waldo Emerson. He wrote a series of philosophical essays, including *On Self-Reliance* (1841). Although the transcendentalists were critical of the direction of mainstream society, they did not gravitate toward the reform movements of the day. Some transcendentalists separated themselves from mainstream society; several utopian communities were started by transcendentalist thinkers during this period. The most well-known one was Brook Farm, established outside of Boston in 1841.

ABOLITIONISM

The reform spirit of the Second Great Awakening inspired the modern movement to abolish slavery. Abolitionism was a minority opinion among northern whites in the antebellum period. However, it had a major impact on America, opening up sectional divisions that contributed to the Civil War.

David Walker

An important early figure was the African American David Walker. In 1829, he issued a pamphlet entitled *David Walker's Appeal To the Coloured Citizens of the World.* This radical tract called on people of African descent to resist slavery by any and every means. His praise of self-defense made southerners furious.

William Lloyd Garrison and Immediate Emancipation

In 1831, the white abolitionist William Lloyd Garrison, began publication of *The Liberator*. Garrison quickly became the key figure in the movement for the immediate and uncompensated abolition of slavery. Antislavery sentiment existed before that, but most antislavery groups advocated a more gradual approach to ending slavery. That is, slave owners would keep their current slaves but would not be able to enslave additional people. Slavery would therefore gradually end as the current slaves died. Additionally, most antislavery activists before Garrison advocated colonization, or sending freed slaves to Africa. Advocates of colonization believed that slaves either could not or should not receive treatment as equals in the United States. Garrison broke with both of these approaches. He said all slaves should be immediately freed, that there should be no compensation to their owners, and that freed slaves were entitled to the same rights as white people.

TIP

Support for Colonization
The American Colonization Society was started by antislavery Quakers, but it also had the support of many southern slave owners who wanted to rid the South of its free black population. Southern slave owners saw this population as a threat.

Abolitionism and Electoral Politics

A group of abolitionists formed the Liberty Party in 1840. This minor third party put forth the idea that the Constitution was essentially an antislavery document and that the United States should live up to the ideals contained in the document. In this, the party differed from Garrison, who insisted that the Constitution protected slavery and, therefore, should be condemned. The Liberty Party hoped to influence public opinion through the electoral arena. Garrison, on the other hand, rejected participating in electoral politics.

The Lovejoy Incident

A violent incidence in 1837 sent a chill over the abolitionist movement. Elijah Lovejoy, an abolitionist newspaper publisher in Illinois, was killed by a proslavery mob. He had been the subject of harassment. Mobs had destroyed his printing press three times before they killed him.

Frederick Douglass

Starting in the 1840s, the prominent figure in the abolitionist movement was Frederick Douglass. Douglass was born into slavery (1818) and escaped to the North in 1838. He had learned to read and write, and he soon became a powerful speaker in the antislavery movement. Douglass remained an important figure before, during, and after the Civil War until his death in 1895.

TIP

Shifting Defense of Slavery
Between the era of Jefferson and the era of Fitzhugh, we can say that the defense of the slavery system shifted from slavery being a "necessary evil" to it being a "positive good."

Southern Defense of Slavery

As the abolitionist movement attacked the system of slavery, southern public figures emerged to give a vigorous defense of the institution. Arguments took a variety of approaches. Some contrasted the factory system of the North with the slave system of the South, arguing that northern "wage slaves" were not taken care of or fed and were fired when business was slow. Other southerners argued that slavery was sanctioned in the Bible. The most well-known defender of slavery in the 1850s was George Fitzhugh. This movement went so far as to claim that slavery was a "positive good" for the slaves—that it provided them with skills, discipline, and "civilization."

GENDER AND THE CULT OF DOMESTICITY

Antebellum society defined women as intellectually inferior and insisted that the proper role for women was maintaining the house and caring for children. This "cult of domesticity" insisted that women keep a proper, Christian home—separate from the male sphere of politics, business, and competition. This ideal discouraged women from participating in public life. The laws of the country relegated women to a second-class status. Women could not vote or sit on juries. Women were not entitled to protection against physical abuse by their husbands. When women married, any property they owned became the property of their husbands. Under the legal doctrine of *femme covert*, wives had no independent legal or political standing.

Seneca Falls Convention

A group of women challenged the cultural and legal restrictions on women in the antebellum period. Many of these women met in the Seneca Falls Convention (1848). The meeting is often considered the birth of the women's rights movement. The convention was organized by Lucretia Mott and Elizabeth Cady Stanton. The genesis of the convention was their exclusion from an abolitionist conference in London in 1840. Mott and Stanton began thinking not only about the abolition of slavery but also about the conditions of women in the United States. The convention issued a Declaration of Sentiments modeled after the Declaration of Independence. The document declared that "all men and women are created equal."

TIP 

The Women's Rights Movement
Be aware of continuities and discontinuities between the movement of the period 1848–1920 and the movement of the 1960s and 1970s. Tactics and priorities shifted once the right to vote had been attained. The earlier movement grew out of the abolitionist movement; the latter was inspired by the civil rights movement.

The American Renaissance in Literature

The antebellum period experienced a renaissance in literature. Some of the greatest literature in American history comes out of the decades before the Civil War, especially 1850 to 1855. The literature of that period included Herman Melville's *Moby Dick*, the first edition of Walt Whitman's *Leaves of Grass*, Nathaniel Hawthorne's *The Scarlet Letter* and *The House of the Seven Gables*, and Thoreau's *Walden*. This literature is uniquely American. It grappled with religious and existential questions raised by the legacy of the Puritans. It also focused on the promise and the contradictions of America's experiment in building a democratic nation in the New World.

Subject to Debate

Historians have disagreed over the nature of the reform movements in the antebellum period. Some have focused on the democratic and egalitarian impulses of the movement. The women's rights movement and the abolitionist movement were certainly attempts to push America in a more democratic direction. However, other historians have focused on the more judgmental, restrictive nature of the reform movement. One can see some of the Puritan dogma still present in the antebellum period. The temperance movement reflects the more restrictive aspect of the movement. The push for public education can be seen in both lights. On the one hand, it embodies the democratic spirit of providing free education to all—a prerequisite for meaningful participation in the democratic process. At the same time, the lessons and the rote learning were meant to reinforce a rigid set of middle-class Protestant values.

Practice Multiple-Choice Questions:

Directions: Pick the letter that best answers the following questions.

1. Which is an accurate description of people who were most likely to be involved in the reform movements of pre–Civil War America?

   (A) Very wealthy merchants and industrialists
   (B) African-American slaves
   (C) Western and southern rural farmers
   (D) Middle-class northerners
   (E) Impoverished immigrants and factory workers

2. Horace Mann was an antebellum public figure most known for

   (A) advocating for free public education.
   (B) writing transcendentalist literature.
   (C) publishing an antislavery newspaper.
   (D) founding the first mental asylum in the United States.
   (E) preaching at revival meetings.

3. William Lloyd Garrison gained prominence in the 1830s by arguing that

   (A) slavery was a "positive good," not just a "necessary evil."
   (B) slaves should be sent to the African colony of Liberia.
   (C) slavery should be abolished immediately.
   (D) "wage slavery" in the North should be irradicated.
   (E) the slave system should be gradually ended.

4. Who of the following does not belong in the following list?

   (A) Frederick Douglass
   (B) George Fitzhugh
   (C) Elijah Lovejoy
   (D) David Walker
   (E) William Lloyd Garrison

Practice Free-Response Questions:

1. Analyze the rise of the temperance movement in the United States in the nineteenth century.

2. Assess the impact of the Second Great Awakening on American society in the period from 1820–1860.

Answers and Explanations to Multiple-Choice Questions:

1. **(D)** The reform movements of the antebellum period were composed primarily of middle-class northerners. Factory workers (E) were too exhausted at the end of the day to go to a reform meeting.

2. **(A)** Horace Mann was a key figure in the movement for free public education in the United States. He served for a period as the Secretary of Education in Massachusetts.

3. **(C)** William Lloyd Garrison is associated with the movement for the immediate abolition of slavery. He was uncompromising in his views. He began publishing *The Liberator* in 1831.

4. **(B)** All the men on the list were opponents of slavery in the antebellum period except for George Fitzhugh. He defended slavery as a "positive good."

Territorial Expansion, 1820–1854

CHAPTER 13

TIMELINE	
1822	Stephen Austin established the first American settlement in Texas
1836	The Battle of the Alamo
	Texas independence
1844	James Polk elected president
	Texas annexation
1846	Resolution of the dispute with Great Britain over the Oregon Territory
	Beginning of the Mexican War
1848	The Treaty of Guadalupe Hidalgo ends Mexican War
	Gold found in California
1854	Ostend Manifesto

As the American economy grew in the decades between the War of 1812 and the Civil War, many Americans continued the push farther and farther into the continent. This westward movement had ominous implications for neighboring nations and as well as for Native-American nations within the borders of the growing United States. Finally, the acquisition of additional territory inflamed sectional tensions as the debate over the expansion of slavery intensified in the decade before the Civil War.

MANIFEST DESTINY AND THE MOVEMENT WEST

The term *Manifest Destiny* was coined in an 1845 newspaper article by John O'Sullivan. It captured the fervor of the westward expansion movement, implying that it was God's plan that the United States take over and settle the entire continent. Americans who did settle out West were probably driven more by economic factors, such as cheap land or precious metals, than they were by a desire to fulfill a divine plan.

TEXAS—FROM SETTLEMENT TO STATEHOOD

Americans had been settling in Texas as far back as the 1820s. Mexico was eager to attract settlers to its northern frontier, in part to provide a buffer from incursions by Native-American groups. Settlers mostly from the American South were led by Stephen Austin. They were attracted to Texas because of an abundance of affordable land that could be used for cotton cultivation.

The Alamo and Texas Independence

Mexico allowed these settlers a degree of self-government in the 1820s, but tensions began to develop in the 1830s. The Texas settlers routinely flouted Mexican law—most notably in practicing slavery, which was banned in Mexico. The new president of Mexico, General Antonio López de Santa Anna, sought to bring the Texans in line with Mexican laws and customs. In 1836, the Texans rebelled. At first they suffered major setbacks. Almost 200 died at the Alamo in San Antonio, a former mission where the rebels had taken refuge. Weeks later, almost 400 rebels were killed by Mexican forces near the town of Goliad. The rebels, under the leadership of General Sam Houston, regrouped and emerged victorious. Texans fought for and won independence from Mexico, establishing the independent Lone Star Republic in 1836.

Texas Annexation and the Politics of Slavery

Texans were eager for their Lone Star Republic to join the United States. One of the first official acts of the Texas president was to send a delegation to Washington to offer to join the United States. Democratic President Andrew Jackson, however, did not want to add to sectional tensions by admitting a large slave state. So he blocked annexation. His successors likewise did not want to open the contentious debate that would accompany Texas annexation. Democratic President Martin Van Buren (1837–1841), and Whig Presidents William Henry Harrison (1841) and John Tyler (1841–1845) all avoided the issue.

The Election of 1844 and the Annexation of Texas

The election of 1844 put the issue of Texas annexation on the national agenda. Democratic candidate James K. Polk promised to push for Texas annexation as well as a resolution of a border dispute with Great Britain over Oregon (see below), offering something to both southern and northern voters. By 1844, the Democrats were clearly emerging as more expansionistic and more proslavery than the Whigs. Polk defeated President Tyler, and even before Polk took office, the outgoing president saw Polk's victory as a mandate for Texas annexation and pushed Texas annexation through Congress. Texas joined the United States as the fifteenth slave state in 1844.

WAR WITH MEXICO

The annexation of Texas was an important catalyst for the Mexican War (1846–1848) between the United States and Mexico. The Mexican government was furious that Texas had become part of the United States. Meanwhile, President Polk and American expansionists were eager to incorporate the remainder of Mexico's northern provinces into the United States. The immediate cause of the war was a border dispute. Mexico and the United States disagreed over the southern border of the new United States territory of Texas. Mexico said it was at the Nueces River. The United States insisted it was at the Rio Grande, 150 miles to the south. Skirmishes in the disputed area led to war between Mexico and the United States.

Victory on the Battlefield

The United States won several early battles in the war. One prong of the war, in the area of Mexico south of Texas, was led by General Zachary Taylor. United States forces also won victories in present-day California. However, Mexico was very reluctant to part with its northern provinces after having lost Texas. An attack on the Mexican capital Mexico City, led by General Winfield Scott, was needed to force the Mexican government to capitulate.

The Treaty of Guadalupe Hidalgo

In 1848, the Mexican government signed the Treaty of Guadalupe Hidalgo, giving up its claims to the disputed territory in Texas. Mexico also agreed to sell the provinces of California and New Mexico, known as the Mexican Cession, to the United States for $15 million. This territory includes present-day California, Nevada, Utah, and parts of Arizona, New Mexico, Colorado, and Wyoming.

The Wilmot Proviso

Northern politicians tried, unsuccessfully, to ban slavery in the Mexican Cession by putting forth the Wilmot Proviso (1846). These politicians were not, for the most part, abolitionists. They believed in the free-soil ideal. They wanted additional land for white settlers to set up homesteads, without competition from the slave system. The proviso was passed by the House of Representatives, where politicians from the populous northern states dominated. However, the proviso failed in the Senate.

TIP 

A Divided Congress
In the antebellum period, the Senate tended to be friendlier to the slave system than was the House. The southern states had more power in the Senate than they did in the population-based House.

SETTLING THE WEST

Manifest Destiny alluded to the political extension of United States territory. However, it also referred to the movement of individuals to newly acquired lands.

The California Gold Rush

The Gold Rush began when gold was discovered at Sutter's Mill in Coloma, California, in 1848. That year, California became United States territory as a result of the Mexican War. As word spread, thousands of people came to California to try to strike it rich. A large percentage of the 300,000 people who migrated to California came in 1849, thus their nickname "forty-niners." A few people did strike it rich. Very soon though, the easily accessible gold was panned from riverbeds. To get access to gold beneath the surface, capital-intensive methods were required. This expensive machinery was beyond the reach of ordinary prospectors.

Competing Motivations
Be aware of the variety of motivations that drew people to the West. Some were small farmers inspired by the free soil ideal. Some were drawn to Texas to find a place as slave-owning cotton growers. Some were part of the Mormon exodus to Utah. Some were gold seekers drawn to California.

The Mormon Exodus

In 1847, the religious group the Church of the Latter-Day Saints, known as the Mormons, settled along the banks of the Great Salt Lake in Utah. The land at the time was Mexican territory. When the Mormons arrived, the Mexican War had already begun. After the United States' victory in the war (1848), Utah and the remainder of the Mexican Cession territory became United States territory. (See more on the Mormons in Chapter 12.)

SETTLING BOUNDARIES

The current boundaries of the continental United States became official by 1854. Political concerns precluded expanding beyond the continental boundaries until well after the Civil War.

Gadsden Purchase

The final land acquisition in what would become the continental United States was the Gadsden Purchase, acquired from Mexico in 1853, five years after the Mexican War. It added an additional area to the vast swath of land obtained by the United States following the war. The Gadsden Purchase was sought by the United States as a possible southern route for a transcontinental railroad.

Border Dispute with Great Britain over Maine

The United States settled a dispute in 1842 with Great Britain over the border between Maine and British-ruled Canada. The Webster-Ashburn Treaty split the disputed territory and also settled a dispute over the border between the Minnesota territory and Canada.

Fifty-four Forty or Fight: Tensions over Oregon

Both Great Britain and the United States made historic claims to the lands of the Pacific Northwest. In 1818, the two nations agreed on a joint occupation of the Oregon Country. In the 1830s and 1840s, adventurous Americans began traveling west along the Oregon Trail and settling in the lush valley of the Willamette River. In 1844, politicians pushed for sole U.S. ownership of the entire Oregon Country, the northern boundary of which was the north latitude line at 54° 40'. "Fifty-four forty or fight" was the rallying call of those who wanted the United States to own the entire territory. Great Britain balked at giving up all the territory. In 1846, the Polk administration reached a compromise with Great Britain, establishing the border at the 49th parallel. That line is the current boundary between the United States and Canada.

TIP

Cuba and the United States Cuba, ninety miles off the coast of Florida, has loomed large in American diplomatic history from the French and Indian War, through the *Ostend Manifesto*, to the Spanish-American War, and then to the age of Fidel Castro.

Cuba and the Ostend Manifesto

For many expansionists, the Manifest Destiny of the United States did not stop at the Pacific. Southern expansionists hoped to extend their slavery empire farther south. Cuba, with its profitable sugar plantations, came into their sights in the 1850s. President Polk offered to purchase it from Spain. When Spain balked, some American adventurers tried to take it by force. American diplomats, sent by pro-southern President Franklin Pierce to Ostend, Belgium, again tried to buy Cuba secretly. Their goals, written up as the Ostend Manifesto (1854), provoked anger from northern politicians when it was released to the press.

Subject to Debate

History textbooks implicitly grapple with a major issue of interpretation—how should the expansion of the United States be discussed? Territorial expansion at the expense of indigenous people and neighboring nations would generally win the disfavor of textbook writers if the subject were not the United States. These books, for instance, might discuss the arrogance of Napoleon's actions or the brutality of Japanese expansion in Asia in the 1930s. By contrast, the era of Manifest Destiny is often shrouded in the language of idealism, democracy, adventure, and optimism. However, historical interpretation, to be taken seriously, should try to maintain fair and consistent criteria in evaluating parallel actions committed by different nations.

Practice Multiple-Choice Questions:

Directions: Pick the letter that best answers the following questions.

1. An important cause of the Mexican War was
   (A) competing claims for gold in California.
   (B) Mexico's refusal to trade with the United States.
   (C) Mexico's arming of Native Americans in the American Southwest.
   (D) rumors that Mexico was forming a secret alliance with Great Britain.
   (E) a border dispute between the United States and Mexico.

2. The most important reason that the Mormon church settled in Utah was

   (A) Utah's liberal laws in regard to polygamy.
   (B) to escape from persecution they received in more settled areas.
   (C) to fulfill a prophecy that Joseph Smith had of building a religious community by a "great salt lake."
   (D) the fertile soil in Utah.
   (E) the desire to spread their faith among Native Americans.

3. Many Americans went to Texas in the 1820s because of Mexico's

   (A) system of self-government.
   (B) promise of cheap, fertile cotton land.
   (C) acceptance of slavery.
   (D) the discovery of gold.
   (E) policy of religious intolerance.

4. The Ostend Manifesto (1854) expressed the goal of

   (A) acquiring Alaska from Russia.
   (B) building a canal through Central America.
   (C) purchasing Cuba from Spain.
   (D) opening up China to trade.
   (E) abolishing slavery throughout the United States.

Practice Free-Response Questions:

1. Assess the political, economic, and social motivations that influenced the drive for Manifest Destiny.

2. Assess how Manifest Destiny shaped the political debates of the 1840s and 1850s.

Answers and Explanations to Multiple-Choice Questions:

1. **(E)** The Mexican War was caused by a dispute between the United States and Mexico over the border between the two countries. In all probability, the United States was simply provoking a war so that it could acquire Mexican territory.
2. **(B)** The Mormons suffered from constant abuse and violence from their neighbors in New York and then in Illinois. They believed that they could practice their faith freely only in an isolated area.
3. **(B)** Texas attracted migrants who hoped to gain a small plot of land and grow cotton. Perhaps with some luck, these settlers would make enough money to purchase a slave or two. Texas provided a way for poor white folks to emulate the grandees of the Old South.
4. **(C)** The Ostend Manifesto was a document written by American diplomats in Ostend, Belgium. The manifesto expressed a wish of southerners to purchase Cuba and turn it into a slave state.

Section Tensions and the Crisis of Union, 1848–1860

CHAPTER 14

TIMELINE

1848	The Treaty of Guadalupe Hidalgo ends the Mexican War
1850	Compromise of 1850
1852	Publication of *Uncle Tom's Cabin* by Harriet Beecher Stowe
1856	Beginning of "Bleeding Kansas"
	The beating of Senator Charles Sumner
1857	*Dred Scott* v. *Sanford* decision
1859	John Brown's raid on Harper's Ferry arsenal
1860	Election of President Abraham Lincoln
	South Carolina secedes from the United States

The acquisition and settlement of new territories in the western half of the North American continent opened up a question that politicians had sought to avoid—should these new territories allow slavery? Most northern politicians were not abolitionists; indeed, abolitionism was a minority position in the North in 1850. However, the issue of the expansion of slavery became increasingly divisive in the 1850s. Some northerners adopted the free-soil ethos—the idea that lands out west should be open to small-scale farming, without competition from large-scale plantation agriculture using slave labor. By the end of the decade, more northerners were grappling with the moral issues around slavery. Positions became decidedly more entrenched on the eve of the Civil War.

THE AFTERMATH OF THE MEXICAN WAR

The Treaty of Guadalupe Hidalgo (1848) following the Mexican War granted the United States a huge portion of Mexico for a mere $15 million. Very soon after, gold was discovered in California, leading to a huge growth in the population of California. The question of whether the newly acquired territory would be free or slave became a pressing issue in the years following the war. The Wilmot Proviso (introduced in 1846), banning slavery from the Mexican Cession, never became law (see Chapter 13).

Popular Sovereignty

Senator Lewis Cass proposed a compromise measure on the question of slavery in the newly acquired territories. He came up with the idea that the question of slavery should be left to the people of a particular territory. This idea became known as popular sovereignty. Though Congress failed to act on his idea, popular sovereignty became an important issue in the 1850s.

The Election of 1848

In the election of 1848, both the Whigs and the Democrats avoided taking strong stands on the issue of slavery. Cass was the Democratic candidate, but he lost to Whig candidate Zachary Taylor, one of the heroes of the Mexican War. In response to the marked silence from the major parties on the slavery question, antislavery men in both parties founded the Free-Soil Party in 1848.

TIP 

Divisiveness in Congress
The lack of agreement on the Compromise of 1850 highlights the hardening of sectional tensions.

California and the Compromise of 1850

In 1849, President Taylor urged California and New Mexico to apply for statehood. Both areas had antislavery majorities. California was ready to apply for statehood. The population of California quickly grew to over 300,000 in the wake of the discovery of gold (see Chapter 13).

By 1850, California had enough people to form a state. Californians wrote up a constitution to submit to Congress in which slavery would be illegal. Southern senators objected to the admission of an additional free state. Senate negotiators, led by the aging Henry Clay, worked out a series of measures to resolve this extremely contentious problem. These measures became known as the Compromise of 1850. The most important elements of the compromise were the admittance of California as a free state, which pleased northern politicians, and a more stringent Fugitive Slave Law, which pleased southern politicians. Other measures included allowing New Mexico and Utah to decide the question of slavery based on popular sovereignty, accepting a new boundary between Texas and Mexico, and banning the slave trade (but not slavery) in Washington, D.C. Senate negotiators put forth these measures as an omnibus bill. However, it soon became clear that neither antislavery senators from the North nor proslavery "fire-eaters" from the South would vote "yes" on the Omnibus Bill. Stephen Douglas, a Democratic Senator from Illinois, proposed "unbundling" the legislative package and voting on each measure separately. The measures all passed. President Millard Fillmore (who assumed the presidency in 1850 upon the death of President Taylor) signed them into law.

SLAVERY AND SECTIONALISM

The "compromise" of 1850 allowed the United States to move forward, but the series of legislative acts did little to settle the question of slavery.

The Fugitive Slave Act and Personal Liberty Laws

Many Northerners grew alarmed at the enforcement of the Fugitive Slave Act. Previously, the majority of Northerners could ignore the brutality of the slave system, but following 1850, slave catchers brought the system to the streets of northern cities. In response, many northern states passed personal liberty laws offering protection to fugitives. Many whites and free African Americans in northern cities even formed vigilance committees to prevent the slave catchers from carrying out their orders. The Supreme Court protected slave catchers from state restrictions on their activities. In *Prigg* v. *Pennsylvania*, the Court overturned the abduction conviction of Edward Prigg, a slave catcher, on the grounds that federal law—the Constitution itself and the Fugitive Slave Law of 1793—was superior to state law. This approach was reinforced in the decision in *Ableman* v. *Booth* (1859). In this case, the Court overturned a Wisconsin Supreme Court ruling. The Wisconsin court had ruled that Sherman Booth, who had interfered with the carrying out of the 1850 Fugitive Slave Act, was not guilty. It declared the act itself unconstitutional. The United States Supreme Court reversed this decision, asserting the supremacy of federal court decisions over state courts.

Uncle Tom's Cabin

Sectional tensions were further inflamed by the publication in 1852 of the novel *Uncle Tom's Cabin.* The novel, written by Harriet Beecher Stowe of the antislavery Beecher family, depicted in graphic and sentimental detail the brutality of slavery. For many Northerners, slavery now had a human face. The novel outraged southern supporters of slavery, who attempted to ban it.

THE SLAVERY QUESTION AND PARTY POLITICS

As the 1850s progressed, both the Whigs and the Democrats sought to decrease sectional tensions, but new controversies continued to divide the parties.

The Election of 1852

The 1852 presidential election was won by the Democrat Franklin Pierce, who was able to take advantage of a divided Whig Party. Pierce, an enthusiastic expansionist, hoped to put sectional divisions aside by acquiring additional foreign territory. He authorized the Gadsden Purchase in 1853, which was approved by the Senate the following year. This purchase added territory south of present-day New Mexico and Arizona. The land was level enough for the United States to begin contemplating a continental railroad along the southern edge of the country.

The Kansas-Nebraska Act

Pierce's desire to unite the sections unraveled in 1854. Senator Stephen Douglas of Illinois introduced the Kansas-Nebraska Act to the Senate. Douglas, who owned significant tracts of land in Chicago, hoped that the first transcontinental railroad would have a more northern route, using Chicago as a hub. The act called for dividing the northern section of the Louisiana Purchase territory into two organized territories, Kansas and Nebraska. Any railroad construction would have to be carried out in organized territory. The most contentious part of the act was allowing for the possibility of slavery in the territories of Kansas and Nebraska—areas that had been closed to slavery by the Missouri Compromise (1820). The act mandated that the question of slavery in these territories be decided by popular sovereignty. Many Northerners were angry at the act and at Douglas.

Nativism over Time
Anti-immigrant sentiment has surfaced several times in American history, usually targeting the most recent immigrants: Irish immigrants in the 1850s; Chinese immigrants in the 1880s; the "new immigrants" of eastern and southern Europe at the turn of the twentieth century; and Latino immigrants at the turn of the twenty-first century.

Party Realignment

The Kansas-Nebraska Act became a lightning rod for sectional divisions. The Whigs became bitterly divided between pro-slavery "Cotton Whigs" and anti-slavery "Conscience Whigs." Meanwhile, the Democratic Party became increasingly a regional southern, proslavery party.

The "Know-Nothings" and the Rise of Nativism

Several new political parties attempted to fill the void left by the collapse of the national parties. The Know-Nothing Party (formally known as the American Party) emerged in the 1840s. By the 1850s, it achieved electoral success in several states, especially in the Northeast. The defining issue of the Know-Nothing Party was opposition to immigration. The party was the political wing of a growing anti-Catholic, anti-Irish nativist movement that gained traction in the wake of the large-scale Irish immigration of the late 1840s and 1850s.

The Birth of the Republican Party

In 1854, the modern Republican Party was born. This party was made of many different factions—former members of the Know-Nothing Party, "Conscience Whigs," free-soilers, abolitionists, and former Democrats, to name a few. Though the party was critical of slavery, it did not advocate the abolition of slavery. Rather, it adopted the position that slavery should not be allowed to spread to the new territories.

Republicans, Then and Now
The Republican Party born in 1854 is the same party that exists today; however, its politics have changed considerably. The party that was born in opposition to the spread of slavery now gets less than 10 percent of the African-American vote. Since the 1920s, it has been more conservative and pro-business than the Democratic Party.

The Election of 1856

The election of 1856 made clear that the stability of the Democrat-Whig two-party system was over. With the Whig Party dissolved and the Know-Nothing Party divided over the slavery issue, the Republican Party emerged as a major party just two years after its birth. The Democratic Party won the election by shrewdly picking a northern candidate who had southern sympathies, James Buchanan. It was clear after the election that a new two-party system was emerging, the Democrats and the Republicans. Though these two parties have dramatically changed in the last century and a half, they remain the two main parties.

THE IMPENDING CRISIS

By 1856, it became clear that compromise on the issue of slavery would be very difficult. In the following years, the tensions between North and South became increasingly acute and even violent.

Bleeding Kansas

Violence erupted in Kansas as proslavery and antislavery men fought for control of the state. In keeping with the dictates of the 1854 Kansas-Nebraska Act (see above), elections were held for a territorial legislature in 1855. Even though only 1,500 settlers were recognized as legal voters, more than 6,000 votes were cast as thousands of proslavery Missourians came over the border for the day to cast votes. In response to such a clearly fraudulent election, antislavery Kansans chose their own shadow legislature. Each side wrote up a constitution for Kansas. Antislavery men wrote up the Topeka Constitution; proslavery men created the Lecompton Constitution. President Pierce recognized the proslavery government and called the antislavery government traitorous. A proslavery posse of Missourians, under the auspices of a federal marshal, sacked the antislavery town of Lawrence in May 1856.

Several days after the sack of Lawrence and just two days after the beating of Senator Charles Sumner (see below), the deeply religious antislavery activist John Brown initiated a bloody massacre of proslavery men along the banks of the Pottawatomie Creek. Brown, his sons, and several followers used knives to kill five men.

Open violence continued in the Kansas territory, on and off, for the next several years. In many respects, bleeding Kansas can be seen as a dress rehearsal for the Civil War. The question of slavery in Kansas was unresolved when Lincoln was elected. After southern secession began, Kansas quickly joined the Union as a free state in January 1861.

The Beating of Senator Charles Sumner

The growing tensions between North and South were evident in a violent incident that occurred on the floor of the Senate in 1856. Senator Charles Sumner from Massachusetts had given a pointed antislavery speech, called "Crimes Against Kansas," in which he singled out Senator Andrew P. Butler of South Carolina. Butler's nephew, a South Carolina representative named Preston Brooks, heard about the speech and came over to Sumner's desk in the Senate chamber and beat him repeatedly with a heavy cane. The injuries left Sumner incapacitated for four years. Northerners saw the beating as a further sign of Southern barbarity; Southerners made Brooks a hero.

The Dred Scott Decision

Northern and southern relations were further pushed apart by the Supreme Court decision in the case of *Dred Scott* v. *Sanford* (1857). The case involved the fate of a slave named Dred Scott. Scott was owned by a doctor serving in the United States army. Scott and his wife, along with their owner, lived for a time in the state of Illinois and in the Wisconsin Territory, areas in which slavery had been banned by the Northwest Ordinance. Years after returning to Missouri, Scott sued for his and his wife's freedom on the grounds that they had lived for a time in free areas and that made them free. The Supreme Court did not find Dred Scott's arguments persuasive. First, the court ruled that Scott was still a slave and did not even have the right to initiate a lawsuit. Next, the court ruled that Congress had overstepped its bounds in declaring the northern portion of the Louisiana Purchase territory off limits to slavery. It therefore invalidated the Missouri Compromise of 1820. Finally, the decision declared that that no African Americans, not even free men and women, were entitled to citizenship in the United States because they were, according to the Court, "beings of an inferior order." Northerners were astounded at the sweep of the decision. The decision seemed to argue that slavery was a national, rather than a regional, institution and that Congress could do little to stop it.

Was Slavery Becoming National?
Antislavery politicians wondered if slavery was becoming a national rather than a sectional institution. They worried that the Supreme Court would hamper any attempts to stop the spread of slavery.

John Brown and the Raid on Harper's Ferry

In the fall of 1859, John Brown carried out a raid on an armory in Harper's Ferry, Virginia (now West Virginia), that pushed North-South relations to the breaking point. Brown, with ties to many of the leading abolitionists of the day including Frederick Douglass, planned to recruit a small group of men to overtake the armory and then to distribute the weapons inside to slaves. Brown believed that this would initiate a massive slave rebellion that would topple slavery. The men managed to overtake the armory but were soon overwhelmed by reinforcements. Brown was tried and executed later in 1859.

Although the event did not accomplish its stated goal, its impact on history is undeniable. It convinced proslavery southerners that there was a conspiracy afoot among northerners to interfere violently with the institution of slavery. The truth of the matter was that Brown's raid was roundly condemned by most northern politicians. However, the perception of a united front among northerners persisted in the mind of the South.

Was John Brown Insane?
Be careful about referring to John Brown as crazy, wild, or insane. Strong evidence does not support such a claim. His lawyer claimed he was insane in court, but that was to prevent Brown from getting the death sentence. Brown protested at his lawyer's tactics. It's safe to say that Brown was deeply religious and committed to the cause of antislavery.

The Election of 1860

The election of 1860 demonstrated the fractured nature of the American political system on the eve of the Civil War. The Democratic Party was divided between a northern wing and a southern wing. The northern Democrats, rallying around the idea of popular sovereignty, nominated Stephen Douglas for president, who carried only Missouri and part of New Jersey. The southern Democrats, who strongly endorsed slavery, carried the deep South. A third formation, the Constitutional Union, which endorsed maintaining the Union and avoided the slavery issue, won the upper South.

The Republican Party chose Abraham Lincoln as their standard bearer. Lincoln had served briefly as a Whig congressman from Illinois, speaking out against the war with Mexico. He ran for the Senate in 1858, losing to Stephen Douglas, but impressing the public with his oratory skills. In seven debates in different parts of Illinois, Lincoln repeatedly asked Douglas whether he favored the spread of slavery. Douglas avoided the issue, putting forth popular sovereignty as a cure-all to the slavery question and race baiting Lincoln. Lincoln had been opposed to the institution of slavery his entire life and had been an advocate of the American Colonization Society. As he ran for president, he indicated that he would not, nor could he, tamper with slavery where it already existed. He promised, however, to block its expansion to new territories in the West. Lincoln won 40 percent of the popular vote but carried the electoral vote, winning virtually all the states of the North as well as California and Oregon.

Even if Lincoln kept his promise not to interfere with slavery in the slave states, many southern slaveholders would still not have been satisfied. In many ways, slavery needed to grow in order to remain economically viable. Even before Lincoln was inaugurated, the states of the deep South began seceding. The process set the stage for Civil War.

Subject to Debate

The events of the 1850s have assumed a central place in one of the most contentious historiographical discussions about American history. How should the coming of the Civil War be understood? Central to that question is the role of slavery in the coming of the Civil War. Partisan historians from the South and from the North have tended to blame the other side. Southern partisans blame the North for interfering with their domestic institutions. Northern partisans blame the extreme language of the Dred Scott decision, the violence done to Senator Sumner, and the strident defense of slavery as indicators of intransigence on the part of the South.

Many historians for decades after the war held that the war was an "irrepressible conflict." The phrase was actually coined before the war by Senator William H. Seward, discussing the possibility of a future conflict between the sections—one he saw as inevitable. The war was inevitable, the theory held, because of slavery. Slavery was both at the heart of the issue and was beyond compromise. The "irrepressible conflict" school has gotten more recent backing from contemporary historian Eric Foner. Foner focuses less on northern moral concerns about slavery and more on the free-labor ideology. The free-labor ideology, which was a central part of the culture of the North, held that the lands out West should be for small-scale farming, without competition from slave labor.

Several historical schools have questioned the centrality of slavery in the conflict. Progressive historians Mary and Charles Beard, writing in the 1920s, argued that the conflict was actually between a capitalist industrial North and an agrarian, almost feudal, South. Other historians have blamed the conflict on blundering politicians—asserting that slavery and other issues were compromisable. This school of thought gained adherents from the 1920s onward but has been challenged more recently in the post–civil rights movement era.

Practice Multiple-Choice Questions:

Directions: Pick the letter that best answers the following questions.

1. In the Dred Scott case (1857), the Supreme Court included which idea as part of its decision?
   (A) Slavery could continue to exist in the South, but it cannot expand to the new territories of the West.
   (B) An African American had no rights a white man was bound to respect.
   (C) The Fugitive Slave Law violates a states' right to legislate on the question of slavery.
   (D) Separate but equal facilities are inherently unconstitutional.
   (E) It is not permissible for African Americans and whites to wed in the United States,

2. The formation of the Republican Party in 1854 was significant in that it
   (A) was the first major party to support the immediate abolition of slavery.
   (B) was the first major political party that appealed to voters in only one region of the country.
   (C) was the only political party in the 1850s to take a strong stand against nativism.
   (D) won the presidency in only two years after its formation.
   (E) was the only American political party to have started in a foreign country.

3. The Kansas-Nebraska Act's provisions for deciding the slavery question in Kansas and Nebraska made obsolete the
   (A) Compromise of 1850.
   (B) Wilmot Proviso.
   (C) Missouri Compromise.
   (D) Northwest Ordinance.
   (E) Ostend Manifesto.

4. Stephen Douglas was only able to assure passage of the Compromise of 1850 by
   (A) agreeing to drop the provision that California be admitted as a free state.
   (B) promising the two South Carolina senators that the next Supreme Court nominee will be from their state.
   (C) assuring southern senators that the first transcontinental railroad would be built in the South.
   (D) agreeing to end Reconstruction.
   (E) unbundling the parts of the compromise so that each one would be voted on separately.

Practice Free-Response Questions:

1. How did the evolution of political parties in the 1850s reflect worsening sectional tensions?

2. Assess the impact of TWO of the following on sectional tensions in the 1850s.

   Publication of *Uncle Tom's Cabin*
   The beating of Senator Charles Sumner
   John Brown's raid at Harper's Ferry

Answers and Explanations to Multiple-Choice Questions:

1. **(B)** The Dred Scott decision essentially denied citizenship rights to all African Americans, slave or free. The decision was a real blow to those who were seeking some sort of compromise between the regions.

2. **(B)** The Republican Party was the first major party to appeal to people in only one region of the country. The Democratic Party soon followed suit and became solely a southern party. With only regional political parties, it was very difficult to reach compromise.

3. **(C)** The Kansas-Nebraska Act stipulated that the question of slavery in Kansas and Nebraska would be resolved by popular sovereignty (a territorial vote). However, these areas had been closed to slavery by the Missouri Compromise. So the Missouri Compromise was nullified.

4. **(E)** The Compromise of 1850 wasn't actually a compromise. All the elements of the package were voted on separately, so congressmen did not have to vote "yes" on parts of the package they found objectionable. There were enough congressmen in the middle to assure passage of each element.

CHAPTER 15

The Civil War and Reconstruction, 1860–1877

TIMELINE

1860	The election of Abraham Lincoln
	South Carolina secedes
1861	The inauguration of Lincoln
	Six more states, all from the Deep South, secede
	Fighting at Fort Sumter
	Four more states, from the Upper South, secede
1862	Homestead Act
1863	The Emancipation Proclamation goes into effect
	New York City draft riots
1864	Sherman's March to the Sea
1865	Freedman's Bureau is established
	13th Amendment is ratified
	Lincoln is assassinated
	Southern states begin to pass Black codes
1866	Civil Rights Act passed
	Ku Klux Klan is formed
1867	Reconstruction Acts passed; beginning of Congressional Reconstruction
	Tenure of Office Act
1868	Johnson is impeached
	14th Amendment is ratified
1870	15th Amendment is ratified
1877	Agreement ends Reconstruction; Hayes becomes president

The importance of the Civil War to American history cannot be overstated. The bloody war settled one of the most vexing issues in American history—the existence of slavery in an otherwise democratic country.

THE ONSET OF WAR

Abraham Lincoln's electoral victory in 1860 alarmed southern defenders of slavery to the point that leading political figures in the South were ready to secede. Even before Lincoln was inaugurated, seven southern states seceded.

Once inaugurated, Lincoln made clear that he would not tolerate southern secession, but he also did not want to initiate a war with the breakaway states. The continued presence of United States troops at Fort Sumter, in the harbor of Charleston, South Carolina, proved to be the match that ignited the war. The leadership of the nearly formed Confederate States of America decided that they would not tolerate the presence of the United States flag flying over Fort Sumter. Confederate President Jefferson Davis ordered Confederate soldiers to bombard the fort. This action constituted the opening shots of the Civil War. Lincoln reacted to this situation with resolve. In April 1861, he issued a proclamation calling up 75,000 troops to "cause the laws to be duly executed." Soon the United States and the seceded southern states, calling themselves the Confederate States of America, were at war.

War Without a Declaration of War

TIP

What Happened to the "United States"? When textbooks discuss the Civil War, they often call the United States the Union. This is fine, but it is also fine to use "the United States" in your essays. The United States did not disappear. Perhaps historians use the Union for the sake of clarity; however, the decision also has political overtones.

President Lincoln faced an unprecedented legal dilemma as the Civil War began. He did not ask for a declaration of war from Congress, because doing so would acknowledge the legitimacy of the Confederate States of America. Lincoln did not recognize the Confederacy; he insisted the rebellious states were participating in an insurrection. However, without a declaration of war, would Lincoln's wartime actions be recognized as legitimate? This issue came to the Supreme Court. The Union army had seized several ships bound for southern ports. Typically the seizing of ships, absent a declaration of war, is considered piracy. The Court ruled in the *Prize Cases* that a *de facto* state of war existed and that Lincoln was within his bounds to have ordered the seizure of the ships.

Taking Sides

Once the war had begun, the states of the upper South were faced with a difficult choice. Slavery in the states of the upper South was not as prominent a component of the economy as it was in the deep South. However, if the upper-South states stayed with the Union, they would be thrust into a war against fellow southerners. Soon Arkansas, Tennessee, North Carolina, and Virginia joined the Confederacy. Missouri, Kentucky, Maryland, and Delaware ultimately stayed with the Union. Lincoln took extensive measures to assure that Maryland would not secede. If it did, the capital of the United States would be surrounded by Confederate states. Lincoln suspended habeas corpus in Maryland and arrested several anti-Union political figures.

Strengths and Weaknesses of the Two Sides

The Union side had some key advantages in the war. It had a far greater population than that of the rebellious southern states (22 million to 6 million, excluding slaves). It also had a far greater military capacity than the South, a more diverse economy, and an extensive network of railroad tracks. All of these advantages would become especially significant in a lengthy war. The Union had the capability to resupply its troops and to recruit reinforcements for fallen soldiers.

The main advantage of the Confederacy was that it simply had to fight a defensive war. It did not have to invade and conquer the North in order to declare victory. The Union, on the other hand, had to fight an offensive war in southern territory. Another advantage of the Confederacy was the rich military tradition of the South. It had able generals and a cohort of military men to draw from.

Fighting the Civil War

The Union had a three-part strategy for the war. First, the navy would blockade southern ports. The intent of this plan, labeled the Anaconda Plan, was to cut off supplies from reaching the South. The second part was to divide Confederate territory in half by taking control of the Mississippi River. Finally, a contingent of troops would march on the Confederate capital of Richmond, Virginia, and achieve victory.

Lincoln and much of the northern populace expected that the war would be quick and victory would be easy. These illusions were shattered after the First Battle of Bull Run (Virginia). Confederate troops successfully pushed back advancing United States troops. The Confederacy continued to hold the advantage on the battlefield for the remainder of 1861 and throughout 1862. President Lincoln went through several generals-in-chief to lead the Union army before, in 1864, settling on General Ulysses S. Grant. Union forces suffered defeats at the Second Battle of Bull Run, the Battle of Fredericksburg, and other encounters. The Battle of Antietam is considered a Union victory by historians, but a more aggressive Union general could have inflicted heavier damage. The early years also saw the first encounter between two ironclad ships, the Confederacy's *Merrimac* and the United States' first ironclad ship, the *Monitor*. The fighting between the two ships resulted in a draw, but it pointed the way toward the future of naval battles.

An important turning point in the war was the Battle of Gettysburg (1863). The battle, in Pennsylvania, was the high-water mark for the Confederacy. After Gettysburg, the Confederacy was in retreat. Another important Union victory was at Vicksburg, Mississippi. With that victory, Union forces gained control of the Mississippi River, cutting the Confederacy in half. In 1864, General Sherman's March to the Sea broke the spirit of the South. General Robert E. Lee finally surrendered to General Grant at Appomattox Courthouse in Virginia (1865).

TIP 

Military History
The material in this section about the military aspects of the war is, more or less, the extent of what you need to know. For this and other wars, there might be a question about strategy, diplomacy, or turning points. However, the AP exam rarely includes a question about the inner workings of a specific battle. The AP exam does not usually test purely military history.

BEHIND THE BATTLE LINES

Emancipation

Perhaps Lincoln's greatest wartime achievement was playing a key role in the liberation of the slaves. Lincoln was partly motivated by the desire to keep Great Britain at bay during the war. While Great Britain may have aided the Confederacy to ensure the steady flow of southern cotton, it would not join the South in continuing slavery. However, Lincoln did not achieve this historic goal on his own. Abolitionists, radical Republicans, and of course the slaves themselves all pushed the envelope and put the issue of liberation on the wartime agenda. Lincoln was able to usher in this historic event while guiding the country through a wrenching war. He was able to convince a reluctant country that ending slavery was consistent with the most basic American tenets.

TIP 

Toward Emancipation
The evolution of Lincoln's thinking in regard to emancipation is a complex process. Historians cite a variety of circumstances—military, ideological, political, and ethical—that entered into the equation. Certainly a complete understanding of the process cannot leave out the role of the slaves themselves in advancing the process.

At first, Lincoln was reluctant to take action against slavery for fear of pushing the border states toward secession. When Congress passed the Confiscation Acts in 1861 and 1862, Lincoln was opposed although he did not veto them. These acts were framed as military measures. The first declared that any slaves pressed into working for the Confederacy could be taken as "contraband of war," meaning confiscated property. The second act allowed for the seizure of the slaves owned by Confederate officials.

By the summer of 1862, Lincoln had come to believe that the time was right for moving forward in regard to emancipation. He waited until the Union had achieved a victory on the battlefield. The Battle of Antietam in September 1862 was enough of a Union victory to prompt the president to issue the Emancipation Proclamation on September 22, 1862. The edict ordered the freeing of all slaves in rebel-held territory as of January 1, 1863. The order significantly exempted slaves in the loyal border states and even in Union-held areas of Confederate states. Of course, orders from the United States government did not hold any weight for Confederate leaders, so the Emancipation Proclamation did not actually free any slaves. However, the order clearly changed the goals and tenor of the war. It made clear that this was as much a war for the liberation of the slaves as it was a war to preserve the Union.

New York City Draft Riots

President Lincoln had to deal with a great deal of resistance to the war within the borders of the loyal states. One of the most significant episodes of resistance to Union policies was rioting against the wartime draft in New York City in July 1863. Protests initially began against government draft offices. Protesters were particularly angry about the rule that one could pay $300 to avoid serving in the draft. This substantial sum was well beyond most working-class men. In subsequent days, the protests turned violent and the target became the city's African-American population. At least 120 people were killed in the riots.

Industrialization

The Civil War spurred rapid industrialization of the North. During the Civil War, the Union government required an enormous amount of war materials, from guns and bullets to boots and uniforms. Manufacturers rose to the occasion by rapidly modernizing production. These changes in production sped up the process of industrialization that was in its beginning stages before the war. Industrialization stimulated a long period of economic growth, turning the United States into a world economic power.

The Republican Agenda

With the Democrats absent from Congress, the Republicans had a free hand to implement legislation that would further their vision of the United States. Congress passed the Homestead Act in 1862, granting people up to 160 acres as an enticement for moving west. This act was part of the "free-labor, free-soil" ideal of the Republicans. A second act was the Morrill Land Grant Act, also passed in 1862, which promoted secondary public education. The federal government provided states with federal land on which they could build public colleges or sell the land to fund the building of public colleges.

Civil Liberties

Lincoln suspended the writ of habeas corpus in 1863, authorizing the arrest, without due process, of rebels and traitors. Lincoln was responding to riots and threats of militia action in the border state of Maryland. After the war, the Supreme Court in *Ex Parte Milligan* (1866) ruled that the suspension of habeas corpus did not empower the president to try to convict citizens before military tribunals. Civilians can be tried in military courts only if civilian courts are not operating.

Civil Liberties During Wartime
Before condemning Lincoln as being authoritarian or heavy-handed for suspending *habeas corpus*, keep the following in mind. In most civil wars in human history, it has been common for authorities simply to shoot enemy sympathizers. Arresting them without due process is relatively civil for a civil war.

PLANS FOR RECONSTRUCTION

As the Civil War was coming to an end, President Lincoln and the Republican Party began to address several questions regarding the postwar world. What accommodations would be made for the freed men and women of the South? How would the secessionist South be reintegrated into the United States? What punishments, if any, would be meted out to those who rebelled against the United States? Finally, who held responsibility for reuniting and reconstructing the country—the president or Congress? Did, as the president argued, the secessionist states still exist as political entities, simply awaiting new governing personnel? Instead, had they committed "state suicide?" Many congressional Republicans argued that the states had ceased to exist and therefore needed to be readmitted by Congress. The answers to these questions formed the basis of competing visions of what Reconstruction would entail.

Wartime Reconstruction

Lincoln was eager to restore the Union quickly. An initial goal of his was restoring southern representation in Congress. In 1863 he announced his 10 percent plan. If 10 percent of the 1860 voters in a southern state took an oath of allegiance to the United States and promised to abide by emancipation, that state could establish a new government and send representatives to Congress. This was a low bar for these states to comply with. In 1864, he vetoed the Wade-Davis Bill, which would have established much stricter standards for the southern states to meet. The bill would have required half of the voters in a state to sign a loyalty oath to the United States before Reconstruction could begin and would have guaranteed equal treatment before the law for former slaves. Finally, in 1865, in his Second Inaugural Address, Lincoln announced that he wanted to reunite the country "with malice toward none; with charity for all." This approach was consistent with Lincoln's broader goals of ending the war as soon as possible. Lincoln was assassinated less than a month after his second inauguration, so it is difficult to surmise how he would have negotiated the difficulties of the Reconstruction era.

Presidential Reconstruction

After Lincoln's assassination, Vice President Andrew Johnson assumed power. Johnson had been tapped for the vice presidency by Lincoln because Johnson did not vacate his seat in the Senate when his native Tennessee declared secession in 1861. Although Johnson had broke with the planter class in the South, it became clear that he had no affinity for the Republican Party nor for emancipation and equality for African Americans. He continued with the lenient and rapid approach to Reconstruction that Lincoln had mapped out. Johnson quickly recognized the new southern state governments as legitimate after they repudiated secession and ratified the Thirteenth Amendment banning slavery. In the South, many members of the old slave-owning class were now back in power. These men tried to replicate the conditions of the old South, including passing a series of restrictive laws known as the Black Codes. Postwar conditions were so similar to prewar conditions that many northerners wondered if they had won the war, but lost the peace.

Congress and the President Clash Over Reconstruction

In 1866, tensions between the president and Congressional Republicans intensified. Johnson vetoed two measures passed by Congress—an extension of the Freedman's Bureau and a Civil Rights Act that was designed to overturn the Black Codes that the southern states had implemented. Congress ultimately overrode both vetoes. The biggest fight, however, was over the Fourteenth Amendment. This amendment made all people born in the United States citizens. In doing this, it undid the Dred Scott decision, which held that African Americans were not citizens of the United States. The amendment further guaranteed all citizens "equal protection under the law" and prohibited states from denying any citizen "life, liberty, or property without due process of law." Although the amendment did not extend voting guarantees to African Americans, it did allow Congress to reduce the representation of states that withheld the vote from African-American males. In this section, the Constitution mentions the word "males" for the first time, much to the consternation of women who had hopes that the amendment would also extend voting privileges to them.

RADICAL RECONSTRUCTION

Johnson tried to mobilize skeptical white voters against the Fourteenth Amendment in the 1866 midterm elections. However, the strategy backfired. Republicans won a resounding victory in the 1866 elections and embarked on more sweeping measures.

Reconstruction Acts of 1867

Republicans were able to push through the Reconstruction Acts of 1867. These sweeping acts divided the South (with the exception of Tennessee) into five military districts. These areas could rejoin the United States only if they guaranteed basic rights, especially the right to vote, to African Americans. The radicals were not able to carry out their program fully. They were not able to extend land ownership to African Americans, nor did they carry out mass arrests of former Confederates.

The Fifteenth Amendment

The Fifteenth Amendment, granting African Americans voting rights, was ratified in 1869. The Fifteenth Amendment states that the vote may not be denied to someone based on "race, color, or previous condition of servitude." African-American women, of course, still could not vote. Women were not granted the right to vote until 1920. Voting rights for African Americans was a key element of the Reconstruction program of the radical Republicans.

Civil Rights Act of 1875

The final congressional Reconstruction act was the Civil Rights Act of 1875. This act guaranteed equal treatment for African Americans in public accommodations, such as hotels and restaurants. It also prohibited the exclusion of African Americans from juries. The act was poorly enforced. Already by 1875, northern Republicans were losing their enthusiasm for carrying out broad reforms in the South.

Impeachment of President Johnson

The clash between President Andrew Johnson and Congressional Republicans resulted in the Republicans impeaching Johnson in 1868. The House charged the president with violating the Tenure of Office Act, an act the Republicans had passed to protect their ally, Secretary of War Edwin Stanton. The act prohibited the president from firing cabinet members without Senate approval but is of questionable legality. Johnson fired Stanton anyway, initiating the impeachment trial. The Senate narrowly fell short of finding Johnson guilty, but the whole procedure rendered Johnson powerless to stop Congress's Reconstruction plans.

RECONSTRUCTION IN PRACTICE

The record of the Reconstruction governments in the South is still a subject of controversy, almost a century and a half later. White southerners at the time and afterward complained bitterly about the burdens imposed by the Reconstruction governments and about corruption and ineptitude. More recently, however, historians of the period have pointed out that corruption was less pronounced than it was in other parts of the country and that these governments accomplished a great deal against great odds.

The southern governments were composed of a variety of elements. Democrats still served in state legislatures, often in the minority, during the Reconstruction period. The Republicans were made up of several different groups. Southern whites that joined the Republicans were labeled "scalawags" by their Democratic opponents. Many southern white Republicans were former Whigs and sought to promote economic progress for the South. Many northerners came to the South to participate in Reconstruction. Some of these northern Republicans sought personal advancement in coming South; many were motivated by a desire to assist the former slaves in their adjustment to life as freed men and women. Southern Democrats labeled these Northerners "carpetbaggers," implying that they hurriedly threw all their belongings into a bag and traveled south to make a quick fortune. Finally, many of the Republican legislators were African Americans. Only in South Carolina, and only briefly (1873), did African Americans control the majority of seats in even one legislative chamber. They were consistently in the minority. However, that African Americans were elected to public office in the South at all was a major accomplishment. It was not until after the Civil Rights era of the twentieth century that significant numbers of African Americans held public office again. Two African Americans were elected to the United States Senate—Hiram Revels and Blanche K. Bruce. Over a dozen African-American representatives were elected to the House of Representatives.

Scalawags and Carpetbaggers
If you use these terms in an essay, do so with caution. Remember, they are not neutral descriptions; they are disparaging terms to describe those who cooperated with Reconstruction. When you use them, at least use quotation marks. Perhaps modify them with the phrase "so-called."

The accomplishments of the Reconstruction period included the establishment of schools for African Americans. Attaining an education was a burning desire for many of the freed African-American men and women. Schools thrived in this period despite the costs involved and despite the personal risk incurred by participants. Important African-American institutions such as Howard University and Morehouse College were established during the Reconstruction period. In addition, the Reconstruction governments established hospitals that served the African-American community, rewrote constitutions, undated penal codes, and began the physical rebuilding of the war-torn South.

Development of the Sharecropping System

Economically, most African Americans were still engaged in agricultural work. Immediately following the Civil War, plantation owners sought to hire gangs of African-American workers to labor under the supervision of a white overseer. African Americans chafed at this arrangement—with its stark resemblance to the slavery system. African Americans desired a plot of their own—forty acres and a mule. Some radical Republicans urged the government to divide the former slave plantations and distribute the land to freedmen. This radical proposal did not gain sufficient support to become reality. Short of this, African Americans began to rent land. They would customarily pay rent with a portion of their yearly crop—usually half. This sharecropping system was somewhat of a compromise. African Americans did not have to work under the direct supervision of an overseer, and white plantation owners generated cotton to be sold on the open market. After paying back loans for seed money and tools, sharecroppers were left with very little for themselves. The system created a cycle of debt, which prevented African Americans from acquiring money and owning land.

The End of Reconstruction

Several factors contributed to the end of the Reconstruction after only a dozen years. Southern conservative Democrats, who called themselves "redeemers," aggressively sought to regain power state by state. The redeemers were aided by networks of white terrorist organizations that used violence to silence African Americans and to intimidate African Americans from participating in public life. Also, northern whites simply lost their zeal for reforming the South. By the 1870s, many whites in the North were more interested in the industrial development of the North than in the race problem in the South.

The final nail in the coffin of Reconstruction was the disputed presidential election of 1876. With both sides claiming victory, an agreement was reached. The Democrats would let the Republicans have the White House, and the Republicans would end Reconstruction. In 1877, Rutherford B. Hayes became president and the last Union troops were brought out of the South.

Subject to Debate

For decades, the southern myth of the lost cause has influenced mainstream historical writing on the Civil War. The lost cause myth holds that the Confederate cause was a noble and honorable one. The South had a rich tradition of military skill and chivalry. The only reason the South lost the Civil War was because of the overwhelming forces of the North. The North had greater industrial capacity and a larger population to draw from. This understanding completely ignores the centrality of the slavery question. Even among northerners in the first half of the twentieth century, the question of slavery was left out of discussions of the war. It is only in the last third of the twentieth century that the history field has fully rejected the lost cause myth.

Traditional historical accounts of the Reconstruction period criticize the Republican Party for imposing crushing burdens on the South, for occupying it with troops, and for saddling it with inept and corrupt governments. Recent historical accounts have moved away from this grim representation by emphasizing the real progress made by African Americans under Reconstruction. The short-lived gains made under Reconstruction helped to inspire civil rights activists throughout the late nineteenth and twentieth centuries.

Practice Multiple-Choice Questions:

Directions: Pick the letter that best answers the following questions.

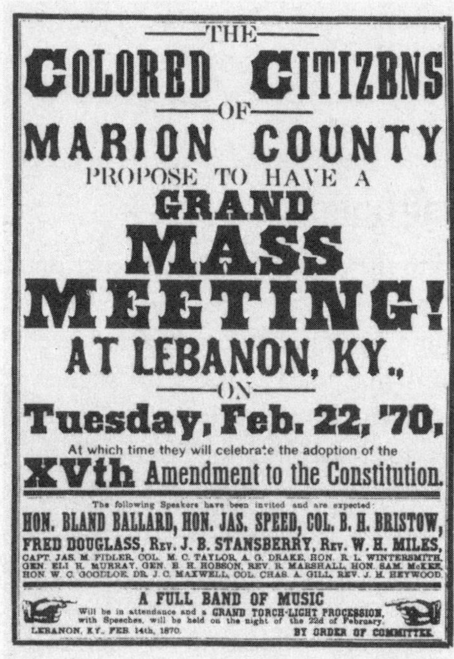

1. The purpose of the meeting announced in the flyer pictured above was to celebrate

   (A) the electoral victory of Abraham Lincoln for president.
   (B) the issuing of the Emancipation Proclamation.
   (C) the ending of the Civil War.
   (D) the extending of suffrage to African-American men.
   (E) the opening of an African-American school.

2. The Morrill Land Grant Act, passed during the Civil War in 1862, was important in that it

   (A) set aside land in Kansas on which freed slaves could build a community.
   (B) provided the states with federal land on which they were to build public colleges.
   (C) provided land to widows of fallen Union soldiers.
   (D) granted railroad companies wide swaths of land on which they were to build new rail lines.
   (E) set aside of millions of acres in southern states for national forests and national parks.

3. Copperheads were

    (A) escaped slaves who made their into Union army camps.
    (B) units of currency used by the Confederacy.
    (C) southern whites who helped with Reconstruction.
    (D) northern workers who went on strike during the Civil War.
    (E) northern Democrats who wanted to settle with the Confederacy and end the war.

4. In order to end the impasse over the 1876 presidential elections, the Republicans agreed to

    (A) pardon all Confederate officers.
    (B) let the Democrats choose the new secretaries of war and state.
    (C) extend money to help the South rebuild.
    (D) end Reconstruction by withdrawing all Union troops from the South.
    (E) suspend the Fourteenth and Fifteenth Amendments.

Practice Free-Response Questions:

1. How successful was President Lincoln in dealing with challenges on the homefront during the Civil War?

2. To what degree were the plans for Reconstruction successful in aiding the freed men and women of the South?

Answers and Explanations to Multiple-Choice Questions:

1. **(D)** This document shows the active participation of African Americans in the political process. They are meeting to celebrate the passage of the 15th Amendment, banning voting restrictions based on race.

2. **(B)** The Morrill Land Grant Act promoted higher education by providing federal land on which states could build colleges. The Republicans in Congress were able to pass many parts of their agenda after the Democrats left Washington, D.C.

3. **(E)** The copperheads were northern Democrats who wanted to negotiate an end to the Civil War. Negotiating an end to the war would entail accepting secession. A copperhead is a type of snake.

4. **(D)** The disputed election of 1876 led an agreement between the Democrats and the Republicans. The Democrats would let the Republicans have the White House if the Republicans agreed to withdraw the last federal troops from the South and end Reconstruction.

CHAPTER 16

The New South and the "Closing" of the Western Frontier, 1865–1900

TIMELINE

1865	The beginning of the Great Sioux War
1866	Medicine Lodge Treaty establishes the reservation system
1876	Custer's Last Stand
1881	Helen Hunt Jackson publishes *A Century of Dishonor*
1887	Dawes Severalty Act
1890	Beginning of Ghost Dance movement
	Massacre at Wounded Knee
1896	*Plessy* v. *Ferguson*

In the decades between the end of the Civil War and the turn of the twentieth century, a series of important developments transformed the South and the West. White and African-American southerners both shaped the New South as it left behind plantation slavery. Ultimately, white southerners were able to create a series of laws and customs that relegated African Americans to a second-class status. At the same time, government policies and economic opportunity encouraged waves of settlers to make their way west. The Midwest became a major agricultural region and the center of a politicized and determined farmers' movement. As settlers ventured farther west, clashes ensued with Native-American groups who lived on lands coveted by others. These clashes led to the demise of autonomous Native-American groups within the United States borders.

THE NEW SOUTH

After the Civil War, several public figures in the South argued for a New South. The most prominent of these spokesmen was Henry Grady, an Atlanta journalist. He argued for a mixed economy in the South that would include industrialization.

He wanted to move away from the single-crop plantation agriculture of the Old South. It was hoped that southern industrialists could join forces with northern businessmen and bankers. There were pockets of industrialization in the South, especially textile production. For the most part, though, the promise of a New South proved to be hollow. For the remainder of the century and well into the twentieth century, the South remained mired in poverty and underdevelopment.

Segregation in the New South

Jim Crow laws segregated public facilities, such as railroad cars, bathrooms, and schools. These laws relegated African Americans to second-class status in the South. These state and local laws first appeared in the South after Reconstruction ended (1877). Jim Crow laws became more prevalent after 1896 when the Supreme Court, in the case of *Plessy* v. *Ferguson*, accepted segregation as Constitutional.

Plessy v. *Ferguson* and the Separate but Equal Doctrine

In the case of *Plessy* v. *Ferguson* (1896), the Supreme Court decided that racial segregation did not violate the equal-protection provision of the 14th Amendment. The decision was a setback for those who sought an end to the Jim Crow system of racial segregation in the South. Jim Crow laws were state and local ordinances that first appeared after Reconstruction ended (1877). Typical laws called for separate schools or separate train cars for African Americans. Opponents of racial segregation argued that Jim Crow laws violated the 14th Amendment (1868). This amendment, ratified during Reconstruction, stated that no person shall be denied "equal protection of the laws." Jim Crow laws, opponents argued, violated the 14th Amendment because the laws relegated African Americans to inferior public accommodations and had the effect of making African Americans second-class citizens. However, the Court disagreed. The decision stated that segregation was acceptable as long as the facilities for both races were of equal quality. "Separate but equal" facilities were deemed constitutional.

TIP 

From *Plessy* to *Brown*
The "separate but equal" doctrine in the *Plessy* decision allowed for the continuation of the Jim Crow system of segregation until the 1950s and 1960s. The beginning of the end to the system came with the *Brown* v. *The Board of Education of Topeka* decision of 1954.

The Exclusion of African Americans from the Political Process

A series of actions effectively removed African Americans from the political process. Literacy tests and poll taxes limited their ability to vote. Poor whites got around these rules with the grandfather clause, guaranteeing a man the right to vote if he or his father or grandfather had the right to vote before the Civil War. In addition, the Democratic Party often held whites-only primaries, thus legally excluding African Americans from the only election that really mattered in the solidly Democratic South. African Americans who spoke out against this were targets of violence and even death. The Ku Klux Klan was first organized in 1866. Thousands of African Americans were killed by lynch mobs as the local authorities looked the other way.

THE TRANSFORMATION OF THE WEST

As more and more white settlers made their way to the West, Native Americans felt their world narrowing. By the 1880s, the last independent Native-American groups were defeated and brought under U.S. control.

The End of Autonomous Native-American Nations

The period between the end of the Civil War and the turn of the twentieth century saw the last large-scale military conflicts between the United States and Native-American groups. These Indian Wars resulted in defeat for Native Americans as the last autonomous Native-American groups came under the control of the U.S. government. From the earliest encounters between white people and Native Americans, white settlers have encroached upon Native-American lands. By using superior firepower, whites pushed Native Americans farther into the interior of the continent. American attitudes and policies toward Native Americans sometimes emphasized assimilation, sometimes removal, and sometimes extermination. All these approaches saw Native Americans as a problem that needed to be rectified.

By 1865, settlers were pushing beyond the Mississippi River in large numbers. Many were headed to the west coast, following the annexation of the lush agricultural lands of the Oregon territory (1848) and the discovery of gold in California (1849). However, the trails west went right through Native American lands, creating tension and conflict.

TIP 

The "Wise Indian"
In your writing, be careful of stereotyping Native Americans, even if the stereotypes seem positive. It is patronizing to assume all Native peoples are "wise" or are "stewards of the environment." A speech attributed to Chief Seattle that reflects environmental ethics was probably invented long after Chief Seattle lived.

The Treaty of Fort Laramie (1851)

In 1851, the United States government and over 10,000 Plains Indians came together in Fort Laramie in Wyoming and came to an agreement that Native Americans would provide a corridor for the passage of wagon trains to the west. In exchange, the United States government promised that the remainder of Native-American lands in the West would not be encroached upon.

The Great Sioux Uprising (1862)

White settlers refused to honor the Treaty of Fort Laramie. In 1862, Sioux Indians, led by Chief Little Crow, challenged white encroachments onto their lands. The Sioux ended up killing over 1,000 settlers before being defeated by the military.

The Sand Creek Massacre (1864)

In 1864, Colonel John M. Chivington led an American attack upon a Cheyenne village, killing 270, mostly women and children. Chivington ignored the villagers' surrender flags.

The Growth of the Reservation System

After the Civil War, the government attempted to solve the "Indian problem" through peaceful means rather than through more warfare. The center of this policy was pushing Native Americans onto reservations—confined areas that were set aside by the government. This policy made Native Americans wards of the government until they learned "to walk on the white man's road." Often the lands set aside for reservations were incapable of sustaining crops, reducing the inhabitants to utter poverty. Many tribal groups resisted being put onto reservations.

Destruction of the Buffalo

As railroads pushed west, herds of the American bison (commonly known as the buffalo) were decimated. Railroad workers and passengers went on a killing spree, shooting buffalo for food and mostly for sport. Also, industrial uses for the hides of buffalo put pressure on their numbers. In a matter of decades, the buffalo herds on the Plains were virtually exterminated. This greatly weakened the Plains peoples that depended on the buffalo for spiritual and physical sustenance.

Treaty of Medicine Lodge (1867)

Southern Plains Indians signed a treaty with the government at Medicine Lodge, Kansas, in 1867, agreeing to move to a reservation in exchange for government protection of their land from white encroachment.

Helen Hunt Jackson and the Call for Reform

By the 1880s, white sympathizers of Native Americans pushed for a change in government policy. A prominent reformer was Helen Hunt Jackson, whose 1882 book *A Century of Dishonor* chronicled the abuses of the United States Government committed against Native Americans. She sent a copy of the book to each member of Congress.

The Dawes Act

TIP

The Dawes Act and the Dawes Plan
Do not confuse the Dawes Act of 1887 with the Dawes Plan of 1924. The Dawes Plan was an international economic program.

Efforts at reform resulted in a shift in American policy toward Native Americans. The Dawes Act (1887) abandoned the reservation system and divided tribal lands into individually owned plots. The goal of the policy was for Native Americans to assimilate into white culture. This reform proved to be as damaging to Native Americans as the earlier reservation policy. The government eventually undid this destructive policy with the Indian Reorganization Act (1934), allowing autonomy for Native-American tribal lands.

The Ghost Dance Movement

In the midst of the apocalyptic losses suffered by Native Americans in the 1870s and 1880s, some Native Americans adopted a spiritual practice known as the Ghost

Dance. The Ghost Dance movement was developed by a Native American named Wokova. It drew on traditional Native-American rituals. It emphasized cooperation among tribes, clean living, and honesty. It wasn't successful in stopping white incursions, but it led to a spiritual revival that had a profound effect on Native-American tribes into the twentieth century.

TIP

Indian Wars
Historians discuss the Indian Wars as occurring during the post–Civil War years, but violence between whites and Native Americans had been happening since the early days of the Jamestown colony. The fighting had moved farther West, generally on the frontier of white settlements.

Massacre at Wounded Knee

The last battle of the Indian Wars was at Wounded Knee, South Dakota, in 1890. U.S. forces surrounded a group of Sioux Indians and proceeded to open fire on them. In all, 200–300 Native Americans were killed.

Subject to Debate

There has been a major disconnect between the West of popular memory and the West of the historical record. Generations of western movies have presented a morality play between virtuous pioneers and conniving Indians. Only in the last generation has the popular memory of the West shifted. Movies such as *Dances With Wolves* (1990) have served as correctives. In your writing, try to avoid the stereotypes and clichés of the "cowboy and Indian" genre.

Practice Multiple-Choice Questions:

Directions: Pick the letter that best answers the following questions.

1. During the post-Reconstruction period (1877–1900), the Supreme Court declared that
   (A) African Americans were beings of "inferior order," and were not entitled to citizenship rights.
   (B) sharecropping violated the Constitution on the grounds that it did not allow freedom of movement.
   (C) separate schools for African Americans was unconstitutional and inherently unfair.
   (D) the Fifteenth Amendment was unconstitutional because voting rights were a state issue, not a federal issue.
   (E) segregation was acceptable as long as the facilities for both races were of equal quality.

2. The 1887 Dawes Severalty Act redefined United States policy toward Native Americans by calling for

   (A) relative legal autonomy for Native Americans within their ancestral homelands, even if certain practices violated United States law.
   (B) the removal of Native Americans from states east of the Mississippi River to reservations in Oklahoma and South Dakota.
   (C) the denial of United States citizenship to Native Americans.
   (D) the assimilation of Native Americans into American society by transferring tribal lands to individually owned plots.
   (E) open warfare against Native Americans of the Great Plains in the wake of the killing of General George Custer.

3. The Indian Wars of the nineteenth century came to an end at

   (A) Fort Laramie.
   (B) Sand Creek.
   (C) Alcatraz Island.
   (D) Fallen Timbers.
   (E) Wounded Knee.

4. Atlanta journalist Henry Grady is most closely associated with which of the following phrases?

   (A) "The 'closing' of the frontier"
   (B) "Waving the 'bloody shirt'"
   (C) "The New South"
   (D) "The Great Migration"
   (E) "An injury to one is an injury to all"

Practice Free-Response Questions:

1. To what degree did Henry Grady's hope for a New South materialize in the years 1880–1920?

2. Discuss changes in government policy in regard to the "Indian question" in the nineteenth century.

Answers and Explanations to Multiple-Choice Questions:

1. **(E)** This question is alluding to the case of *Plessy* v. *Ferguson*. That decision said that it was permissible to segregate if the facilities for African Americans and for whites are of equal quality. Of course, in practice, facilities were not equal.

2. **(D)** The Dawes Act (1887) is associated with the government push for assimilation. Today, such an approach seems disrespectful of Native-American traditions. In the nineteenth century, assimilation was a more progressive approach than its alternative—extermination. The act was inspired, in part, by the book *A Century of Dishonor* (1881) by Helen Hunt Jackson. The U.S. government eventually undid this destructive policy with the Indian Reorganization Act (1934), allowing autonomy for Native-American reservations.

3. **(E)** The last fighting of the Indian Wars occurred at Wounded Knee, South Dakota. The army opened fire, killing over 200 Sioux people.

4. **(C)** Henry Grady proposed a New South. This New South would have a diverse economy, including industry. The concept implied a break with the plantation economy. The hopes of the New South backers went mostly unfulfilled.

CHAPTER 17

The Growth of Industrial America, 1865–1900

TIMELINE

1869	Founding of the Knights of Labor
1873	The Panic of 1873
1876	Alexander Graham Bell develops the telephone
1877	Great Railroad Strike
	Munn v. *Illinois*
1879	Thomas A. Edison develops the lightbulb
1882	The formation of the Standard Oil Trust
1886	Founding of the American Federation of Labor
	Haymarket bombing
	Wabash, St. Louis and Pacific Railway Company v. *Illinois*
1887	Interstate Commerce Act
1890	Sherman Antitrust Act
1892	Homestead lockout
1893	Panic of 1893
1894	Pullman strike
1895	*United States* v. *E. C. Knight Company*

The United States economy expanded tremendously in the late 1800s as the country experienced an industrial revolution. Before the Civil War, businesses generally served local or regional markets. After the war, we see the development of businesses with a national and even an international reach. The era of industrial expansion after the Reconstruction period is known as the *Gilded Age.* Although

The Gilded Age
The term alludes to gold gilding on cheap statues. These statues are shiny like gold, but beneath the surface is cheap plaster. The age had great wealth, but beneath the surface was desperate poverty. The term was coined by Mark Twain and Charles Dudley Warner in their book *The Gilded Age: A Tale of Today* (1873).

the nation as a whole enjoyed an increase in its wealth, that wealth was not equally distributed. The owners of big businesses, labeled robber barons by their critics, enjoyed unparalleled wealth. In contrast, many of the workers lived in squalid condition in working-class slums. The contrast between the mansions of Andrew Carnegie and Henry Frick along New York City's Fifth Avenue and the tenements depicted in Jacob Riis's *How the Other Half Lives* (1890) startled many Americans.

THE ERA OF BIG BUSINESS

During the Gilded Age of the late 1800s, the era of small, local-oriented businesses began to give way to large corporations and trusts that came to dominate entire industries. The three most important industries of the era were the railroad industry, the steel industry, and the oil industry.

The Robber Barons

The men who controlled the major industries in the United States came to be known as robber barons, a scornful title meant to call attention to their cutthroat business activities and their attempts to control the government.

Andrew Carnegie and Vertical Integration (or Consolidation)

Andrew Carnegie came to dominate the steel industry by investing in all aspects of steel production, from mining to transportation to processing to distribution. This type of organization is called vertical integration.

Rockefeller and Horizontal Integration (or Consolidation)

Horizontal integration entails creating a monopoly, or near monopoly, in a particular industry. A common way that corporations gained monopoly control of an industry was by establishing trusts. A trust consisted of trustees from several companies involved in the same industry acting together rather than in competition with one another. John D. Rockefeller organized the most well-known trust in the oil-processing industry.

Other Robber Barons

Carnegie and Rockefeller were the most well-known robber barons but certainly not the only ones. Others included Collis P. Huntington, a railroad magnate, Mark Hanna, a coal and iron merchant who became a leading senator from Ohio, Philip Armour, a meat-processing giant in Chicago, and Stephen Elkins, a magnate in mining, railroads, and politics.

Regulation Versus Laissez-Faire

Critics of corporate power pushed the government to take steps to reign in these massive corporations. However, these efforts at regulation were often hampered by the courts and by lax enforcement. Take, for example, the case of railroad regulation. In 1886, the Supreme Court in the case of *Wabash, St. Louis and Pacific Railway Company* v. *Illinois*, limited the ability of states to regulate railroads, asserting that such regulations could not impose "direct" burdens on interstate commerce. In response, the federal government created in 1887 the Interstate Commerce Commission (ICC) to regulate railroads. However, the ICC was chronically underfunded and was, therefore, ineffective. A similar pattern can be seen in antitrust legislation. In 1890, the Sherman Antitrust Act was passed to break up trusts. The act, however, had limited usefulness. In the case of *United States* v. *E. C. Knight Company* (1895), the Supreme Court greatly limited the scope of the act by making a distinction between trade (which would be subject to the act) and manufacturing (which would not).

IDEOLOGIES OF THE GILDED AGE

In many ways, the rise of giant corporations ran counter to traditional American ideas about the economy and society. The free-labor ideology of the pre–Civil War era put forth the idea that working for another man was a temporary condition; eventually each employee would accumulate enough money to start his own farm or shop. However, with the army of unskilled workers flooding into the massive firms of the Gilded Age, it became increasingly clear that these men, and their offspring, were not going to rise to be become independent entrepreneurs. As older ideas about the nature of the American economy became anachronistic, new ones gained traction. Some of these ideas unabashedly embraced the new corporate order; others challenged it.

TIP

The Appeal of Social Darwinism
Social Darwinism, with its call for a laissez-faire approach to the economy, appealed to owners of large corporations, because it both justified their wealth and power and also warned against any type of regulation or reform.

Social Darwinism

Social Darwinism was an attempt to apply Charles Darwin's ideas about the natural world to social relations. Social Darwinism was popularized in the United States by William Graham Sumner. Sumner was attracted to Darwin's ideas about competition and survival of the fittest. He argued against any attempt at government intervention into the economic and social spheres. Interference, he argued, would hinder the evolution of the human species. The inequalities of wealth that characterized the late 1800s were part of the process of survival of the fittest. This hands-off approach to economic activities is known by the French phrase *laissez-faire*.

Andrew Carnegie and the Gospel of Wealth

Andrew Carnegie asserted in an essay entitled "Wealth" (1899) that the wealthy have a duty to live responsible, modest lives and to give back to society. This gospel of wealth asserted that wealthy entrepreneurs should distribute their wealth so that it could be used for good rather than frivolously wasted. Carnegie ended up donating the majority of his fortune to charity and public-oriented projects. Carnegie believed in a laissez-faire approach to social problems. He did not want the government interfering in the social and economic spheres. That is, in part, why he urged his fellow millionaires to take action on behalf of the community. In this way, the government wouldn't have to.

Horatio Alger and the Myth of the Self-Made Man

Horatio Alger wrote a series of dime novels that often featured a poor boy who achieves success in the world. That success is usually the result of a bit of luck and a bit of pluck—fortuitous circumstances as well as determination and perseverance. These rags-to-riches novels, such as *Ragged Dick*, put forth the idea that anyone could make it in Gilded Age America. The reality, of course, was quite different.

Henry George and the Single Tax on Land

Henry George was a thinker, economist, and politician who was critical of the persistence of poverty in a nation of such technological and industrial progress. In his book *Progress and Poverty* (1879), he criticized the vast resources, especially land, controlled by the wealthy elite. He argued for a single tax on land values, which he believed would create a more equitable society.

Socialism and Anarchism

Many Americans began to question the basic assumptions of capitalism and embraced alternative ideologies, such as anarchism and socialism. These radical ideas never gained the number of adherents in the United States that they did in Europe. Occasionally, conservative newspapers and politicians exaggerated the strength of these movements in the United States. Newspapers often conflated the labor movement in general with these "dangerous" movements in order to delegitimize or stigmatize the labor movement. Still, these movements had adherents in the United States. After the utter failure of the Pullman strike (see below), Eugene V. Debs moved away from the labor movement and toward socialism. He was one of the founders of the Socialist Party of America in 1901.

The most famous American socialist tract of the nineteenth century was Edward Bellamy's *Looking Backward, 2000–1887* (1888). This novel imagined a man who falls asleep in 1887 and awakens in 2000 to find a socialist utopia in which the inequities and poverty of the Gilded Age have been eradicated.

THE RISE OF ORGANIZED LABOR

The Gilded Age saw some of the fiercest workplace conflicts in American history. Workers saw their position and status erode during this period as cutthroat competition and mechanization of the work process pushed down wages and worsened working conditions. The wealth generated by the rapid expansion of industry in the post–Civil War period was certainly not evenly distributed. However, workers' grievances during the Gilded Age went beyond low wages. Workers were alarmed at how the changing workplace eroded their sense of autonomy and control on the work process. This loss of control was both a blow to workers' sense of pride and their ability to control the pace and conditions of work. Many workers responded by forming and joining labor organizations, or unions, to advance their cause through collective bargaining and, if all else fails, through striking.

Labor Battles of the Gilded Age

The fierce labor battles were almost exclusively won by management, with its near monopoly on firepower, the support of the government and the courts, and vast numbers of poor, working-class men willing to serve as strike breakers. These battles often occurred in the wake of announced pay cuts announced during the economic downturns of the 1870s and of the 1890s.

The Great Railroad Strike of 1877

In 1877, The Baltimore and Ohio Railroad (B&O) announced a 10 percent pay cut for its workers. Wages had already been falling during the economic depression that followed the Panic of 1873. Railroad workers in West Virginia went on strike. Workers down the line—in Pittsburgh, Chicago, even San Francisco—followed suit. At its height, the Great Railroad Strike involved over 100,000 railroad workers and over half a million other workers. Violence erupted in nine states. President Rutherford B. Hayes called out federal troops, many recently withdrawn from enforcing Reconstruction policies in the South. Many observers thought a second civil war was unfolding.

TIP 

Reassignment of Troops
Many of the soldiers assigned to put down the Great Railroad Strike of 1877 had just been released from duty in the South as Reconstruction ended earlier that year.

The Haymarket Incident

In 1886, a strike at the McCormick Harvesting Machine Company turned violent. Unskilled workers at McCormick struck and were quickly replaced by scab—or replacement—workers. The striking workers attacked several of the scabs on May 3, two days after a large May Day rally in Chicago for the eight-hour workday. The police and Pinkerton guards opened fire on the strikers, killing or injuring six men. The strikers called for a rally on May 4 in Haymarket Square. Toward the end of the rally, a bomb exploded in the midst of the police ranks. Several police were killed. The police responded by opening fire on the rally. Eight men were tried and convicted on scanty evidence; four were executed. At the time, many Americans shied away from the perceived violence of the labor movement. The Knights of Labor was especially hard hit.

The Homestead Strike

Another momentous labor battle took place at Carnegie's steel works in Homestead, Pennsylvania. Though Carnegie had the reputation of being a friend of labor, he was determined to break the union—the Amalgamated Association of Iron and Steel

Workers, a powerful craft union under the American Federation of Labor (A.F.L.) umbrella. When Amalgamated's contract expired in 1892, Carnegie announced that he would not renew its contract—in effect ending the union. Carnegie traveled outside of the country in the summer of 1892 and left the plant under the charge of manager Henry Clay Frick, a notorious antiunion man. Frick built a fence around the plant, locked out the workers, brought in scabs, and hired Pinkerton guards to enforce his edicts. A battle ensued between the "Pinks" and the workers. The workers won a temporary victory and took over the plant. However, the governor then called in 8,000 National Guard troops to retake the plant. Frick was able to reopen the plant, without union workers, in a devastating blow for organized labor.

TIP

The Courts and Strikers
During the Gilded Age, the courts generally sided with management over labor. *In re Debs* (1895) and *Loewe* v. *Lawlor* (1908) are two examples of Supreme Court cases that went against labor.

The Pullman Strike: Strife in a Company Town

The Pullman strike occurred during the economic downturn following the Panic of 1893. The Pullman Company, which built railroad cars, cut wages several times in 1893 and 1894. Pullman was also the name of the town in Illinois where the workers lived. The town was built by the Pullman Company in 1880 as a model company town. The housing was better than most working-class housing but was also more costly. The town exemplified the two sides of company towns. On the one hand, they provided decent housing. On the other hand, they allowed the company to have a great deal of control over their workers and to deny housing to "troublemakers" (such as prounion workers). The company owned all the housing in the town. Rent was taken directly out of wages. When wages were cut in 1893 and 1894, rents were not cut. Workers appealed to the American Railway Union (ARU), led by Eugene V. Debs, to come to their aid. In May 1894, three organizers were fired. Soon most of the 3,300 workers were on strike. ARU members across the nation voted to support the strike by refusing to handle trains that contained Pullman cars. Railroad traffic was brought to a standstill. Courts issued two injunctions against the strike. President Cleveland eventually called out federal troops to put down the strike. Violence immediately ensued, leading to the death of 25 strikers. The strike ended in defeat for the union, with new workers hired by Pullman. In the wake of the incident, the Supreme Court, in *In re Debs* (1895) decided that the government was justified in stopping the strike.

TIP

Company Towns
Pullman, Illinois, was one of many company towns built during the industrialization of America in the late nineteenth and early twentieth centuries. They shared certain features with Pullman: slightly better living conditions in exchange for being under the control and watch of the company.

Subject to Debate

A central point of contention in interpretations of the Gilded Age is the place of the owners of big business. The image that has stuck is that of the bloated robber baron. This image was promoted by many contemporaries during the Gilded Age. The accumulation of such wealth and power was unprecedented and seemed at odds with the ideal of the yeoman farmer or the urban artisan. Further, the lavish spending habits of these men—illustrated by the gaudy mansions of New York's Fifth Avenue—also seemed outside the American tradition of thrift and humility. This image of greed and excess was kept alive by progressive-era historians and is still part of the collective memory of the era. Recently, some historians have begun to question this representation of the Gilded Age. For one, even in the late nineteenth century, most of the big companies were incorporated and run by boards of directors. The age of an arbitrary proprietor, ordering his employees around, was an anachronism even in the late Gilded Age. Second, recent historical interpretations have noted the tremendous wealth generated during this period. Eventually, this rising tide of wealth helped lift all individuals. It is not by accident that so many new immigrants came to the United States—it truly was a land of opportunity at the turn of the twentieth century. In your essay writing, keep in mind the origins of the image of the robber baron and its usefulness in understanding the realities of the Gilded Age.

Practice Multiple-Choice Questions:

Directions: Pick the letter that best answers the following questions.

1. After the Pullman Company defeated the American Railway Union in the 1894 Pullman Strike, ARU President Eugene V. Debs
   (A) grew impatient with mass action and made an assassination attempt on Henry Clay Frick, manager of the United States Steel Company.
   (B) moved to Paris and became an impressionistic painter.
   (C) quit union work and got an upper-level management job with the Pullman Palace Car Company.
   (D) grew frustrated with the piecemeal approach to social change and become one of the founders of the American Socialist Party.
   (E) retired from public life and wrote his memoirs.

2. In the last third of the nineteenth century, steel became a more widely used material after
   (A) the Bessemer process made it easier to convert iron to steel.
   (B) the Sherman Antitrust Act broke up the steel trust.
   (C) the United States lowered tariffs on steel from Japan.
   (D) the Environmental Protection Agency relaxed pollution control rules on the steel production industry.
   (E) major iron ore deposits were discovered in Pennsylvania and West Virginia.

3. Henry George, in his 1879 book *Progress and Poverty* (1879),
   (A) portrayed a young man who makes it in the modern commercial world with a combination of "luck and pluck."
   (B) called for the government to take a laissez-faire approach in regard to industrial capitalism.
   (C) imagined a utopian future that was brought about by a transition to socialism.
   (D) set forth the principles of scientific management.
   (E) proposed a single tax on land values because land belonged equally to all humanity.

4. What is the main point of the 1883 cartoon pictured above?
   - (A) Middle-class men of the late nineteenth century were experiencing a crisis of masculinity, brought on by office work and domesticity.
   - (B) Workers were not sufficiently appreciative of the progress brought to American society by the Industrial Revolution.
   - (C) Organized labor was at a distinct disadvantage in challenging the owners of corporations in the labor battles of the Gilded Age.
   - (D) The goals of the Populist Party were unrealistic, similar to the fictional character, Don Quixote, "tilting at windmills."
   - (E) The development of railroad lines in the West was leading to the destruction of the pristine natural world.

Practice Free-Response Questions:

1. "The owners of large corporations in the Gilded Age were more beneficial than they were harmful in regard to American Society." Assess the validity of this statement.

2. Assess the reasons for the failure of organized labor to improve wages and conditions significantly for workers in the Gilded Age.

Answers and Explanations to Multiple-Choice Questions:

1. **(D)** After the Pullman strike, Debs left the union movement. He came to believe that fundamental changes were necessary in the United States if the workers were to get decent treatment. He was one of the founders of the Socialist Party in the United States. He ran for president on the Socialist ticket in 1900, 1904, 1908, 1912, and 1920. His last campaign was conducted from his jail cell. He had been convicted under the Espionage Act for opposing World War I.
2. **(A)** Steel become cheaper and more readily available with the development of the Bessemer process. The process was an efficient method of converting iron ore to steel. Steel is stronger and lighter than iron. It is impossible to build tall buildings without steel.
3. **(E)** Henry George proposed a steep tax on unproductive land. This would force speculators to sell that land. With so much more land on the market, the price would drop and land would be available to everyone. Choice A describes Horatio Alger; choice D describes Frederick Winslow Taylor.
4. **(C)** The cartoon depicts the unequal forces involved in the labor battles of the late 1800s. Workers consistently lost these battles. Owners had in their corner "the corruption of the legislature" (the shield) and a "subsidized press" (the sword). Looking on approvingly were the railroad tycoon William H. Vanderbilt, the financier and railroad mogul Jay Gould, and other "robber barons."

Politics in the Gilded Age, 1865–1900

CHAPTER 18

TIMELINE

1872	Republican Ulysses S. Grant is elected president
1873	U.S. stops coining silver; goes on gold standard
	Panic of 1873
1877	Compromise of 1877; Republican Rutherford B. Hayes assumes presidency
1878	Formation of the Greenback Party
1880	Republican James Garfield is elected president
	Assassination of President Garfield; Chester Arthur assumes presidency
1883	Passage of the Pendleton Act
1884	Democrat Grover Cleveland is elected president
1888	Republican Benjamin Harrison is elected president
1892	Democrat Grover Cleveland is reelected president
1892	Formation of the People's (Populist) Party; Omaha Platform
1893	Economic downturn following the Panic of 1893
1894	Coxey's Army march to Washington, D.C.
1896	William Jennings Bryan's "Cross of Gold" speech
	Republican William McKinley is elected president

In many ways, the Gilded Age saw the two main political parties, the Democrats and the Republicans, become increasingly removed from the concerns of ordinary Americans. Both parties seemed more responsive to the priorities of the newly formed trusts and industrial giants than to needs of farmers, workers, or the urban poor. Corruption permeated political life from the backrooms of local political clubhouses to the corridors of power in Washington, D.C. A spate of reform movements was developed to address this situation, most notably the People's Party, better known as the Populist Party, in the last decade of the nineteenth century.

DEMOCRATS AND REPUBLICANS

Neither the Democrats nor the Republicans, the two main political parties from the Civil War to the present, were able to dominate national politics during the Gilded Age. The Republicans controlled the White House for most of the period from 1869 to the turn of the century. (The one exception was the two nonconsecutive terms of Grover Cleveland.) However, the elections were extremely close, with no presidential candidate receiving a clear majority of the popular vote in any election between 1872 and 1896. Control of Congress was split. The Republicans controlled the Senate for most of the period, and the Democrats controlled the House. Only briefly, for three different two-year periods, did one of the parties control the White House and both houses of Congress.

Ideology Takes a Backseat

Neither of the two political parties took strong stands on most of the pressing issues of the day. Neither party showed a willingness to deal with any of the various problems associated with the industrial expansion of the age. Issues like child labor, the consolidation of industries, workplace safety, and abuses by railroad companies were either avoided or dealt with in a superficial fashion. Neither party did much to protect the rights of African Americans (especially after the end of Reconstruction) or Native Americans. Neither party addressed the call of many women for the right to vote. The one issue that consistently divided the parties was the tariff. Democrats wanted lower tariff rates, and Republicans wanted higher tariff rates.

Both parties seemed aligned with the priorities of big business. Owners of major companies openly curried favor with congressmen with contributions, gifts, and outright bribery. Political leaders, even the presidents of the age, seemed to shrink in importance when compared with the towering industrial figures of the day. Cornelius Vanderbilt, John D. Rockefeller, and Andrew Carnegie are far more clearly imprinted on the national collective memory than the "forgotten presidents" of the day.

TIP 

Corruption and the History of Reconstruction
Corruption in American politics seemed to be everywhere during the Gilded Age. However, traditional histories of Reconstruction tended to single out state Reconstruction governments for extravagance and corruption. More recent histories of the period look at such claims with a critical eye.

Corruption and the Grant Administration

American political life was rife with corruption during the Gilded Age. This was true on the local level, as evidenced by the illegal schemes of "Boss" Tweed in New York, as well as on the national level. The administration of Ulysses S. Grant was tainted by corruption. Historians assess Grant's ability as a president far below his abilities on the battlefield. The Republican president was not decisive on the issue of Reconstruction (see chapter 15). In addition, he surrounded himself with incompetent and corrupt advisors and appointees. He rewarded friends, army contacts, and party loyalists with jobs that required political experience. Though Grant was not directly charged with corruption, key members of his administration were, including his vice president.

The Contested Election of 1876

The election of 1876 was perhaps the most contentious and tumultuous in American history, with the possible exception of the election of 2000. The Democratic candidate Samuel J. Tilden won the majority of the popular vote. However, neither he nor his Republican opponent, Rutherford B. Hayes, was able to claim enough electoral votes to be declared the winner. In three states—South Carolina, Louisiana, and Florida—the Democrats and the Republicans both claimed victory. A special electoral commission, with a Republican majority, declared Hayes the winner in the three contested states. Democrats protested, with some threatening to block Hayes's inauguration. Party leaders reached an informal compromise, known as the Compromise of 1877, that allowed the Republican Hayes to win the presidency. In return, the Republicans agreed to end Reconstruction, paving the way for rule by the Democratic Party in the South.

TIP 

The Electoral College
A working understanding of the electoral college is essential for understanding some of close elections in American history, especially those in which the winner of the national popular vote did not end up winning the presidency. This occurred in 1824, 1876, 1888, and 2000.

The Presidency of Rutherford B. Hayes

Hayes did not accomplish a great deal as president. He was partly handicapped by the perception that he had come into office fraudulently and partly by the prevailing understanding that the role of the president should be limited. Presidents of the Gilded Age did not forge broad visions—nothing akin to Franklin Roosevelt's New Deal or Lyndon Johnson's Great Society. Hayes did send in federal troops to suppress the Great Railroad Strike of 1877 (see Chapter 17), but he did not leave a significant legislative legacy.

Civil Service Reform

Civil service reform became a major issue in the Gilded Age. The civil service is the workforce of government employees. Attempts were made to reform the civil service in the 1880s so that jobs would be allocated to the most qualified people rather than to friends and relatives of powerful politicians.

Mugwumps, Stalwarts, and Half-Breeds

The issue of civil service reform divided the Republican Party in the wake of the scandals of the Grant administration. Reform-minded Republicans, mainly from Massachusetts and New York, were nicknamed "mugwumps" by their critics after the Algonquin word for "chief." They wanted to move away from the corruption of the Grant years and create a merit-based civil service. Those most resistant to abandoning the spoils system were nicknamed "stalwarts." Those loyal to the Republican leadership but wanting some degree of reform were known as "half-Breeds." Hayes, who won the disputed election of 1876, was not well liked by any of the factions and chose not to run for reelection in 1880.

The Election of 1880 and the Assassination of President Garfield

The Republicans nominated James A. Garfield for president in 1880. He had served as major general in the Civil War and was elected to the House in 1863. During Reconstruction, he was aligned with the Radical Republicans. He was still a member of the House in 1880 and was no longer closely associated with any of the Republican Party's factions. He won the presidency but was shot four months after his inauguration in 1881. Garfield died from the wound two months later. The assassin was no doubt unbalanced. However, the reason he gave for his actions was that he was passed over for a government job, despite his work on the Garfield campaign.

Passage of the Pendleton Act

The events of the summer of 1881 made civil service reform a more pressing issue. Congress finally passed the Pendleton Act in 1883 to set up a merit-based federal civil service, a professional career service that allots government jobs on the basis of a competitive exam. This system still covers most of the bureaucratic jobs in the federal government. Upper-level, policy-oriented positions are still rotated when new presidential administrations come into office.

The Presidency of Chester Arthur

Chester Arthur, who assumed the presidency after the assassination of President Garfield, surprisingly championed the Pendleton Act and signed it into law. Arthur also broke with Republican orthodoxy and looked into lowering tariffs. The rate of taxation on imported goods had long divided many Americans. Industrialists tended to encourage higher tariffs to keep out foreign competition. Farming interests tended to support a lower tariff rate. They sold cotton and wheat to Europe and benefited from increased international trade; high tariffs impeded international trade. Republicans had pushed tariffs higher during the Civil War to fund the war effort. By the 1880s, the government was awash in money from tariffs, and tariff reformers argued that lowering tariffs would put more money into circulation and stimulate economic activity. Tariff reform foundered in Congress. Ultimately, a small decrease in tariff rates was passed.

The Election of 1884, President Cleveland, and Tariff Reform

In 1884, Republican insiders abandoned Chester Arthur and picked the half-breed leader James Blaine. Blaine endorsed keeping high tariffs, appealing to both industrialists and workers. The Democratic candidate, Grover Cleveland, advocated lowering tariffs, arguing that high tariffs placed an added burden on American consumers. Cleveland won the election, in part because many mugwump Republicans abandoned the Republican Party altogether because of Blaine's resistance to civil service reform and tariff reform.

Economic Issues Continue to Dominate National Politics

The tariff issue remained contentious during Cleveland's first administration. Many Democrats, including Cleveland, began to push for lower rates. These tariff reformers became increasingly critical of the power of trusts and large corporations in dominating the economy. They saw high tariff rates as benefiting these big business interests at the expense of consumers and small producers. Cleveland also signed into law an act creating the Interstate Commerce Commission, further challenging the power of big business (see Chapter 17).

The Election of 1888 and the Harrison Presidency

In 1888, the Republican Party nominated for president Benjamin Harrison, grandson of President William Henry Harrison. Business interests poured money into the Harrison campaign. Cleveland edged out Harrison in the popular vote, but Harrison won the all-important electoral vote.

In 1890, Harrison signed into law the highest tariff in the nation's history. That year, the Republicans were punished in the midterm elections. Harrison also signed into the law the Sherman Antitrust Act (1890), which had bipartisan support in Congress.

The Election of 1892

By the time of the 1892 presidential election, voters rebelled against the Republican-backed high tariff rates. Also, many voters flocked to the Democratic Party in protest of Republican support for prohibition of alcohol consumption. In 1892, Democrat Grover Cleveland returned to the White House, becoming the only president to serve two nonconsecutive terms.

The Panic of 1893
This economic crisis was the worst one in American history up until the Great Depression of the 1930s.

The Panic of 1893 and the Currency Issue

The vibrant economic growth that characterized much of the Gilded Age came to a screeching halt in 1893. The Philadelphia and Reading Railroad went bankrupt, followed by other railroads as well as banks that had lent the railroads money. The stock market followed suit as Wall Street panicked. Millions of workers were unemployed by 1894.

Many observers, both contemporaries and historians, cite the inadequate amount of currency in circulation as one of the underlying weaknesses in the economy. The money supply in the Gilded Age did not have the ability to grow as the economy expanded. The United States used metallic money, as stipulated in the Mint Act of 1792. The act allowed for the "free and unlimited coinage" of gold and silver. Individuals could coin gold or silver at a fixed ratio (the amount of silver in a silver dollar was to weigh fifteen times as much as the amount of gold in a gold dollar). However, in 1873, Congress changed this policy, allowing for the coinage of only gold. The amount of gold being coined

Currency and Inflation
Be familiar with basic economic concepts involving the currency supply. An expansion of the currency supply increases inflation. This would tend to benefit farmers but would hurt consumers.

in the 1870s and 1880s could not keep up with the growing economy. This was especially hard on farmers as it depressed the prices they received for their goods and made it difficult to repay loans. The situation was beneficial to bankers, who wanted a relatively stable currency so that money repaid on loans retained its value.

FARMERS CHALLENGE THE TWO-PARTY SYSTEM

During the post–Civil War period, midwestern farmers felt they were being squeezed from all sides. Railroad companies were overcharging farmers for carrying their produce to Chicago and other destinations. Also, the tight supply of currency in the United States was both making it difficult for farmers to pay off their debts and driving down the commodity prices they received for their crops. Also, banks were foreclosing on farms. These problems led farmers to seek solutions through political action. Some of their political agitation was carried out within the two-party system. Significantly, they also decided to work outside of mainstream politics.

Third Parties in American History
It is very difficult for a third-party candidate to win election in the American political system. The system favors the two main parties. So why join a third party? They often put issues on the national agenda even if they don't win the election. This has been true from abolitionism to environmentalism.

The Greenback Party

An early political formation that sought an expansion of the currency supply was the Greenback Party. Founded in 1878—during the economic downturn following the Panic of 1873—the party advocated issuing paper money that was not backed by gold or silver. This was done briefly during the Civil War, and farmers received higher prices for their goods. The party received a million votes in the 1878 congressional elections. The party soon disbanded, but the call for an expanded money supply was taken up again following the Panic of 1893.

The Grange and Granger Laws

The Grange was a farmers' organization that pushed for state laws to protect farmers' interests. In many midwestern states, they were successful in passing laws that regulated railroad freight rates and made certain abusive practices illegal. These laws came to be known as Granger laws. Initially, the Supreme Court, in *Munn* v. *Illinois* (1877), upheld these laws, asserting that it was within the government's permissible powers to regulate private industry. Later, the court overruled itself. In *Wabash* v. *Illinois* (1886), the Court ruled that individual states could not regulate railroads because they cross state lines. This led to the federal government establishing the Interstate Commerce Commission to regulate railroads (1887).

The "Hayseed" Versus the Populist
Farmers have been represented throughout history as slow and dim-witted. Their participation in the Grange, in farmer co-ops, and in the populist movement demonstrate a level of sophistication at odds with the image of the "hayseed." Avoid using condescending stereotypes.

The Populist Party

The call for the government to undo the "crime of '73"—to move away from a gold standard and again allow for the "free and unlimited coinage" of silver—became loud in the 1890s, especially after the Panic of 1893 hit. It became one of the main rallying cries of the Populist Party, which was born in 1892. The Populists were able to harness growing discontent following the panic of 1893 and gave a voice to a radical program for change that included increased democracy, a graduated income tax, and regulation of the railroads. This program was included in their Omaha Platform, written at their founding convention in 1892. The party did remarkably well in the presidential election later in 1892, garnering over one million votes and twenty-two electoral votes. The party made solid gains in the midterm election of 1894, electing six senators and seven representatives from the farming regions in the South and the West. The Populists were perhaps the most successful third party in the nineteenth century, but their popularity was short-lived.

Coxey's Army

In 1894, Coxey's Army—a group of disgruntled workers, many of whom were recently laid off by railroad companies—marched from Ohio, through Pennsylvania, and into Washington, D.C., to demand that the government take action to address the economic crisis. There were similar protests of populist-inspired working-class men.

Was Coxey Ahead of His Time?
In 1894, the Coxeyites were ridiculed and ignored. However, a generation later, the New Deal consisted of exactly the types of programs Coxey and his men were encouraging. It shows that social movements influence government policies, but sometimes the process takes a while.

The Election of 1896 and the "Cross of Gold" Speech

The election of 1896 was significant in several ways. It resulted in the demise of the Populist Party, and it helped to establish the identity of the major political parties in the twentieth century. The most contentious issue in the election was the amount of currency in circulation. William Jennings Bryan ran for president in 1896 on the ticket of the Democratic Party. He broke with the more conservative elements in the party and endorsed the call for the "free and unlimited coinage of silver." In his famous "Cross of Gold" speech, he promised not to let the American people be crucified "upon a cross of gold." He was also endorsed by the farmer-oriented Populist Party because of his support for the free coinage of silver. The Republican candidate William McKinley appealed to banking and business interests by promising to keep the country on the gold standard. McKinley's victory was devastating to the Populist Party, which had thrown its support to Bryan. The positions of the two parties shaped the political landscape well into the twentieth century. The Republican Party continued to be more aligned with pro-business interests, and the Democratic Party continued to present itself as the champion of the "little guy."

The "Cross of Gold" Speech
Be familiar with Bryan's speech; it appears frequently on the AP exam.

Subject to Debate

Historians have long debated the "revolt of the farmers" in the 1880s and 1890s. You should be familiar with the different poles in the debate. On the one hand, some historians have looked admiringly on the populist movement. These historians note the dire situation farmers found themselves in and see the movement as a reasonable response. This approach also looks approvingly at the legacy of the movement. Some of its goals were taken up by the progressive movement in the early decades of the twentieth century, and even by the New Dealers in the 1930s. Other historians paint the movement as an irrational, emotional rebellion against the modern world. These historians cite the racism, anti-Semitism, antiurbanism, and anti-immigrant sentiment evident in certain corners of the movement. In this light, the populist movement is a precursor of the Ku Klux Klan in the 1920s and McCarthyism in the 1950s.

Practice Multiple-Choice Questions:

Directions: Pick the letter that best answers the following questions.

1. "Mugwumps" and "stalwarts" took different positions on

   (A) civil service reform.
   (B) the immediate abolition of slavery.
   (C) United States imperialism.
   (D) the expansion of currency.
   (E) the theory of evolution.

2. A principal goal of Coxey's Army was to

   (A) defeat Spanish forces at San Juan Hill in the Spanish-American War.
   (B) pressure the government to provide assistance to the unemployed during the depression of 1893.
   (C) aid in the defeat of fascism during the Spanish Civil War.
   (D) register African Americans in the rural South to vote.
   (E) eradicate Native Americans from the Black Hills of South Dakota.

3. The Populist Party's decision to endorse the Democratic candidate for president in 1896 proved to be a

   (A) terrible decision as the Democrat lost and the Populists lost support and momentum.
   (B) bad decision as the Democrat won the election but ignored the concerns of the farmers.
   (C) good decision as the Democrat won and a populist was named Secretary of the Interior.
   (D) great decision as the Democrat won but died one month after taking office and a Populist became president.
   (E) neutral decision as the Democrat lost but the Populist Party gained strength in the following years.

4. The only president to serve nonconsecutive terms has been

   (A) Rutherford B. Hayes.
   (B) Chester Arthur
   (C) Grover Cleveland.
   (D) Benjamin Harrison.
   (E) Theodore Roosevelt.

Practice Free-Response Questions:

1. "The Democrats and the Republicans were two sides of the same coin during the Gilded Age (1865–1900)." Assess the validity of this statement.

2. Assess the legitimacy of the grievances of the Populist movement in the 1880s and 1890s.

Answers and Explanations to Multiple-Choice Questions:

1. **(A)** A major political debate in the Gilded Age was whether to reform the civil service. Reformers argued that the method for allocating civil service government jobs should be changed so that it was done on a merit basis. At the time, many jobs were given to supporters, friends, and relatives of powerful political figures. (This system is called the spoils system.) Reformers (the mugwumps) thought it was inefficient for so many jobs to change hands every time a new administration came to power.

2. **(B)** Coxey's Army was a march of the unemployed from the Midwest to Washington, D.C. The marchers urged the government to help people who had been thrown out of work by the depression that followed the Panic of 1893.

3. **(A)** The Populist Party backed the wrong horse in 1896. They endorsed the Democratic Party instead of remaining independent of the two main political parties. Their decision led to a real loss of momentum for the party. By the turn of the century, the movement had virtually disappeared.
4. **(C)** Grover Cleveland was the only president to serve two nonconsecutive terms. He was also the only Democratic president between Andrew Johnson and Woodrow Wilson.

Society and Culture in the Gilded Age, 1865–1900

CHAPTER 19

TIMELINE	
1882	Chinese Exclusion Act
1883	Opening of the Brooklyn Bridge
1887	Opening of the first subway system in the United States (Boston)
1893	World's Columbian Exposition (Chicago World's Fair)

The era of rapid industrial and economic expansion in the late-nineteenth century dramatically transformed American culture and society. Americans experienced new cultural products, new patterns of work and leisure, and new class and ethnic divisions. These new aspects of American life were most evident in America's growing cities. Cities became centers of industrial production and magnets for the large number of immigrants coming into the United States. At the same time, agriculture was becoming more mechanized, requiring fewer people in rural areas. New York retained its stature as the largest American city, with Chicago, Cleveland, Detroit, and other cities of the Midwest and the Northeast also growing rapidly.

URBANIZATION AND THE PHYSICAL CITY

The pre–Civil War city of densely packed, low-lying wood and brick buildings was virtually unrecognizable by the end of the nineteenth century. Steel-framed skyscrapers, electric lighting, suspension bridges, and rail lines propelled cities upward and outward.

The Skyscraper

The development of tall buildings required two important developments: the steel frame and the elevator. A steel-framed building, in which the weight of the building hangs on the steel structure, became a reality after the development of the Bessemer process. Operable elevators were developed by the 1850s. Due to popular resistance, they were not used extensively until the 1880s. Elisha Otis developed a "safety elevator"—one that would not fall if the rope or cable failed—and became the largest purveyor of elevators. Chicago can lay claim to the first skyscraper, the ten-story Home Insurance Building (1885); New York was soon to follow.

Brooklyn Bridge

The Gilded Age saw the building of large-scale suspension bridges, using steel cables to bridge wide expanses. The most famous bridge of the era was the Brooklyn Bridge (completed in 1883), connecting the then-independent cities of New York and Brooklyn. The bridge was designed and begun by John Roebling. His son Washington took over upon John's death. After Washington became ill with the bends, his wife, Emily Warren Roebling, took over day-to-day supervision of the project, allowing her bedridden husband to retain the status of chief engineer.

Mass Transit

The nation's first subway system was built in Boston and completed in 1897. The separation of mass transit rail lines from street traffic allowed for the rapid movement of large numbers of urban dwellers and contributed to the development of outlying areas of cities. Previously, both horse-drawn and mechanical trolley cars plied the streets of cities. New York City opened its subway system in 1904. Cities also built elevated train systems. Large portions of Chicago's "L" rapid transit system, begun in 1892, are elevated.

TIP 

Remembering the Civil War
The most popular subject for monuments in this era was the Civil War. Most monuments, however, forgot the main result of the Civil War—the abolition of slavery. In an age of Jim Crow laws and "scientific" racism, the cause of African Americans was jettisoned. In its place was a focus on heroism and shared sacrifice.

Monuments and Memorials

The last decade of the 1800s and the first decade of the 1900s was the age of monument building in American history. Monuments served two broad purposes. The first purpose was local. Cities built monuments as a point of civic pride. A major monument announced that a particular city had "arrived." The second purpose was broader. Monuments reflected a bold nationalism and a unity of purpose in an era of imperial ambitions and growing immigration.

SOCIAL CLASSES IN THE GILDED AGES

The Gilded Age is characterized by a division of the city between working-class districts and wealthy enclaves. Before the Civil War, different classes lived in close proximity to one another. An owner of a printing shop, for example, might live on the second and third stories above his street-level shop. His apprentices might live in his attic—owner and workers under one roof. After the Civil War, the middle class and the wealthy class moved from the low-lying industrial zones, away from the factories, the docks, and the slaughterhouses. In New York City, the wealthy moved uptown. Elsewhere, they moved away from the urban core. In the divided city, the working-class districts tended to become utterly squalid while the wealthier areas had the nicest amenities—wider streets, large parks, and sunlight.

The Wealthy Class

The Gilded Age saw the growth of a well-to-do class that greatly surpassed previous wealthy classes in terms of money, cohesiveness, and power. These wealthy businessmen built gaudy mansions along New York's Fifth Avenue and on other city's "gold coasts." They built equally sumptuous summer "cottages" in Newport, Rhode Island, and other exclusive spots. The social critic and economist Thorstein Veblem's book *The Theory of the Leisure Class* (1899) coined the phrase "conspicuous consumption" to describe the lavish spending habits of the wealthy.

The Working Class and the Poor

At the other end of the social spectrum, often living just blocks or miles from the wealthy class, was the Gilded Age's have-nots—the working class and the poor. The densest neighborhood in the world in the late 1800s was the Lower East Side of New York. Conditions there were typical of many similar districts in other cities—many people packed into small apartments in substandard tenement buildings, lack of ventilation and lights, streets thick with horse dung, and lack of basic municipal services such as sewer lines, running water, and garbage removal.

The conditions of the poor were chronicled in Jacob Riis's *How the Other Half Lives* (1890). His photographs, often criticized for their condescension and stereotyping, did draw many people's attention to the plight of the poor.

TIP 

Was Jacob Riis a Racist?
Not exactly. But he reflected contemporary middle-class perceptions of different ethnic groups. His depictions could be read as condescending and sentimental.

The Middle Class

Although the contrasts between the very wealthy and the very poor were stark, the middle class was growing in the late 1800s. Industry needed managers, accountants, and marketers. Further, there were more doctors, teachers, and lawyers in American society.

THE NEW IMMIGRATION

After 1880, a major new source of labor to work in American factories was immigrants from southern and eastern Europe. This so-called new immigration of southern and eastern Europeans was differentiated from the old immigration of northern and western Europeans. The large wave of immigrants who came to the United States between 1880 and 1920 was essential to the industrialization of the United States. An estimated 20 million people, from Russia, Italy, Poland, the Balkan region, and elsewhere, immigrated to the United States, most settling in industrial cities such as New York, Pittsburgh, and Chicago.

The Rise of Nativism

These new immigrants heightened fears among conservative, Protestant public figures, such as Henry Cabot Lodge and Madison Grant. These nativists feared that Anglo-Saxon Americans were committing race suicide by allowing "inferior" races to enter America in large numbers.

Chinese Exclusion Act (1882)

Chinese Americans were especially targeted by nativists. The 1882 Chinese Exclusion Act represents the only instance in which a particular national group has been explicitly excluded from entrance into the United States by legislation. Later, in the 1920s, the government imposed quotas on immigrants that greatly reduced the overall number of immigrants allowed into the United States (see Chapter 23).

URBAN POLITICS AND THE RISE OF MACHINE POLITICS

Politics in major cities came to be dominated by political machines. In the aftermath of the Civil War, political parties on the local level created smooth-running organizations whose main purpose was to achieve and maintain political power. Ideology was barely a concern in these bare-knuckled electoral contests. New York City was dominated by the Democratic Party machine, headquartered at Tammany Hall. The most famous Tammany chief was "Boss" William M. Tweed. Tweed and other political bosses earned a reputation for corruption. Tweed's complicated schemes included the building of a courthouse that involved millions of dollars in kickbacks to Tammany Hall. Tweed's nefarious doings were exposed by the press, most notably by cartoonist Thomas Nast. The Tammany Hall political machine was popular with German and Irish immigrants. Under the Democratic Party, the city initiated massive municipal projects that provided jobs to thousands of immigrants.

TIP 

Immigrants and Political Machines
Don't be too quick to condemn political machines for exploiting immigrants. The relationship is complicated. Political machines were corrupt, but they provided real benefits to immigrant communities.

LEISURE FOR THE MASSES

City life and a slightly shorter workday provided more opportunities for leisure time activities for the masses of urban residents.

The Saloon

The most popular leisure time activity for working-class men was drinking in saloons. Saloons were often part social hall, part political club, and part community hub. The attacks on saloons, and on alcohol consumption in general, were seen as attacks on working-class immigrant culture as much as they were on drunkenness (see more on the temperance movement in Chapters 12 and 21).

TIP 

Muckraking Journalism Versus Yellow Journalism
Don't confuse these two terms. Muckrakers were genuinely interested in exposing social ills. Yellow journalism was simply a technique to sell newspapers.

Newspapers

As printing costs went down and literacy went up, newspaper circulation increased dramatically in the Gilded Age. Papers with a large circulation in the later decades of the nineteenth century, such as Joseph Pulitzer's *New York World* and William Randolph Hearst's *New York Journal*, gained readership through exaggerated, sensationalistic coverage of events. This yellow journalism played a role in pushing public opinion toward support for the Spanish-American War (1898) (see Chapter 20).

The Health of the City and the Parks Movement

As cities became denser and more disease ridden in the Gilded Age, reformers sought to provide more opportunities for working-class men, women, and children to enjoy outdoor recreation. Older notions of disease causation—that disease, for example, was divine punishment for sinful behavior—gave way to the idea that our environment played a significant role in our health. Later, doctors adopted the germ theory of disease causation, put forth by Robert Koch (who worked from the 1870s to the 1900s). Public parks were part of a strategy to provide an alternative to dirty streets and alleyways, as well as saloons, for people to recreate.

Frederick Law Olmsted and New York's Central Park

The most important park project of the nineteenth century was New York City's Central Park (1858). The design competition was won by Frederick Law Olmsted and Calvert Vaux. The park embodies some of the contradictions of the parks movement. On the one hand, Olmsted sought to create a democratic meeting place where the city's different classes could congregate and enjoy the benefits of nature. On the other hand, working-class advocates wondered aloud why the park was built so far from the working-class districts of the city. Also, the rules and regulations of the park made the park seem, to some people, more about control than enjoyment.

Recreation and Spectator Sports

Park grounds soon became centers for a variety of recreation activities. Several of these activities went from being participatory activities to spectator sports.

- Baseball: Developed in 1845, baseball became the national pastime by the Gilded Age. The first truly professional team was the Cincinnati Red Stockings (1869).
- Tennis: Lawn tennis was developed in Great Britain (1873) as a women's sport. It gained popularity in America among men and women during the Gilded Age.
- Croquet: Croquet was a popular activity in public parks during the last third of the nineteenth century. It was often played by mixed-sex groups.
- Cycling: Wheeling—bicycle riding—became very popular in the Gilded Age. The difficult penny-farthing bicycles, with their enormous front wheel, gave way to the modern design of the safety bicycle in the 1880s. Wheeling was especially popular among women, who enjoyed the freedom from male supervision that bicycle riding offered.
- Football: College football games became popular in the Gilded Age. The first contest was between Rutgers and the College of New Jersey (Princeton) in 1869.

The Romanticization of the West
Be aware of the differences between the real history of the West and the romanticization of the West. "Buffalo Bill" Cody was romanticizing the West when people still had memories of the real West.

Coney Island and the Commercialization of Leisure

The growth of cities went hand in hand with the commercialization of leisure-time activities. The community-sponsored town fairs and dances of rural America were replaced by for-profit ventures in the city.

The most successful large-scale amusement area was Brooklyn's Coney Island. Coney Island consisted of three main amusement parks as well as a boardwalk, vaudeville theaters, and other assorted attractions.

Other successful amusements included "Buffalo Bill" Cody's Wild West show (starting in 1883), which mythologized the old West even before the Indian Wars of the actual West had ended.

Circuses became popular in the Gilded Age. P. T. Barnum created the most popular circus of the era (1871), labeling it "the greatest show on earth."

Subject to Debate

Historians have debated the impact of machine politics in the nineteenth century. Starting in the progressive era, historians wrote disparagingly about the corruption of the political bosses of the Gilded Age. In this narrative, these bosses undermined democracy until progressive reformers rose up and cleaned up the political process. There is certainly truth to the narrative. However, reality is always more complicated. Social historians have recently examined the positive impact the political machines had on immigrant communities. The machines may have been corrupt, but they were the only safety net and jobs program for recently arrived immigrants. In some ways, the attacks on the political machines were attacks on the structure of the immigrant community. In your essay writing, it would be wise to exercise caution when talking about the political bosses of the Gilded Age.

Practice Multiple-Choice Questions:

Directions: Pick the letter that best answers the following questions.

1. William Randolph Hearst gained fame as

   (A) a newspaper publisher.
   (B) a landscape architect.
   (C) an inventor.
   (D) an urban planner.
   (E) a political boss.

2. Leisure activities for city dwellers in the Gilded Age (1870–1900) included all of the following EXCEPT

   (A) visiting P. T. Barnum's circus.
   (B) attending talkie movies.
   (C) swimming at Coney Island.
   (D) watching college football games.
   (E) wheeling (cycling) in public parks.

3. The 1871 cartoon by Thomas Nast shown above is commenting upon

   (A) the power of the robber barons.
   (B) the arrogance of United States imperial policies.
   (C) the intellectual capabilities of the new immigrants.
   (D) the greed of urban political bosses.
   (E) the underhanded tactics of organized labor.

4. The only national people that were specifically excluded from the United States during the nineteenth century were immigrants from

   (A) Japan.
   (B) Ireland.
   (C) Russia.
   (D) China.
   (E) Mexico.

Practice Free-Response Questions:

1. To what degree were reformers successful in addressing TWO of the following urban problems during the Gilded Age?

   Corrupt political bosses
   Sanitation
   Tensions over immigration

2. Analyze the social, economic, and political factors that contributed to the nativist movement (1888–1920).

Answers and Explanations to Multiple-Choice Questions:

1. **(A)** Hearst was known for the practice of yellow journalism. In the run-up to the Spanish-American War, he and fellow publisher Joseph Pulitzer excited the American public with lurid accounts of the treatment of the Cuban people and of the sinking of the *USS Maine.*

2. **(B)** People in the Gilded Age participated in all of the activities listed in the question except attending talkie movies. The first real talkie, *The Jazz Singer,* wasn't released until 1927.

3. **(D)** The cartoonist Thomas Nast is attacking political bosses, specifically "Boss" Tweed of New York's Tammany Hall. Nast published many cartoons attacking Tweed and the Tammany machine. The public finally turned on Tweed. He died in jail.

4. **(D)** The question is alluding to the Chinese Exclusion Act (1882). Chinese and Japanese immigrants were especially targeted by nativists. Racist assumptions of the time held that Asian immigrants would never fully assimilate into the United States. Japanese immigration (A) ended with the Gentlemen's Agreement, but that occurred during the twentieth century (1907).

CHAPTER 20

The United States and Its Empire, 1890–1917

TIMELINE

1893	Queen Liliuokalani is toppled by a coalition of U.S. marines and businessmen
1898	Spanish-American War
	Annexation of Hawaii
	Formation of the American Anti-Imperialist League
	Treaty of Paris
1899–1900	Secretary of State John Hay establishes the Open Door policy in China
1899–1902	Philippine-American War
1903	The United States acquires the Panama Canal Zone (canal completed in 1914)
1906	Theodore Roosevelt wins the Nobel Peace Prize
1914–1917	United States intervention in Mexico

History texts generally cite the 1890s as the beginning of America's imperialistic ventures. It is true that after 1890, the United States began to play a more aggressive role on the world stage, intervening in Hawaii, Cuba, Panama, Mexico, and beyond, and acquiring possessions from Puerto Rico to the Philippines. But the beginning date of 1890 only works if one excludes previous United States military engagements and territorial acquisitions. One must define all the Native American nations that the United States fought with and acquired territory from as nonentities in order to state that United States imperialism began after 1890. Also, the U.S. acquisition of territory from Mexico as a result of the Mexican War (1848) must be discounted. Therefore, this chapter shall examine U.S. imperialist ventures beyond what would become the continental United States. These ventures raised the profile of the United States on the world stage and established it as one of the world's major powers.

TIP

Interrogate Sources
In a DBQ about the causes of American imperialism, be careful to note the source of a document. The pronouncements of a president or a senator might not explain actual motivation. Often a public rationale for an event is different from the actual rationale. Look carefully, for instance, at President McKinley's assertion that the war in the Philippines was motivated by a desire to "civilize" the Filipino people.

REASONS FOR OVERSEAS IMPERIALISM

The United States entered the overseas imperialism scramble a little after the major European powers began carving up Africa and Asia. Many Americans resisted the idea of the United States embarking on overseas expansion. After all, the United States was born in a war against a major imperial power. However, several factors led United States political leaders to engage in overseas expansion.

Alfred Thayer Mahan and the Importance of Naval Power

Alfred Thayer Mahan stressed the importance of naval power in achieving and maintaining power on the world stage. This idea might seem commonplace. However, throughout the nineteenth century, the United States was more focused on domestic issues and expansion over the American continent. Mahan pushed for the United States to develop a strong navy, maintain military bases and coaling stations throughout the world, and administer an overseas empire. These ideas were central to his book *The Influence of Sea Power Upon History, 1660–1783* (1890).

TIP

Imperialism Versus Colonialism
The two terms are not always interchangeable. Colonialism usually implies the effort of one country to establish a settlement in another land. Imperialism usually implies the effort to rule territory that is already occupied and organized.

Industrialization and the Depression of 1893

Contributing to the push for imperialism was the unprecedented growth of American industry. Some policy makers thought that imperialism would become necessary if the United States were to become the world's predominant industrial power. Imperial holdings would provide American industry with important raw materials. Also, the people in these new American possessions could provide a market for the growing output of consumer products that American industry was turning out. The desire for new markets intensified with the onset of the Panic of 1893. This economic downturn left Americans unable to absorb additional consumer items. The economy did not begin to improve until 1896.

"The White Man's Burden"

Imperialist ventures were motivated by a particular cultural set of ideas that created a racial hierarchy. Mainstream thinking in the United States in the late 1800s posited the superiority of the descendents of the Anglo-Saxon people and the inferiority of the nonwhite peoples of the world. This racist notion was widely held, but it led to divergent impulses. Some white Americans felt it was the duty of the "civilized" peoples of the world to uplift the less fortunate. Others felt that the inferior races would simply disappear in a struggle for the survival of the fittest. The push to uplift the peoples of the world was made clear in Rudyard Kipling's famous poem, "The White Man's Burden" (1899). Josiah Strong, a Protestant clergyman, echoed Kipling's sentiment. He argued that the "Anglo-Saxon race" had a responsibility to "civilize and Christianize" the world.

The racial hierarchy implicit in "The White Man's Burden" was starkly displayed at the World's Fair in Chicago in 1893 as a sideshow of the "exotic" people's of the world was presented to fairgoers. These displays of "natives" were contrasted with the industry and progress of the advanced civilizations. The obvious implication was that the advances of civilization must be made available to the rest of the world. Frederick Douglass attended the fair and, with Ida B. Wells, wrote a scathing critique of the racist assumptions of the fair.

TIP 

Consensus and Conflict in the Past

Students often assume that the unpleasant ideas of earlier eras—such as slavery or racism—were simply accepted by all of society. However, it is important to recognize that these ideas were not universally accepted. In regard to both slavery and to notions of white supremacy, important voices challenged the mainstream thinking of the day.

Christian Missionaries

Christian missionary work went hand in hand with American expansion. Missionaries were eager to spread the Christian gospel and introduce new populations to Christianity. Many of these missionaries targeted China's large population.

HAWAII

American missionaries arrived in Hawaii as early as the 1820s. Later in the century, American businessmen established massive sugar plantations, undermining the local economy. Discord between the American businessmen and the ruler of the island, Queen Liliuokalani, emerged after 1891. The pineapple grower Sanford Dole urged the United States to intervene. American businessmen staged a coup in 1893, toppling Queen Liliuokalani. U.S forces immediately protected a new provisional government led by Dole. The provisional government hoped for U.S. annexation of the islands, but that did not occur until 1898.

THE SPANISH-AMERICAN WAR AND ITS AFTERMATH

In the 1890s, Spain was still in control of Cuba. However, a Cuban independence movement was trying to break its ties to Spain. The Spanish governor of Cuba, Valeriano Weyler, used brutal tactics to suppress the rebellion. Thousands of Cubans were crowded into concentration camps. By 1898, approximately a quarter of Cuba's population had died in the revolution.

United States Interest in Cuba

Many Americans wanted the United States to intervene on Cuba's side in its struggle against Spanish rule. Some Americans saw parallels between the Cuban struggle for independence from Spain and America's struggle for independence from Great Britain. Also, some American businessmen were angered by the interruption of the sugar harvest caused by the fighting between Cuban rebels and Spanish forces.

Yellow Journalism and the Call to War

Events in Cuba were brought to the attention of ordinary Americans through mass-produced and mass-distributed newspapers. Industrialization and increased literacy set the groundwork for America's first mass media. To attract customers, newspapers began printing bold, sensationalistic headlines, often disregarding accepted journalistic practices and even the truth. This sensationalistic journalism came to be known as yellow journalism. News organizations used these techniques of exaggeration and innuendo to build support for war with Spain. These newspapers breathlessly followed events in Cuba, with lurid accounts of Spanish wrongdoing and condemnations of "Butcher" Weyler—the Spanish governor.

The Sinking of the *Maine*

The event that led directly to the Spanish-American War was the destruction of a United States warship, the USS *Maine*, in the harbor of Havana, Cuba. Many in the United States thought that the destruction of the ship was the work of Spain, especially after American newspapers bluntly accused Spain of the crime despite the scarcity of evidence.

The Spanish-American War

The Spanish-American War was brief. American forces landed in Cuba on June 22, 1898, and Spain surrendered on July 17. Fighting in the Philippines—also held by Spain—lasted just days, as Admiral George Dewey led American forces in taking the capital Manila. Theodore Roosevelt led a charge up San Juan Hill in a key battle for Cuba. The colorful Roosevelt and his men—known as the Rough Riders—made headlines in American papers. This elevated Roosevelt's status in the political realm.

The Treaty of Paris

The United States and Spain negotiated the Treaty of Paris (1898) following the war. In the treaty, Spain agreed to cede the Philippines, Puerto Rico, and Guam to the United States; in return, the United States agreed to pay Spain $20 million.

Cuba and the Platt Amendment

Cuba gained its independence after the Spanish-American War. In many ways, Cuba became independent in name only. The United States wanted to ensure that American economic interests would not be challenged by a future Cuban administration. The United States, therefore, insisted that the Platt Amendment be inserted into the Cuban Constitution. This amendment allowed the United States to intervene militarily in Cuban affairs if it saw fit. The amendment limited the Cuban government's ability to conduct its foreign policy and to manage its debts. Also, the amendment allowed the United States to lease a naval base at Guantanamo Bay. Americans troops intervened in Cuba three times between 1902 and 1920.

CRITICS OF AMERICAN IMPERIALISM AND THE DEBATE OVER THE TREATY OF PARIS

As the dust settled after the Spanish-American War, the American public realized that the Treaty of Paris would grant the United States ongoing control of several lands beyond America's existing borders. The United States had recently annexed Hawaii (1898). The Treaty of Paris (1898) would give the United States control over Puerto Rico, Guam, and the Philippines. Although Cuba was technically independent, the Platt Amendment made it a U.S. protectorate. To many Americans, these acquisitions were markedly different from earlier acquisitions. These new islands were densely populated and were far away from the settled parts of the United States, unlike the Louisiana Purchase (1803) or the Mexican Cession (1848). Perhaps the distinction amounted to splitting hairs, but critics did surmise one additional key difference. The earlier territorial gains of the United States were intended to absorb American citizens and eventually to achieve statehood and equal footing with the existing states. There was no expectation, on the other hand, that the Philippines would absorb large numbers of American citizens. The United States would, indefinitely, rule over a foreign population.

The American Anti-Imperialist League

In 1898, as the Treaty of Paris was debated in the Senate, a group of critics of American imperialism formed the American Anti-Imperialist League. The league was a coalition of conservative Democrats (known at the time as Bourbon Democrats) as well as more progressive elements. The league included the American author Mark Twain, who became increasingly radical as he grew older. He was the vice president of the league from 1901 to 1910 and wrote some of the league's more scathing condemnations of imperialism.

The league suffered a major schism in 1900 as the more conservative members rejected the candidacy of Democrat William Jennings Bryan for president of the United States while the more progressive elements embraced it. Jennings was an anti-imperialist. However, many of his other positions, especially his criticism of the gold standard, alienated many of the conservative Bourbon Democrats. The Republican William McKinley won reelection, continuing an aggressive foreign policy.

The debate over imperialism—over whether the United States Constitution permitted the American government to make rules for peoples who were not represented by lawmakers—nearly imperiled ratification of the Treaty of Paris. Democratic opponents of imperialism rallied against the treaty, which barely achieved the necessary two-thirds majority in 1899.

DOES THE CONSTITUTION FOLLOW THE FLAG?

The question of whether constitutional provisions applied to people in the new American territories continued in the courts after the ratification of the Treaty of Paris. Expansionists argued that the Constitution did not necessarily follow the flag. Anti-imperialists insisted that it should. The Supreme Court settled this issue in a series of cases in 1901 that have come to be known as the insular cases ("insular" means *island related*). The Court agreed with expansionists that the United States need not grant its colonial subjects constitutional rights. The decisions were based on the racist assumption that the colonial subjects were of an inferior race and the colonial power had the responsibility to uplift these peoples before granting them autonomy.

WAR IN THE PHILIPPINES

Many Filipinos were surprised and disappointed to learn that the United States decided to hold onto the Philippines as a colony. They had seen the United States as a liberating force that would help rid the nation of Spanish rule and usher in independence. This was not the intent of the United States. Following the ratification of the Treaty of Paris, a bitter, three-year war, known as the Philippine-American War, ensued that was far more lengthy and deadly than the Spanish-American War. (Filipino forces continued to resist American control for another decade.) Filipino forces were led by Emilio Aguinaldo. The war cost the American forces 4,000 lives; over 20,000 Filipinos died in the conflict. Estimates of Filipino civilian deaths vary greatly. The United States held onto the Philippines until after World War II (1946).

TIP

A Tale of Two Wars
In writing about American imperialism, don't forget about the war in the Philippines. It lasted longer (three years) and resulted in more casualties (over 4,000 American deaths, approximately 20,000 Filipino combat deaths, and estimates of 100,000 to 600,000 civilian deaths) than the more well-known Spanish-American War (four months, less than 400 American deaths, less than 15,000 combined Cuban and Spanish deaths).

CHINA AND THE OPEN-DOOR POLICY

The bitter conflict in the Philippines was in many ways designed to provide the United States with a stepping stone to an even greater prize—trade with China. China's large population and natural resources made it a target for the imperialist nations. The major powers of Europe had previously begun carving up China. Britain, Japan, Germany, Russia, and France each proclaimed a sphere of influence—a port city and surrounding territory—in which other foreign nations would be excluded. The United States asserted that all of China should be open to trade with all nations. Secretary of State John Hay wrote a series of notes to the major powers asserting an open-door policy for China. The United States claimed to be concerned for the territorial integrity of China but was more interested in gaining a foothold in trade with China. The open-door policy was begrudgingly accepted by the major powers.

The Boxer Rebellion

Christian missionaries had come to China in large numbers but met with little success there. The number of converts was small, and the presence of the missionaries inspired militant antiforeign secret societies. The most well known of these societies was the Boxers, or the Society of Righteous and Harmonious Fists. The Boxers led a rebellion that resulted in the death of over 30,000 Chinese converts as well as 250 foreign nuns. The United States participated in a multination force to rescue westerners held hostage by the Boxers (1900).

THEODORE ROOSEVELT AND THE BIG STICK

In September 1901, President McKinley was shot at the Pan-American Exposition in Buffalo, New York, by anarchist Leon Czolgosz. McKinley soon died from the wound, just six months into his second term as president. His vice president, Theodore Roosevelt, became president. (See more on Roosevelt's domestic agenda in Chapter 21.) Roosevelt was an adventurer, an expansionist, and a Spanish-

American War hero. His foreign-policy approach is neatly summed up in his famous adage that the United States should "speak softly, but carry a big stick" when dealing with other nations. (Roosevelt had borrowed the phrase from an African proverb.) The "big stick" implied the threat of military force. He envisioned the United States acting as the world's policeman, punishing wrongdoers. He asserted that the "civilized nations" had a duty to police the "backward" countries of the world. He claimed that the United States had the right to intervene militarily in the nations of Latin America. This assertion of American might is known as the Roosevelt Corollary to the Monroe Doctrine. In 1902, he sternly warned Germany to stay out of the Americas after Venezuela failed to repay a loan to Germany and Germany threatened military intervention.

TIP

Foreign Policy and Economic Priorities
Often in American history, economic priorities drive foreign policy decisions. A Central American canal was a major priority for American commercial and industrial interests at the beginning of the twentieth century.

Panama and the Panama Canal

Roosevelt's aggressive approach to Latin America is clearly evident in regard to Panama. With the acquisition of Pacific territories and with an increased interest in trade with China, American policy makers became interested in a shortcut to the Pacific. Merchant ships and naval vessels had to travel around the southern tip of South America to reach the Pacific Ocean. The building of a canal through Panama, therefore, became a major goal of Roosevelt.

Before 1903, Panama was a department of Colombia. American investors picked the narrow piece of land as an ideal location for a canal to facilitate shipping between the Atlantic and Pacific Oceans. When Colombia refused the U.S. offer of $10 million to build a canal, American investors, with the backing of President Roosevelt and the United States military, instigated a "rebellion" in Panama against Colombia. Panama became an independent country and immediately negotiated the Hay-Bunau-Varilla Treaty (1903) with the United States to build a canal. President Roosevelt boasted that he "took Panama."

Roosevelt, Diplomacy, and the Nobel Peace Prize

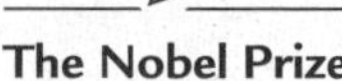

TIP

The Nobel Prize
Three other presidents besides Theodore Roosevelt have won the Nobel Peace Prize: Woodrow Wilson in 1919, Jimmy Carter in 2002, and Barack Obama in 2009.

President Roosevelt was interested in establishing the United States as a major player in world diplomacy. Toward this end, he acted as a mediator between France and Germany in their conflict over Morocco (1905). Roosevelt was also interested in maintaining a balance of power among the other world powers. That same year, Roosevelt offered to mediate an end to the Russo-Japanese War (1904–1905). A peace conference was held in Portsmouth, New Hampshire, with Roosevelt presiding. Despite Roosevelt's aggressive actions in Latin America, he was granted the Nobel Peace Prize (1906) for his diplomatic efforts.

The Gentleman's Agreement

In 1907, the diplomatic gains that Roosevelt had achieved with Japan were threatened by discriminatory legislation passed in California, restricting the rights of "Orientals." Roosevelt quietly worked out a Gentleman's Agreement with Japan, in which Japan agreed to limit immigration to the United States and Roosevelt agreed to pressure California to end its discriminatory practices.

PRESIDENT TAFT AND DOLLAR DIPLOMACY

President William Howard Taft (1909–1913) continued to pursue an aggressive foreign policy. However, he put more emphasis on expanding and securing American commercial interests than on pursuing the global strategic goals that Roosevelt championed. Taft's foreign policy has come to be known as dollar diplomacy. He sent troops to Nicaragua and the Dominican Republic to coerce them into signing commercial treaties with the United States. In general, he tried to substitute dollars for bullets in pursuing American interests. He failed to stem revolution in Mexico in 1911.

PRESIDENT WILSON'S FOREIGN POLICY

President Wilson's initial focus as president was on domestic concerns (see Chapter 21). However, his administration became increasingly drawn into foreign policy matters, from problems in the Americas to war in Europe (see Chapter 22). Wilson was driven by both a desire to secure American economic interests abroad and by a strong moral compass; often these impulses clashed with one another.

Wilson immediately signaled a break with his Republican predecessors by appointing the anti-imperialist William Jennings Bryan to be secretary of state. Bryan sought peaceful accommodation of differences with many nations, but he and Wilson were not above flexing America's military muscle in the Americas. Wilson authorized the occupation of Nicaragua by American marines to suppress a rebellion against the American-backed president of the country. He sent troops to Haiti in 1915 and to the Dominican Republic in 1916 to ensure that American business interests were not challenged.

Wilson and the Mexican Revolution

President Wilson became enmeshed in the convulsions of the Mexican Revolution, which lasted through the 1910s. The revolution began with the ousting of an autocratic leader in 1910 but soon degenerated into a civil war that left nearly a million Mexicans dead. In 1914, Wilson challenged the legitimacy of the new Mexican leader, General Victoriano Huerta. He sent 800 marines to Mexico. Huerta fled the country. A new government, more amenable to American interests, came to power. This new government was challenged by an uprising led by the rebel leader Francisco "Pancho" Villa. Villa successfully intercepted a train carrying American gold and led a raid into American territory that left 18 Americans dead. Wilson authorized over 12,000 troops to invade Mexico to capture Villa. Villa eluded the American forces. In early 1917, the United States began preparations for World War I.

Subject to Debate

History textbooks can take one of several approaches in discussing American imperialism. You should be familiar with these approaches in order to write about events and documents from this period within a broader intellectual framework.

James Loewen, in his survey of American history textbooks, identifies three approaches to talking about American imperialism. Critics of American imperialism often discuss the United States as if it were a colossus, imposing its will on the world. This American colossus approach asserts that any talk of spreading democracy around the world is cynical window dressing to hide the actual motives of American imperialism: economic exploitation. A competing view acknowledges that economic motives drive foreign policy but is not troubled by that fact. This hard-nosed "realpolitik" approach holds that America must expand if it wants to maintain the standard of living that Americans have come to appreciate. A third view, which Loewen calls the international good guy approach, ignores economic motives altogether. It asserts that American motives in the world are altruistic and noble. This view takes the words of public figures at face value.[1]

These approaches are useful when confronted with a document such as President Wilson's call for intervention in World War I. You should be able to interrogate his claims that we are entering the war to "make the world safe for democracy." You should be able to discuss the intent of such a document rather than simply recounting information contained within it as fact.

---

[1]James Loewen, *Lies My Teacher Told Me: Everything Your American History Textbook Got Wrong* (New York: New Press, 1995).

Practice Multiple-Choice Questions:

Directions: Pick the letter that best answers the following questions.

1. Following the Spanish-American War, Puerto Rico
   (A) retained its political ties to Spain.
   (B) became a possession of the United States.
   (C) attained independence.
   (D) was divided into two nations, one communist and one democratic.
   (E) joined the Axis powers.

2. When President Wilson took office, he initially displayed his sense of idealism in regard to foreign policy by

   (A) granting control of the Panama Canal to Panama.
   (B) reducing the size of the American military by 70 percent.
   (C) appointing anti-imperialist William Jennings Bryan as secretary of state.
   (D) issuing his Fourteen Points Speech in regard to creating a peaceful world order.
   (E) eliminating import duties.

3. In 1906, President Theodore Roosevelt won the Nobel Peace Prize for his efforts to

   (A) establish a Jewish state in the Middle East.
   (B) reduce armaments among the world's powerful nations.
   (C) deal fairly with Native Americans within United States borders.
   (D) prevent an armed coup in Panama.
   (E) mediate an end to the Russo-Japanese War.

4. The American assertion of an open-door policy in regard to China was a challenge to

   (A) Japanese domination of China.
   (B) the League of Nations.
   (C) the spheres of influence system that was in effect.
   (D) communist control of China.
   (E) Republican isolationists in the Senate.

Practice Free-Response Questions:

1. Assess the behavior of America as an imperialist power with reference to THREE of the following:

   The Open-Door Policy
   The Platt Amendment
   The Insular Cases
   Dollar Diplomacy

2. Compare the approaches of Presidents Theodore Roosevelt and Woodrow Wilson in regard to foreign policy in the Americas.

Answers and Explanations to Multiple-Choice Questions:

1. **(B)** After the Spanish-American War, Spain ceded Puerto Rico, Guam, and the Philippines to the United States. This was stipulated in the Treaty of Paris (1898). Cuba was granted independence, but strings were attached. The Platt Amendment allowed for U.S. intervention in Cuban affairs.

2. **(C)** William Jennings Bryan had a long and colorful career. He gave the Cross of Gold speech when he ran for president in 1896. He was the secretary of state under President Wilson. He was part of the prosecution team in the Scopes Trial (1925), arguing for a literal interpretation of the Bible. Bryan was consistent in his opposition to imperialism.

3. **(E)** Roosevelt successfully mediated an end to the Russo-Japanese War. Roosevelt was known for an aggressive foreign policy, especially in regard to Panama and the Panama Canal (D). In this case, he acted to bring about peace.

4. **(C)** The open-door policy was put forth by President McKinley's Secretary of State John Hay in 1900 in order to open up China to American trade. In the 1890s, the major European powers had established spheres of influence in China. The European nations eventually accepted the concept.

CHAPTER 21

The Progressive Movement, 1900–1920

TIMELINE

1904	Republican Theodore Roosevelt elected president
1905	Founding of the Niagara Movement
1906	Publication of *The Jungle* by Upton Sinclair
	The Meat Inspection Act
	Passage of the Pure Food and Drug Act
	The Hepburn Act
1908	RepublicanWilliam Howard Taft elected president
1909	Creation of the National Association for the Advancement of Colored People
1910	The Mann Act
1912	Democrat Woodrow Wilson elected president
1913	The Sixteenth Amendment (federal income tax) is ratified
	The Seventeenth Amendment (direct election of senators) is ratified
1914	The Federal Reserve Act
	The Federal Trade Commission
	The Clayton Antitrust Act
1915	The release of D. W. Griffith's film *Birth of a Nation*
1916	The reelection of Woodrow Wilson
1919	The Eighteenth Amendment (prohibition) is ratified
1920	The Nineteenth Amendment (women's right to vote) is ratified

The progressive movement was an essentially middle-class response to the excesses of rapid industrialization, political corruption, and unplanned urbanization. Progressivism existed at the grass-roots level as well as in the corridors of power. Two influential presidents, Theodore Roosevelt and Woodrow Wilson, took on the progressive mantle. The movement was more an amalgam of interests, ideas, groups, and individuals rather than a tight-knit cohort of activists with a cohesive ideology and a clearly articulated vision of the future. The movement was a bundle of contradictions. It championed reforms to benefit the working class but looked at the actual working class with a mix of paternalism and suspicion. The movement challenged women's exclusion from the political process but largely accepted the prevailing social views of African Americans. To some degree, progressivism challenged the abuses of unbridled capitalism. At the same time, many industrialists embraced progressive legislation in order to rationalize the freewheeling nature of the capitalist system. The movement claimed many legislative victories and ultimately influenced both the New Deal and twentieth-century liberalism.

THE WORLDVIEW OF THE PROGRESSIVE MOVEMENT

Middle-Class Progressivism

The progressive movement was essentially a middle-class phenomenon. Not only were the primary activists in the movement middle-class college graduates, but also the tone and tenor were decidedly middle class.

Women and the Progressive Movement

A large percentage of progressive activists were women. The progressive movement provided a means for women to become engaged in public issues in an era when the vote was still restricted to men in most states. Women often framed their participation in the movement as "social housekeeping." In this way, it did not seem like such a radical break from the traditional domestic activities in which women were expected to find fulfillment. Prominent women in the progressive movement included: Florence Kelly, an activist for the reform of factories and Chief Factory Inspector for Illinois (1893); Frances Perkins, head of the New York Consumers' League (1910) and later secretary of labor under President Franklin Roosevelt (1933–1945); and Jane Addams, founder of Hull House in Chicago (1897).

Scientific Management and the Quest for Efficiency

Many progressive reformers embraced the goals of expertise and efficiency. Progressives tended to believe that expert management in the workplace and in government would benefit society as a whole. This system of expert managers would replace systems based on cronyism, nepotism, and favoritism. Many progressives looked favorably to the scientific management techniques developed by Frederick Winslow Taylor. Taylor carefully watched workers, noted the most efficient techniques, and wrote down in exacting detail how a particular task was to be done. Work tended to become monotonous under rigid scientific management but also, no doubt, more efficient. The movement held the optimistic belief that experts, with the backing of the government, could address a variety of social ills using scientific and rational criteria. Many of these ideas are articulated in Walter Lippmann's book *Drift and Mastery* (1914).

Pragmatism

Progressives gravitated toward the pragmatist philosophical ideas of William James and John Dewey. Pragmatists questioned the philosophical quest for eternal truths. Rather, they argued, the value of an idea lay in its ability to have a positive impact on the world. Experimentation was central to the pragmatists' work. Dewey put this idea into practice in an experimental school he started in Chicago. The school put much more of an emphasis on the process of learning and on student participation than on the content of the curriculum.

Reform Darwinism

Progressive activists rejected the ethos of social Darwinism, which applied Charles Darwin's ideas about the natural world to the world of human interactions (see Chapter 17). Progressives embraced the Darwinian idea of evolution but thought that the evolution of human society to its highest ideals required active intervention and cooperation rather than a laissez-faire approach. This call to active intervention in the evolution of the social order is called reform Darwinism.

Muckrakers and the Birth of Investigative Journalism

Progressives believed in the power of the newly developed mass print media to shed light on social ills and to inspire action. The practitioners of this new investigative form of journalism were known as muckrakers. *McClure's*, *Harper's*, *Cosmopolitan*, and several other magazines became staples of middle-class homes by the turn of the twentieth century. Readers were increasingly drawn to articles detailing the corruption and scandal of the modern world. Many of these muckrakers saw themselves on a mission to shine a light on the sordid business and political practices of the day. Important muckrakers included Upton Sinclair, Ida Tarbell, Lincoln Steffens, and Frank Norris. (All of them are discussed in the pages that follow in the context of the topics they wrote about.)

PROGRESSIVES AND MUNICIPAL REFORM

Progressive activists were alarmed at the inefficiency and corruption of municipal government. The political machines that developed in large American cities in the nineteenth century continued to dominate cities in the early twentieth century. The most famous nineteenth-century political machine was the Democratic Party machine in New York City—headquartered in Tammany Hall and dominated by "Boss" William M. Tweed (see Chapter 19).

The Galveston Flood and the Commission Form of Government

The issue of municipal inefficiency and corruption came to the fore in the aftermath of a devastating hurricane and flood that struck Galveston, Texas, in 1900. More than 6,000 people died in the disaster. The ineffective response by the city government in Galveston convinced locals to create commissions to spearhead the cleanup and rebuilding of the city. This commission form of government soon spread from Galveston to other cities. In this form of government, voters elect a group of commissioners who run the city and head various departments, such as public works, fire, and sanitation. In this way, city officials are not beholden to the largess and patronage of powerful political bosses.

The inefficiencies of urban governance were also highlighted in Lincoln Steffens' 1904 muckraking book, *The Shame of the Cities.* The book is a collection of pieces he had written for *McClure's Magazine.*

THE DEMOCRATIZATION OF AMERICA

The reform of municipal government was part of a larger effort by progressive activists to make local, state, and national government more responsive to the popular will. Perhaps the most important reform to come out of the progressive era was the Nineteenth Amendment to the Constitution, which gave women the right to vote (discussed in the context of World War I in Chapter 22).

The Referendum, the Recall, and the Initiative

Reformers hoped that by expanding democracy, the power of political machines would be lessened. In states across the United States, progressives proposed and often implemented reforms to expand democracy. The referendum was a progressive-era reform that allowed people to vote directly on proposed legislation. A proposed referendum item would appear on the ballot on election day. Voters would vote either "yes" or "no" on the referendum. Several states still have the referendum. The recall empowered the people of a city or state to remove an elected official before his or her term ended. Several states still have the recall. In 2003, Californians recalled Governor Gray Davis and replaced him with Arnold Schwarzenegger. The initiative allowed citizens to introduce a bill to the local or state legislature by petition.

Direct Primaries

In the nineteenth century, party machines generally picked the candidates that would run in the general election. This practice removed a key element of the electoral process from public participation. The progressive movement pushed for the adoption of direct primaries, which empowered voters to choose party candidates to run for elected public office. In 1903, Wisconsin was the first state to adopt a direct primary. Most other states had also adopted direct primaries by 1916.

Direct Election of Senators

Progressives pushed for the Seventeenth Amendment (1913), which called for the direct election of senators. Previously, senators were chosen by state legislatures.

TIP 

Progressive-Era Amendments
Four important amendments to the Constitution came out of the Progressive era. The Sixteenth Amendment allowed for a federal income tax. The Seventeenth Amendment provided for the direct election of senators. The Eighteenth Amendment called for prohibition. The Nineteenth Amendment extended the vote to women.

The Australian Ballot

In the nineteenth century, political machines routinely printed ballots with their candidates on them. Voters would then deposit these ballots in voting boxes, allowing anyone who was interested to see which ballot a voter deposited. This system allowed for voter intimidation. In 1888, Massachusetts adopted a secret ballot, which was already in use in Australia. These ballots, printed by the state instead of by the parties and filled out by voters in curtained booths, became the norm in America by 1910.

PROGRESSIVISM AND INDUSTRIAL CAPITALISM

During the Gilded Age of the late nineteenth century, America's industrial output grew exponentially with virtually no government regulation. Industrialists and their allies championed laissez-faire, the idea that government should stay out of economic activities. By the early twentieth century, it became evident that unregulated industry could be harmful to individuals and communities and even to the health of industrial capitalism itself. If people lost confidence in the products of the industrial system, sales would suffer.

The Jungle and the Meatpacking Industry

A public outcry about the conditions of the meat-processing industry was generated by Upton Sinclair's 1906 novel *The Jungle*, which vividly depicted the horrible conditions in the meatpacking industry. The novel takes place in Chicago and follows a Lithuanian immigrant family through the stockyards of Chicago. The novel, based on extensive research by Sinclair, brought to light the unsanitary and dangerous conditions of the meatpacking industry. The socialist message of the book was largely ignored by the public, but the depiction of meat processing was not. The public uproar that followed publication of the book led Congress to pass the Meat Inspection Act (1906) and the Pure Food and Drug Act (also 1906), which helped to establish the Food and Drug Administration.

The History of the Standard Oil Company

The Standard Oil Company, a giant trust assembled by John D. Rockefeller, had come to dominate the petroleum-processing industry by the end of the nineteenth century (see Chapter 17). Ida Tarbell detailed the rise of Standard Oil in a series of articles in *McClure's Magazine* and then in the book, *The History of the Standard Oil Company* (1904). Her research exposed the ruthlessness of John D. Rockefeller's oil company. The book contributed to the government breaking up the Standard Oil Trust in 1911.

The Triangle Factory Fire

The progressive movement was spurred to take action after a tragic fire swept through the Triangle Shirtwaist Factory in 1911. The factory, which produced women's blouses (then known as "shirtwaists"), was located in the upper floors of a factory building in the Greenwich Village section of New York City. The employees were mostly young women, many of who were recent Italian or Jewish immigrants. A fire began in one of the scrap bins and soon spread. The workers discovered that one of the entrances was blocked by the flames and another was locked (perhaps to keep the workers in or to keep union organizers out). Some escaped by elevator; some by a fire escape before it collapsed. Ultimately, 146 workers died. The tragedy led to the creation of fire safety laws in New York and to the rapid growth of the International Ladies Garment Workers' Union.

Muller v. *Oregon* and the Brandeis Brief

Progressives tackled the dual issues of long working hours and child labor. In the late-nineteenth century, workdays of twelve hours or more were not uncommon and child labor had become a common practice in large factories. The movement had some successes, but federal fair-labor standards would not become a reality until the New Deal era of the 1930s. The movement suffered a setback in 1905 when the Supreme Court shot down a New York State law restricting hours for bakers in the case of *Lochner* v. *New York*. The court cited the sanctity of private contracts between employers and employees. However, the progressive movement achieved a major boost in another Supreme Court decision just three years later, in the case of *Muller* v. *Oregon* (1908). That decision upheld an Oregon law limiting the number of hours women could work. This decision cited the supposed physical limitations of women and the threat to their health that long workdays posed. The decision specifically cited women's role as child bearers. The case is significant because of the brief written by future Supreme Court justice Louis Brandeis. On behalf of the state of Oregon, Brandeis prepared a brief citing copious scientific, psychological, and sociological studies to bolster the case for limiting women's hours of work. This type of legal argument has come to be known as a Brandeis brief. The use of nonlegal information in legal matters would become increasingly common in the twentieth century, including in *Brown* v. *Board of Education of Topeka* (1954).

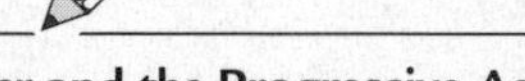

***Muller* and the Progressive Agenda**

The Muller decision represented a major victory for the progressive movement. The decision also reflected differing attitudes about gender within the movement. Although many progressives challenged traditional understandings of gender, this decision reinforced traditional notions of female frailty.

PROGRESSIVISM AND THE POOR

Many progressive activists actively sought to improve the lives of the nation's poorest residents.

Jane Addams and the Settlement House Movement

The settlement house movement was the most visible example of this alliance between middle-class reformers and working-class men and women. Settlement houses were established to aid immigrants, especially immigrant women. By 1911, over 400 settlement houses existed in the United States, usually run by women. Jane Addams ran Hull House in Chicago.

PROGRESSIVISM AND MORAL REFORM

The progressive zeal to attack social ills led many to campaign against "sin" and "vice." These middle-class reformers were more than ready to impose their notions of proper behavior on the society as a whole. Reformers tackled excessive drinking, prostitution, rowdy behavior, and cheap entertainment in their attempt to "civilize" the urban environment.

The Campaign Against Prostitution

The issue of prostitution tapped into progressive concerns in several ways. Religious progressives saw it as sinful. Campaigners for gender equality saw a double standard in society's acceptance of male extramarital sexual activities (including with prostitutes). Public health advocates saw prostitution as a means of spreading venereal disease. Antipoverty activists saw prostitution as reinforcing a cycle of poverty for working-class women. These forces united in pressuring local authorities to close red-light districts. Nationally, progressives successfully lobbied for the Mann Act (1910), which cracked down on the transport of women across state lines to engage in prostitution.

The Temperance Campaign

The movement to ban alcohol from American society had been one of the largest reform movements in the nineteenth century. It gained new enthusiasts among progressives who sought to harness the power of the government to change social behavior. The Anti-Saloon League (founded in 1895) and The Women's Christian Temperance Union (founded in 1874) headed the temperance campaign in the early twentieth century. The temperance movement was especially popular among women. Many women were troubled by the large amount of alcohol their husbands drank. Women, who had the responsibility of putting food on the table, were also troubled by the fact that their husbands often literally drank away their paychecks. Another reason for the popularity of the temperance crusade was that it complimented the growing nativist, or anti-immigrant, movement. Progressives with nativist tendencies thought that the new immigrants, who were mostly non-Protestant, lacked the self-control of "proper," middle-class Protestant Americans.

The final victory for the temperance movement came as the United States entered World War I. The movement successfully equated the prohibition of alcohol with the quest to bring democracy to the world. The United States would purify the world of undemocratic forces and purify its citizens of alcohol. Also, with wartime shortages of grain, it made sense to ban grain-based alcoholic beverages. The anti-German sentiment that developed during World War I also played a role because many American breweries had German names. All these factors led to the ratification of the Eighteenth Amendment, which banned alcohol production, sales, and consumption as of January 1, 1920. (See more on the effects of prohibition in Chapter 23.)

PROGRESSIVISM IN THE WHITE HOUSE

The progressive movement was primarily a grassroots movement of thousands of activists, but in the early-twentieth century, progressivism entered the discourse of the national political parties. President Theodore Roosevelt, a Republican, embraced many progressive reforms, but his handpicked successor, President William H. Taft, proved to be a disappointment to the progressive movement. The divisions within the Republican Party over Taft led to the electoral victory in 1912 of the Democrat Woodrow Wilson. The pervasiveness of the progressive ideology crossed party lines, and Wilson implemented some important progressive reforms.

THEODORE ROOSEVELT AND THE SQUARE DEAL

Theodore Roosevelt assumed the presidency following the assassination of William McKinley (1901) and quickly began to move the Republican Party and the nation itself in a progressive direction. His domestic agenda was known as the Square Deal. He championed the cause of conservation of natural resources and came to be known as "the trust buster." Roosevelt also pursued an aggressive foreign policy (see Chapter 20). Roosevelt had a colorful, forceful personality. He was a historian, having written *The Naval War of 1812* (1882), and became a high-ranking official in the Department of the Navy. Roosevelt led a small group of men, known as the Rough Riders, in a battle in Cuba in the Spanish-American War. In addition, he was an active outdoorsman and a boxer, despite being an asthmatic.

Roosevelt and the Regulation of Business

Roosevelt's Square Deal approach to public issues is reflected in his handling of the anthracite coal strike in 1902. Roosevelt called representatives from both management and labor to the White House. He even threatened to take over the mines if owners did not negotiate in good faith. Ultimately, the miners received a 10 percent wage increase but not union recognition. Roosevelt also pushed for important consumer protections in the wake of the publication of *The Jungle* (see page 211). Also, Roosevelt pushed for stronger regulation of the powerful railroad industry. The power of the railroad industry was the subject of Frank Norris's novel *The Octopus: A California Story* (1901). Roosevelt strengthened the Interstate Commerce Commission (created in 1887) with the Elkins Act (1903), which targeted the railroad practice of granting rebates to favored customers, and the Hepburn Act (1906), which gave the commission greater latitude to set railroad rates.

Roosevelt as Trust Buster

Roosevelt saw the concentration of economic power in a few hands as potentially dangerous to the economy as a whole. Though the Sherman Antitrust Act (1890) was passed to limit monopolistic practices, the act was not enforced with a great deal of enthusiasm. Roosevelt made a point of using the act to pursue "bad trusts"—ones that interfered with commerce—not necessarily the biggest trusts. One of his first targets was the Northern Securities Company, a railroad holding company. His efforts were challenged in court. In *Northern Securities Co.* v. *United States* (1904), the Supreme Court upheld the power of the government to break up Northern Securities under the Sherman Antitrust Act. The case was a victory for Roosevelt. His efforts at challenging monopolies earned him the nickname "the trust buster."

Roosevelt and Conservation

Roosevelt became increasingly concerned with the rapid destruction of much of the nation's pristine wilderness. Logging and mining operations were taking a toll on forested areas starting in the late 1800s. He therefore embraced the cause of environmental conservation. This view endorses using natural resources in a responsible way so that these resources continue to exist for future generations. This view can be contrasted with the views of environmental preservationists. Preservationists want society to have a hands-off approach in regard to the remaining relatively untouched natural areas. An early preservationist was John Muir, one of the founders of the Sierra Club (1892). Both conservationists and preservationists were concerned about the rapid disappearance of natural areas in the United States. However, the two positions clashed in controversies such as the destruction of the Hetch Hetchy Valley in Yosemite National Park in California. In pursuit of his conservationist agenda, Roosevelt set aside millions of acres as protected areas. These included six national parks. In keeping with the progressive reliance on expertise, he appointed the scientifically trained Gifford Pinchot to head government conservation efforts effectively.

THE ADMINISTRATION OF WILLIAM HOWARD TAFT

After Roosevelt's nearly two terms in office, he picked his secretary of war, William Howard Taft, to succeed him. Taft readily won the nomination of the Republican Party and defeated the Democratic candidate, William Jennings Bryan, in the election in 1908.

Progressives were repeatedly disappointed by Taft. Taft was not an adroit politician and failed to develop a base of support. He agreed to higher tariff rates by signing the Payne-Aldrich Tariff into law (1909), despite the progressive goal of lowering tariff rates to reduce consumer prices. He also ended up firing Gifford Pinchot after Pinchot's clashes with Taft's development-minded Secretary of the Interior Richard Ballinger. Taft did pursue antitrust suits, even though his public rhetoric did not emphasize this. He initiated 90 antitrust cases, including a major case against U.S. Steel.

Taft, Roosevelt, and the Election of 1912

Roosevelt came to regret his decision to throw his support behind Taft. After 1910, a wide rift developed within the Republican Party between Taft and Roosevelt. By 1912, this rift became a civil war within the party. Roosevelt and his supporters walked out of the Republican Party nominating convention in 1912 after the party nominated Taft to run for reelection. Roosevelt and his loyalists founded the Progressive Party (more commonly known by its nickname, the Bull Moose party), and nominated Roosevelt to run as a third-party candidate in the general election. The election was further complicated by the candidacy of Eugene V. Debs of the Socialist Party (see below). The split within the Republican Party allowed the Democratic Party candidate, Woodrow Wilson, to win the presidency. He won the majority of the electoral votes, despite winning only 41 percent of the popular vote. Roosevelt won 27 percent of the popular vote, Taft won 23 percent, and Debs won 6 percent.

PROGRESSIVISM AND WOODROW WILSON

Woodrow Wilson was an anomaly in the White House. He was only the second Democrat to serve since Andrew Johnson (1865–1869). Republicans had repeatedly "waved the bloody shirt"—alluded to the role of the Democratic Party in the Civil War—and won several close presidential elections during the Gilded Age. Wilson was also the first southerner to occupy the White House since 1844 (he was from Virginia). Wilson was an historian and a scholar. He had been the governor of New Jersey and the president of Princeton University before assuming the presidency. He is noted as a man of convictions with a stubborn streak. Wilson had an established track record as a progressive reformer when he entered the White House.

Wilson and the Federal Reserve Act

President Wilson grew increasingly suspicious of the banking industry. He believed that it was inflexible and in the service of the stock market more than in the service of the American public. To rectify this situation, he pushed for passage of the Federal Reserve Act, which created the Federal Reserve Bank (the Fed) in 1913. The Federal Reserve Bank is a national bank that is partly privately controlled and partly government controlled. One of its main functions is to regulate economic growth. Its policies can expand or contract the currency supply. If the economy is sluggish, the Fed will attempt to stimulate economic growth by expanding the amount of currency in circulation. If inflation occurs, the Fed will attempt to slow down economic activity by contracting the currency supply. An important mechanism for regulating economic growth is raising or lowering the interest rate at which the Fed loans money to other banks. Other banks follow suit, raising or lowering the interest rates at which they loan money to the public. For example, by lowering interest rates, the Fed stimulates economic activity by making it more attractive for people to make major purchases.

Regulation of Business

Wilson was a strong supporter of small business and took a dim view of the growing power of big business. He readily took on the mantle of regulation of big business that had been central to the agenda of the progressive movement from its inception. Progressives had become increasingly alarmed at the power of unregulated business during the era of rapid industrialization in the late nineteenth century. In 1890, the Sherman Antitrust Act had been passed but was used with limited success. Wilson strengthened the antitrust powers of the federal government with the Clayton Antitrust Act (1914). A key difference in the new act is that it specifically exempted labor unions from being targeted by antitrust actions. The Sherman Antitrust Act had often been used to break up strikes.

Wilson also pushed for the creation of the Federal Trade Commission (1914) to regulate business practices. Among the regulatory responsibilities of the commission is reducing the power of trusts. Another is guarding against unfair trade practices.

THE LIMITS OF PROGRESSIVE REFORM

The progressive movement put forth many innovative ideas in regard to improving society and was able to enact important legislation. However, many working-class Americans felt the movement did not go far enough; they turned to more radical solutions. Finally, the movement turned a blind eye to one of the gravest problems of twentieth-century America—white supremacy and the legal separation of the races.

Radical Alternatives

To some Americans, the progressive movement was more interested in placing bandages on difficult problems, not in looking at the fundamental dynamics of an industrial capitalist society. In the first decades of the twentieth century, several important groups and parties developed with a more radical agenda. These groups both reacted to the limited nature of the progressive agenda and, ultimately, made some of the progressive's initiatives seem more palatable to mainstream Americans.

The Persistence of White Supremacy

The one major injustice in the United States that the progressive movement largely ignored was the plight of African Americans. Since the end of Reconstruction (1877), southern states had passed a series of Jim Crow laws, segregating African Americans from whites in public facilities. Further, voting laws and intimidation had virtually excluded African Americans from voting, despite passage of the Fifteenth Amendment (1870). Violence by the Ku Klux Klan and others had become the backdrop to life in the South for African Americans.

African-American activists attempted to put the issue of race and racism on the national agenda. Ida B. Wells was a journalist who meticulously documented the extent of lynching in the United States and campaigned for civil rights for African Americans. W. E. B. Du Bois was a militant civil rights activist who wrote about the injustices carried out against African Americans in the South. He was one of the founders of National Association for the Advancement of Colored People (NAACP). The NAACP was formed in 1909. The leadership of the organization first met in 1905 on the Canadian side of Niagara Falls, where they formed the Niagara Movement. Du Bois's call for full political equality and civil rights for African Americans was in marked contrast to the more accommodationist approach of Booker T. Washington. Washington encouraged African Americans to gain training in vocational skills. Toward this end, he was selected to be the first leader of the Tuskegee Institute (1881). He argued that confrontation with whites would end badly for African Americans; he counseled cooperation with supportive whites and collective self-improvement.

However, white progressives turned a blind eye toward the plight of African Americans. Progressive President Woodrow Wilson was, in fact, an outspoken racist. He ordered the segregation of government offices, including post offices, throughout the country. His advocacy of white supremacism went even further than contemporary social attitudes. He praised the racist film *Birth of A Nation* (1916) by D. W. Griffith, with its positive portrayal of the Ku Klux Klan during the Reconstruction period.

Subject to Debate

For much of the twentieth century, the progressive movement was treated quite favorably by historians. Historians generally accepted the self-descriptions of the progressive movement—that it was a movement devoted to eliminating corruption, inefficiencies, inequalities of wealth, and unhealthy working and living conditions. It would be hard to find fault with such a movement, especially because a large percentage of historians would probably consider themselves progressive and would probably share many of the same ideas about society that members of the progressive movement did. However by the 1960s, we begin to see questions being raised about the movement.

Some historians argue that the progressive movement did not pose a serious challenge to the profitability of business. They contend that much of the impetus to reform business either originated with the business community or was shaped by it. Members of the business community were interested in reigning in the worst elements of the business world. The example of the meat-packing industry demonstrates this point well. After the publication of *The Jungle*, the public's confidence in the entire industry declined. Industry leaders wanted to reform their world—rationalize and standardize it—so that people would continue to buy meat. Rather than resisting reform, industry leaders initiated it in order to save their industry.

A second avenue of critique of the movement had to do with the attitude of the progressive movement toward the poor. This critique painted the progressive movement as elitist and condescending toward the working class it was trying to help. The movement was ready to impose its idea of proper behavior on others. This is most evident in the prohibition movement, middle-class activists telling working-class people that they shouldn't drink. The crusade against "immoral" behavior—gambling, prostitution, and smoking—also raises this issue of elitism. The nature of reform movements in general continues to divide historians.

Practice Multiple-Choice Questions:

Directions: Pick the letter that best answers the following questions.

1. One issue that the progressive movement failed to address was
   (A) the power of trusts.
   (B) the unhygienic processing of meat.
   (C) political corruption.
   (D) the segregation of the races in public facilities.
   (E) the problems of democratic participation.

2. What is the main point of the cartoon shown above?
   (A) The government should extend funding to child-care facilities to enable women to enter the workplace.
   (B) Parents should use traditional methods of child-rearing in order to instill discipline and good behavior in the next generation.
   (C) Granting women the right to vote would have the effect of upending traditional gender roles in families.
   (D) Immigrant families should practice birth-control to reduce family size.
   (E) Women should be granted the right to vote because they had gained equal stature in the business world.

3. The publication of *The Jungle*, by Upton Sinclair, contributed to rapid passage of the
   (A) Pure Food and Drug Act.
   (B) Interstate Commerce Act.
   (C) Federal Trade Commission.
   (D) Fifteenth Amendment.
   (E) Clayton Antitrust Act.

4. The adoption of the Australian ballot and the ratification of the Seventeenth Amendment to the U.S. Constitution could both be seen as attempts to
   (A) right the wrongs of racism by extending voting rights to African Americans.
   (B) limit the influence of German Americans in the political process during World War I.
   (C) include women in the political process.
   (D) check the power of big business.
   (E) make the American political system more democratic.

Practice Free-Response Questions:

1. Assess the relationship between progressive reform and the working class.

2. To what degree was the progressive movement successful in reforming American society?

Answers and Explanations to Multiple-Choice Questions:

1. **(D)** The progressive movement did not the address the issues that we might expect a progressive movement to address—racism and segregation. Many members of the progressive movement shared many of the racial prejudices of the public at large. African-Americans activists, such as Booker T. Washington, W. E. B. Du Bois, and Ida B. Wells, addressed the issue of Jim Crow segregation, but white activists were largely silent.
2. **(C)** The cartoon is opposed to granting women the right to vote. The implication is that if women gain the right to vote, traditional gender roles would be rendered obsolete. The woman in this cartoon is ignoring her role as mother and homemaker. The father, emasculated, is forced to deal with crying children. The cartoonist is arguing for maintaining traditional gender roles.
3. **(A)** The publication of *The Jungle* contributed to passage of the Pure Food and Drug Act (1906). *The Jungle* exposed the public to the horrors of the meatpacking industry. The public then demanded that the government take action to rectify the situation.
4. **(E)** Both moves were intended to enhance democracy. The progressives were challenging the power of corrupt machine politicians and putting power in the hands of ordinary people. The Seventeenth Amendment called for the direct election of senators. The Australian ballot is a secret ballot.

The United States and World War I, 1914–1920

CHAPTER 22

TIMELINE	
1914	The beginning of World War I
1917	The Espionage Act
1918	The Sedition Act
	Armistice ends World War I
1919	The creation of the Comintern
	The deportation of Emma Goldman
	Schenck v. *United States*
	The Seattle General Strike
1919–1920	The Boston Police Strike
1920	The height of the Palmer raids
	Ratification of the Nineteenth Amendment (women's right to vote)

When the Great War, later known as World War I, began in Europe in August 1914, most Americans were not eager to join the conflict. The war seemed to be a continuation of the age-old rivalries of the European nations. As the conflict dragged on, a number of factors pushed America toward intervention. In addition the war ushered in some important domestic changes. Culturally, the country became more jingoistic and conservative; the war saw the last gasp of the progressive era. The war expanded the role of the federal government, and it contributed to the Great Migration of African Americans. On the world stage, American participation in the war strengthened the position of the United States, even though it withdrew into isolationism in the years following the war.

THE WORLD AT WAR

Historians cite several factors that created an unstable—even dangerous—situation in prewar Europe. History teachers often graphically represent these factors as sticks of dynamite. The sticks in such a drawing are labeled nationalism, imperialism, militarism, and the alliance system. By the end of the nineteenth century, one can certainly see a rise in nationalism among the European powers. The nations of Europe began to see themselves as actors in a Darwinian struggle to be the "fittest." Inexpensive newspapers and rising literacy rates allowed for the dissemination of patriotic sentiments to an entire nation. This sense of nationalism was fueled by a competition to imperialize the remaining independent areas of Asia and Africa. A scramble occurred among the major powers, setting the stage for tensions and conflict. The situation was made more dangerous by an ominous arms buildup among the European nations, especially the rival nations of Great Britain and Germany. The two nations built larger and larger warships, including Great Britain's HMS *Dreadnought*, which ushered in an era of similarly massive battleships. Finally, the situation was made more volatile by a series of alliances that guaranteed that any conflict between two belligerents would soon degenerate into a broad conflagration as mutual defense treaties would drag more nations into the conflict.

If the long-term causes of World War I are presented as sticks of dynamite, the fuse would be the assassination of the heir to the throne of the Austro-Hungarian Empire, Archduke Franz Ferdinand. The archduke was assassinated by a Pan-Slavic nationalist while visiting the city of Sarajevo, in Bosnia, part of Austria-Hungary. The assassination resulted in Austria-Hungary declaring war on Serbia. The alliance system brought Germany into the conflict on the side of Austria-Hungary. Russia, and then France and Great Britain, were brought into the conflict on the opposing side. As the war began, Russia, France, and Great Britain were known as the Triple Entente. By the time the United States joined the war effort in 1917, this side was known as the Allied Powers. Austria-Hungary, Germany, and Italy were known as the Triple Alliance as the war began. Over time, Germany, Austria-Hungary, and their allies came to be known as the Central Powers. The conflict would last four years and result in the deaths of an astounding 8.5 million soldiers.

Understanding Neutrality
Be familiar with the variety of social, economic, political, and historical factors that contributed to United States neutrality during the first years of World War I.

UNITED STATES NEUTRALITY

The United States initially assumed that it could stay neutral in World War I. Several factors kept the United States neutral in the war for its first three years. The United States, from the time of Washington's Farewell Address, has attempted to stay aloof from the ongoing conflicts of Europe. This has not always been easy. The United States got into wars with Great Britain at the beginning of the nineteenth century (1812,) and with Spain at the end of it (1898). Both of these wars, however, were fought in the Americas (and in Asia in the case of the Spanish-American War), not in Europe. Isolationism in regard to European affairs remained strong. Neutrality also allowed the United States to trade with both sides during the conflict.

Immigration Patterns

Immigration patterns did not immediately predispose the United States toward support for either side in World War I. The United States was home to millions of people who were from the belligerent nations on both sides of the conflict. On the one hand, German and Irish immigrants tended to favor the Central Powers.

Progressives and the War

Progressives, such as John Dewey, were initially very leery about American involvement in the war. They predicted that participation in a major war would distract the nation from domestic reform and would unleash a jingoistic fervor that would result in a conservative shift in the United States.

FROM NEUTRALITY TO INTERVENTION

Although several factors initially kept America out of World War I, important developments propelled the United States toward intervention.

Trade with Great Britain

President Wilson emphasized the principle of freedom of the seas. Wilson indicated that the United States would trade and sell weaponry to either side in the conflict, but Great Britain had effectively blockaded Germany. Trade therefore shifted to Great Britain as the war progressed. Between the start of the war in 1914 and 1917, U.S. trade with Britain increased by 300 percent, while trade with Germany shrank to almost nothing.

Germany responded by warning that U.S. ships in the waters off of Great Britain would be subject to attack by U-boats, or submarines. The sinking of the British ocean liner *Lusitania* infuriated many Americans (128 Americans were among the dead). Germany, however, wanted to keep the United States out of the war and agreed in the Sussex Pledge (1916) to make no surprise submarine attacks on U.S. ships. The United States took advantage of this pledge and traded extensively with Great Britain, much to the consternation of Germany.

Wilson, Public Opinion, and the War

As the war dragged on in Europe, public opinion began to shift toward the Allied Powers. This was partly brought about by wartime news coverage, which tended to present Germany as aggressive and even barbaric in its execution of the war. Also, the Allied Powers seemed to be more clearly the democratic side of the war after Czarist Russia was no longer part of the alliance. (The Czar was toppled in February 1917, and soon after Russia withdrew from the war.) Wilson's approach to the conflict changed rapidly. During his reelection campaign in 1916, he repeatedly reminded voters that he "kept us out of war." After his reelection, Wilson became increasingly convinced that United States participation in World War I was necessary to make the world "safe for democracy."

Wilson's shift to a prowar stance divided Americans. Some joined Wilson on his intellectual journey. They too began to think of participation in the war as an idealistic crusade to create a new world order based on peace and autonomy. However, many opposed the drive for war. The government went to great lengths to alter public opinion in regard to the war (see below).

The Zimmermann Note and Unrestricted German Submarine Warfare

Many Americans moved toward a prowar position after the secret Zimmermann Note became public. The intercepted telegram from German Foreign Secretary Arthur Zimmermann indicated that Germany would help Mexico regain territory it had lost to the United States if Mexico joined the war on Germany's side. Americans took this as a threat to their territory.

Finally in early 1917, Germany announced that it would rescind the Sussex Pledge and that it would resume unrestricted submarine warfare against Great Britain and its allies, including the United States. In February and March of 1917, hundreds of American ships were sunk by German submarine attacks. This proved to be the final straw for the United States. In April 1917, the United States declared war on Germany.

THE UNITED STATES AT WAR

The United States entered the war late in the game. It provided the allied countries—Great Britain and France—with much-needed support. France and Great Britain had been at war for nearly three years when the United States joined the conflict. The 2 million soldiers of the American Expeditionary Force that the United States provided proved to be crucial in the allied victory. By the time the United States had entered the war, the war had bogged down into a brutal stalemate. Both sides had dug themselves into trenches, separated by a strip of no-man's land. One side might attempt a frontal attack on the other. As soon as the soldiers were ordered out of their trench, however, they would be subjected to machine gun fire, barbed wire, and poison gas attacks. Perhaps one side or the other would capture a few miles of desolate land only to be subsequently pushed back. The Battle of the Somme (1916), for example, resulted in over a million casualties and no substantial gains for either side.

TIP 

Lack of Volunteers
The tepid response to President Wilson's call to join the military reflects the mixed feelings Americans had about the war.

Filling the Ranks of the Military

Thousands of men volunteered to join the military, but the volunteers fell far short of American goals. Therefore, the government passed the Selective Service Act (1917) to organize a draft of American men.

African-American Troops

African-American troops were organized into the 92nd Division. The commander of the American forces, Major General John Pershing, allowed these American troops to fight under French auspices; he wanted his white troops to fight only under American command. African-American troops fought side by side with French troops for over six months. The 369th Regiment of the 92nd Division was the most decorated American combat unit of the war.

Allied Victory

American forces under American command did not see action until 1918. In June, American forces saw action at Chateau-Thierry on the Marne River in France, helping to halt the last major offensive by Germany. Throughout the summer and into the fall, Americans participated in driving the German army back toward the German border, especially at St. Mihiel. The exhausted German army surrendered and signed an armistice on November 11, 1918, ending World War I. American troops were engaged in combat for only the last battles of the war but lost over 100,000 men in the battlefield and to disease. Over 8.5 million soldiers in total died.

THE WAR AT HOME

American participation in World War I impacted the America home front in significant ways. President Wilson ushered in an era of expanded government power. He created several agencies to handle different aspects of the war effort. These new agencies pleased progressive advocates of a more activist government. The war also resulted in the unprecedented migration of African Americans out of the rural South, and it challenged traditional notions of gender. The war created an environment conducive to sweeping reform. The Eighteenth Amendment called for the prohibition of the consumption, production, and sale of alcoholic beverages in the United States (see Chapter 23). The Nineteenth Amendment allowed women to vote.

Shaping Public Opinion

TIP

World War I and Modern Advertising
The campaign organized by the Committee on Public Information could be considered one of the first major national advertising campaigns in United States history.

The government created the Committee on Public Information (CPI) to organize prowar propaganda. It was led by George Creel, a former muckraking journalist. The CPI sent Four-Minute Men around the country to give brief, impassioned speeches in favor of the war effort to schools, civic groups, churches, and any gathering that would have them. The CPI also produced a series of evocative posters to convince Americans to support the war. Several of these posters specifically targeted the supposed brutal actions of German soldiers, often labeling them as "Huns," a derogatory term that alludes to the Germanic tribes of the ancient world that attacked Rome. One of the posters, created by the American artist and illustrator James Montgomery Flagg, featured the image of Uncle Sam pointing directly at the viewer of the poster with the famous tag line "I Want You for U.S. Army."

Civil Liberties During Wartime

The various measures to reshape public opinion during the war certainly had an impact, but the government still felt the need to enact restrictive measures to force

Americans into compliance. The Espionage and Sedition Acts were passed during World War I to put limits on public expressions of antiwar sentiment. The Espionage Act (1917) along with the Sedition Act (1918) made it a crime to interfere with the draft or with the sale of war bonds as well as to say anything "disloyal" in regard to the war effort.

TIP

Civil Liberties in Comparison
The debate over civil liberties during wartime is an ongoing issue. Be prepared to compare restrictions on civil liberties in the context of the quasi-war with France, the Civil War, World War I, World War II, and even the current war on terrorism.

These acts were upheld by the Supreme Court in the decision in *Schenck* v. *United States* (1919). Charles Schenck and other members of the Socialist Party had been arrested for printing and distributing flyers opposing the war and urging young men to resist the draft. The Supreme Court argued that freedom of speech is not absolute and that the government is justified in limiting certain forms of speech during wartime. The court argued that certain utterances pose a "clear and present danger." By analogy, the court reasoned that one is not allowed to falsely shout "Fire!" in a crowded theater.

Federal Agencies and War Production

The War Industries Board was created by the government to direct industrial production. The agency was led by Bernard Baruch. He sought to bring together labor and management in order to ensure uninterrupted production of armaments, uniforms, and other needed items. The Food Administration, with future president Herbert Hoover at the helm, was created to ensure sufficient food production to feed the troops as well as the civilian population. The National War Labor Board dealt with labor disputes. This constellation of government agencies was exactly what progressive reformers hoped to create on a permanent basis.

TIP

World War I and the New Deal
While the constellation of wartime agencies were disbanded after the war, a similar set of agencies was created by President Franklin Roosevelt as part of his New Deal during the Great Depression.

Women and the War

The war presented unprecedented opportunities for women. Over 25,000 women served in Europe as nurses and ambulance drivers. Back home, over a million women found employment in war-related industries.

Woman Suffrage

The opportunities afforded women during World War I encouraged many activists to push for the right of women to vote. This demand had been raised at the Seneca Falls Convention (1848). After the Civil War, two organizations emerged—the American Woman Suffrage Association and the National Woman Suffrage Association. The two groups grew out of disagreements within the movement over the Fifteenth Amendment. In 1890, the groups merged as the National American Woman Suffrage Association. In 1917, the National Woman's Party emerged.

Suffragists won voting rights for women in several of the states by the turn of the twentieth century, but women were still prohibited from participating in national elections. Most western states granted women suffrage prior to adoption of a constitutional amendment. Life on the western frontier demanded great physical efforts by both men and women. This equality of effort, historians argue, often translated into a rough political equality. Wyoming granted women full voting rights in 1869, Utah in 1870, Colorado in 1893, and Idaho in 1896. Suffragists urged the president and political leaders to push for an amendment to the United States Constitution guaranteeing women the right to vote. In 1913, women held a suffrage parade to publicize their cause. However, it was not until the war that the movement fully got the ear of President Wilson. The suffrage movement was successful in achieving its goal with the ratification of the Nineteenth Amendment to the Constitution in 1920.

The Great Migration

The needs of industry for labor during World War I led to the Great Migration of African Americans out of the South, which lasted from the 1910s until the onset of the Great Depression. (A second wave of the migration occurred during and after World War II.) There are several important reasons for the migration of African Americans from the rural South to the urban North. A basic factor was the mistreatment that African Americans received in the South. White southerners created a series of Jim Crow laws that separated African Americans from whites in schools, buses, trains, and other facilities. A rigid system of segregation persisted in the South well into the twentieth century and constantly reminded African Americans of their second-class statue. In addition, African Americans were excluded from the political system in the South. A series of obstacles, such as literacy tests and poll taxes, limited their ability to vote. Further, economic conditions for African Americans worsened in the South during the 1910s and 1920s due to a devastating infestation of the cotton crop by the boll weevil.

The main factor that drew African Americans north was jobs. By the turn of the twentieth century, the industrial revolution was in full swing in northern cities such as New York and Chicago. Factories using new mass production techniques were able, at first, to fill the jobs with local people and European immigrants. However, World War I created a labor crisis for these factories. Factories were producing goods around the clock. Even before the United States entered the war in 1917, American factories were producing war goods for Great Britain. After entering the war, demand for these goods increased. In addition, European immigration to the United States dropped significantly due to the war. Millions of potential factory hands were also pressed into the U.S. military. Factory agents from the North frequently made recruiting trips to the South, offering immediate employment and free passage to the North.

THE UNITED STATES AND THE POSTWAR WORLD

President Wilson was determined to shape the structure of the postwar world. He felt strongly that the causes of war should be identified, addressed, and alleviated.

Wilson's Fourteen Points

Wilson put forth a document, known as the Fourteen Points (1918), that emphasized international cooperation. He envisioned a world order based on freedom of the seas, removal of barriers to trade, self-determination for European people, and an international organization to resolve conflicts. These ideas were rejected by the victorious European powers except for the creation of the League of Nations.

United States Rejection of the Treaty of Versailles

Ironically, the United States did not end up joining the League of Nations. This international body was the one component of President Wilson's Fourteen Points document that was embraced by the victorious European nations. The United States would have had to approve the Treaty of Versailles in order to join the League. Despite Wilson's enthusiasm for passage of the treaty, some senators wanted to isolate the United States from world affairs and opposed membership in the league. These isolationists, led by Senator Henry Cabot Lodge of Massachusetts, announced that they would vote to reject the treaty. Some senators took a middle position. They would agree to vote to approve the treaty if the senate put certain conditions on U.S. participation in the League of Nations. Wilson refused to compromise with these senators and urged his allies in the Senate to reject any conditions. Without these senators in the middle, the Treaty of Versailles was rejected by the Senate.

POSTWAR SOCIETY

The early predictions by progressive thinkers that participation in World War I would derail domestic reform efforts and create a conservative backlash against the progressive movement proved to be accurate. A postwar wave of strikes and a general fear of things foreign led to the Red scare. Conservative and isolationist politicians came to dominate political discourse throughout the following decade (see Chapter 23). The aftermath of the war also led to the worst disease pandemic in the world and in American history as well as an epidemic of racial violence.

The Spanish Flu

Peacetime brought a major influenza pandemic to the United States. The disease was brought to the United States by returning soldiers. The Spanish flu was a global pandemic, accounting for 22 million deaths—the most of any disease, famine, war, or natural disaster in world history. In the United States, the toll was 675,000, more than six times the number of American combat deaths in World War I.

The Wave of Strikes in 1919

When World War I ended, the government disbanded the agencies that it had created to regulate economic activity during the war. For instance, workers no longer had the protections of the National War Labor Board. In addition, inflation was no longer kept in check by the government. In 1919, prices roses nearly 75 percent. In these conditions, workers across America organized and fought to protect wartime gains. The year 1919 saw the biggest wave of strikes in American history. There were over 4,500 strikes, involving 4 million workers. The biggest strike was the Seattle General Strike in February. The radical Industrial Workers of the World and the more moderate American Federation of Labor (AFL) worked together to virtually close down Seattle. In September, over 340,000 steelworkers went on strike. Late in 1919 and into 1920, the police force in Boston went on strike. In all three of the strikes and in countless others, the workers were defeated. In many cases, management was able to paint the striking workers as would-be Bolsheviks. It was not until the New Deal Era of the 1930s that the labor movement was able to regain momentum.

The Red Scare

The backlash against the wave of strikes in 1919 combined with the virulent strain of patriotism unleashed by World War I set the groundwork for the Red scare of the late 1910s and early 1920s, a crusade against suspected communists, anarchists, labor leaders, and other radicals. The Red scare was both a grassroots sentiment expressed by ordinary Americans as well as a government-orchestrated campaign. The movement can be traced to the successful Bolshevik revolution in Russia that brought the Communist Party to power and led to the establishment of the Soviet Union. In 1919, the Bolsheviks created the Comintern, an international organization of Communist Party leaders determined to duplicate the success of the Bolsheviks in other countries. Conservative Americans took the pronouncements of the Comintern at face value, even though the Communist movement in the United States was extremely small.

In December 1919, Russian-born anarchist and activist Emma Goldman was deported by the Justice Department. In January 1920, Attorney General A. Mitchell Palmer began a broad hunt for suspected radicals. Palmer's Justice Department carried out unwarranted raids, known as Palmer raids, of suspected radicals' homes. Palmer's men identified 6,000 alleged radicals. Although Palmer did not uncover the makings of an uprising, he did end up deporting over 500 noncitizens. The movement spread to the local level as radical newspapers were shut down, libraries were purged of radical books, and even elected officials were removed from office. The Supreme Court decision in *Schenck* v. *United States*, which established the "clear and present danger" guideline for limiting free speech, gave cover to such excesses (see above). Soon Americans began to question the aggressive tactics of Palmer, but suspicions of "Reds" persisted throughout the 1920s.

Racial Violence

The postwar period saw a spike in racial violence. There were at least 25 significant race riots in 1919 alone. This racial antagonism was, in part, an offshoot of the reactionary political backlash against progressivism following the war. The tensions can also be connected to the fact that African Americans had been relocating to northern cities throughout the war. In July, a riot against African Americans occurred in Washington, D.C. An even more violent riot in Chicago left 38 people dead and over 500 injured. Racial violence also occurred in the South, including in Longview, Texas, and Elaine, Arkansas.

Subject to Debate

World War I often gets relegated to the back seat in standard history curricula to World War II. World War II is imbued with a sense of mission—it was a "good fight" carried out by the "greatest generation." On the mall in Washington, D.C., a new, large World War II memorial occupies a prominent place between the Washington Monument and the Lincoln Memorial. The World War I monument, by contrast, is a modest gazebo tucked away to the side of the mall. It is not even a national monument—it commemorates local residents who perished in the conflict. One reason World War I has been ignored is that there isn't a clearly identifiable evil that the United States was trying to stop. The history of World War I does not read like a morality play.

That said, it would be unwise for a student preparing for the AP exam to ignore World War I. There are several crucial questions to consider. For instance, how do we account for the fact that the American political landscape completely changed from the beginning of the war to the end of the war? In 1914 on the eve of the war, the progressive movement was enjoying its heyday. In 1919 as the war ended, America had become violently conservative. The Red scare was paving the way for the rise of the Ku Klux Klan, restrictions on immigration, and attacks on secularism. Students should be cognizant of the role that war plays in changing the political climate.

Practice Multiple-Choice Questions:

Directions: Pick the letter that best answers the following questions.

1. The War Industries Board, the Committee on Public Information, and the Espionage and Sedition Acts are similar in that they all
   (A) were attempts to silence opposition to World War I.
   (B) reflect the expanded power of the federal government during World War I.
   (C) failed to achieve their stated goals.
   (D) were welcomed by organized labor.
   (E) continued to exist beyond World War I and were incorporated into the New Deal.

2. The 1917 cartoon shown above is making the point that
   - (A) Americans should collectively cheer for the American troops going "over there" to participate in World War I.
   - (B) a coalition of powerful forces in American society is unwisely pushing the United States to enter World War I.
   - (C) prohibition laws are allowing politicians and organized-crime figures to make huge profits.
   - (D) factory owners and political figures are working together to prevent unions from winning decent wages for their members.
   - (E) President Wilson's stated reasons for joining the League of Nations are not his actual reasons.

3. Which of the following is <u>not</u> true of Wilson's Fourteen Points speech?
   - (A) It encouraged the reduction of military arms.
   - (B) It encouraged the maintenance of wartime alliances.
   - (C) It called for the establishment of an international peacekeeping organization.
   - (D) It called for a reduction and eventual elimination of tariffs.
   - (E) It called for a fair settlement of colonial claims.

4. In the case of *Schenck* v. *the U.S.*, the Supreme Court

   (A) invalidated the War Industries Board as
   (B) expanded the constitutional rights of people within the U.S. empire.
   (C) upheld the legality of the Pure Food and Drug Act to regulate private industry.
   (D) restricted speech that presented a "clear and present danger."
   (E) struck down segregation in the armed forces.

Practice Free-Response Questions:

1. Assess the attitude of the progressive movement toward World War I (before, during, and after the war).

2. Analyze TWO of the following presidents in regard to the expansion of federal power:

   Andrew Jackson
   Abraham Lincoln
   Woodrow Wilson

Answers and Explanations to Multiple-Choice Questions:

1. **(B)** The three agencies all reflect an expanded role for the federal government. This activist government was exactly what some progressive reformers were hoping for. Ironically, the patriotic fervor of World War I crushed the progressive spirit of reform.

2. **(E)** The cartoon reflects an isolationist stance. It is implying that powerful institutions in American society—the news media, business interests, corrupt political bosses, and even the church—were pressuring America to get involved in World War I. The stated reasons for intervention, such as making the world "safe for democracy," are not the actual reason for intervention. The figures in the cartoon toss those altruistic reasons aside. The actual reason is greed. War will benefit the wealthy.

3. **(B)** All of the choices are part of Wilson's Fourteen Points speech except choice B. The alliance system was one of the reasons World War I occurred. All of the mutual defense agreements among the world powers turned a local conflict into a global one. In place of the alliance system, Wilson proposed an international peacekeeping body—a League of Nations.

4. **(D)** The decision in *Schenck* v. *United States* upheld the Espionage and Sedition Acts, passed during World War I to limit public expressions of anti-war sentiment. Charles Schenck had been arrested for printing and distributing flyers opposing the war and urging young men to resist the draft. The Supreme Court argued that the government is justified in limiting certain forms of speech during wartime. The court argued that certain words pose a "clear and present danger."

CHAPTER 23

Tradition and Modernity in the 1920s

TIMELINE

1913	Henry Ford introduces the conveyor belt to automobile production
1919	Ratification of the 18th Amendment (prohibition)
1920	Election of Warren G. Harding
1921	Emergency Quota Act
	Beginning of the Teapot Dome Scandal
1924	National Origins Act
	Election of Calvin Coolidge
1925	Scopes Trial
1927	Execution of Sacco and Vanzetti
1928	Election of Herbert Hoover
1933	Ratification of the 21st Amendment (repeal of prohibition)

During the 1920s, we see the development of some of the cultural divisions that have roiled Americans since that time. Many historians note the resurgence of traditional values in the United States in response to the unfolding of a more modern America. This tension between tradition and modernity has shaped much of the historical work on the 1920s. Not all the elements of the 1920s fit neatly into this model of tradition versus modernity. The experiment in prohibition comes to mind. Its origins were both in the Progressive movement's push for government-sponsored social engineering as well as in the religious crusade to eradicate "immoral" habits. Still, the tradition-versus-modernity model is a useful lens through which to examine the 1920s.

THE CONSERVATISM OF THE 1920s

In many ways, the 1920s was a conservative decade. The aftermath of World War I unleashed the Red scare against suspected radicals and labor activists (see Chapter 22). The conservative impulses of the postwar period continued into the 1920s. Key elements of the decade included a strong fundamentalist Christian movement, anti-immigrant legislation, a large and active Ku Klux Klan, and a resurgence of rural, traditional values. Not all Americans subscribed to these conservative values, but these values shaped public debates in the 1920s and propelled three conservative Republicans into the White House.

Anti-Immigrant Sentiment and the Quota System

Nativism, or opposition to immigration, rose steeply in the years after World War I. This nativist impulse led to the passage of the Emergency Quota Act (1921) and the National Origins Act (1924). These acts greatly reduced the number of immigrants allowed into the United States. A large wave of immigrants from southern and eastern Europe had arrived in the United States between 1880 and 1920. Nativists resented this new wave of immigration for several reasons. Some nativists focused on the fact that most of the new immigrants were not Protestant. Poles and Italians tended to be Catholic, Russians and Greeks tended to be Eastern Orthodox, and Jews came from several countries in eastern Europe. Some nativists objected to the cacophony of languages heard on the streets of New York or Chicago. Some Americans were anti-European after the trauma of World War I. Some nativists associated the immigrants with either radical movements or drunkenness. Finally, working-class people feared that low-wage immigrant laborers would take jobs from native-born American workers.

The Trial of Sacco and Vanzetti

The trial of Nicola Sacco and Bartolomeo Vanzetti for robbery and murder illustrated the intolerance that many Americans had toward immigrants and toward radicals in the 1920s. The two men were accused of robbing and killing a payroll clerk in Massachusetts in 1920. The evidence against them was sketchy. The judge was openly hostile to the two men, who were not only immigrants but were also anarchists. After they were found guilty, many Americans protested the verdict and wondered if an immigrant, especially with radical ideas, could get a fair trial in the United States. Despite protests, the two men were executed in 1927.

The Resurgence of the Ku Klux Klan

The original Ku Klux Klan, a violent, racist group with its roots in the immediate aftermath of the Civil War, had died out by the 1870s. In 1915, a new Ku Klux Klan was born. Part of the inspiration for the new Klan was the movie *Birth of a Nation* (also 1915), which depicted the original Klan in a heroic light. The organization was a genuine mass movement. By 1925, it grew to 3 million members by its own estimates. The Klan was devoted to white supremacy and "100 percent Americanism."

The Experiment in Prohibition

The movement to ban alcohol from American society was one of the largest movements in the nineteenth century. It finally achieved success in 1919 when prohibition became national policy with the ratification of the Eighteenth Amendment to the Constitution. The amendment called for a ban on the manufacture, sale, and transportation of alcoholic beverages. The temperance movement was especially popular among women. The movement complimented the growing nativist, or anti-immigrant, movement. Nativists thought that the new immigrants, who were mostly non-Protestant, lacked the self-control of "proper," middle-class Protestant Americans.

The final victory for the temperance movement came as the United States entered World War I. The movement successfully equated the prohibition of alcohol with the quest to bring democracy to the world. The United States would purify the world of undemocratic forces and purify its citizens of corrupting alcohol. Also, with wartime shortages of grain, it made sense to ban grain-based alcoholic beverages. The anti-German sentiment that developed during World War I also played a role because many American breweries had German names. All these factors led to the ratification of the Eighteenth Amendment, which banned alcohol production, sales, and consumption as of January 1920. The victory of the movement proved to be hollow, though. Although the per capita consumption of alcohol went down during the Prohibition era, the amount of lawlessness in America went up. Criminal activity became so widespread that the nation agreed to ratify the Twenty-First Amendment (1933), which repealed Prohibition.

The Scopes Trial

During the 1920s, a large number of Americans, especially in the South, adopted a fundamentalist, literal approach to the Bible and to religion. The Scopes Trial of 1925 illustrated the conflict between Protestant fundamentalism and modern science. The Scopes trial involved the teaching of evolution in public schools. John Scopes, a Tennessee biology teacher, was arrested for violating the Butler Act, a state law forbidding the teaching of evolution. The case turned into a national spectacle, with the famous lawyers Clarence Darrow representing Scopes and William Jennings Bryan representing the state. It is one of several important events that highlighted cultural divisions in the 1920s.

THE ADVENT OF MODERNITY

While the 1920s saw the resurgence of conservative, traditional values in the United States, the decade also witnessed unprecedented technological and cultural changes that ushered in the modern world.

Gender in Flux

The changing image of women during the 1920s was symbolized by the popularity of the flappers and their style of dress. Flappers were independent-minded young women of the 1920s who openly defied Victorian moral codes about "proper" ladylike behavior. The typical flapper of the 1920s was characterized by a short haircut,

Women and Public Life
When traditional history texts discuss women and gender, they often discuss fashion and appearance. In your writing, try to avoid limiting your discussions of gender to these topics.

called a bob, and short dresses. Women of the 1920s also moved away from the heavy, matronly dresses of the Victorian era. However, there was more to the "new" woman of the 1920s than new fashions. The new woman of the 1920s was engaged in public issues. She might have participated in the political struggles of the progressive movement and gained a new sense of confidence in participating in public issues, especially after women achieved the right to vote in 1920.

Radio and the Development of Mass Culture

Radio grew from being virtually nonexistent at the beginning of the decade to becoming an extremely popular medium by the end of it. The medium was begun by amateurs who sent out music or sermons to the few scattered people who had "wireless receivers." Soon, Westinghouse and other corporations saw the potential to reach the masses with radio. By 1923, there were almost 600 licensed radio stations. Early successful programs included *The Amos 'n' Andy Show* (1928), a holdover from "blackface" minstrel shows of the nineteenth century.

Hollywood in the 1920s

Movie attendance achieved staggering levels in the 1920s. By the end of the decade, three-fourths of the American people (roughly 90 million) were going to the movies every week. The first talkie, *The Jazz Singer*, came out in 1927.

The Lost Generation Writers

The Lost Generation literary movement expressed a general disillusionment with American society, commenting on everything from the narrowness of small-town life to the rampant materialism of American society. Several writers were troubled by the destruction and seeming meaninglessness of World War I. *The Great Gatsby* (1925) by F. Scott Fitzgerald exposed the shallowness of the lives of the wealthy and privileged of the era. Sinclair Lewis's novels, such as *Main Street* (1920) and *Babbitt* (1924), mocked the narrowness of the middle class. Ernest Hemingway's *A Farewell to Arms* (1929) critiqued the glorification of war.

The Harlem Renaissance

The Great Migration of African Americans from the rural south to the urban North (see Chapter 22) contributed to the Harlem Renaissance. This was a literary, artistic, and intellectual movement centered in the African-American neighborhood of Harlem, in New York City. A key goal of the movement was to increase pride in African-American culture by celebrating African-American life and forging a new cultural identity among African-American people. Contributions included the poetry of Langston Hughes, Claude McKay, and Countee Cullen and the jazz music of Louis Armstrong, Duke Ellington, and Bessie Smith. Langston Hughes's poems include "Harlem," "The Negro Speaks of Rivers," and "I, Too, Sing America." He wrote an essay that became a manifesto for Harlem Renaissance writers and artists entitled "The Negro Artist and the Racial Mountain." Duke Ellington is perhaps the most important figure in twentieth-century jazz. Some of his most important compositions include "Mood Indigo," "Don't Get Around Much Anymore," and "Take the A Train."

MASS PRODUCTION AND MASS CONSUMPTION

The production and consumption of consumer goods stoked the American economy for much of the 1920s. New products, such as automobiles and radios, captured the public's imagination. New production techniques increased industrial output. Yet by 1927, manufacturers noticed that warehouse inventories were on the rise. Consumption just couldn't keep up with production. Manufacturers made the logical decision of beginning layoffs. Of course, unemployed workers had even less ability to purchase goods. Further, many farmers failed to share in the general prosperity of the 1920s mainly because they received low prices for crops due to overproduction. Farmers had put more acres under cultivation during World War I to meet increased demand for agricultural goods. By the 1920s, Europe was back on its feet, yet American farmers did not cut back on production. Mechanization and expansion left the farmers of the 1920s in a cycle of debt, overproduction, and falling commodity prices. In addition, increased tariff rates and an isolationist foreign policy further reduced the international market for American agricultural goods.

Thus a spiral of economic problems began that resulted in the Great Depression of the 1930s, which will be discussed in Chapter 24.

The De-skilling of the Labor Process
Mass production and assembly line work weakened the position of workers in terms of bargaining for better wages and conditions.

Henry Ford and Mass Production

The most important figure in the development of new production techniques was Henry Ford. In 1913, he opened a plant in Michigan with a continuous conveyor belt. The belt moved the chassis of the car from worker to worker so that each did a small task in the process of assembling the final product. This mass production technique reduced the price of his Model T car and also dealt a blow to the skilled mechanics that previously built automobiles. Unskilled assembly line workers gradually replaced skilled craft workers in American industry.

Scientific Management

An important aspect of mass production was the scientific management techniques developed by Frederick Winslow Taylor. Taylor carefully watched workers, noted the most efficient techniques, and wrote down in exacting detail how a particular task was to be done. Work became more efficient but also more monotonous. (See more on scientific management in Chapter 21.)

Advertising and Mass Consumption

If the quality of work deteriorated for factory workers in the 1920s, the availability of consumer goods to average workers greatly increased. Cars, radios, toasters, health and beauty aids, and other consumer goods filled the shelves of stores. The advertising industry also changed a great deal in the 1920s. Advertising men tapped in the ideas of Freudian psychology to reach the public on a subconscious level. Easy credit and layaway plans also helped move merchandise.

REPUBLICAN DOMINANCE IN THE 1920s

The Republican Party controlled the White House for twelve years, from 1921 to 1933. The presidents of the 1920s, Harding, Coolidge, and Hoover, all tended to pursue pro-business policies. Coolidge once said, "The man who builds a factory, builds a temple."

Warren G. Harding and the "Return to Normalcy"

Harding had been an undistinguished senator from Ohio before he received the Republican nomination for president in 1920. During the campaign, he promised a "return to normalcy," a somewhat bland commitment to move away from the experimentation of the Progressive Era and from the internationalism of World War I.

Teapot Dome Scandal (1921–1923)

Several of Harding's appointees, known as the Ohio Gang, turned out to be unscrupulous figures. His secretary of the interior, Albert Fall, crafted a complicated scheme that involved transferring oil reserves in Teapot Dome, Wyoming, and at another location in California, from the U.S. Navy to the Department of the Interior. Fall then leased the valuable land to two businessmen who, in turn, "loaned" Fall half a million dollars. Harding died of a heart attack in the summer of 1923 before investigations into the scandal began.

The Coolidge Presidency

Harding was succeeded by his vice president, Calvin Coolidge, a former governor of Massachusetts. Coolidge espoused a philosophy of nonintervention in the economy. Coolidge easily won election in 1924, defeating a little-known Democrat as well as the Wisconsin progressive reformer Robert La Follette. In his full term in office, Coolidge spent his time lowing tax rates and blocking congressional initiatives.

The Politics of Isolationism

Isolationist sentiment ran high in the United States. Many Americans were disillusioned about World War I while others had grown resentful of the wave of "new immigrants" that had come to America. The United States remained outside the League of Nations. (See Chapter 22 for information about the rejection of the Treaty of Versailles.)

Tariff Rates in History
Debates about tariff rates have existed throughout American history, from Alexander Hamilton's "Report on Manufactures" (1791) to the passage of the North America Free Trade Agreement (1994). Tariff rates were passionately debated in the nineteenth century.

Higher Tariff Rates

The isolationist Republican presidents of the 1920s enacted higher tariffs to keep out foreign goods. In 1922, the Fordney-McCumber Act dramatically raised tariff rates. In 1930, in the midst of the Great Depression, isolationist legislators pushed through the Smoot-Hawley Tariff Act, which increased tariffs to their second-highest rate in United States history, exceeded only by the Tariff of Abominations (1828).

Washington Conference

The presidents of the 1920s attempted to isolate the United States from world affairs and reduce spending on war munitions. President Harding successfully pressed for a reduction of naval power among Britain, France, Japan, Italy, and the United States at the Washington Disarmament Conference in 1921.

The Kellogg-Briand Pact

The United States was one of 63 nations to sign the Kellogg-Briand Pact, renouncing war in principle. The pact was unenforceable, negotiated outside of the League of Nations, and ultimately meaningless.

Subject to Debate

The decade of the 1920s poses problems for historians in the consensus tradition. Consensus history asserts that there is a broad consensus among Americans around basic ideas and feelings. According to consensus historians, Americans share a belief in democracy and individual liberties, believe that hard work leads to advancement, believe in God but do not try to impose their beliefs on others or on society as a whole, and are a tolerant, welcoming people. Consensus history gained traction in the 1950s. This broad set of ideas set America apart from the Soviet Union—an essentially different system developed by people from an essentially different background. Consensus historians acknowledge that there have been conflicts, but, they argue, these conflicts have not been over essential values.

Consensus historians have a great deal of difficulty explaining the 1920s. Here is a decade in which the Ku Klux Klan claimed to have 3 million members in a country of 100 million people. Even if the membership figures are inflated, the Ku Klux Klan was a huge organization. Three million Americans joined a violent, racist, intolerant, anti-Semitic organization. In addition, there were many cases of German-American residents being beaten in their homes by mobs of Americans in the early 1920s. These violent episodes challenge the assumptions of the consensus historians. Some historians have tried to minimize the importance of these facts or stress the fun of the jazz age. Others have seen the reactionary impulses of the decade as responses to rapid social change. However, the undercurrent of intolerance and violence in the 1920s is difficult to fit into the traditional consensus model of American history.

Practice Multiple-Choice Questions:

Directions: Pick the letter that best answers the following questions.

1. Which candidate ran for the presidency by promising Americans a "return to normalcy?"
   (A) Eugene V. Debs
   (B) Warren G. Harding
   (C) Franklin D. Roosevelt
   (D) Henry Wallace
   (E) John F. Kennedy

2. The Republican presidents of the 1920s tended to
   (A) raise tariffs to keep foreign goods out of the country.
   (B) lower barriers to immigration to allow more workers into the country.
   (C) push for a belligerent foreign policy in regard to the nations of Europe.
   (D) actively pursue antitrust litigation.
   (E) extend public health care to the urban poor.

3. Frederick Winslow Taylor developed a set of ideas that promoted
   (A) the teaching of the theory of evolution in public schools.
   (B) creativity in public school classrooms.
   (C) migration of African Americans from the rural South to the urban North.
   (D) an open-door policy in regard to trade with China
   (E) efficiency at the workplace using time and motion studies.

4. The Teapot Dome scandal involved
   (A) exchanges of gifts between American and Chinese diplomats.
   (B) the selling of government positions to the highest bidder.
   (C) transfers of land with oil reserves in Wyoming.
   (D) spying on political opponents.
   (E) an arms for hostages deal with Mexico.

Practice Free-Response Questions:

1. Describe economic transformations that occurred in both production and consumption in the 1920s.

2. Assess why the Ku Klux Klan became a major organization in the 1920s.

Answers and Explanations to Multiple-Choice Questions:

1. **(B)** Harding's promise of a "return to normalcy" involved a rejection of the experiments of the progressive era as well as a move away from the internationalism of World War I. It was a call to steer the country in a more conservative direction. Apparently the rather bland promise resonated with the public; Harding won the election in 1920.
2. **(A)** High tariff rates were an expression of isolationism. There was sentiment among conservatives to remove the United States from the affairs of Europe. Many isolationists were bitter over the experience of World War I; others were simply suspicious of all things foreign.
3. **(E)** This question deals with the principles of scientific management. Taylor popularized this idea of creating the most-efficient processes at work. Workers resented the intrusion of management into the most minute details of the work process. Scientific management took any skill away from the worker and put it in the hands of management.
4. **(C)** The Teapot Dome Scandal involved financial improprieties related to oil reserves in Wyoming. Although President Harding was not directly involved, it damaged his reputation.

CHAPTER 24

The Great Depression and American Society, 1928–1939

TIMELINE

1928	Herbert Hoover elected President
1929	The stock market crash
	The Great Depression begins
1930	The Hawley-Smoot Tariff
1931	The Marx Brothers' movie *Duck Soup* is released
1932	The Bonus March
	The Reconstruction Finance Corporation is established
	Franklin D. Roosevelt elected president
1933	Prohibition is repealed (Twenty-First Amendment)
1934	Clifford Odets writes the play *Waiting for Lefty*
1936	Charlie Chaplin's *Modern Times* is released
1939	The movie *Mr. Smith Goes to Washington* is released
	John Steinbeck writes *The Grapes of Wrath*

The Great Depression was the most devastating economic downturn in American history. It is one of several downturns in American history—notable ones include the Panics of 1819, 1837, 1857, 1873, and 1893. However, in none of these panics did the country reach the depths of despair that it did during the Great Depression. The Great Depression is a frequent topic on the Advanced Placement exam because it provides an opportunity to introduce economic theory into this history exam. A basic understanding of introductory economic concepts, such as supply and demand, Keynesianism, and the business cycle, will come in handy when answering questions about the Great Depression and responses to it.

CAUSES OF THE GREAT DEPRESSION

The precise reasons for the Great Depression are still debated by historians. However, the following explanations are frequently mentioned.

Overproduction and Underconsumption

Industrial production greatly expanded in the 1920s. New products, such as automobiles and radios, captured the public's imagination. New production techniques, such as the assembly line and scientific management, increased industrial output. For much of the 1920s, the public, induced by easy credit and seductive advertising, was able to absorb this increased industrial output. However, by 1927 manufacturers noticed that warehouse inventories were on the rise. Consumption just couldn't keep up with production. A weak labor movement in the 1920s led to stagnant wages. Ordinary Americans did not share in the economic expansion of the 1920s. The gap between the wealthy and the poor grew. During the 1920s, income for the top 1 percent of the population increased by nearly 75 percent, while the bottom 90 percent of the population saw their income rise by less than 10 percent. By the late 1920s, manufacturers made the logical decision of beginning layoffs, worsening a bad situation.

Problems Down on the Farm

Throughout the 1920s, the agricultural sector lagged behind the rest of the economy. Farmers had put more acres under cultivation during World War I to meet increased demand for agricultural goods. By the 1920s, Europe was back on its feet yet American farmers did not cut back on production. Mechanization and expansion left American farmers of the 1920s in a cycle of debt, overproduction, and falling commodity prices.

Increased tariff rates and an isolationist foreign policy further reduced the international market for American agricultural goods.

TIP

Speculation and the Stock Market
Many accounts of the economy in the 1920s fault the speculative practices of the stock market. Try to avoid an overemphasis on the speculative nature of the 1920s stock market. Speculation is, of course, at the heart of the stock market, then and now.

An Inflated Stock Market

Investing in the stock market is always something of a gamble. In the 1920s, though, people gambled recklessly with other people's money. In the 1920s, people increasingly bought stocks on margin, paying only 10 percent of the purchase price upfront with the promise of paying the remainder in the future. This practice worked as long as stock prices rose, which they did throughout most of the 1920s. By the late 1920s, however, serious investors began to see that stock prices were reaching new heights as the actual earnings of major corporations were declining. This discrepancy between the price per share and the actual earnings of corporations led investors to begin selling stocks, which stimulated a panic. In late October 1929, the stock market crashed, destroying individuals' investments and signaling the beginning of the Great Depression.

THE GREAT DEPRESSION'S IMPACT

Urban Poverty

The Great Depression hit city dwellers especially hard. Between 1929 and 1933, wages fell by 60 percent and unemployment tripled to over 12 million. With no safety net in place, families were forced out of their homes. Most cities had makeshift communities of shacks known derisively as Hoovervilles. People picked through garbage cans for food and formed long lines at soup kitchens. The situation was desperate, especially in contrast to the seeming prosperity of the 1920s.

Dust Bowl

From 1934 to 1937, parts of Texas, Oklahoma, and surrounding areas of the Great Plains suffered from a major drought. The area became known as the Dust Bowl. The Dust Bowl was caused by unsustainable overfarming coupled with a devastating drought. The natural grass cover of the region had been removed in the years leading up to the Dust Bowl, as wheat farmers increased the number of acres under cultivation. With this natural root system gone, the fertile topsoil simply blew away when drought struck from 1934 to 1937. The government, through the Soil Conservation Service, encouraged farmers to replant trees and grass. The government also purchased land to be kept out of cultivation.

The Dust Bowl prompted some significant cultural responses, such as the "Dust Bowl ballads" of the folk singer Woody Guthrie (1940) and the novel *The Grapes of Wrath* (1939) by John Steinbeck. These cultural responses chronicled the plight of Dust Bowl refugees, including the "Okies" who fled from Oklahoma.

TIP 

Tariffs in the 1920s

Tariffs in the 1920s were at their highest rate in American history other than in the period following the Tariff of Abominations. Raising tariff rates during the 1920s was exactly what the country didn't need. The United States needed to trade more with Europe in order to sell excess goods. Tariffs closed off trade with Europe.

HOOVER'S RESPONSE TO THE GREAT DEPRESSION

President Herbert Hoover seemed to be the right man to deal with the problems associated with the Great Depression. He demonstrated his organizational skills as head of the Food Administration during World War I. However, contemporaries and historians have questioned his decisions and his leadership qualities. Hoover was very reluctant to harness the power of the central government to intervene in economic matters. He signed into law the restrictive Hawley-Smoot Tariff (1930), which dramatically raised tariff rates on goods imported into the United States. In response, other nations instituted retaliatory tariffs against the United States, thereby reducing demand for American-made goods. He feared that government intervention into the Great Depression would stifle individual initiative. The belief that government should stay out of economic affairs is known as laissez-faire.

Hoover and Rugged Individualism

Hoover refused to initiate programs that would provide direct relief for individuals. Rather, he invoked the idea of rugged individualism—the belief that the problems of the nation could best be solved by the determination and resolve of the American people. When people were unable to help themselves, Hoover encouraged voluntary cooperation and private charities to step in.

TIP

Hoover's Economic Policies
Hoover's approach to the economy and his rhetoric set a template for Republican economic policy for much of the twentieth century.

Reconstruction Finance Corporation

Hoover's most important initiative designed to address the economic crisis was the Reconstruction Finance Corporation (1932). This government agency extended loans to struggling railroads, banks, insurance companies, and other firms. He refused, however, to extend direct relief to individuals.

The Bonus March

Hoover's inaction in regard to direct relief led many Americans to believe that Hoover did not empathize with the plight of ordinary workers and the unemployed. This perception was reinforced by his handling of the Bonus March in 1932. The Bonus Marchers were World War I veterans who demanded that the federal government pay them a bonus that Congress had promised to pay them in the future. When Hoover refused to meet with the Bonus Marchers, the marchers set up an encampment on the mall in Washington, D.C. Finally, the army was called in to clear out the encampment. The sight of soldiers shooting tear gas at and removing veterans further damaged Hoover's standing among the American people. Most historians assert that Hoover's attachment to the ideas on rugged individualism and laissez-faire proved inadequate in the face of the Great Depression.

TIP

Movies in the Pretelevision Era
Movies would never draw as large a percentage of the public as they did in the 1930s and 1940s. Some thought that television would destroy the movie industry. The predictions did not come true, but television certainly made deep cuts into the movie industry's audience.

THE CULTURE OF THE 1930s

Cultural developments of the 1930s must be seen in the context of the economic hardships of that decade. Some cultural products offered escape from the drudgery of everyday life, while others looked squarely at the plight of the downtrodden.

Movies

The movie industry, which had entered the talkie era in the late 1920s, thrived during the Great Depression. Between 60 percent and 90 percent of the American public went to the movies every week. Escapist musicals with lavish sets and spectacular numbers, such as *Golddiggers of 1933* (1933) and *42nd Street* (1933), proved popular. In *The Wizard of Oz* (1939), Dorothy, played by Judy Garland, escapes an impoverished Kansas farm and is transported, along with the audience, to the magical land of Oz, which was shot in color. The Marx Brothers produced and starred in anarchic comedies, such as *Monkey Business* (1931) and *Duck Soup* (1933), which mocked authority figures and the pretensions of the wealthy. Charlie Chaplin's comedy *Modern Times* (1936) satirized the entire capitalist system, from the drudgery of assembly line work to the corruption of the law enforcement system. Some movies attempted to grapple with the wrenching public issues of the time. *The Grapes of Wrath* (1940), the film version of John Steinbeck's novel, chronicled the conditions of Dust Bowl farmers fleeing to California. Frank Capra's *Mr. Smith Goes to Washington* (1939) depicted the triumph of a decent, "everyman" politician.

Radio

Radio, which had become a popular medium in the 1920s, continued its popularity in the 1930s. Americans listened to weekly serials such as *The Shadow* and *The Lone Ranger*, comedians such as Jack Benny and George Burns, and soap operas. In addition, big band swing music became very popular. Americans listened to big bands led by Duke Ellington, Tommy Dorsey, and Glenn Miller. Radio and movies tended to create a more homogenous culture in the United States in the 1930s.

Literature

Pearl Buck's *The Good Earth* (1931)—a story of peasants in China, Steinbeck's tale of the Dust Bowl—*The Grapes of Wrath* (1939), and Margaret Mitchell's account of the Old South—*Gone With the Wind* (1936) have endured as classics of 1930s literature. Several novels of the 1930s reflected the influence of the Communist Party on American culture. Antifascist novels included *It Can't Happen Here* (1935) by Sinclair Lewis. Proletarian literature included the novel *The Disinherited* (1933) by Jack Conroy and the play *Waiting for Lefty* (1935) by Clifford Odets.

Subject to Debate

Historians have debated the legacy of President Herbert Hoover in recent years. History textbooks tend to give Hoover a bad name. He is presented as aloof and rigid in the face of economic disaster. Hoover is remembered for what he didn't do (provide direct relief to the poor) rather than what he did do.

Hoover's legacy in historical work tells us a great deal about historical writing. Many historians have come to lionize Hoover's successor, President Franklin D. Roosevelt. Roosevelt both saved the country from the worst ravages of the Great Depression at home and from the fascist menace abroad. In the process, he created the modern liberal welfare state. This adoration of Roosevelt has influenced historical writing about Hoover. Hoover, in this context, has become the anti-Roosevelt, representing the negative side of the coin. Hoover is lumped in with the two other Republican presidents of the 1920s, Harding and Coolidge. However, a brief look at the record would indicate that Hoover was not the incompetent that he has often been portrayed as. He was an exceptionally competent administrator, running the successful Food Administration during World War I. When the Great Depression hit, he did not sit by idly. He implemented the far-reaching Reconstruction Finance Corporation, which provided needed funds to key components of the economy. Later he implemented public works programs. Even his handling of the Bonus March is not as heavy-handed as usually portrayed. The most aggressive acts were carried out by General Douglas MacArthur, without the permission of Hoover.

Practice Multiple-Choice Questions:

Directions: Pick the letter that best answers the following questions.

1. Hoover's handling of the Bonus Marchers in 1932 left many Americans with the impression that he

   (A) had the best interests of poor people at hand.
   (B) did not sympathize with the plight of ordinary people.
   (C) was able to balance conflicting demands.
   (D) was not in control of the government.
   (E) gave in to radical demands too easily.

2. Which of the following was <u>not</u> a weakness of the American economy on the eve of the Great Depression?
   (A) Government spending programs and war had produced inflation, making consumer products unaffordable to many Americans.
   (B) Farmers were growing too much food, sending prices down.
   (C) Investors continued to invest in a volatile stock market, with many people buying their shares on margin.
   (D) Mass production had created surpluses of automobiles and appliances, leading to cutbacks in production of these major items.
   (E) There was a widening gap between the annual earnings of the wealthiest 10 percent and the poorest 10 percent of the population.

3. In response to calls that he should initiate programs of direct relief to the people, Hoover asserted the idea of
   (A) welfare capitalism.
   (B) Keynesian economics.
   (C) the social gospel.
   (D) whip inflation now.
   (E) rugged individualism.

4. Woody Guthrie was a prominent cultural figure in the 1930s best known for
   (A) writing and singing folk songs about the downtrodden and forgotten.
   (B) directing films that portrayed an undying optimism in the face of economic disaster.
   (C) writing a series of novellas about a cowboy known as the Lone Ranger.
   (D) painting murals in post offices and schools portraying the economic hardships of the 1930s.
   (E) performing minstrel shows in blackface.

Practice Free-Response Questions:

1. Analyze the cause of the Great Depression.

2. "Hoover's main problem was not the Great Depression; it was his inability to craft a positive image of himself." Assess the validity of this statement.

Answers and Explanations to Multiple-Choice Questions:

1. **(B)** Hoover was not a bad president (see Subject to Debate, above). However, the public perceived him as uncaring. His handling of the Bonus Marchers, impoverished World War I veterans, was a public relations disaster. The event clinched the election later that year for Franklin D. Roosevelt.

2. **(A)** All of the choices indicate major weaknesses in the economy of the 1920s except for choice A. The Republican presidents of the 1920s, Harding, Coolidge, and Hoover, did not believe in extensive government programs. In addition, there was no war on the eve of the Great Depression. World War I was a decade earlier; World War II was a decade later.

3. **(E)** Hoover stubbornly clung to the idea of rugged individualism in the face of a massive economic disaster. There were limits as to what a rugged individual could do when unemployment was 20 percent. Roosevelt was more flexible in his approach to politics.

4. **(A)** Woody Guthrie was a folk singer who sang songs about many of the victims of the Great Depression. His "Dust Bowl Ballads" put the story of the Joad family (from *The Grapes of Wrath*) to music. He said that he figured there were people who would enjoy the story but who couldn't read.

CHAPTER 25

The New Deal and the Politics of the 1930s, 1932–1940

TIMELINE

1932	Franklin D. Roosevelt elected president
1933	The 100 Days
	Bank holiday
	Agricultural Adjustment Act (AAA)
	Glass-Steagall Act (Federal Deposit Insurance Corporation established)
	National Industrial Recovery Act (NIRA)
	Civilian Conservation Corps (CCC)
1934	Share Our Wealth clubs started by Huey P. Long
	Securities and Exchange Commission
1935	National Labor Relations Act (Wagner Act)
	Social Security Act
	Schechter decision strikes down the NIRA
	Works Progress Administration
1936	Butler decision strikes down the AAA
	Roosevelt's court-packing plan
	Roosevelt elected to a second term
1937	Roosevelt Recession
	Farm Security Administration
1940	Roosevelt elected to unprecedented third term

The Great Depression and the New Deal have been increasingly important topics on the Advanced Placement exam in the last few years. There have been three DBQs that have been either partly or completely about Franklin D. Roosevelt's New Deal and over 20 standard essay questions about the era. The 1930s witnessed the emergence of the political and ideological alignment that has existed, to some extent, to the present. Hoover's generally conservative laissez-faire approach has been echoed in the policies of Republican President Ronald Reagan and both Presidents Bush, while Roosevelt's generally liberal interventionist approach inspired Democratic President Lyndon Johnson's Great Society. Today, Democratic leaders debate how closely their party should be associated with New Deal liberalism, while Republicans brand their opponents as tax and spend liberals. So the debates of the 1930s are still part of the political culture.

THE ELECTION OF FRANKLIN D. ROOSEVELT AND THE NEW DEAL

In 1932, Franklin Delano Roosevelt offered the public a marked contrast to President Hoover. Roosevelt was from a wealthy New York family. He was a distant cousin of Theodore Roosevelt. In 1928, Roosevelt won the governorship in New York and introduced a number of innovative programs to help New Yorkers as the Great Depression deepened. Though Roosevelt was from a wealthy background, he was able to convey to the public a sense of empathy and warmth. Further, his openness to experimentation allowed for a more flexible response to the Great Depression than did Hoover's more ideological approach. Roosevelt won the presidential election of 1932 easily, garnering 57 percent of the popular vote and 472 out of 531 electoral votes.

Roosevelt took the federal government in a new direction by asserting that it should take some responsibility for the welfare of the people. The Roosevelt administration developed a series of programs that are known as the New Deal. Previously, churches, settlement houses, and other private charities helped people in times of need. However, the levels of poverty and unemployment during the Great Depression were unprecedented. Roosevelt believed that the government needed to take action. The New Deal provided relief to individuals through a variety of agencies.

The Newness of the New Deal
The extension of the federal government into the economic lives of individuals represented a marked departure from the traditional role of the government.

THE FIRST NEW DEAL

The Roosevelt administration developed a remarkable array of programs during its first hundred days in 1933 and in the months immediately following. These programs, which comprise the first New Deal, reflected Roosevelt's willingness to experiment and the scope of problems that faced the nation. Below are some of the more important programs.

Glass-Steagall Act (1933)

One of the most pressing problems that Roosevelt faced was the instability of the banking industry. Many people had lost confidence in the banking system and withdrew their money in fears that their bank might fold. With thousands of people withdrawing their money at the same time, many banks actually did close, turning their fears into a self-fulfilling prophecy. The Federal Deposit Insurance Corporation, created by the Glass-Steagall Act, insures deposits so that if a bank does fold, people will not lose their savings.

National Industrial Recovery Act (1933)

The National Industrial Recovery Act called for representatives from labor and competing corporations to draw up a set of codes. These codes were designed to eliminate discount selling, shorten hours for workers, and establish minimum wage levels. The idea was that cutthroat competition hurt the economy and pushed down workers' wages, and their ability to purchase goods.

Agricultural Adjustment Act (1933)

The Roosevelt administration took the counterintuitive measure of paying farmers not to grow crops. The goal of the Agricultural Adjustment Act was to reduce production in order to bolster sagging commodity prices and strengthen the agricultural sector. Commodity prices did increase, but the AAA had an unintended negative effect. Landowners often evicted tenant farmers and sharecroppers in order to take land out of cultivation. This hurt many of the nation's poorest farmers, including many African-American farmers.

Tennessee Valley Authority (1933)

This innovative program, which is still in existence, was the federal government's first experiment in regional planning. The TVA built dams, generated electricity, manufactured fertilizer, provided technical assistance to farmers, and fostered economic development in the Tennessee Valley.

Federal Emergency Relief Act (1933)

FERA was created to distribute over $500 million to state and local governments, that would, in turn, distribute aid to the poor. It was intended to provide temporary relief for people in need.

Civilian Conservation Corps (1933)

Roosevelt created the Civilian Conservation Corps to provide outdoor work for young men between the ages of 18 and 24. CCC projects included soil conservation, flood control, trail and road building, and forest projects. During the 1930s, approximately 2.75 million men worked on CCC projects.

Securities and Exchange Commission (1934)

Many people lost confidence in the stock market after the 1929 crash, which was partly caused by unsound practices. The Securities and Exchange Commission was established to oversee stock market operations by monitoring transactions, licensing brokers, limiting buying on margin, and prohibiting insider trading. The SEC still functions today.

THE SECOND NEW DEAL

By 1935, Roosevelt was facing several problems. The economy had improved slightly between 1933, when Roosevelt took office, and 1935. Average weekly earnings had increased for workers, and unemployment had dropped from about 25 percent to 20 percent. With over 10 million people out of work, though, Roosevelt could not claim that the New Deal had resolved the nation's economic woes. In addition, The Supreme Court had declared key New Deal legislation unconstitutional. The *Schechter* decision (1935) ended the National Industrial Recovery Act. Several months later, the *Butler* decision (1936) declared the Agricultural Adjustment Act unconstitutional. With mounting pressure from a variety of populist and left-wing forces and with a presidential election looming in 1936, Roosevelt introduced a second set of programs that are known as the second New Deal. This second phase of the New Deal was less about involvement with the different sectors of the economy and more about providing assistance and support to the working class.

The Supreme Court and Politics
Throughout history, note the connections between Supreme Court decisions and contemporary political currents. The justices are products of their society; they don't make their decisions in a vacuum.

Works Progress Administration (1935)

The Works Progress Administration was a massive initiative that created jobs for millions of unemployed men and women. The jobs ranged from construction work to theatrical productions to writing guidebooks about each of the states. Earlier jobs programs, such as the Civilian Conservation Cords, were piecemeal compared with the immense WPA.

Social Security Act (1935)

Social Security is perhaps the initiative that has had the largest long-term impact on American society. The Social Security Act was designed to help the unemployed, the elderly, and the disabled. The most important element of the plan was retirement benefits, funded by taxes on workers and employers, which workers collect after they turn 65.

The Wagner Act (1935)

The Wagner Act encouraged the formation of unions. The act established the National Labor Relations Board, which is still in existence, to oversee union elections and to arbitrate conflicts between workers and owners. It also prohibited owners from taking punitive actions against workers who sought to organize unions. The act led to a tremendous increase in union activity.

The Second New Deal and the Supreme Court

President Roosevelt feared that the Supreme Court would invalidate key elements of this second New Deal as it had earlier New Deal acts. In 1937, he proposed a bill to alter the composition of the Supreme Court by allowing him to appoint six additional justices. This court-packing bill generated a great deal of opposition.

Congress rejected this plan, but the Court became friendlier to the president anyway. Over the next few years, some of the more conservative justices retired and Roosevelt was able to appoint seven new justices, including the liberal Hugo Black.

THE END OF THE NEW DEAL

In late 1937 and 1938, Roosevelt took the New Deal in a new direction that, many historians believe, hurt the economy. By 1937, the economy was showing signs of improvement. Unemployment was going down, and banks and businesses were showing signs of stability. Roosevelt took the advice of some of the more conservative members of his cabinet and cut back on spending with the goal of balancing the budget.

The Roosevelt Recession

Roosevelt's move to cut spending on New Deal programs contributed to a further downturn in economic activity in 1938 known as the Roosevelt recession. Later in 1938, Roosevelt shifted direction again and increased government spending. The economy did show signs of growth. However, the real boost to the economy came in 1939 as the United States began producing armaments and supplies for World War II.

Keynesian Economics

When Roosevelt cut back spending to balance the budget in the middle of the Great Depression, he was rejecting the advice of the economist John Maynard Keynes. Keynes's most important book, *General Theory of Employment, Interest and Money* (1936), argued that deficit spending by the government was acceptable and even desirable as a means of increasing overall demand and stimulating economic activity. This idea of using the tools of the government—the Federal Reserve Bank, and spending and taxation policies—to influence economic activity is known as Keynesian economics.

TIP 

Keynes and Government Policy
Be familiar with Keynesian economics. His theories have influenced government policy in the twentieth century, especially during Democratic administrations. Republicans have focused on cutting spending.

THE POLITICAL CLIMATE OF THE 1930s

President Roosevelt had to negotiate the New Deal through the tumultuous political currents of the 1930s. A variety of social and political movements emerged, each offering different solutions to the economic crisis. To some degree, these movements hindered the New Deal. To some degree, they influenced it.

The Growth of the Communist Party

Although the Communist Party never attracted a large following in the United States, it attracted new members and exerted influence beyond its numbers in the 1930s. Some Americans were impressed with the achievements of the Soviet Union, and some simply felt that the capitalist system was not working. The Communist Party also attracted members by dropping talk of impending revolution and adopting Stalin's Popular Front strategy (in effect 1934–1939). This approach called for the Communist Party to cooperate with a spectrum of antifascist groups and governments, including Roosevelt's New Deal.

Populist Opposition to the New Deal

Although Roosevelt could count on support from the Communist Party, other voices from the left criticized the New Deal as being overly cautious. Upton Sinclair (author of *The Jungle*) ran for governor of California in 1934 under the banner "End Poverty in California" by proposing sweeping, somewhat socialistic solutions. Francis Townsend, also from California, proposed a tax to generate enough money to give everyone over 60 a monthly stipend. The most serious threat to Roosevelt from the left came from Huey P. Long, the flamboyant populist governor and then senator from Louisiana. His Share Our Wealth Society, begun in 1934, proposed breaking up the fortunes of the rich and distributing them to everyone else. His slogan was "Every Man a King." He talked of running against Roosevelt in 1936 but was assassinated in 1935.

Conservative Critics Denounce Creeping Socialism

Some conservative critics saw the New Deal as socialism in disguise. The New Deal, they argued, had pushed the government too far into new realms. Roosevelt's court-packing scheme seemed especially heavy-handed to many Americans. The most prominent group on the right was the American Liberty League (founded in 1934), which consisted primarily of conservative businessmen. The group supported conservative politicians of both parties. It promoted the open shop—a business in which the employees are not required to join a union. Father Charles Coughlin, using his popular national radio show, attacked Roosevelt as being a communist and a dictator. Coughlin had initially supported Roosevelt in 1932 but grew increasingly critical of the New Deal, adding anti-Semitic and even fascistic elements to his broadcast.

THE DEPRESSION AND AFFECTED GROUPS

Different sectors of society were affected by the Great Depression and the New Deal differently. Although the 1930s was certainly a dismal time economically, some groups in the United States were able to put forth agendas for change and to achieve gains.

The Growth of Organized Labor

Roosevelt encouraged union membership in order to increase the purchasing powers of workers. Section 7A of the National Industrial Recovery Act and later the Wagner Act legalized union membership in the United States. Union membership, which had been falling in the 1920s and early 1930s, rose from 3 million in 1933 to 10.5 million by 1941. By the end of World War II, 36 percent of nonagricultural American workers were in unions.

The Growth of the Congress of Industrial Organizations

The drive to organize workers led to tensions within the labor movement. The fifty-year-old American Federation of Labor (AFL), a coalition of craft unions, had never shown much interest in organizing unskilled assembly line workers. Labor leaders such as John L. Lewis of the United Mine Workers wanted the AFL to do more organizing in this growing sector of the labor force. In 1935, he and other leaders from primarily unskilled unions organized the Committee for Industrial Organization within the AFL. The committee's task of organizing basic industries met the ire of AFL leadership, which ordered the committee to disband in 1936. When it refused, the AFL leadership expelled the committee unions in 1937. In 1938, the committee reconstituted itself as the independent Congress of Industrial Organizations (CIO). It grew rapidly, surpassing the AFL by 1941. The CIO had about 5 million members compared with the AFL's 4.6 million.

TIP 

The CIO and the AFL
The CIO started out as the Committee for Industrial Organization within the AFL in 1935. In 1938, it became the independent Congress of Industrial Organization. In 1955, the CIO merged with the AFL to form the AFL-CIO.

The Sit Down Strike

Although unions were legal in America, employers were still under no compulsion to accept union demands. A wave of strikes ensued in the late 1930s. A new, militant tactic that CIO unions engaged in was the sit down strike, in which workers stopped work and refused to leave the shop floor, thus preventing the employer from reopening with replacement workers (or scabs in the parlance of the labor movement). The most famous sit down strike took place at the General Motors plant in Flint, Michigan, in the winter of 1936–1937.

African Americans

African Americans, who were in a vulnerable position in American society before the Great Depression, were especially hard hit by the economic difficulties of the 1930s. Many New Deal programs ignored African Americans, such as the Agricultural Adjustment Act, which did not help tenant farmers. Roosevelt was leery of losing the support of the southern wing of the Democratic Party, so he did not push for civil rights legislation. Neither did he endorse federal antilynching legislation (which Congress never passed).

Despite President Roosevelt's reluctance to take the lead in civil rights legislation, many African Americans switched their allegiance from the party of Lincoln (the Republicans) to the Democratic Party. There are several reasons for this historic shift. First Lady Eleanor Roosevelt and Interior Secretary Harold Ickes did champion civil rights causes. The most dramatic gesture by Eleanor Roosevelt was organizing a concert by Marian Anderson in 1935 on the steps of the Lincoln Memorial after she was blocked by the Daughters of the American Revolution from performing at their concert hall. Also, the president met periodically with a group of African-American advisors, called the Black Cabinet. In 1941, Roosevelt issued an executive order banning discrimination in government jobs. Finally, African Americans believed that Roosevelt, despite his shortcomings, was attempting to improve conditions for poor and working-class people.

Slow Steps Toward Civil Rights
We can see Roosevelt and the Democratic Party just beginning to shift toward support for civil rights in the 1930s. This was a major shift for a party that in the 1860s pushed the southern states to secede in order to defend slavery.

THE SCOTTSBORO BOYS CASE

The racial biases of the justice system were demonstrated in the highly publicized Scottsboro Boys case (1931–1935). Nine African-American youths were convicted of rape in Alabama on flimsy evidence. In 1932, the Supreme Court reversed most of the convictions on the grounds that the defendants' due process rights had been violated because they were denied effective counsel. The cases were then sent back to state court for retrial. The defendants were again found guilty, even after one of the alleged victims admitted fabricating the story. Charges were later dropped for four out of the nine defendants.

Women

Women suffered a double burden during the Great Depression. They were responsible for putting food on the table during difficult times, and they were scorned if they "took a job away from a man" by working outside the home. Further, New Deal programs tended to slight women. The Civilian Conservation Corps—a New Deal program that sent young men out of urban areas to work on federal lands—excluded women. NIRA set lower wage levels for women than for men. Nonetheless, individual women such as Frances Perkins—the first female cabinet member (Secretary of Labor)—and Eleanor Roosevelt, one of the most active and public First Ladies, opened doors for women. Despite criticism, more women were working outside the home in 1940 than in 1930.

Native Americans

New Deal legislation profoundly affected Native Americans. The Indian Reorganization Act (1934) largely undid the 1887 Dawes Act. The Dawes Act had attempted to "Americanize" Native Americans by breaking up reservations and dividing the land into small plots for individual Native Americans. The Indian Reorganization Act reversed this policy by restoring tribal ownership of reservation lands and recognizing the legitimacy of tribal governments. The act also extended loans to Native-American groups for economic development.

Mexican Americans

Many Mexicans had moved to the Southwest United States in the 1920s to work in agriculture. These Mexican Americans saw their wages plummet in the 1930s, and New Deal programs did little to help. For instance, the CCC and the WPA excluded migrant farm workers by requiring a permanent address. Many Mexicans returned to their homeland. The Mexican-American population decreased by almost 40 percent during the Great Depression.

Subject to Debate

The nature of the New Deal has been a subject of much debate among historians, as it was among contemporaries. Conservative critics in the 1930s railed against creeping socialism. Liberals championed the expansion of the state to help society cope with economic dislocation. Radicals asserted that the New Deal was essentially a conservative scheme to prop up capitalism. Historians often have in mind contemporary debates about government intervention in the economy when they are looking at the New Deal.

Historians have tried to understand the intellectual and political origins of the New Deal. Some look to the reform impulses of the Populist and Progressive movements of the late 1800s and early 1900s. They see continuities between the reform programs of Presidents Theodore Roosevelt and Woodrow Wilson and the reform impulses of the New Deal. They note that many New Dealers were active in the progressive era. Some historians see more of a break between earlier reform efforts and the New Deal. The progressives were mostly middle-class men and men, imposing their values on society. The New Deal, some argue, was driven more by working-class concerns.

Was the New Deal successful or not? Some historians have noted that the New Deal did not solve the problems of the Great Depression. They see the creation of a bloated government bureaucracy that was too large and impersonal to address the concerns of ordinary people. These historians note that the Great Depression ended only when the United States began producing materials for World War II. Other historians, more sympathetic to Roosevelt and the New Deal, argue that the New Deal restored hope among the American people and prevented more widespread suffering. Defenders of the New Deal also note that organized labor made great strides because of New Deal legislation. These debates parallel contemporary debates about the efficacy of government efforts at solving social and economic problems.

Practice Multiple-Choice Questions:

Directions: Pick the letter that best answers the following questions.

1. When the Supreme Court declared some New Deal programs unconstitutional, President Franklin D. Roosevelt
   (A) refused to disband the programs, arguing that the Supreme Court had become irrelevant.
   (B) sent the Supreme Court on an extended holiday until they agreed to revisit the cases in question.
   (C) shifted policy priorities from addressing the Great Depression to challenging Nazi aggression in Europe.
   (D) attempted to add additional justices to the Supreme Court.
   (E) moved to impeach Chief Justice Charles Evans Hughes.

2. In the 1930s, Francis Townsend influenced New Deal legislation by proposing
   (A) a series of dams along the rivers of the South to generate electricity.
   (B) federal oversight of the stock market.
   (C) using federal funds to bring art to those without access to art.
   (D) relocating Dust Bowl refugees to California.
   (E) creating a program to provide monthly pensions to senior citizens.

3. First Lady Eleanor Roosevelt arranged for singer Marian Anderson to perform on the steps on the Lincoln Memorial
   (A) because the Daughters of the American Revolution rescinded an offer for Anderson to perform because she is African American.
   (B) in order to entertain the Bonus March protesters who had set up an encampment on the mall in Washington, D.C.
   (C) because Anderson was a direct descendent of Abraham Lincoln.
   (D) as part of the a birthday celebration for Eleanor's husband, Franklin.
   (E) in order to generate enthusiasm for President Roosevelt's run for reelection in 1936.

4. The economic theories of John Maynard Keynes
   (A) encouraged maintaining a balanced budget at all costs.
   (B) inspired Ronald Reagan's economic program.
   (C) called for massive tax cuts for large corporations.
   (D) called for deficit spending in order to generate demand.
   (E) encouraged the enactment of high tariff rates.

Practice Free-Response Questions:

1. Analyze the changes that took place between the First New Deal (1933) and the Second New Deal (1935). Account for the factors that led to the changes.

2. Analyze the reasons for a shift in voting patterns among African Americans in the 1930s.

Answers and Explanations to Multiple-Choice Questions:

1. **(D)** Roosevelt's court-packing scheme was a major political misstep. Roosevelt was growing increasingly frustrated with a conservative Supreme Court that was shooting down some of the centerpieces of the New Deal, including the National Industrial Recovery Act and the Agricultural Adjustment Act. Roosevelt's court-packing scheme would have upset the balance of the three branches by making the Supreme Court a rubber stamp for New Deal legislation. Congress opposed the plan. After much criticism, Roosevelt eventually backed away from it.
2. **(E)** Townsend put the issue of pensions for senior citizens on the national agenda. The New Deal addressed the welfare of retired people and people with disabilities by creating the Social Security system in 1935.
3. **(A)** Eleanor Roosevelt was more outwardly supportive of civil rights for African Americans than was her husband. President Roosevelt did not want to lose the support of southern Democrats for the New Deal, so he was vey tentative on civil rights.
4. **(D)** Keynesian economics asserts that the government should increase spending during economic downturns in order to stimulate demand. Keynesian theory has been very influential to the policies of most Democratic presidents since the 1930s. Republican administrations have put more emphasis on balancing the budget.

CHAPTER 26

World War II: From Isolationism to Intervention, 1928–1945

TIMELINE

1928	The Kellogg-Briand Pact
1935	The First Neutrality Act
1936–1939	The Spanish Civil War
1937	The *Panay* incident
	The Quarantine Speech
1939	Cash-and-Carry Policy
	Nazi-Soviet Pact
1940	Selective Service Act
	Lend-Lease Act
	Tripartite Pact
1941	Lend-Lease Act
	Japanese attack on Pearl Harbor
1942	The Battle of Midway
1943	The Teheran Conference
1944	*Korematsu* v. *United States*
	The Bretton Woods Conference
1945	Battles of Iwo Jima and Okinawa
	The Yalta Conference
	The Potsdam Conference
	Dropping of the atomic bomb on Hiroshima and Nagasaki

After World War I, public sentiment in the United States pushed the nation away from engagement in the affairs in Europe. Isolationists carried the day in 1920 in the American rejection of the Treaty of Versailles, which precluded American membership in the League of Nations. This isolationist sentiment continued into the 1930s. However, as the world moved toward war in the 1930s, President Roosevelt guided the United States into a more engaged position. After the attack on Pearl Harbor (1941), neutrality was no longer an option.

TIP

Europe in the 1930s
Even though it is not American history, the events in Europe in the 1930s should be familiar to you. Often, events abroad have an impact on the United States—fighting between France and Great Britain at the turn of the nineteenth century; European imperialism in the late-nineteenth century, the World Wars, and the Cold War to name just a few.

AN INCREASINGLY DANGEROUS WORLD

The United States existed in an increasingly dangerous world in the 1930s. The Fascist Party, led by Benito Mussolini, had taken power in Italy in 1922. Adolf Hitler came to power in Germany in 1933. A civil war in Spain led to the rise of a government run by the dictator Francisco Franco in 1939. In Japan, militaristic leaders set Japan on an aggressive course. These dictatorial governments all took aggressive actions in the 1930s. Japan attacked China in 1931. Germany occupied the demilitarized Rhineland in 1936, annexed Austria in 1937, and occupied Czechoslovakia in 1939. Italy conquered Ethiopia in 1936. The League of Nations protested, and Great Britain and France objected. However, not until Germany attacked Poland in September 1939 was Hitler seriously challenged. Great Britain and France declared war on Germany, beginning World War II. Germany, Italy, and Japan formed the Axis Powers with the signing of the Tripartite Pact (1940).

The Pull of Isolationism

As events degenerated into war in Europe, a debate occurred in the United States about America's role. Isolationists argued strongly that the United States should stay out of world affairs. Many of these isolationists looked back to World War I as a lesson in the futility of getting involved in European affairs. America lost 50,000 men in World War I for no apparent reason, they argued. World War I hadn't made the world safe for democracy. Almost as soon as the war ended, antidemocratic forces emerged and set Europe once again on the path toward war.

TIP

Politics and Literature
Some of the antiwar novels written in the wake of World War I, such as *All Quiet on the Western Front* (1929) by the German writer Erich Maria Remarque and *A Farewell to Arms* (1929) by Ernest Hemingway, added fuel to the isolationist sentiment of the 1930s.

The Argument for Intervention

While isolationism remained strong in the 1930s, many Americans came to believe that it would be a mistake for the United States to isolate itself from world affairs. They mocked the idea that the Atlantic Ocean would indefinitely protect the United States from dangerous trends in Europe. Interventionists believed that the United States could no longer stand apart. Airplanes and submarines could bring the war to the United States very quickly. If Great Britain were defeated, nothing would be standing between Hitler and America. Interventionists believed that the Atlantic Ocean would not be a barrier for Hitler. Rather, it would be a means for him to bring his war machine farther west to the United States. Also, many interventionists believed that the war in Europe was different from earlier European quarrels over territory or national pride. They believed that if Hitler and Mussolini were successful, civilization itself would be threatened. They were convinced that the Axis Powers were determined to defeat democratic forces all over the world.

President Franklin Roosevelt Proceeds with Caution

President Franklin Roosevelt was cautious in his responses to the conflict in Europe. He was sympathetic to the countries defending themselves against fascism. However, he knew he couldn't commit the United States to an interventionist position without the support of the public. Early on in 1937, Roosevelt recognized that a European war could engulf people far from Europe. He was not ready to commit the United States to intervene, but he didn't pretend that the United States could isolate itself from the affairs of Europe.

The Onset of World War II—From Cash-and-Carry to Pearl Harbor

The question of the international role of the United States grew more intense in 1939 as World War II formally began. The war began after Germany attacked Poland. Great Britain and France quickly declared war on Germany. As soon as the war began, Roosevelt pushed for legislation allowing the United States to send armaments to Great Britain with the condition that Great Britain pay for the weapons first and transport them in their own ships. The policy of cash-and-carry allowed the United States to support Great Britain without the risk of U.S. ships being destroyed.

By mid-1940, the American public began to shift toward a more interventionist stance. The situation in Europe grew dire. Americans were shaken by the defeat of France at the hands of the Nazis in June 1940. They saw how easily one of the democratic powers could be defeated by the Nazi war machine. Would Great Britain fall next? Would the United States be the next target? By 1941, 70 percent of the American public was ready to directly help Great Britain, even if it meant risking getting involved in World War II. In 1940, Roosevelt pushed for the enactment of the Selective Service Act, calling for compulsory military service for males between 21 and 35. With this shift in public opinion and with his victory in the presidential election of 1940, Roosevelt was ready to take more direct action. In March 1941, Congress approved his Lend-Lease Act, which allowed the United States to ship armaments to Great Britain in American ships. Though officially neutral, the United States was moving steadily toward intervening on the side of Great Britain.

The public was not unified in its support of intervention. Isolationists such as the renowned aviator Charles Lindbergh continued to argue against any U.S. steps toward helping Great Britain. He was a leader of the America First Committee and, historians argue, a Nazi sympathizer. Even as late as 1941, it was clear that many Americans still had major reservations about America entering World War II. Debates about intervention ended abruptly on December 7, 1941. On that date, Japanese planes attacked the U.S. naval base at Pearl Harbor, Hawaii. Almost immediately, the United States entered World War II. With American involvement in World War II, the isolationist position was largely silenced.

THE UNITED STATES AT WAR

Staffing the Army

The Roosevelt administration began a push to enlarge the size of the army even before Pearl Harbor. The Selective Service Act was passed in September 1940, creating the first peacetime draft in American history. By the summer of 1941, almost 1.5 million men were in the armed forces. During the course of the war, more than 15 million men and women served in the armed forces.

African Americans participated in the war effort in unprecedented numbers. The National Association for the Advancement of Colored People (NAACP) encouraged African Americans to take part in the "double V" campaign—promoting victory against fascism abroad and victory against racism at home. Ultimately, 125,000 African-Americans served overseas during World War II. The most famous segregated African-American units were the Tuskegee Airmen and the 761st Tank Battalion. African American effectiveness on the battlefield later encouraged President Truman to desegregate the armed services with Executive Order 9981 in 1948.

Women contributed to the effort in many ways during World War II. Women served in the armed forces as nurses. In addition, over 150,000 women served in the Women's Army Auxiliary Corps (later, the Women's Army Corps) and in the WAVES, the women's unit of the Navy.

WAR IN THE PACIFIC THEATER

Through the first year of the war, the United States sent more of its troops to the Pacific theater than to Europe. Even though the defeat of Hitler was a top priority for the United States, Japan had directly attacked the United States. The United States suffered several setbacks at the hands of the Japanese military in the first few months of the war. Japan took over the Philippines at the end of December 1941. By May 1942, Japan controlled a massive empire and had Australia in its sights.

Turning Points in War
Although extensive knowledge of battles in not required for the AP exam, be aware of key turning points in wars, such as the Battle of Saratoga in the American Revolution and the capture of Vicksburg and the Battle of Gettysburg in the Civil War.

The Battles of Coral Sea and Midway (1942)

The United States turned the tide of the war in the Pacific in two naval battles in 1942. In May, the United States stopped a Japanese fleet as it was headed to New Guinea in the Battle of the Coral Sea. In June, the United States achieved a victory over the Japanese fleet in the Battle of Midway. After the Battle of Midway, the United States slowly began to push Japanese forces back toward the Japanese home islands.

Island Hopping

By the end of 1943, the United States began employing a strategy called leapfrogging (also known as island hopping) in regard to defeating Japan in the Pacific. The basic idea of leapfrogging was that the United States and its allies would avoid attacking some of the most heavily fortified islands in the Pacific. Instead, it would focus on islands that were important in the drive toward the Japanese home islands but that were not as well defended. The United States then hoped to isolate the Japanese-held islands that it had leapfrogged over by blockading supply ships. The Japanese forces on these islands would, according to this strategy, wither on the vine.

WAR IN EUROPE

Before June 1944, most of the fighting against Germany was carried out by the Soviet Union in Eastern Europe. Joseph Stalin, the leader of the Soviet Union, had been urging the United States and Great Britain to open a second western front in Europe against Germany. At a meeting in Teheran, Iran held in November 1943, President Roosevelt and British Prime Minister Winston Churchill assured Stalin that they would open up a second European front. (The Teheran Conference is discussed in detail below.)

The Washington and Casablanca Conferences

In June 1942, Roosevelt and Churchill met in Washington, D.C., to discuss strategy. In January 1943, they met again in Casablanca, Morocco. Stalin did not attend either meeting, but he let it be known that he hoped the allies would soon open up a major second front in Europe. The brunt of the fighting against Hitler's forces was carried out by the Soviet Red Army. Nearly 90 percent of German casualties came at the hands of Soviet troops. At both meetings, Churchill opposed the idea of immediately invading France. The British did not want to initiate prematurely a repeat of the trench warfare of World War I. Churchill and Roosevelt agreed to open a front in North Africa, followed by an attack on "the soft underbelly" of the Axis, Italy.

Fighting in North Africa

The first offensive involving American troops in Nazi-occupied areas occurred in North Africa in November 1942. American forces, led by General Dwight D. Eisenhower, landed in Morocco and Algeria. They pushed back the forces of the French Vichy Government, which collaborated with the Nazis. Americans also fought Nazi troops in Tunisia and Libya. By May 1943, North Africa was in Allied hands.

The "Soft Underbelly" of the Axis

Approximately a quarter of a million Allied forces landed in Sicily in June 1943. The allies captured Sicily by August, which led to the Italian king dismissing Mussolini as prime minister. The new Italian Government left the Axis and eventually joined the Allies. Germany, however, not ready to accept Allied occupation of Italy, sent reinforcements into Italy. The Allies finally marched into Rome in June 1944.

D-Day

In June 1944, allied troops landed on the beaches of Normandy, France, and began pushing Hitler's forces back toward Germany. By August 1944, Allied forces had liberated Paris from Nazi occupation.

V-E Day

Hitler made a last attempt to stop the Allied assault in the winter of 1944–1945. German forces drove through Allied lines into Belgium in the Battle of the Bulge before being stopped by Allied forces. American and British troops approached Germany from the west as Soviet troops approached from the east. By April 1945, Soviet troops were on the outskirts of Berlin. On April 30, 1945, Hitler committed suicide. On May 7, 1945, Germany surrendered, ending the war in Europe.

The Holocaust

As the war in Europe was ending, the Allies became aware of the full extent of the barbaric crimes against civilians committed by the Nazis during the war. The Holocaust was the systematic murder of over 6 million European Jews and other "undesirables" by the Nazis. In 1939, the German dictator Adolf Hitler and other leading Nazis developed the "final solution of the Jewish question," a plan to eliminate the Jewish population. After the Germans took over most of continental Europe, this plan went from being the scheming of a madman to a horrible, deadly reality. The plan also included other groups, such as gypsies and homosexuals. Nazis rounded up Jews first into crowded urban areas called ghettos, then to concentration or labor camps, and finally to death camps, where gas chambers and incineration ovens were built to carry out the "final solution."

THE WAR AT HOME

In many ways, World War II required the participation of the entire American public, not simply members of the military. Workers were needed in munitions factories, people were asked to buy war bonds, and the government rationed important resources such as meat and fuel. These efforts created a sense of unity and common cause in the country.

Rationing and Recycling

During the war, there were shortages of key items because of the needs of the military. Starting in 1942, the Office of Price Administration began rationing key commodities to civilians, such as gasoline and tires. Next, the government began rationing food—sugar, meat, coffee, lard, butter, and many other items. Families were given ration books and would use ration stamps, along with cash, when they purchased the affected items. In addition, children organized Tin Can Clubs to collect scrap metal to be melted down to produce weapons and ammunition.

Funding the War Effort

The Roosevelt Administration paid for the war effort through the sale of war bonds and increases in taxes. The government went into massive debt during the war. The debt increased sixfold between 1940 and 1949. The experience of World War II demonstrates that massive government spending and the ensuing deficits can play a significant role in stimulating a sluggish economy.

War Production

If the United States were to become the "arsenal for democracy," as President Roosevelt promised in a speech in 1940, it would have to step up the production of war-related materials dramatically and rapidly. In 1942, he created the War Production Board and later the Office of War Mobilization to oversee the conversion from civilian industry to war production. Almost overnight, the persistent unemployment of the 1930s disappeared. After the United States entered World War II, in December 1941, the country faced the opposite problem—labor shortages. With millions of men and women in the armed forces, the Roosevelt Administration took several important steps to ensure a sufficient supply of factory workers. To ensure uninterrupted production, labor unions agreed to refrain from striking during the war. This promise was kept, with the exception of a few strikes in the coal industry.

Latinos and the War

The administration initiated the *bracero* program in 1942 to bring temporary contract workers from Mexico into the United States. The Mexican government pushed the United States to guarantee that these temporary workers would not be drafted. Over 200,000 Mexicans participated in the program. It is estimated at least that amount came into the United States as undocumented workers.

Mexicans and Mexican Americans were the object of discrimination, harassment, and violence during World War II. In California, whites frequently targeted Mexican Americans for violent attacks. White teenagers and servicemen especially targeted Latinos wearing colorful zoot suits, then in style among Latinos and African Americans. A serious zoot suit riot occurred in Los Angeles in 1943.

African Americans and War Production

Initially, many war-related industries were reluctant to hire African Americans. An important African-American labor leader, A. Phillip Randolph, the president of the Brotherhood of Sleeping Car Porters, planned a public demonstration in Washington, D.C., in 1941 to protest discrimination in war-related industries. When the Roosevelt Administration heard of these plans, it worked out a bargain. Roosevelt issued Executive Order 8802, banning discrimination in war-related industries, and Randolph called off the march.

African Americans joined millions of other Americans in moving toward industrial centers. The Great Migration that began in World War I continued, with African Americans moving to the West coast in addition to moving to northern industrial cities.

Rosie the Riveter

The government also made a concerted effort to recruit women to participate in the war effort. Women were needed because factories were working around the clock producing military goods and much of the male work force was in the military. Many images were produced by the government, usually through the Office of War Information, showing women in industrial settings. The fictional Rosie the Riveter was often featured in this public relations campaign. These female workers were presented in a positive light—helping the nation as well as the men in combat abroad. Such a campaign was needed because prewar societal mores discouraged women from doing industrial work. During the Great Depression of the 1930s, women were encouraged to leave the job market so that there would be enough jobs available for male bread winners. The campaign was successful. By 1945, one-third of the work force was female.

Civil Liberties During Wartime
The *Korematsu* case is often on the AP exam. Be prepared to discuss it in the context of the broader question of civil liberties during wartime.

The Japanese Relocation

In 1942, President Roosevelt issued Executive Order 9066, authorizing the government to remove over 100,000 Japanese Americans from West Coast states and relocate them to camps in Arizona. The order applied to both Issei (Japanese Americans who had emigrated from Japan) and Nisei (native-born Japanese Americans). Most of their property was confiscated by the government. In *Korematsu* v. *United States* (1944), the Supreme Court ruled that the relocation was acceptable on the grounds of national security. Much later, in 1988, the U.S. Government publicly apologized to the surviving victims and extended $20,000 in reparations to each one. The Korematsu decision is one of several rulings by the Supreme Court that have curtailed civil liberties in times of war. Another is the *Schenck* v. *United States* decision (1919), where the Court upheld restrictions on free speech during World War I.

American Engagement
Note the marked difference between American disengagement following World War I and American engagement following World War II.

SHAPING THE POSTWAR WORLD

The United States participated in a number of conferences among the Allied countries that played a significant role in shaping the postwar world. The most significant ones follow.

Teheran Conference

Stalin, Churchill, and Roosevelt, met in Teheran, Iran, in November 1943. The allies agreed that the D-Day invasion would coincide with a major Soviet offensive. Also, Stalin pledged that the Soviet Union would join the war in Asia following the defeat of Germany. The allies agreed in theory to forming an international peacekeeping organization.

Bretton Woods Conference

In 1944, delegates from 44 nations met at Bretton Woods, New Hampshire, to discuss the basis of the global economy following the war. The International Monetary Fund was established at this meeting.

Yalta Conference

The Yalta Conference, held in 1945, was the most significant and last meeting of Churchill, Stalin, and Roosevelt. At Yalta, a coastal city in Ukraine, the "big three" agreed to divide Germany into four military zones of occupation (the fourth zone would be occupied by France). Also, Stalin agreed to allow for free elections in Poland in the future, with a Soviet-dominated interim government immediately following the war. Also at the meeting, secret agreements were made allowing for Soviet control of Outer Mongolia, the Kurile Islands, and part of Sakhalin Island as well as for Soviet railroad rights in Manchuria. In exchange, Stalin reaffirmed his commitment to help the United States defeat Japan following the surrender of Germany. Critics later faulted Roosevelt and Churchill for "abandoning" Poland and the rest of Eastern Europe to communist forces. However, there was little the United States and Great Britain could do dislodge the Red Army from Eastern Europe, short of starting a third world war.

Potsdam Conference

In 1945, at this final meeting of the United States, the Soviet Union, and Great Britain, Stalin, President Truman in place of Roosevelt (who died in April 1945), and British Prime Minister Clement Atlee in place of Churchill, hammered out the details of the administration of occupied Germany. These details included the process of denazification of Germany, which led to the Nuremburg War Crimes Trials. The victorious nations set up this international tribunal to try leading Nazis for waging aggressive war and for committing crimes against humanity. At these trials, about 30 American judges participated. The chief justice of the U.S. Supreme Court was a chief lawyer for the prosecution. Many of the Nazis defended themselves by claiming that they were merely following orders.

VICTORY IN THE PACIFIC

Iwo Jima and Okinawa

By February 1945, American forces had taken most of Japan's empire from Japanese control. Two small, heavily fortified islands stood between American forces and the Japanese home islands—Iwo Jima and Okinawa. Capturing these two islands proved to be onerous tasks for American forces. The battle for Iwo Jima lasted six weeks in February and March 1945. Approximately 7,000 Americans died in the battle. The battle for Okinawa was even more deadly. The island of Okinawa was to be a staging area for an attack on the Japanese home islands. Fighting there lasted from early April until mid-June 1945. The United States mobilized 300,000 troops for the battle. Approximately 12,000 American troops died, while Japan lost approximately 140,000 troops. After these bloody battles, Japan was reduced to its home islands.

The Decision to Drop the Atomic Bomb and Japanese Surrender

After the Battle of Okinawa, the Japanese emperor urged the Japanese prime minister to attempt to negotiate an end to the conflict with the United States. Around the same time, President Harry S. Truman learned that the United States had successfully tested an atomic bomb and that more bombs were ready to be used. The United States had been working on this awesomely deadly weapon since 1940. The top secret research program was known as the Manhattan Project. The project involved research labs at different sites. The facility at Los Alamos, New Mexico, headed by physicist J. Robert Oppenheimer, was charged with the actual construction of the bomb.

The United States used this new weapon twice on Japan. On August 6, 1945, the United States dropped an atomic bomb on Hiroshima. On August 9, a second bomb was dropped on Nagasaki. Soon after, Japan surrendered, thus ending World War II. At the time, the decision to drop the atomic bomb did not generate much public debate. The atomic bombing swiftly ended a bloody conflict that consumed 50 million lives. In the decades since the war, some Americans have raised questions about the decision. Critics argue that it was morally wrong for the United States to have targeted civilian populations and that the Japanese were ready to surrender anyway. Many stand by the decision to drop the bombs. Virtually every Japanese city was involved in some way with military production. Further, it is not clear that the Japanese were on the verge of surrendering. Some members of the Japanese military argued against surrendering even after the second bomb was dropped.

Impact of World War II

World War II was a cataclysmic event that profoundly transformed the nations that had participated, including the United States. World War II set in motion a series of demographic, political, and social trends that would shape American history for the remainder of the twentieth century. A large percentage of the millions of returning soldiers soon settled down, married, and had the children that would comprise the baby boom generation. The country shifted in a westward direction as workers headed for California for war-related industrial jobs. The war brought the United States out of the Great Depression and set the country on a generation of sustained economic growth. Wartime experiences inspired both African Americans and women, setting the stage for the civil rights movement and the women's liberation movement. The United States did not retreat into an isolationist stance after the war as the wartime alliance of the United States and the Soviet Union would soon degenerate into a cold war.

Subject to Debate

Two of the most heated historical questions involving the World War II era both have to do with issues of morality, justice, and war. Historians have recently had heated debates over both the Holocaust and the dropping of the atomic bomb on Japan. Some historians have insisted that the United States could have done more to save European Jews. These historians cite prewar immigration restrictions that prevented Jewish refugees from coming into the United States. In 1939, the State Department did not allow the passenger ship *St. Louis* to dock in Florida. The ship was carrying over a thousand Jewish refugees seeking asylum. The ship was forced to return to Antwerp, where most of the Jews aboard ended up dying in concentration camps. This question has resonated in the contemporary world as Americans have debated how much their country should intervene in human rights crises abroad, such as in Kosovo or Darfur.

The debate over the dropping of the atomic bomb has also generated a great deal of controversy. In 1994, the Smithsonian Museum announced plans for an exhibit to open the following year to commemorate the fiftieth anniversary of the dropping of the atom bomb on Hiroshima and Nagasaki. When the floor plans and the text of the proposed exhibit were released to the public, there was a firestorm of controversy. Veterans groups and conservative historians accused the Smithsonian of "revisionism" by portraying the United States in a bad light. The plans revealed a balanced exhibit, but it was not the heroic exhibit that critics had hoped for. The text asked troubling questions, such as whether Japan was actually ready to surrender. The exhibit also showed scenes of death and destruction, which one would expect at an exhibit about a nuclear explosion. Ultimately, the entire exhibit was scrapped. The museum ended up displaying the *Enola Gay* (the plane that dropped the bomb on Hiroshima), but it left out any context or thought-provoking questions.

Practice Multiple-Choice Questions:

Directions: Pick the letter that best answers the following questions.

1. During World War II, working people

   (A) saw their wages drop.
   (B) went on strike frequently.
   (C) organized many protests against U.S. involvement in the war.
   (D) benefited from the policies of the War Labor Board.
   (E) faced high unemployment as factories mechanized production.

2. Some of the participants in the civil rights movement of the 1950s had been inspired by the "double V" campaign of World War II, which urged a victory over both

   (A) fascism abroad and racism at home.
   (B) the Nazis in Europe and the militarists in Japan.
   (C) sexism and racism.
   (D) psychological and political oppression.
   (E) de jure and de facto segregation.

3. At the end of World War II, the main purpose of the conference held at Bretton Woods, New Hampshire, was to

   (A) organize a concerted response to Soviet aggression among the nations of Western Europe and North America.
   (B) plan criminal trials against leading members of the Nazi Party.
   (C) discuss the framework of the United Nations.
   (D) coordinate plans for the reintegration of over 1 million returning soldiers into civilian life.
   (E) regulate the international monetary and financial order through mechanisms such as the International Monetary Fund.

4. The *bracero* program, introduced in 1942, was designed to

   (A) bring temporary contract workers from Mexico into the United States to contribute to the war effort.
   (B) improve relations with Mexico, which had grown strained in the wake of the revelation of the Zimmerman telegram.
   (C) protect the Mexican–United States border from illegal immigrants.
   (D) relocate the Mexican-American population in California to internment camps in the interior of the United States.
   (E) outsource production of military equipment to firms operating in Mexico.

Practice Free-Response Questions:

1. Analyze the debates between isolationists and interventionists in the decade before the Japanese attack at Pearl Harbor (1930–1941).

2. How did the experience of World War II affect the lives of American women?

Answers and Explanations to Multiple-Choice Questions:

1. **(D)** The War Labor Board made sure that war-industry workers received decent wages. All of a sudden when the United States started gearing up for World War II, the Great Depression ended. Stimulus spending ended the depression. Apparently, the New Deal wasn't enough of an expansion to jump-start the economy.
2. **(A)** The "double V" campaign reminded the world about the plight of African Americans. Many historians look to World War II to find the origins of the civil rights movement. Participation in the war effort empowered many African Americans. The contradiction between African-American troops putting their lives on the line to topple a racist regime in Europe and then coming home to a racist system in America became too much to bear.
3. **(E)** The Bretton Woods conference was designed to organize the postwar global economy. The International Monetary Fund and its sister organization, the World Bank, still exist. Choice D was accomplished by the G.I. Bill.
4. **(A)** The *bracero* program brought temporary workers into the United States from Mexico. There was an acute shortage of workers in munitions factories during World War II. The government encouraged women to join the workforce with its Rosie the Riveter campaign.

CHAPTER 27

The Cold War, 1945–1960

TIMELINE	
1947	Publication of the "X Article" ("Sources of Soviet Conduct") by George Kennan
	The Truman Doctrine (containment) is announced
	$400 million in military aid to Greece and Turkey
	House Un-American Activities Committee begins investigations of Hollywood
1948	Beginning of the Berlin Blockade
	Election of Harry S. Truman
1949	Formation of the North Atlantic Treaty Organization (NATO)
1950	Senator Joseph McCarthy gains public spotlight on the issue of anticommunism
	NSC-68 is adopted
	The beginning of the Korean War
	Passage of the McCarran Internal Security Act
1951	Truman fires General Douglas MacArthur
	The United States tests the world's first hydrogen bomb
1952	Execution of Julius and Ethel Rosenberg
	Army-McCarthy hearings
	Election of Dwight D. Eisenhower as president
1955	Creation of Warsaw Pact
1957	Soviet launch of the *Sputnik* satellite
1960	Soviet Union shoots down U-2 spy plane

The Cold War began after World War II when two former allies, the United States and the Soviet Union, emerged as rival superpowers. The perceived threat of communist aggression presented several challenges to the United States. The United States changed in many ways as a result of the Cold War. The country became much more engaged in the affairs of the world and assumed the leading role in the opposition to communism. In addition, the nation changed domestically. New programs were initiated during the Cold War. Some of these programs helped allay people's concerns about the threat of communism, while some initiatives might have added to people's fears.

ORIGINS OF THE COLD WAR

Tensions existed between the United States and the Soviet Union from the time of the Russian Revolution (1917). However, historians tend to date the beginning of the Cold War from the close of World War II.

The Soviet Army Occupies Eastern Europe

The United States believed that the Soviet Union was intent upon extending its control over Europe. As the war ended, the Soviet Union left its Red Army troops in the nations of Eastern Europe. These nations became satellites of the Soviet Union. The Soviet Union indicated that it would allow free elections in Poland. Even there, the Soviet Union imposed its will and installed a puppet regime. The United States was worried that the Soviet Union would try to push into Western Europe. The leader of the Soviet Union, Joseph Stalin, insisted that he wanted to have only friendly nations on the border of the Soviet Union. After numerous attacks from western powers throughout history, from Napoleon to Hitler, the Soviet Union was wary of the West.

Containment

A sophisticated essay might draw comparisons between Truman's policy of the containment of communism in the 1940s and 1950s and Lincoln's policy of the containment of slavery in the 1860s. The position of the Republican Party, starting in 1854, was to contain slavery within its then-present borders.

Containment and the Truman Doctrine

In order to block any further aggression by the Soviet Union, Truman issued the Truman Doctrine (1947), in which he said that the goal of the United States would be to contain communism. The containment approach to the Soviet Union had been spelled out in an article entitled "Sources of Soviet Conduct," published in *Foreign Affairs* (1947). The article was also known as "X Article" because it was published using the pseudonym "X." Later it was learned that the author was George Kennan, a diplomat who had served in the United States embassy in Moscow (1944–1946). Containment remained the cornerstone of American foreign policy for decades to come.

Military Aid to Greece and Turkey

The United States extended military aid to Greece and Turkey in 1947 to further the policy of containment. The aid was successful. It helped the Greek monarchy put down a communist-influenced rebel movement. Further, the move quieted

Republican criticism of Truman and improved Truman's standing in public opinion polls; he won reelection the following year. The United States demonstrated that it was committed to a policy of containment.

TIP

Postwar Policies
Be prepared to compare United States foreign policy following each of the two world wars. After World War I, the United States retreated into isolationism. After World War II, the United States maintained its involvement in world affairs with the containment policy.

The Marshall Plan

The United States further demonstrated its commitment to global engagement with the massive Marshall Plan. The plan, developed by Secretary of State George Marshall, allocated almost $13 billion for war-torn Europe to rebuild. A total of 17 nations received aid between 1948 and 1951, with West Germany, France, and Great Britain receiving the bulk of it. The plan stabilized the capitalist economies of Western Europe and contributed to remarkable growth, as the standard of living in the countries improved. The goal was to provide a viable alternative to Soviet-style communism, and it worked.

The Berlin Blockade and the Berlin Airlift (1948)

In 1948, the United States decided to challenge the Soviet blockade of West Berlin. West Berlin was part of West Germany (an American ally), but it was completely within the territory of East Germany (a Soviet ally). In 1948, the Soviet Union decided it would prevent any food or other supplies from entering West Berlin. The goal was for the Soviet Union to take over West Berlin and make it part of East Germany. The United States did not stand by idly when it learned of the Berlin blockade. President Truman decided to send thousands of planes filled with supplies into West Berlin, in an action known as the Berlin Airlift. The Berlin Airlift prevented West Berlin from starving and prevented the Soviet Union from taking over the city.

The Formation of NATO (1949)

The United States demonstrated its commitment to protect Western Europe when it participated in the founding of the North Atlantic Treaty Organization (NATO) in 1949. The members of NATO vowed to collectively resist any aggressive actions by the Soviet Union. This marked the first time that the United States joined a peacetime alliance.

NSC-68 (1950)

A National Security Council Paper, known as NSC-68, called for a more aggressive defense policy for the United States. It recommended raising taxes and devoting more money to military spending. The document largely shaped United States foreign policy during the Cold War through the 1960s.

Espionage and the U2 Incident (1960)

The United States began an extensive program of spying on the military capabilities of the Soviet Union. At first, the United States denied the program. After a U2 plane was shot down over Soviet territory in 1960, Eisenhower admitted the program existed and defended its goals. These actions all demonstrated that the United States would take a more active role in challenging the Soviet Union.

THE COLD WAR IN ASIA

The initial conflicts of the Cold War occurred in Europe. By the late 1940s, American policy makers became increasingly concerned about events in Asia. The United States' Cold War policies had mixed results in Asia. The United States successfully ushered Japan toward democracy and economic self-sufficiency. The United States also granted independence to the Philippines in 1946. However, China proved to be a difficult problem for President Truman.

"Soft on Communism"
In your essays, try to make connections between foreign-policy issues and domestic politics. After communism triumphed in China, Republicans accused Truman of being "soft on communism." This hurt the Democrats and helped Senator Joseph McCarthy gain an audience.

Communism in China

China had been roiled by an ongoing civil war. The conflict abated during the Japanese occupation during World War II but began again after the war. The United States had allied itself with the Nationalist side, led by Jiang Jieshi (Chiang Kai-shek). However, it became increasingly clear that the opposition Communist Party, led by Mao Zedong, was amassing a huge following among the poor rural population of China. Mao's forces won in 1949, and the People's Republic of China was established.

The news that China, the most populous nation in the world, became communist shocked many Americans. Republicans accused Truman of "losing" China, although in reality he could not have done much to prevent the eventual outcome.

The Korean War (1950–1953)

The next hotspot in the Cold War was Korea. Korea had been divided at the 38th parallel after World War II, with the United States administering the southern half and the Soviet Union administering the northern half (similar to the division of Germany). In 1948, this arrangement was formalized with the creation of two nations, North Korea (a communist country) and South Korea (an American ally). In June 1950, North Korean troops, using Soviet equipment, invaded South Korea. President Truman decided to commit troops to support South Korea and managed to secure United Nations sponsorship. United Nations forces, led by U.S. General Douglas MacArthur, pushed the North Korean troops back to the 38th parallel and then marched into North Korea. When U.N. troops got within 40 miles of the border of between North Korea and China, China sent 150,000 troops over the Yalu River to push back the U.N. forces. After intense fighting, the two sides settled into positions on either side of the 38th parallel.

THE FIRING OF GENERAL MACARTHUR

During the Korean War, General Douglas MacArthur made it clear that he thought the United States could successfully invade China and roll back communism there. Truman was convinced that initiating a wider war so soon after World War II would be disastrous. MacArthur made public pronouncements about strategy, arguing that "there is no substitute for victory." Truman fired MacArthur for insubordination and other unauthorized activities.

ARMISTICE IN KOREA

The Korean War ended as it began—with North Korea and South Korea divided at the 38th parallel. By 1953, an armistice was reached accepting a divided Korea, although a formal treaty ending the war was never signed.

THE DOMESTIC COLD WAR

The Cold War also affected the United States domestically. Americans became increasingly concerned about communist "infiltration" in the United States. The 1963 song "Talkin' World War III Blues" by the folk singer Bob Dylan captured the sense of paranoia that had overtaken the United States. The narrator of the song imagines the aftermath of a nuclear war. As he walks through the devastation, he comes across another living person but that person immediately screams and runs from the narrator. "Must have thought I was a communist," the narrator wryly speculates. This song was issued after the most intense period of anticommunism in the early 1950s. It is doubtful if a major record label would have even released this song a decade earlier.

Federal Employee Loyalty and Security Program

The Federal Loyalty and Security Program barred communists and fascists from serving in federal government positions. This loyalty program was created by President Truman with Executive Order 9835. It also allowed for investigations into the political affiliations of current employees.

Employees had to promise to uphold the Constitution and promise that they were not members of the Communist Party or other "subversive" organizations.

The McCarran Internal Security Act (1950)

The McCarran Internal Security Act mandated that communist groups in the United States register with the government. It also allowed for the arrest of suspected security risks during national emergencies. Truman saw this act as a grave threat to civil liberties and vetoed it. However, Congress passed it over his veto.

Senator Joseph McCarthy

The most prominent elected figure in the anticommunist movement of the 1950s was Senator Joseph McCarthy, a republican from Wisconsin. He was so closely identified with the anticommunist movement that it is often referred to as *McCarthyism.* McCarthy rose to national prominence in 1950 when he announced that he had a list of of 205 "known communists" who were working in the State Department. He later reduced that figure to 57, but he encouraged a mindset where people began to suspect those around them of being communists. This and similar claims, mostly baseless, created a name for McCarthy and set the stage for a host of measures to halt this perceived threat.

THE ATTACK ON HOLLYWOOD

Senate and House anticommunists put a great deal of effort in investigating the movie and television industry, fearing that communists would subtly get their message out through television and movies. In 1947, a group of prominent directors and writers, subsequently known as the "Hollywood 10," was summoned to testify in Washington. They refused, citing their First Amendment rights to freedom of speech and assembly. These ten and others who refused to cooperate were blacklisted in the 1950s, unable to find work in Hollywood.

The Threat of Nuclear War

Although the fear of communist plots might have been overstated, the threat of nuclear war was a constant presence in American life during the Cold War. Both nations invested large sums of money into nuclear weapons programs. Americans were never sure whether a conventional conflict, such as the Korean War, would turn into a nuclear war. Many Americans built bomb shelters in their basements or backyards. Local authorities established civil defense programs to built bomb shelters in public buildings and prepare the public for a nuclear emergency.

DUCK AND COVER

The government took a series of actions in regard to the threat of nuclear war. One action taken by the government was conducting air raid drills in public schools. When an alarm sounded, students would either be ushered to a fallout shelter in the basement of the school or would be ordered to duck and cover under their desks.

The Rosenberg Case

When the United States learned that the Soviet Union had built and tested a nuclear bomb, many Americans were convinced that communists in the United States, loyal to the Soviet Union, had provided the Soviets with essential information about the bomb. Ethel and Julius Rosenberg were an American couple who were accused of passing secrets of the nuclear bomb to the Soviet Union. The Rosenbergs, who were members of the Communist Party, insisted on their innocence but were sent to the electric chair in 1953. Evidence has emerged since the end of the Cold War that suggests that Julius had been involved in some sort of espionage on behalf of the Soviet Union.

The Smith Act and the Communist Party

Government prosecutors used the World War II–era Smith Act to arrest leading members of the Communist Party in several states on the grounds that they conspired to organize and advocate the overthrow of the government by force. Between 1949 and 1957, over 140 communists were arrested, including the leader of the party, Eugene Dennis.

The Fall of McCarthyism

Eventually, critics began to assert that some of the anticommunist measures violated people's constitutional right to freedom of speech. Criticism became more common after the conclusion of hostilities in the Korean War (1953). Finally McCarthy himself went too far, accusing members of the military establishment of being communists. The Senate voted to censure him in 1954, thus ending the worst excesses of what many people referred to as a witch hunt. In the case of *Yates* v. *United States* (1957), the Supreme Court overturned the convictions of members of the Communist Party under the Smith Act.

Understanding NASA

Be aware of the different, and often competing, goals of NASA. On the one hand, it was created to engage in scientific research for the benefit of humanity. On the other hand, it helped further the military goals of the United States during World War II.

The Launching of *Sputnik* (1957)

The launching of the Soviet unmanned satellite *Sputnik* into space in 1957 caught many Americans off guard and led to several important domestic developments.

Sputnik alarmed United States government officials because they realized that the same type of rocket that launched the satellite could also be used to deliver atomic weapons quickly to any location on Earth.

CHANGES IN EDUCATION

The launching of *Sputnik* led the American government to devote more resources to teaching science and math to young people. Americans had assumed that the United States was technologically superior to the Soviet Union. The government was determined not to be outdone in regard to science and technology by the Soviet Union.

THE SPACE RACE

After the launch of *Sputnik*, the United States engaged in a race to explore outer space. The United States created the National Aeronautics and Space Administration (NASA) in 1958 to carry out the nation's space program. In 1961, President John F. Kennedy announced the goal of landing a man on the moon before the close of the 1960s. This goal was accomplished. In 1969, the United States was the first nation to land men on the moon successfull

Subject to Debate

Many of our understandings of the Cold War were developed by American historians during the height of the Cold War. As might be expected, these historians saw American actions in a positive light and Soviet actions in a negative light. "Our" side stood for democracy, freedom, and progress; "their" side stood for repression, aggression, and coercion. Since the fall of the Soviet Union, historians have reevaluated this standard narrative. Some historians have put renewed emphasis on covert operations by the United States during the Cold War, such as the 1954 CIA-backed coup in Iran that toppled Mohammed Mosaddegh and installed the Shah. These covert operations complicate the story. In addition, historians have also looked at Soviet moves in a slightly different light. Stalin's occupation of Eastern Europe following World War II is still seen as an unfortunate move, but some historians have begun to put Stalin's actions in a larger historical context. After all, perhaps the moves are less reprehensible when looked at in the context of the history of attacks on Russia that came through Eastern Europe.

On the other side of the political spectrum, historians of the Cold War period have revisited debates about the nature of the American communist movement in the 1940s and 1950s. For many years, historians looked at the Communist Party as victims of an irrational witch hunt. More recently, since the fall of the Soviet Union, a group of historians, led by Harvey Klehr and John Earl Haynes, have scoured old Soviet archives and found some damning evidence against the Communist Party. Klehr and Haynes have found, for instance, transcriptions that seem to implicate Julius Rosenberg in spying for the Soviet Union.[1] Their findings have forced a reevaluation of the assumption that members of the Communist Party were innocent victims.

[1]John Earl Haynes and Harvey Klehr, *Venona: Decoding Soviet Espionage in America* (New Haven: Yale University Press, 1999).

Practice Multiple-Choice Questions:

Directions: Pick the letter that best answers the following questions.

1. The central tenet of the Truman Doctrine was
   (A) the United States would not tolerate imperialist ventures by European powers in the Americas.
   (B) the United States and the Soviet Union should cooperate to explore space and land a man on the moon.
   (C) the United States would extend foreign aid only to countries that respect human rights.
   (D) the United States would not use nuclear weapons in a first-strike basis; it would use them only in response to a nuclear attack.
   (E) the United States would extend military and financial resources to contain communism.

2. Julius and Ethel Rosenberg were accused of and were executed for
   (A) spying for Nazi Germany.
   (B) inciting opposition to World War II.
   (C) being members of the Communist Party.
   (D) providing information about the atomic bomb to the Soviet Union.
   (E) organizing the bombing of an Army recruiting station during the Vietnam War.

3. The McCarran Internal Security Act was
   (A) passed by Congress over President Truman's veto.
   (B) signed by President Harding as part of the Red Scare.
   (C) derided by Senator Joseph McCarthy as "soft on communism."
   (D) passed by President Bush in the wake of the September 11, 2001, terrorist attacks.
   (E) pushed by President McKinley after the assassination attempt on Henry Clay Frick.

4. The immediate cause of United States military involvement in the Korean peninsula in 1950 was the
   (A) acquisition of nuclear weapons by North Korea.
   (B) Japanese invasion of Manchuria.
   (C) sinking of a United States Navy destroyer off the coast of North Korea.
   (D) execution of Red Cross observers by the North Korean government.
   (E) attack by North Korea on South Korea.

Practice Free-Response Questions:

1. To what degree were public fears about communist infiltration in the United States justified?

2. Analyze the degree to which civil liberties were abridged in TWO of the following situations:

   World War I
   The Red Scare of the 1920s
   World War II
   McCarthyism in the 1950s

3. Discuss the relationship between foreign affairs and domestic politics during the Truman presidency (1945–1953).

Answers and Explanations to Multiple-Choice Questions:

1. **(E)** The Truman Doctrine set forth the policy of containment. The policy asserted that the United States would accept communism where it already existed but would challenge it elsewhere. Truman extended military aid to Greece and Turkey as part of the containment policy. He also extended economic aid to Western Europe as part of the Marshall plan.
2. **(D)** The Rosenbergs were arrested for spying for the Soviet Union. The government asserted that they conveyed the secret of the atomic bomb to the Soviets. The couple insisted on their innocence until the very end. They were both executed. Subsequent evidence indicates that Julius did spying work for the Soviet Union. There is no evidence, however, that Ethel participated.
3. **(A)** The McCarran Internal Security Act was a Cold War measure that was passed by a congressional override of Truman's veto. Truman was anticommunist, but he also supported civil liberties. He thought this act went too far.
4. **(E)** The Korean War began when North Korea attacked South Korea. The United States entered the conflict, with the backing of the United Nations to defend South Korea. The United States was successful in its limited mission of removing North Korean forces from South Korea. General Douglas MacArthur wanted to go further and attack North Korea and China. Truman, however, wanted to keep it a limited war.

American Society in the Post–World War II Era, 1945–1960

CHAPTER 28

TIMELINE

1944	The G.I. Bill is passed
1946	*Baby and Child Care* by Dr. Benjamin Spock is published
	Largest wave of strikes in United States history
1947	Taft-Hartley Act
1948	President Truman issues the order to desegregate the military
	Truman wins presidential election
1952	Dwight D. Eisenhower wins the presidential election
1954	Interstate Highway Act
	Brown v. *The Board of Education of Topeka*
1956	Rosa Parks is arrested for not giving up her seat; Montgomery Bus Boycott
	Reelection of Eisenhower
1957	Founding of the Southern Christian Leadership Conference
	Crisis in Little Rock, Arkansas, over school desegregation
	On the Road by Jack Kerouac is published

In many ways, World War II was a watershed in American society. The postwar world was almost indistinguishable from the prewar world. A more modern, more affluent society emerged in the postwar era—one unimaginable in the depth of the Great Depression.

ABUNDANCE IN POSTWAR AMERICA

Perhaps the most remarkable development of the postwar years was the unprecedented growth of the economy and the rising living standard for millions of Americans. The gross domestic product of the country—the total value of goods and services produced in the United States in a year—rose dramatically between 1945 and 1960, from $200 billion to $500 billion. Such growth was unprecedented in American society. In this period, we see a dramatic rise in the middle class. Millions of Americans from working-class backgrounds were able to achieve many of the markers of middle-class life—home and car ownership, a college education, and a comfortable income.

The Wave of Strikes in 1946

Immediately following World War II, the United States experienced the largest wave of strikes in its history as 5 million workers walked off their jobs. Unions, which had refrained from striking during the war, feared that the gains they had made during the war would be taken away. The wave of strikes was largely successful, boosting wages for factory workers and allowing them to partake in the consumer culture of the era.

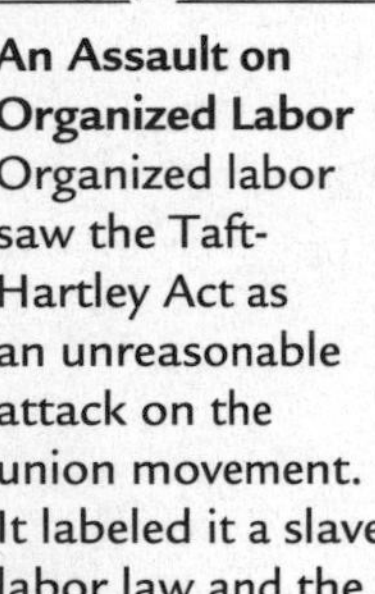

TIP

An Assault on Organized Labor Organized labor saw the Taft-Hartley Act as an unreasonable attack on the union movement. It labeled it a slave labor law and the "Tuff-Heartless" Act.

The Taft-Hartley Act

The Taft-Hartley Act (1947) was designed to monitor and restrict the activities of organized labor. The law was passed, over President Truman's veto, by a conservative Republican-dominated Congress that had been elected in 1946. The law imposed restrictions on unions that made it more difficult to strike. It allowed states to pass "right to work" laws, banning union shops (a union shop is a workplace in which all the workers are required to join the union after a majority voted for it). The law also required union leaders to pledge that they were not members of the Communist Party.

The G.I. Bill

The federal government helped returning veterans adjust to the peacetime economy with the Servicemen's Readjustment Act (1944), more commonly known as the G.I. Bill. The act provided low-interest loans for veterans to purchase homes and to attend college.

The Growth of Suburbia

An important postwar trend was the growth of suburbs. Suburbs were not a new phenomenon in the postwar period. The earliest residential suburbs were built around commuter railroad stations in the late-nineteenth century. However, a series of factors contributed to the unprecedented growth of these communities. New suburban communities were built just outside of major American cities to meet the housing crunch created by all the returning World War II soldiers. Huge numbers of these soldiers quickly married, had children, and looked for affordable housing.

Race also played a factor in the development of suburbia. Many white people did not want to live in the urban neighborhoods that had become integrated after many southern, rural African Americans had moved north to work in war industries.

Levittown and Suburban Development

Developers facilitated the move to the suburbs. An innovative developer was William Levitt. He took large tracts of land outside of major cities (often farmland) and built huge developments of nearly identical, modest houses. He applied the techniques of mass production to these houses, building them rapidly and cheaply. Levittown, on Long Island, New York, became synonymous with these mass-produced communities. These developments were not without their critics. Songwriter Malvina Reynolds skewered the monotony of life in these developments in the song "Little Boxes" (1962).

The Baby Boom

For several years before 1946, birthrates in the United States had remained relatively low. Couples tended to have fewer children during the lean years of the Great Depression. The dislocation and physical separation caused by World War II kept the birthrate even lower. When the war ended, returning veterans quickly began starting families. The spike in birthrates from 1946 through the early 1960s produced a baby boom that would have lasting repercussions in American society. The baby boom required states to spend more money on public education in the 1950s and 1960s, and expanded college enrollment in the 1960s and 1970s. Today, political leaders are confronted with the economic repercussions of baby boomers reaching retirement age.

Child-Rearing in the 1950s

The parents of the baby boom generation were enthusiastic readers of child-rearing guides. The most influential was Benjamin Spock's *Baby and Child Care* (1946). Spock urged parents to treat their children as individuals, to let them develop at their own pace, and to focus less on discipline and more on affection. When baby boomers joined the counterculture in the 1960s, conservative critics cited Spock's book as part of the problem.

The Interstate Highway Act

Federal and local highway initiatives also made suburbia attractive. One could now drive into cities from the suburbs quickly and easily. With the National Interstate Highway and Defense Act (1956), the federal government initiated a massive highway-building project that resulted in the interstate highway system. The act was also promoted as a defense measure, allowing for the rapid movement of military equipment and personnel. Americans could now feasibly leave cities and enjoy a small piece of land to call their own.

White Flight and the Decline of Older Cities

Not everyone shared equally in the abundance of the 1950s. As middle-class families left urban centers to move to the suburbs, they took with them their ability to pay local taxes. Cities saw their tax bases shrink dramatically. With funds scarce, cities had to cut back on basic services like policing and education. Crime became an unavoidable urban reality, and city schools deteriorated. This decline in city services put more pressure on middle-class people to make the move to the suburbs. By the 1960s, entire sections of cities had become slums.

THE URBAN RENEWAL PROGRAM

To address the decline of older cities, the federal government initiated the Urban Renewal Program. The Urban Renewal Program labeled entire urban neighborhoods as blighted slum areas and provided funds for the destruction of these areas. Often nothing was built to replace the blighted areas. In many cities, the federal government funded large-scale housing projects for low income residents in urban renewal zones. These housing projects proved to be soulless structures that bred crime and unsanitary conditions. Finally in the 1960s, many urban African-American residents, from Watts to Detroit to Newark, responded to their conditions with rioting.

THE CIVIL RIGHTS MOVEMENT IN THE 1950s

One of the most significant reform movements in American history blossomed in the 1950s—the civil rights movement. The movement challenged the legal basis of the segregation of African Americans in the United States, but it also challenged the pervasive racism of American society. This racism justified the existence of slavery and the persistence of Jim Crow segregation. The movement forced America to examine its most cherished institutions and also to reevaluate its patterns of thought.

World War II and Origins of the Civil Rights Movement

World War II was a transformative experience for many African-American men and women. Many returning soldiers felt a sense of empowerment and engagement that they had had not previously felt. These veterans had taken part in the NAACP's Double V campaign during the war—victory against fascism abroad and victory against racism at home. The injustices of American life seemed especially reprehensible to men who had just risked their lives serving their country. In addition, the migration of many African-American men and women from the familiar patterns of rural southern life to the new challenges of urban, industrial America whetted their appetites for change and justice. This was the generation that would become the leaders of the civil rights movement in the decades after the war.

Truman and Civil Rights

President Truman, the Democratic president from Missouri who took office when President Franklin Roosevelt died in 1945, was an early supporter of civil rights. He created the Committee on Civil Rights in 1946, and he pushed Congress to enact the committee's recommendations in 1948. In 1948, Truman issued an executive order to ban segregation in the military. Finally, he issued an executive order to desegregate the armed forces. However, he failed to implement it until the Korean War, when the military needed additional personnel. Truman was motivated to take these steps both out of personal conviction and in response to actions by civil rights activists. Truman felt that he could not go too far because he would lose the support of southern Democrats.

A Favorable Supreme Court and the *Brown* Decision (1954)

Early civil rights activists pressed their cause in a number of ways. However, a very promising one was to bring the issue of segregation in front of the Supreme Court. The movement realized that the Supreme Court in 1954 was more far liberal than the Supreme Court of 1896, which had issued the infamous *Plessy* v. *Ferguson* decision. In 1953, the Supreme Court got a new, more liberal Chief Justice, Earl Warren, appointed by President Dwight Eisenhower. The NAACP and its lead lawyer Thurgood Marshall thought the time was right.

The case of *Brown* v. *Board of Education of Topeka* was actually several cases looked at simultaneously by the court. The *Brown* in the case was the Reverend Oliver Brown, whose eight-year-old daughter had to go an African-American school over a mile away from her house rather than attend a white school nearby. The court heard a variety of types of evidence in the case, including studies on the psychological impact of segregation on young people. The court ruled unanimously that segregation in public schools was unfair and had to end. The *Brown* decision set in motion a major upheaval in American society. It gave great encouragement to the civil rights movement, which believed that the federal government was in favor of civil rights.

State and Federal Power
The crisis in Little Rock brought to the fore the issue of the relationship of federal power to state power. This was a central issue in the Civil War. When President Eisenhower sent troops to Little Rock, Governor Faubus used language that was purposely evocative of the Reconstruction period. The reaction of Faubus brings to mind William Faulkner's quotation, "The past is not dead. In fact, it's not even past."

The Little Rock Crisis (1957) and the Backlash Against the *Brown* Decision

The *Brown* decision unleashed a violent backlash against civil rights on the part of many southern white people. These people vowed to engage in "massive resistance" against efforts toward integration. An example of the backlash was the reaction of the Arkansas Governor Orval Faubus to the desegregation plan at Central High School in Little Rock in 1957. He mobilized the National Guard to block the African-American students from entering the school. This move angered President Eisenhower, who ended up sending army troops to Little Rock to ensure the safety of the African-American students.

Rosa Parks and the Montgomery Bus Boycott (1955–1956)

Rosa Parks was a civil rights activist who refused to give up her seat to a white person on a Montgomery, Alabama, city bus in 1955. She was arrested for this action. Her arrest led to the Montgomery bus boycott, which lasted about a year (1955–1956). The boycott led to the bus company ending its policy of making African Americans give up their seats to whites.

Martin Luther King, Jr. and Nonviolent Civil Disobedience

The Montgomery bus boycott was led by a young Baptist minister, Martin Luther King, Jr., from Atlanta, Georgia. King's leadership during the boycott made him a well-known figure. He soon became the central figure in the civil rights movement of the 1950s and 1960s. King supported directly challenging unjust practices through civil disobedience. In 1963, the civil rights movement held one of the biggest demonstrations in American history in Washington, D.C. Over 200,000 people gathered to march, sing, and hear speeches, including King's "I Have a Dream Speech."

THE CULTURES OF THE 1950s

The 1950s are often presented as a decade of bland conformity. Although there were pressures to conform to mainstream norms for proper behavior, there were also undercurrents of nonconformity and resistance to these norms.

Conformity in a Conservative Decade

Several commentators noted the societal pressures toward conformity in the 1950s. Part of this push toward conformity can be attributed to the domestic Cold War and the dictates of McCarthyism (see Chapter 27). Many Americans felt intimidated from appearing nonconformist in the 1950s. Sociologists David Riesman, Nathan Glazer, and Reuel Denney in their book *The Lonely Crowd* (1950) noted that Americans were more eager to mold their ideas to societal standards than they were to think independently. William H. Whyte's book *The Organization Man* (1956) described the stultifying atmosphere of the modern corporation where employees were pressured to think like the group. The novel *The Man in the Gray Flannel Suit* (1955) by Sloan Wilson depicted a man trapped in the materialistic business world of the 1950s. J. D. Salinger's best-selling novel *The Catcher in the Rye* (1951) railed at the "phonies" who had achieved success in mainstream 1950s society.

Television

Television became an extremely popular medium in the 1950s. By the end of the decade nearly 90 percent of American homes owned a television set. After an initial burst of creativity in the late 1940s and early 1950s, television programming settled into safe, predictable genres. The most emblematic genre of the 1950s was the suburban situation comedy (sitcom), complete with a stay-at-home mother, such as *Leave It to Beaver* and *Father Knows Best.* Westerns, such as *Bonanza* and *Gunsmoke,* and daytime dramas (labeled soap operas because of sponsorship by soap manufacturers) such as *The Guiding Light* and *Search for Tomorrow* dominated the airwaves. Many of these genres were carryovers from radio. *The Ed Sullivan Show,* a variety show, was extremely popular, airing from 1948 to 1971.

TIP

Countercultures
Do not confuse the timeframe for countercultural movements. The beats were in the 1950s; hippies were in the 1960s; and punks were in the 1970s.

Rock 'n' Roll Music

Rock 'n' roll music became extremely popular among young people in the 1950s. Rock 'n' roll developed primarily in the African-American community. It was dubbed "race music" and was deemed dangerous by mainstream white commentators. Elvis Presley, a white singer from Memphis, Tennessee, became a huge cultural force in America. He followed in the footsteps of numerous African-American performers, some famous (Chuck Berry) and some largely forgotten ("Big Mama" Thornton). Rock 'n' roll music was part of a distinct youth culture ushering in a generational divide in American society.

Beat Generation Literature

The beat literary movement represented a subversive undercurrent in the 1950s. The beats represented a rejection of mainstream social values in the 1950s—the suburban lifestyle, the consumer society, and patriotism. The most important text of the beat movement was *On the Road* by Jack Kerouac (1957). Initially written on a scroll—a stream of consciousness screed—the book depicts a life of spontaneity and freedom. Also important is Allen Ginsberg's book of poems *Howl* (1956), which ripped apart the foundations of materialistic American society.

Abstract Expressionism

An important artistic movement of the 1950s came to be called abstract expressionism. Centered in New York City, the movement elevated the process of painting—emphasizing spontaneity, emotion, and intensity over studied, realistic reproductions of the visible world. The most well-known practitioner of abstract expressionism is Jackson Pollock, who poured and dripped paint on his canvasses.

Subject to Debate

When writing about history, beware of clichés. Mainstream media and popular memory often reduce a complex time period to a phrase or an image. When many of us hear "the nineteen twenties," the first thing that pops into our head might be the jazz age. We think of *The Great Gatsby*, martinis, flappers, and speakeasies. But this image has become a cliché, obscuring the complex tensions of the 1920s. Yes, people went to speakeasies, but they also joined Ku Klux Klan rallies. The more we read about the 1920s, the harder it becomes to reduce it to a catchphrase.

The same is true of the 1950s. For many Americans, the image of the 1950s can be reduced to the word "conformity." We look condescendingly at the naïve suburbanites of the decade, blithely watching bland television programs. As students of history, we should be weary of such easy clichés. As in the 1920s, complex social factors were at work. There were many trends in the 1950s that flew in the face of conformity—the most obvious one being the civil rights movement. The 1950s also saw the birth of the beat movement, the popularity of rock 'n' roll, and the beginnings of the folk revival.

On a related note, be careful about identifying the decade too closely with one individual—Joseph McCarthy. Yes, he was a powerful figure. But his power was brief. By 1954, he was largely discredited. Also even at the height he was not the entire anticommunist movement. By focusing on McCarthy, we forget that there was a liberal anticommunist movement, one that was critical of the excesses of McCarthy. Historians are moving away from using the term "McCarthyism" to describe the entire anticommunist movement.

Practice Multiple-Choice Questions:

Directions: Pick the letter that best answers the following questions.

1. William Levitt is often compared to Henry Ford because they both

   (A) invented new products that changed American society.
   (B) standardized production of particular products.
   (C) used extensive government funding to advance particular projects.
   (D) created products that only the wealthy could afford.
   (E) worked closely with labor unions to assure their workers received a living wage.

2. Which was <u>not</u> a form of *de jure* segregation?
   (A) Preventing blacks and whites from sitting at the same lunch counter
   (B) Separating blacks from whites in department store fitting rooms
   (C) Blacks and whites living in separate neighborhoods in cities
   (D) Discrimination in waiting rooms in interstate bus stations
   (E) Requiring blacks and whites to use separate water fountains

3. Beat generation literature
   (A) reflected disillusionment with the materialism of the 1920s.
   (B) showed the economic devastation of the 1930s.
   (C) encouraged support for the war effort of the 1940s.
   (D) represented a departure from the suburban conformity of the 1950s.
   (E) inspired the women's rights movement of the 1960s.

4. A central assertion of David Riesman, Nathan Glazer, and Reuel Denney in their sociological study *The Lonely Crowd* (1950) was that
   (A) Americans were more interested in conforming to social norms than they were to think independently.
   (B) children were becoming increasingly alienated from the adult world.
   (C) Jim Crow legislation and poverty led to African Americans feeling divorced from mainstream society.
   (D) men and women were losing the ability the ability to communicate effectively with one another.
   (E) anti-immigrant legislation contributed to immigrants living a life of isolation in the shadows of society.

Practice Free-Response Questions:

1. "The 1950s was an era of conformity and timidity." Assess the validity of this statement.

2. Assess the social, economic, and politics factors that account for the rise of suburbia (1945–1960).

Answers and Explanations to Multiple-Choice Questions:

1. **(B)** Levitt and Ford standardized production of particular products—cars in the case of Ford and houses in the case of Levitt. Levitt built huge communities of nearly identical homes, the Little Boxes about which Malvina Reynolds sang. He often named communities after himself; there are several suburban Levittowns.

2. **(C)** De jure segregation is segregation mandated by law. All the choices are mandated by law except choice C. The civil rights movement of the 1950s and 1960s brought an end to de jure segregation in the United States. De facto segregation, a pattern of segregation supported by custom, continues to exist in areas of the United States.
3. **(D)** The "beats" mocked the middle-class values of the 1950s. A key beat generation text is Jack Kerouac's *On the Road.* Despite the perception that the 1950s were an age of conformity, there were elements of cultural rebellion.
4. **(A)** *The Lonely Crowd* bemoaned the trend in American society to fit in and to be a team player. The authors argued that the anticommunist crusade and the jingoism of the decade had created a conformist public.

The High Tide of American Liberalism, 1960–1968

TIMELINE

1960	Lunch counter sit-in movement begins
	Election of John F. Kennedy
1961	Bay of Pigs invasion in Cuba
1961	The Freedom Rides begin
1962	Cuban Missile Crisis
1963	The campaign to desegregate Birmingham, Alabama
	The assassination of President John F. Kennedy
	March on Washington, D.C.; King delivers his "I Have a Dream" speech
1964	The Civil Rights Acts passed
	"Freedom Summer" voter registration drive in Mississippi
	The killing of civil rights workers Michael Schwerner, James Chaney, and Andrew Goodman
	The Gulf of Tonkin Resolution
	Election of Lyndon B. Johnson
1965	Voting Rights Act
	Malcolm X is assassinated
	Selma to Montgomery, Alabama march
1966	Founding of the Black Panthers

The election of the youthful John F. Kennedy coupled with a series of decisions by the Warren Court, the implementation of President Johnson's Great Society programs, and the successful passage of landmark civil rights legislation points to the high tide of American liberalism. The 1960s also saw the unraveling of the liberal agenda as the war in Vietnam sucked valuable resources from social programs and urban rioting highlighted the limits of the federal government's ability to address the problems of the African-American underclass.

TIP

Liberalism
Note that liberalism has meant different things at different times. In the nineteenth century, liberalism implied unfettered individual rights. Since the New Deal, liberalism has meant support for government programs to rectify social ills.

THE PRESIDENCY OF JOHN F. KENNEDY

In many ways, Kennedy's election in 1960 symbolized a break from the conservatism of the 1950s. Although Kennedy continued many of Eisenhower's policies, the election represented a symbolic passing of the torch to many Americans. Kennedy's domestic agenda is called the New Frontier. Kennedy's presidency was cut short by an assassin's bullet less than two years into his presidency.

The Election of 1960

The election of 1960 proved to be one of the closest in American history. The Democratic candidate John F. Kennedy and the Republican candidate Richard Nixon each received just under 50 percent of the popular vote. However, Kennedy won by a comfortable margin in the electoral vote.

The 1960 campaign was notable for the growing importance of the mass media in the political process. For the first time, millions of people saw presidential candidates debate. The contrast between the young, confident, handsome Kennedy and the disheveled, nervous Nixon was striking. The image of Nixon, with his five o'clock shadow and with perspiration streaming down his face, did not win over many members of the public. Since that debate, politicians have spent much more time working on their image.

The Peace Corps (1961)

President Kennedy's sense of idealism and his commitment to service are embodied in the Peace Corps. The program was established by Kennedy in 1961 to assist underdeveloped countries in Africa, Latin America, and Asia. Under the program, American volunteers work for two years at a particular site, serving as teachers, health workers, or agricultural advisors. The program still exists.

A.I.D. and the Alliance for Progress

To mend frayed relations with the developing world, Kennedy created the United States Agency for International Development (USAID) to coordinate aid to foreign countries. He also created the Alliance for Progress, a series of development projects in Latin America.

Hostilities with Cuba

Events in Cuba occupied much of Kennedy's brief tenure as president, as Cuba became a Cold War hotspot in 1959. Cuba had been run as a military dictatorship with close ties with the United States from 1933 to 1959. In 1959, Fidel Castro led a successful guerilla movement to topple the dictatorship. By 1960, the relationship between the United States and Cuba grew hostile while the relationship between the Soviet Union and Cuba grew friendly. In the final months of the Eisenhower Administration, advisors planned for the United States to train, arm, and aid a group of Cuban exiles opposed to the communist government of Fidel Castro.

Kennedy adopted the plan and green-lighted its implementation in 1961. The exiles landed at the Bay of Pigs in Cuba in April 1961 but were quickly captured by Cuban forces. The Bay of Pigs incident was the first of several attempts to oust the communist regime from Cuba.

TIP 

Cuba and Florida
Hostilities toward Cuba have persisted since the 1960s, despite the fact that the United States has normalized relations with other communist nations (China and Vietnam). One reason for the continued hostility is that both major political parties fear alienating Cuban Americans in Florida and losing that state in presidential elections.

Cuban Missile Crisis

The Cuban Missile Crisis occurred in 1962 when a United States U2 spy plane discovered that Cuba was preparing bases to install Soviet nuclear missiles. President Kennedy felt that these missiles, in such close proximity to the United States, amounted to an unacceptable provocation. He ordered Soviet Premier Nikita Khrushchev to halt the operation and dismantle the bases. Khrushchev insisted on the right of the Soviet Union to install the missiles. For about a week, the world stood on the brink of nuclear war. Finally a deal was reached in which the Soviet Union would abandon its Cuban missile program and the United States would quietly remove missiles from Turkey.

U.S.-Soviet Relations Under Kennedy

Kennedy made attempts to ease tensions between the Soviet Union and the United States. In the wake of the Cuban Missile Crisis, a Partial Test Ban Treaty was signed by the United States, the Soviet Union, and Great Britain in 1963. The ban exempted underground nuclear tests.

Kennedy and the Race to the Moon

In 1961, President Kennedy boldly predicted that the United States would land a man on the moon by the close of the decade. The budget for the National Aeronautics and Space Administration grew under his administration. The prediction proved correct. In 1969, the United States became the first nation to land a man on the moon.

The Assassination of President Kennedy (1963)

On November 22, 1963, President Kennedy was assassinated by Lee Harvey Oswald while visiting Dallas, Texas. The news of Kennedy's death shocked the nation.

PRESIDENT JOHNSON AND THE GREAT SOCIETY

Lyndon B. Johnson took office upon the assassination of President Kennedy. Johnson, a Texas Democrat, proved to be a remarkably effective president, passing a host of domestic programs that rival the New Deal in scope. However, his administration took a tragic turn as Johnson's hopes for a Great Society were brought down by a costly and unpopular war in Vietnam.

The Election of 1964

Johnson won the election handily in 1964, capturing 61 percent of the popular vote. Although Johnson's opponent, Republican Senator Barry Goldwater, lost, he generated a great deal of grassroots enthusiasm. In many ways, Goldwater's campaign represented the beginning of the ascendency of a conservative movement that would become a force to reckon with later in the twentieth century (see Chapter 31).

TIP 

Federal Programs
Note the continuities between the New Deal of the 1930s and the Great Society of the 1960s. Both expanded the role of the federal government in the lives of ordinary Americans. Both were met with only limited success.

The Great Society

A major goal of President Johnson's Great Society program was to end poverty in the United States. Great Society programs include the development of Medicare and Medicaid, welfare programs, and public housing. Johnson created the Office of Economic Opportunity, which oversaw many of the Great Society initiatives. These programs have had limited success. The cycle of poverty proved to be too difficult to break in a short period of time. Further, the war in Vietnam became increasingly costly, diverting billions of dollars that could have been used for antipoverty programs.

Immigration Reform (1965)

Part of the Great Society program included reforming the restrictive immigration policies that had been put into effect in the 1920s. The Immigration Act of 1965 continued to limit the number of immigrants allowed into the United States. However, it eliminated the quota system based on national origin.

THE WAR IN VIETNAM

Vietnam is a small country hugging the edge of the Indochina peninsula in Southeast Asia. From the mid-nineteenth to the mid-twentieth centuries, it was a colony of France. It was occupied by Japan during World War II. After the war, many Vietnamese hoped to finally be free of foreign control, but France reoccupied it. A resistance movement, led by Ho Chi Minh, intensified in the 1950s. In 1954, French forces were defeated at the Vietnamese town of Dien Bien Phu and began to withdraw from the region. The Geneva Accords (1954) divided Vietnam at the 17th parallel, between communist-controlled North Vietnam, led by Ho Chi Minh, and a western-allied South Vietnam. A rebel movement, known as the Vietcong, continued to press its cause in South Vietnam. American observers came to the conclusion that the government of South Vietnam could very likely fall to communist rebels without outside help.

The Domino Theory

American involvement in Vietnam was influenced by a belief in the domino theory. It asserts that when a nation become communist, its neighbors will be more likely to become communist. The theory presumes that communism is imposed on a country from the outside—that it does not develop as a result of internal conditions.

The United States Sends Advisors to Vietnam

United States interest in Vietnam began in the 1950s when it sent military advisors and assistance to the government of South Vietnam after Vietnam was divided in 1954. The United States feared that South Vietnam would become a communist nation, as North Vietnam had.

The Gulf of Tonkin Resolution

The United States became heavily involved in the Vietnam War after Congress gave President Johnson a blank check with the Tonkin Gulf Resolution (1964). In August 1964, Johnson announced that American destroyers had been fired upon in the Gulf of Tonkin, off the coast of North Vietnam. Later, reports questioned the accuracy of the announcement. However, the incident led Congress to give Johnson a blank check in Vietnam. The Gulf of Tonkin Resolution can be considered the beginning of full-scale American involvement in the war in Vietnam.

The Draft

Starting in 1964, the Selective Service System began drafting young men to serve in the army. In 1965, the number of draftees doubled monthly. The draft made the Vietnam War much more of an immediate concern for millions of young men and contributed to the number of young people participating in the antiwar movement.

A Living Room War

TIP 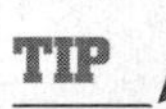

A Lack of Consensus
Note the evolution of popular sentiment in regard to Vietnam and the factors that contributed to antiwar sentiment among many Americans.

The Vietnam War was the first American war to occur in an age when the vast majority of Americans owned television sets (90 percent by 1960). Americans, therefore, were able to see uncensored images of warfare in their living rooms for the first time. Many were shocked at what they saw. A report by Morley Safer in 1965 showed Marines evacuating civilians from their homes and then setting the entire village on fire. More disturbing images followed and contributed to public opinion questioning the wisdom and justness of the war.

The Tet Offensive

In January 1968, the Vietcong and North Vietnamese forces launched a major offensive on U.S. forces. The offensive began on Tet, the beginning of the new year in the traditional lunar calendar. This major offensive left 1,600 American troops dead, while the North Vietnamese and the Vietcong suffered over 40,000 deaths. The offensive was put down by U.S. forces. However, it demonstrated the ability of the Vietnamese to organize a coordinated strike and to push deep into American-held territory.

The My Lai Massacre

In 1968, a company of American troops killed a large percentage of the inhabitants of My Lai. The army covered up the massacre for over a year. In 1971, the commander of the company, Lieutenant William Calley, was tried by the military for the massacre. The incident led many Americans to question the morality of the war in Vietnam even further.

A Working-Class War

In many ways, the war in Vietnam was a working-class war; 80 percent of the troops in Vietnam were working class poor. Middle-class youths often managed to get college deferments or had connections to get a stateside position in the National Guard. In 1967, Martin Luther King gave a speech entitled "Beyond Vietnam," condemning the war and its impact on American society.

The War Drags On

The war in Vietnam became a quagmire that the United States neither could win nor could successfully extricate itself from. Americans began to grow impatient with the war effort as the number of troops and the number of casualties increased. As we shall see in Chapter 30, the war generated a vocal antiwar movement and doomed Johnson's presidency.

THE WARREN COURT (1953–1969)

Earl Warren was the chief justice of the Supreme Court from 1953 to 1969. The Court under his leadership moved in a decidedly liberal direction. The first case Warren dealt with as Chief Justice was the landmark *Brown* case (see Chapter 28). During the 1960s, the Warren Court continued to protect the rights of minorities, reinforced the separation of church and state, established an individual's right to privacy, and protected the rights of people accused of crimes. Liberals have generally welcomed Warren Court decisions, while conservatives have accused him of judicial activism.

TIP

Chief Justices
The AP exam does not require you to know all the chief justices of the Supreme Court, but you should be familiar with John Marshall (1801–1835) and Earl Warren (1953–1969). Both of these courts maintained a consistent ideological approach that is evident in the respective decisions of each.

Expanding the Rights of the Accused

Several important Warren Court decisions expanded the rights of people accused of crimes. The Court ruled in *Mapp* v. *Ohio* (1961) that prosecutors could not use evidence obtained in illegal searches. In *Gideon* v. *Wainwright* (1963), the Supreme Court ruled that the states must provide court-appointed attorneys to impoverished defendants. Previously, this stipulation applied only to federal court procedures. In *Miranda* v. *Arizona* (1966), the Court ruled that arrested people must be read basic rights, now known as Miranda rights, including the right to remain silent and the right to have a lawyer.

The Right to Privacy

Although the right to privacy is not specifically mentioned in the Constitution, the Warren Court asserted that the right is implicit in it. In *Griswold* v. *Connecticut*

(1965), the Court ruled that laws forbidding the use of birth control devices were unconstitutional. The right to privacy would become important in *Roe* v. *Wade*, which insisted that states allow abortions during the first two trimesters of pregnancy (see Chapter 30).

Free Speech

In *Tinker* v. *Des Moines* (1969), the Supreme Court ruled that a school board prohibition against students wearing black armbands in protest of the war in Vietnam was unconstitutional. The Court ruled that students in school had the right to free speech, including symbolic speech, as long as their actions did not interfere with the educational process.

In *Brandenberg* v. *Ohio* (1969), the Court ruled that the government cannot restrict inflammatory speech unless that speech is likely to incite imminent, unlawful action directly. The case revolved around an incendiary interview with a Ku Klux Klan leader. Local authorities arrested him under a criminal syndicalism statute. The decision set the precedent of protecting antigovernment and provocative speech.

Reapportionment and One-Person, One-Vote

In *Baker* v. *Carr* (1966), the Supreme Court ruled that states must periodically redraw legislative districts so that districts have roughly equal numbers of people. Previously, Tennessee had not redrawn its legislative districts for over 60 years. Urban areas such as Memphis had grown much faster than rural districts. Without reapportionment, urban areas would be underrepresented, violating the principle of "one-person, one-vote."

Prayer in Public Schools and the Separation of Church and State

In *Engel* v. *Vitale* (1962), the Supreme Court ruled that the Regents' Prayer, a state-mandated prayer that was recited by public school children in New York State, was unconstitutional because it violated the doctrine of separation of church and state.

TIP 

Church and State in American History
The relationship between church and state has occurred throughout American history from Roger Williams and the founding of Rhode Island in the 1630s to recent controversies about the teaching of evolution in public schools.

THE CIVIL RIGHTS MOVEMENT IN THE 1960s

The civil rights movement continued into the 1960s. As the 1960s began, a younger generation of activists began to play a prominent role in the movement. Over time, rifts developed between the older, church-based leadership of the movement and a younger cadre of activists.

The Lunch Counter Sit-ins (1960)

In 1960, students in Tennessee and North Carolina began a campaign of sit-ins at lunch counters to protest segregation. The sit-ins occurred as some members of the movement grew frustrated with simply protesting and pushed the movement to take direct action to challenge and defy racist practices. The lunch counter sit-ins began in 1960 in Greensboro, North Carolina, when four African-American students challenged the "whites only" policy of Woolworth's lunch counter and sat at the counter. The lunch counter sit-ins spread to other cities, including Nashville, Tennessee. They put the practice of segregation of public facilities on the front page of newspapers and eventually pressured companies to end the practice.

The Freedom Rides (1961)

In 1961, the Congress on Racial Equality (CORE) organized a series of bus rides through the South to challenge segregation on interstate bus routes. The previous year, the Supreme Court had ruled that state laws separating the races on interstate transportation facilities were unconstitutional. Still, states maintained Jim Crow codes that separated African American and white passengers. The Freedom Rides met a great deal of resistance in the South. In Alabama, a mob slashed the tires of one bus and then firebombed it. President Kennedy finally sent federal marshals to Alabama to protect the Freedom Riders and to enforce federal law.

"Bull" Connor and the Birmingham Campaign (1963)

In the spring of 1963, Martin Luther King, Jr., and the Southern Christian Leadership Conference decided to launch a major campaign in Birmingham, Alabama, to protest racial segregation. The campaign proved to be a turning point in the push for federal legislation. The Public Safety Commissioner of Birmingham, Eugene "Bull" Connor, would not tolerate public demonstrations. He used fire hoses, police dogs, and brutal force to put down the campaign. The campaign included a children's march, sometimes called the "children's crusade," in May 1963. Connor used violent tactics to break up the children's march. Images of police brutality brought the Birmingham campaign to the attention of the nation and helped to bring public sympathy to the side of the civil rights movement. During the Birmingham campaign, King was arrested and wrote his famous "Letter from Birmingham Jail," a response to a call by white clergy members to give the legal system time to address the issue of racial injustice. King insisted that the black community had waited long enough for change to happen. The Birmingham campaign made passage of the Civil Rights Act, a year later, more likely.

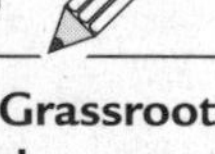

The Grassroots and the Government The civil rights movement vividly illustrates the complex relationship between the grassroots movement and government policy. The movement pushed the government to take action; support from the government emboldened the movement.

Kennedy, Johnson, and the Politics of Civil Rights

For years, the Democratic Party had walked a fine line with African Americans. On the one hand, many Democratic leaders since the Franklin D. Roosevelt Administration believed that extending civil rights to African Americans was the correct and just thing to do. On the other hand, the party did not want to alienate its southern wing. As the civil rights movement put the issue on the national agenda and as violence by white southerners put the issue on the nightly news, Democratic leaders had to react. In June 1963, the same month that civil rights leader Medgar Evers was murdered in front of his house in Jackson, Mississippi, President Kennedy made a national address in which he called civil rights a moral issue and pledged to support civil rights legislation. After Kennedy's assassination in November 1963, President Johnson took up the cause of civil rights legislation with vigor, pressuring reluctant Democrats to support the cause. In a March 1965 speech in support of a voting rights bill, Johnson invoked one of the central slogans of the civil rights movement—"We shall overcome."

The March on Washington (1963)

In 1963, the civil rights movement held one of the biggest demonstrations in American history in Washington, D.C. Over 200,000 people gathered to march, sing, and hear speeches, including Martin Luther King, Jr.'s "I Have a Dream Speech."

Civil Rights Act (1964)

Congress passed and President Johnson signed the Civil Rights Act in the summer of 1964. The act was intended to end discrimination based on race and sex. The Civil Rights Act guaranteed equal access for all Americans to public accommodations, public education, and voting. Another section banned discrimination in employment based on race or sex.

The Selma to Montgomery March (1965)

With passage of the Civil Rights Act, the movement focused on voting rights. A major march from Selma to Montgomery, Alabama, was scheduled for March 1965. As the marchers crossed a bridge over the Alabama River, county and state police blocked their path. After ordering the marchers to turn back, the police attacked them with clubs and tear gas. The incident, known as Bloody Sunday, was broadcast on national television and aroused indignation among many Americans. The march was finally held later in the month. Bloody Sunday and the Selma to Montgomery march raised awareness of the issue of voting rights.

The Voting Rights Act (1965) and the Culmination of a Movement

The Voting Rights Act, passed in August 1965, authorized the federal government to oversee voter registration in counties with low African-American registration. The act also outlawed literacy tests and poll taxes—means of preventing African Americans from voting. By 1968, the number of southern African-American voters jumped from 1 million to over 3 million. In many ways, the Civil Rights Act and the Voting Rights Act were the culmination of the civil rights movement.

From "Freedom Now!" to "Black Power!"

As the civil rights movement achieved success in ending legal segregation (*de jure* segregation) and removing barriers to voting, pervasive problems continued to plague the African-American community. Patterns of segregation enforced by custom rather than law (*de facto* segregation) persisted. Also, the bitter realities of poverty, substandard housing, and lack of decent jobs continued to plague large sections of the African-American community. A younger generation of activists continued to push the movement in a more militant direction and to demand power, not just rights. After 1964, a central rallying cry of the movement, "Freedom now!," was, often replaced by the call for "Black power!"

Malcolm X

Malcolm X was central to the more militant turn the movement took. Between 1952 and 1964, he was a member and then a leader of the Nation of Islam. This is an African-American group that shares certain practices with mainstream Islam but differs from mainstream Islam in several important respects. The organization advocated that African Americans organize among themselves, separate from whites. After making a pilgrimage to Mecca in 1964 and seeing Muslims of different races interacting as equals, Malcolm X revised his views about black separatism. He was killed by assassins from the Nation of Islam in 1965, but his words continued to inspire the movement through the remainder of the 1960s.

The Black Panthers

The Black Panthers Party was formed in 1966. The Panthers took up the call for a Black Power movement, embracing self-defense and militant rhetoric. Initially, the Black Panthers focused on community organizing. However, their activities grew increasingly confrontational.

The Assassination of King (1968)

Martin Luther King, Jr., was killed by an assassin on April 4, 1968, in Memphis, Tennessee. The assassination of King was a source of national mourning and represented the end of the civil rights movement. The movement accomplished much but was unable to provide a fix for many of the problems facing the African-American community. As the 1960s wound down, rioting engulfed many African-American neighborhoods, highlighting the continued frustrations of the black community (see Chapter 30).

Subject to Debate

There has been much historical discussion about the origins of the civil rights movement. One key division in the discussion is between those who stress grassroots activism and those who focus on the actions of the government. Historians that take a more top-down approach elevate the importance of powerful institutions—the courts, the police, and elected officials—in shaping events. This is the more traditional approach. Revisionist historians, many of whom come out of a new left tradition, focus on the agency of ordinary people in shaping historical change. Of late, historians have looked at the interaction between the grassroots level and the halls of power. We see this at play with the Birmingham campaign in 1963. The campaign, which ignited a violent reaction from police (broadcast on the evening news), prompted the Kennedy and Johnson Administrations to take action and to push for the 1964 Civil Rights Act. This act might not have been passed were it not for the events in Birmingham.

Practice Multiple-Choice Questions:

Directions: Pick the letter that best answers the following questions.

1. The book *Silent Spring* (1962) by Rachel Carson was significant in
   (A) raising awareness of the difficulties of being deaf in contemporary American society.
   (B) showing the effects of the atomic bombing of Hiroshima, Japan.
   (C) critiquing the effects of McCarthyism on public discourse and debate.
   (D) spurring the growth of the modern environmental movement.
   (E) exploring the effects of rote memorization and standardized testing of school children.

2. Lyndon Johnson's Great Society programs
   (A) were undermined by the costs of the war in Vietnam.
   (B) were declared unconstitutional by a conservative Supreme Court.
   (C) eradicated poverty in the United States.
   (D) became the basis for Ronald Reagan's New Right agenda.
   (E) consisted primarily of the power of moral suasion.

3. In the 1960s, Bloody Sunday is associated with the
   (A) assassination of Martin Luther King, Jr.
   (B) Tet Offensive.
   (C) Bay of Pigs invasion.
   (D) first boxing match between Mohammed Ali and Sonny Liston.
   (E) Selma to Montgomery March.

4. The main purpose of the Freedom Rides was to protest
   (A) segregation on interstate bus service.
   (B) immigration policies between the United States and Mexico.
   (C) the proliferation of nuclear weapons.
   (D) underfunding for intercity rail service.
   (E) the high price of gasoline.

Practice Free-Response Questions:

1. Analyze the impact of decisions by the Warren Court on American society.

2. Compare the policies and actions of Presidents Lyndon Johnson and Richard Nixon in regard to the Cold War.

Answers and Explanations to Multiple-Choice Questions:

1. **(D)** Rachel Carson's book gave the environmental movement a big boost. The book detailed the harmful effects of toxic chemicals on the environment. She asserted that the big chemical companies spread false information about their products. The book was especially critical of chemical pesticides such as DDT. The title of the book is meant to evoke a future springtime when we won't be able to hear the chirping of birds.

2. **(A)** This question alludes to a speech by Martin Luther King, Jr., in which he said, "The promises of the Great Society have been shot down on the battlefield of Vietnam." The war in Vietnam increasingly occupied President Johnson's time and drained enormous resources from Great Society social programs.

3. **(E)** Bloody Sunday refers to the beginning of a planned march from Selma to Montgomery, Alabama, that was meant to galvanize the movement for African-American voting rights. The issue of voting had become central to the civil rights movement by 1965, especially after the Civil Rights Act (1964) was signed. At the beginning of the march, police began beating the demonstrators, including SNCC leader John Lewis. The march disbanded but finally completed the route a month later. In 1965, President Johnson signed the Voting Rights Act.

4. **(A)** In 1961, the Congress on Racial Equality (CORE) organized a series of interstate bus rides, with African-American as well as white passengers, throughout the South to challenge local segregation codes. The Freedom Rides met a great deal of resistance in the South. In Alabama, a mob slashed the tires of one bus and then firebombed it. President Kennedy finally sent federal marshals to Alabama to protect the Freedom Riders and to enforce federal law.

Conflict, Crisis, and Scandal, 1966–1975

CHAPTER 30

TIMELINE

1967	"Summer of Love"
	Rioting in Detroit, Newark, and other cities
1968	The assassination of Martin Luther King, Jr.
	The assassination of Robert F. Kennedy
	Violence occurs at the Democratic Convention in Chicago
	The Election of Richard Nixon
	The founding of the American Indian Movement
1969	Woodstock Festival
	Stonewall Riot in New York City; birth of the gay liberation movement
	Apollo 11 lands on the moon
1970	President Nixon widens the Vietnam War into Cambodia
	Four students are killed by the National Guard at a Kent State protest
1971	Publication of the *Pentagon Papers* in the *New York Times*
1972	Arrest of burglars at the Watergate Complex
	Reelection of Richard Nixon
1973	Congressional hearings on Watergate
1974	Nixon resigns presidency; Gerald Ford assumes the presidency
	Ford grants Nixon a complete pardon

The late 1960s and early 1970s were some of the more eventful years in American history. These years saw violence in the streets of American cities, a widening and eventual abandonment of the war in Vietnam, assassinations of major public figures, a nationwide energy crisis, and a major political scandal that brought down a sitting president. The period also saw an expansion of grassroots democratic participation, inspired by the civil rights movement, on a number of issues.

THE UNRAVELING OF THE WAR IN VIETNAM

By 1968, the war in Vietnam seemed increasingly unwinnable. The Vietcong and North Vietnamese forces launched the Tet Offensive in January, shocking the American public. Further extensive, uncensored media coverage of the war left many Americans questioning the morality and propriety of the war. Opponents of the war became increasingly vocal as the decade wore on.

TIP

Old Left Versus New Left
The Old Left of the 1930s focused on workers and workplace issues. The New Left of the 1960s focused on participatory democracy and on cultural, social, economic, and political issues. The New Left developed on college campuses rather than in factories.

The Antiwar Movement

The antiwar movement can be traced back to the early 1960s as small peace groups questioned the purpose of the armed advisors that were sent to Vietnam.

Students for a Democratic Society and the Rise of the New Left

The most significant organization in the antiwar movement of the 1960s was Students for a Democratic Society (SDS), with chapters at major college campuses across the country. The name was coined in 1960, with SDS developing out of an earlier organization. SDS held its first national convention at Port Huron, Michigan. At this convention, the organization adopted a guiding manifesto, known as the Port Huron Statement, which became an important document in the development of the New Left. The document, written by Tom Hayden, stressed participatory democracy and direct action. The label "New Left" applies to activist organizations of the 1960s that broke with the worker-oriented, top-down movement that developed in the 1930s. SDS continued to grow throughout the 1960s but disbanded in 1969 after intense factional infighting.

TIP

The Media and War
During the Vietnam War, Americans saw uncensored images of the horrors of war. This contributed to antiwar sentiment among many Americans. Later, during the Iraq War (2003–present), the government kept tight reins on media coverage. If reporters wanted access to the military, they had to agree to be imbedded with a unit. The military would then have control over what was reported. President George W. Bush took a lesson from the Vietnam War.

Vietnam Veterans Against the War

Another significant antiwar group was the Vietnam Veterans Against the War. Born in 1967, the organization harnessed the frustrations of returning veterans of the conflict. Many front-line soldiers grew to question the tactics and even the purpose of the war. There were several incidents of "fragging" in Vietnam—soldiers attacking and even killing commanding officers.

The Shootings at Kent State and Jackson State

The antiwar movement was stunned when four students were killed at Kent State University in Ohio in May 1970 during a demonstration against President Nixon's decision to invade Cambodia. National Guardsmen opened fire on the demonstrators, killing four and wounding ten. A week later, two African-American students were shot and killed by state police at Jackson State University in Mississippi. By the beginning of the school year in September 1970, college campuses were considerably quieter.

The Government and a Free Press
The publication of the *Pentagon Papers* helped to clarify free speech issues in regard to the government's ability to squelch embarrassing information. The Supreme Court upheld the rights of the press.

Publication of the *Pentagon Papers*

Many of the suspicions of the antiwar movement were borne from the publication of the *Pentagon Papers*, a secret study of the Vietnam War written by the Pentagon. The study revealed official deception and secrecy. It was leaked to the press by Daniel Ellsberg, a Pentagon official critical of the direction the Vietnam War was taking. The Nixon Administration tried to block *The New York Times* and the *Washington Post* from publishing the papers. Initially, the Nixon Administration obtained an injunction against publication, but the Supreme Court, in the case of *New York Times* v. *United States* (1971), overruled the injunction and upheld the right of the newspapers to publish the information.

THE NIXON PRESIDENCY

The presidency of Richard Nixon will be remembered for its denouement—scandal and resignation. Opponents of the Vietnam War will remember Nixon bitterly for expanding the war after promising Americans that he would wind it down. Nixon also made significant progress in pursuing a policy of détente with China and the Soviet Union. He also signed important domestic measures into law, such as the Clean Air Act. However, Nixon's paranoia and hunger for power and control led to a series of dirty tricks that, when revealed, weakened people's trust in government.

The Counterculture and Public Opinion
Nixon's victory in 1968 reveals that even at its height, the antiwar movement and the counterculture did not reach large segments of the electorate. This became even more evident in the sweeping reelection of Nixon in 1972.

The Election of 1968

The election campaign of 1968 took place among some of the most turbulent events in American history. The Tet Offensive occurred in January, Martin Luther King, Jr. was killed in April, and revolutionary movements roiled France and Czechoslovakia in the spring.

The Democratic Party was in complete disarray, with different factions vying for control. The Vietnam War seriously divided the party between supporters of President Johnson and Vice President Hubert Humphrey on the one hand and opponents of the war who rallied around the candidacy of Eugene McCarthy. Furthermore, white southern democrats grew frustrated with the direction of the Democratic Party and rallied behind the independent candidacy of Governor George Wallace of Alabama. Johnson withdrew from the race altogether in March after polling numbers indicated he was fading from contention in the face of challenges from McCarthy and Senator Robert Kennedy. Humphrey then entered the race and emerged as the front-runner after Kennedy was assassinated in June. The disarray of the Democratic Party was evident in its August convention in Chicago as antiwar protestors were beaten by Chicago police officers.

Richard Nixon was able to capitalize on the turmoil of 1968, both within the Democratic Party and within society at large. His law-and-order sensibility appealed to many Americans disturbed by the violence in many sectors of American society. Nixon prevailed despite fears that the Wallace campaign would siphon votes from him, with forty-three percent of the popular vote.

Vietnamization of the Vietnam War

Nixon assured the American people that he had a plan for "peace with honor" in the Vietnam War when he ran for president in 1968. Victory proved elusive for the United States in Vietnam. Starting in 1969, Nixon began the policy known as *Vietnamization.* This involved replacing American troops with Vietnamese troops. In 1970, he widened the war to Cambodia. However, all of Nixon's measures would not lead to American victory. The United States pulled out of Vietnam in 1973. By 1975, the side that the United States had supported, South Vietnam, was defeated. Both sides of Vietnam were then reunited as a single communist country.

Détente with China and the Soviet Union

President Nixon's policy of détente represented a thawing in the Cold War and an improvement of relations with the Soviet Union. In 1971, Nixon initiated an agreement with the Soviet Union whereby the Soviet Union accepted the independence of West Berlin and the United States recognized East Germany. The Strategic Arms Limitation Talks (SALT) led to two arms control agreements in 1972. Tensions still existed but détente led to discussion between the two sides, limited arms agreements, and cultural exchanges. In 1972, Nixon visited China. It was the first time an American president visited the country. The visit was an important step in normalizing relations with China's communist government.

The Legacy of President Nixon
Although Nixon is most vividly remembered for the Watergate scandal, there is not a consensus among historians in regard to Nixon's legacy. Many cite his foreign policy accomplishments alongside his scandalous downfall.

Nixon's Domestic Achievements

In 1970, the Nixon Administration created the Environmental Protection Agency and the Clean Air Act to set standards for air quality.

The Energy Crisis

In 1973, the Arab oil-producing nations cut off exports to the United States and the Organization of Petroleum Exporting Countries (OPEC) increased the price of oil. These moves were largely in retaliation for the United States' support of Israel in the 1973 Yom Kippur War between Israel and its Arab neighbors.

Watergate and the Undoing of President Nixon

The Watergate scandal led to the undoing of the Nixon presidency. The scandal began in June 1972 when five men were caught breaking into the headquarters of the Democratic Party at the Watergate Hotel in Washington, D.C. Persistent reporting by Carl Bernstein and Bob Woodward of the *Washington Post* drew connections between the burglars, Nixon's reelection committee, and ultimately the White House. When it became known that Nixon taped conversations in the White House Oval Office, investigators demanded that the tapes be turned over. Nixon argued that executive privilege allowed him to keep the tapes. In *United States* v. *Nixon* (1974), the Supreme Court ordered Nixon to turn over the tapes. Also in 1974, the House Judiciary Committee voted in favor of articles of impeachment against President Nixon. Before the question of impeachment could be addressed by the entire House of Representatives, Nixon resigned. Since the 1970s, the percentage of people voting has declined and opinion polls have shown an erosion of trust in the government.

THE DOOMED PRESIDENCY OF GERALD FORD (1974–1977)

Ford was the only American president to have never been victorious in a national election, not even as a vice presidential candidate. He was appointed vice president when President Nixon's first vice president, Spiro Agnew, resigned. Ford assumed the presidency when Nixon resigned.

The Pardon of President Nixon (1974)

Ford's most well-known action occurred in 1974 when he pardoned Richard Nixon for any crimes he might have committed as president. Nixon would almost certainly have faced criminal proceedings, as over thirty members of his staff did, if it had not been for this pardon. The public was eager to see Nixon on trial and to hear the details of the Watergate episode.

Whip Inflation Now

Stagflation—high inflation coupled with slow economic growth—continued to dog the economy during Ford's brief tenure. Ford's most public initiative was the promotion of the Whip Inflation Now (WIN) campaign. The campaign encouraged people to be more disciplined with their money. Supporters were encouraged to wear WIN buttons.

MOVEMENTS FOR CHANGE

The civil rights movement and the New Left inspired other movements for change. These movements have had varying degrees of success.

The Women's Liberation Movement

In the 1960s, a women's liberation movement developed, challenging inequities in the job market, representations of women in the media, violence against women, and an ingrained set of social values. Many women looked at the circumstances of their own lives and saw connections to the larger society, giving rise to the motto "the personal is political." The movement was inspired by Betty Friedan's 1963 book *The Feminine Mystique*, which challenged the traditional options in life offered to middle-class women. In 1966, Friedan was one of several women to found the National Organization for Women (NOW), the leading liberal organization supporting women's rights. Many women in the movement had come out of New Left organizations, empowered to fight for a better world but frustrated at the treatment women received in these organizations.

PROTEST AT THE MISS AMERICA PAGEANT

Many Americans heard about the women's liberation movement for the first time from news reports of a protest at the 1968 Miss America Pageant. The pageant exemplified, to the protesters, society's attitude toward women. Women were forced to wear skimpy outfits and give vacuous answers to questions in order to win male approval.

ROE V. *WADE* (1973)

Central to the women's liberation movement was a woman's right to control reproduction, including the choice of whether to have an abortion. One of the major successes of the movement was the Supreme Court decision in the case of *Roe* v. *Wade* (1973). The Court declared that states shall not prohibit women from having an abortion during the first two trimesters of pregnancy. Previously, the decision had been left to the states, and many states forbade abortions. The Supreme Court reasoned that the Constitution guaranteed people the right to privacy. Abortion, they argued, was a decision that should be left to the woman with the advice of her physician. This decision echoed the reasoning of an earlier decision, *Griswold* v. *Connecticut* (1965), in which the Court ruled that laws forbidding the use of birth control devices were unconstitutional (see Chapter 29). The issue of abortion has proved to be one of the most contentious issues in America in the late-twentieth and early-twenty-first centuries.

THE EQUAL RIGHTS AMENDMENT

The Equal Rights Amendment would have prohibited the abridgment of "equality of rights under the law . . . on account of sex" either by the federal government or by state governments. It was approved by both the House and the Senate in 1972 but failed to get the required 38 states to ratify it, even after the deadline for ratification had been moved forward to 1982. It therefore did not become part of the Constitution.

TITLE IX (1972)

Another success of the women's liberation movement was passage of Title IX of the Educational Amendments of 1972. Title IX banned sex discrimination in all aspects of education, such as faculty hiring and admissions. It has had a major impact on funding for female sports activities at the high school and college levels.

The Gay Liberation Movement

The gay liberation movement was born in 1969 when patrons at the Stonewall Inn, a gay bar in New York's Greenwich Village, resisted a raid by the police and fought back. The event brought a series of grievances into the open. Gay men and women had suffered discrimination in many walks of life, including in government civil service jobs. Many gays attempted to avoid such discrimination by concealing their sexual identity and remaining "in the closet."

The American Indian Movement

The example set by the civil rights movement also inspired a movement to fight for justice for Native Americans. The American Indian Movement was founded in 1968. The following year, the movement made headlines when several dozen activists seized control of Alcatraz Island in the San Francisco Bay, claiming that the former prison belonged to the first inhabitants of the area—Native Americans. The movement won greater autonomy over tribal lands and affairs.

Cesar Chavez and the United Farm Workers

Cesar Chavez and Delores Huerta founded the United Farm Workers (UFW) in 1962 to protect the interests of migrant farmers, including many Mexican Americans. The UFW organized a nationwide boycott of grapes to pressure farm owners to pay their workers a decent wage. The boycott did result in a wage increase in 1970.

The Environmental Movement

Another important movement for change in the 1960s and 1970s was the environmental movement. The movement became a national phenomenon and led to some important changes in laws and consciousness. Environmental issues were brought to the public's attention by Rachel Carson's 1962 book *Silent Spring*, which vividly described how modern society was poisoning the earth. She described the impact of the agricultural chemical DDT on the environment. Many participants in the environmental movement were veterans of the New Left and of the movement to end the Vietnam War. Many of these New Left activists had developed a critique of corporate power and influence. Finally, the environmental movement was connected to the counterculture of the 1960s. The so-called hippies of the 1960s encouraged people to rid themselves of material possessions and live a more simple life (see below). The movement gained national exposure with the first Earth Day, which occurred in April 1970.

THE COUNTERCULTURE OF THE 1960s

American culture became increasingly fractured in the 1960s. Divisions along generational lines were most apparent. As the baby boom generation came of age in the 1960s, it grew increasingly weary of the cultural products of the previous generation. Mainstream culture seemed inauthentic, shallow, and corporate controlled.

Bob Dylan and the Folk Revival

Despite his protests to the contrary, Bob Dylan was able to verbalize many of the fears and hopes of the younger generation in the 1960s. Even his musical choices—simple, acoustic instrumentation—seemed a welcome break from the bland, overproduced products of the record industry. He cultivated a vocal approach that paid homage to the untrained, indigenous music of rural America, rather than to the smooth crooners of his parents' generation.

The British Invasion

In the 1960s, a series of British bands, most notably the Beatles and the Rolling Stones, transformed American culture. These bands took inspiration from the rich tradition of African-American music—from rhythm and blues to rock 'n' roll—and infused it with a youthful energy. The Beatles inspired a manic following in the United States, known as Beatlemania. The Beatles also generated a backlash in the United States. Conservative Americans were troubled by their long hair, veiled allusions to drug use, interest in Eastern religions, and challenges to traditional notions of propriety. A comment by one of the Beatles, that the band had become more popular than Jesus Christ, added to the backlash.

The Hippie Movement and Haight-Ashbury

The hippie movement became visible in the late 1960s in neighborhoods such as San Francisco's Haight-Ashbury and New York's Lower East Side. In many ways, this counterculture represented a rejection of the materialistic conformity that many young people grew up with in the 1950s (see Chapter 28). A variety of activities came to be associated with the hippie movement—urban and rural communal living, a do-it-yourself approach to the varied tasks of life, mystic spiritual experiences, drug use, experimental music, and avant-garde art. Taking inspiration from sit-ins of the civil rights movement, the counterculture organized be-ins, gatherings of young people in San Francisco's Golden Gate Park or New York's Central Park.

The Sexual Revolution

The 1960s also witnessed the development of more tolerant attitudes toward sexual behavior. In 1960, the birth control pill was introduced to the market, allowing women more control over reproduction and over their sexual lives.

Woodstock and Altamont (1969)

The counterculture reached its peak and showed its limits in two important events, months apart from one another, in 1969. The Woodstock Festival, in August, attracted half a million people to a farm in upstate New York and seemed to provide a glimpse of a utopian future for many participants. In December, promoters tried to duplicate the success of Woodstock with a giant music festival at the Altamont Speedway in California. However, the Altamont event was marred by incidents of violence. One concertgoer, armed and apparently crazed, was stopped and stabbed to death by a member of the Hell's Angels Motorcycle Club security detail as the Rolling Stones performed.

Subject to Debate

Many of the historians active over the last generation not only came of age in the 1960s but were active participants in the events of that decade. The undergraduate and graduate students in history programs in the 1960s were well represented at campus antiwar activities. As might be expected, the legacy of the war in Vietnam has been hotly debated. Historians have argued about whether the conflict in Vietnam was essentially a civil war or an international Cold War struggle. Should the focus be on the rebellion by the indigenous Vietcong and its peasant supporters against an oppressive regime? Instead should the focus be on North Vietnam and China fomenting chaos in South Vietnam? If we accept the first scenario, then American intervention seems misguided and bound for failure. If we accept the second scenario, then American intervention seems entirely reasonable. A related question is whether the war was winnable. To some, the United States was fighting a hopeless war—additional years of extensive bombing would simply steel the resolve of the populace to resist the American occupation. To others, victory was both possible and within sight; President Nixon abandoned the fight at just the wrong moment. Domestic political considerations and the Watergate scandal caused Nixon to make a hasty exit from Southeast Asia.

Historians have also debated the overall legacy of the Nixon presidency. In the popular imagination, the Watergate scandal looms large. However, historians point out, the scandal should not overshadow some of Nixon's real accomplishments, including promoting détente with China and the Soviet Union. Historians have also praised Nixon for avoiding the divisive social and religious issues that characterized subsequent Republican administrations. Other historians insist that Nixon's legacy is irreparably tarnished by the bombing of civilians in Southeast Asia.

Practice Multiple-Choice Questions:

Directions: Pick the letter that best answers the following questions.

1. Which of the following is an accurate description of media coverage of the war in Vietnam?

   (A) Uncensored coverage of the war was widely seen by the American public.
   (B) The government controlled images and limited what the American public saw.
   (C) There was little interest in the war on the part of the media and of the public.
   (D) There was extensive newspaper coverage but very little televised coverage.
   (E) Bloggers from within Vietnam undermined troop morale.

2. A raid at the Stonewall Inn in New York City in 1969

   (A) led to two days of rioting by African Americans in Harlem.
   (B) uncovered a major source for heroine in the United States.
   (C) led to the arrest of members of the Weather Underground.
   (D) sparked the gay liberation movement.
   (E) led to the unraveling of the Tammany Hall machine.

3. Cesar Chavez gained prominence in the 1960s by

   (A) becoming the first Latino to be appointed to a cabinet level position.
   (B) organizing a nationwide boycott of grapes to protest conditions for migrant famers.
   (C) joining forces with Native-American activists in the takeover of Alcatraz Island.
   (D) commanding troops in Vietnam who carried out the My Lai massacre.
   (E) winning an Academy Award for his portrayal of Cuban revolutionary Che Guevara.

4. The Supreme Court decision in the case of *Roe* v. *Wade*

   (A) relied on the principle of separate but equal, established in *Plessy* v. *Ferguson.*
   (B) used reasoning found in Title IX.
   (C) was made possible by the ratification of the Equal Rights Amendment.
   (D) was overturned after President Bush was able to replace Justice William Brennan with Justice David Souter.
   (E) relied on the right to privacy carved out in *Griswold* v. *Connecticut.*

Practice Free-Response Questions:

1. "President Richard Nixon's historical legacy will be shaped more by his foreign policy achievements than by his ignoble fall." Assess the validity of this statement.

2. Evaluate the level of success of social movements in the 1960s with reference to TWO of the following movements:

   Gay liberation movement
   Chicano rights movement
   American-Indian Movement
   Women's liberation movement.

Answers and Explanations to Multiple-Choice Questions:

1. **(A)** Sometimes the war in Vietnam is called the living room war because Americans saw brutal images of the war, uncensored, on the nightly news. These images turned many Americans against the war.
2. **(D)** The raid at the Stonewall Inn, a Greenwich Village bar, led to rioting when the mostly gay clientele fought the police. Previously, gays and lesbians made efforts to remain closeted. Participants in the gay liberation openly celebrated their sexuality. Every year, New York City's Gay Pride March commemorates that event.
3. **(B)** In the 1960s, Cesar Chavez was one of the organizers of the United Farm Workers. He led strikes and boycotts of farm products to advance the cause of migrant farm workers' rights. In the 1980s, Chavez was one of the organizers of a national boycott of grapes in order to protest the use of toxic chemicals used in growing grapes.
4. **(E)** *Roe* v. *Wade* has been the most divisive Supreme Court case of the late-twentieth and early-twenty-first centuries. In that case, the Supreme Court forbade states from prohibiting women from having abortions during the first two trimesters of pregnancy. Previously, the decision to allow or forbid abortions had been left to the states, and many states forbade them. The *Roe* decision was based on the right to privacy. Abortion, the decision reasoned, was a decision that should be left to the woman with the advice of her physician.

CHAPTER 31

The Decline of Liberalism and the Rise of the New Right, 1976–1993

TIMELINE	
1976	The election of Jimmy Carter
1977	Supreme Court decision in *Bakke* v. *University of California*
1978	Panama Canal Treaty
	Camp David Accords
1979	Three Mile Island nuclear accident
	Formation of the Moral Majority
	Soviet invasion of Afghanistan
	Iranian students seize the U.S. embassy; hold hostages for over a year
1980	The United States boycotts the Olympic Games held in Moscow
	Election of Ronald Reagan
1981	Release of American hostages held in Iran
	Reagan fires striking air traffic controllers
1984	Reelection of Ronald Reagan
1987	Iran-Contra hearings
1988	Election of George H. W. Bush
1989	Collapse of communism in Eastern Europe
1991	Operation Desert Storm
	Collapse of the Soviet Union

Starting with the 1964 presidential campaign of Barry Goldwater, there were signs of a growing conservative movement. This movement celebrated when Ronald Reagan was elected in 1980 and has been successful in redefining the terms of political debate in the late-twentieth and early-twenty-first centuries.

PERSISTENT CRISES OF THE 1970s

Stagflation

The economy of the United States remained strong throughout the 1960s, despite the costs of the war in Vietnam. As the 1970s began, however, the economy began to contract. By the early 1970s, economists noted an unusual set of circumstances—both unemployment and inflation were at high levels (both over 6 percent). High unemployment is a sign of a stagnant economy; but high inflation is usually a sign of an active economy. After all, consumer demand pushes up prices. The incidence of both occurring simultaneously was dubbed "stagflation." Stagflation continued throughout the 1970s.

The Energy Crisis and the Limits of Growth

Starting with the OPEC oil embargo in 1973, fuel prices rose dramatically in the 1970s. America had to confront a stark reality—there are limits to the amount of fossil fuels, particularly petroleum, available in the world and much of it comes from the volatile Middle East. Up until the 1970s, Americans assumed that petroleum was a cheap, inexhaustible commodity. The 1970s saw a dramatic spike in petroleum prices and long lines at gas pumps.

Nuclear Energy and Three Mile Island

Some Americans put faith in nuclear energy as an alternative to fossil fuels. Electricity is generated by the spinning of turbines. In power plants, steam spins the turbines. The problem is generating energy to boil water to produce steam. In a nuclear power plant, a nuclear reaction generates that energy, rather than the burning of coal or oil. The material needed for nuclear power, such as uranium, is relatively cheap and plentiful. The nuclear reaction does not produce the greenhouse gas, carbon dioxide. However, problems are associated with nuclear power. The waste product of a nuclear reaction is radioactive and must be safely disposed. Also, accidents can occur that can have devastating effects on the environment. The worst nuclear accident in world history was in Chernobyl, Ukraine (formerly part of the Soviet Union) in 1986. The worst accident in United States history occurred at the Three Mile Island power plant in Pennsylvania (1979). These accidents raised significant concerns among Americans about the safety of nuclear power. Currently, nearly 20 percent of electricity is generated by nuclear power in the United States.

Conservation Measures

While many policy makers were trying to find alternative sources of power to Middle East petroleum, some were looking for ways for the United States to reduce its consumption of energy. Americans are by far the largest consumers of energy, consuming nearly twice the amount as the average resident of Great Britain or France. A National Minimum Speed Law was enacted in 1974 (since repealed). President Jimmy Carter, through the newly created Department of Energy (1977), encouraged conservation measures, such as turning down thermostats and turning off lights when not in use. He also encouraged investment in renewable sources of energy, such as solar power. Americans, however, have proved to be remarkably resistant to adopting conservation measures.

THE RISE AND FALL OF THE CARTER PRESIDENCY

The Election of 1976

The Republican Party nominated President Ford to stand for reelection. Ford survived a challenge from Ronald Reagan, the conservative former governor of California. Reagan appealed to the burgeoning New Right conservative movement, but many Republicans felt that the more moderate Ford had a better chance in the general election.

The Democrats chose Jimmy Carter, the former governor of Georgia, to be their standard-bearer. Carter, a soft-spoken born-again Christian, exuded a sense of honesty and trustworthiness if not charisma. Carter was a moderate Democrat, able to appeal to the southern wing of the party.

The Watergate scandal cast its shadow over the election. Voter turnout dropped from previous elections (and would continue to drop throughout the 1980s), perhaps reflecting Americans' growing distrust of politics. Also, Ford's pardon of Nixon haunted him and contributed to his defeat on election day.

The Camp David Accords (1978)

President Jimmy Carter succeeded in providing a foundation for a peace treaty between Egypt and Israel. The Camp David Accords are considered one of the few triumphs for President Carter's troubled presidency. Since the founding of Israel in 1948, tensions have existed in the Middle East. The Arab nations refused to recognize Israel's right to exist. Four wars occurred between Israel and its neighbors between 1948 and 1973. In 1977, Egyptian President Anwar Sadat broke with the other leaders of the Arab world and flew to Israel to meet with Israeli Prime Minister Menachem Begin. Negotiations ensued between the two leaders, but they were unable to come up with a peace treaty. President Carter invited the two leaders to the presidential retreat Camp David in Maryland. The three men met for 13 days and emerged with the basis for a peace treaty. The treaty resulted in an end to hostilities between Israel and Egypt, but tensions continued to exist between Israel and its other neighbors.

The Panama Canal Zone (1977)

Carter negotiated an agreement with Panama in 1977 to turn the Canal Zone over to Panama. The agreement, ratified by the Senate in 1978, called for the United States to turn over control by December 31, 1999.

United States–Soviet Relations

Relations between the Soviet Union and the United States, which had been improving since Nixon's détente overtures earlier in the 1970s, soured after the Soviet Union invaded Afghanistan (1979). President Carter suspended grain sales to the Soviet Union in protest of the Soviet invasion. He also pushed for a U.S. boycott of the 1980 Summer Olympics in Moscow.

The Iran Hostage Crisis (1979–1981)

In 1979, the U.S.-supported leader of Iran, Shah Pahlavi, was ousted by a revolution led by the Muslim religious leader Ayatollah Khomeini. The United States supported the Shah to the end. Later in 1979, when the United States admitted the deposed Shah to the United States for medical treatment, angry Iranian students took over the U.S. embassy and kept the personnel there hostage. Carter finally secured their release after the election in late 1980, but they were not actually released until 33 minutes into the administration of President Reagan in January 1981.

THE BIRTH AND GROWTH OF THE NEW RIGHT

Ronald Reagan rode the crest of a conservative revolution that had been, by the time of Reagan's election in 1980, at least 15 years in the making. Conservatives had coalesced around Barry Goldwater, the unsuccessful Republican candidate for the presidency in 1964. The movement suffered temporary setbacks with the scandals of the Nixon administration and the ineffectiveness of the Ford administration in the 1970s. However, it continued to grow at the grassroots level, achieving electoral success in 1980.

Elements of the Conservative Movement

The conservative movement has always had three distinct tendencies within it that have sometimes worked in unison and have sometimes been in conflict. First, there are Cold War conservatives, focused on containing or rolling back communist regimes abroad. In the post–Cold War era, interventionists have argued for continued U.S. actions abroad, notably in the Middle East. The second tendency is the pro-business economic conservatives. These conservatives argue for lower corporate taxes, deregulation, and an economic atmosphere friendly to the priorities of big business. Economic conservatives might use the language of laissez-faire economics in regard to rolling back environmental regulations. However, they are ready to use the power of the government to extend military contracts to large corporations, for example.

The third tendency within the conservative movement is the religious and cultural wing. This wing has had the greatest grassroots support, fueling electoral victories for Reagan (twice), George H. W. Bush (once), and George W. Bush (twice). This movement gained steam as tradition-minded people grew frustrated with what they saw as the excesses of the counterculture of the 1960s. They railed against the women's liberation movement for challenging traditional gender roles and against the gay liberation movement. Many were troubled by the assertiveness of African

Americans in the 1960s and pined for an early time in which everyone "knew their place." The public nature of drug consumption in the 1960s also angered tradition-minded people. The issue that propelled the cultural conservatives from the margins to prominence was abortion. In the wake of the *Roe* v. *Wade* decision (1973), religious conservatives found their voice. The issue propelled evangelical Protestants to put aside their long-held suspicions of Catholicism and create a broad Christian conservative movement. This movement found voice in organizations such as the Moral Majority, founded by the Reverend Jerry Falwell in 1979.

THE REAGAN ADMINISTRATION (1981–1989)

Ronald Reagan's presidency was both pivotal and polarizing. Reagan had been a well-known actor in B movies from the 1930s to the 1960s. He was president of the Screen Actors Guild in the 1940s and 1950s. He became increasingly interested in politics, first as a New Deal Democrat. By the 1950s, he became increasingly anti-communist and became an active Republican in the 1960s. He served as governor of California from 1967 to 1975.

Reagan's tenure as president saw a tremendous military build-up and the beginning of the end for the Soviet Union and the communist bloc. He also gave voice to the rising New Right movement.

The Election of 1980

The New Right achieved a remarkable victory in the nomination and election of Ronald Reagan. The election of the conservative Ronald Reagan in 1980 has been seen by many historians as a repudiation of the political and social movements of the 1960s. Reagan's victory can, in part, be attributed to more immediate causes. President Jimmy Carter was seen as ineffective in not securing the quick release of hostages held at the American embassy in Tehran by Iranian militants. However, Reagan projected a sense of hope and optimism that promised to move the United States beyond the scandals and doubts of the 1970s. He promised a new "morning in America," and Americans listened.

Reaganomics

President Reagan advanced a series of economic initiatives that bear the name Reaganomics. He was not the first conservative politician to advance such policies—Reaganomics bear striking similarities to Herbert Hoover's approach to the Great Depression. Reagan supported economic policies that favored big business. He based this on a belief in supply-side economics. This approach to the economy stressed stimulating the supply side of the economy—manufacturing firms, banks, and insurance corporations. The idea is that if there is growth in the supply side, there will be general economic growth and the benefits of that growth will reach everyone. The alternative approach is to stimulate the demand side—consumers. Demand-side economics emphasizes government policies designed to increase workers' wages and expand social programs such as welfare and unemployment benefits. As a believer in supply-side economics, Reagan implemented policies that

Hoover and Reagan
Be familiar with the similarities between Presidents Reagan and Hoover in regard to economics. Both promoted a supply-side approach to economic policy.

he thought would stimulate business. President Reagan cut taxes for corporations and greatly reduced regulations on industry.

Deregulation

Reagan was a staunch proponent of deregulation. He and Secretary of the Interior James Watt were criticized by environmental advocates for dismantling or weakening much of the environmental legislation of the 1970s.

Antiunion Policies

Reagan's approach to the economy included limiting the power of organized labor. When the air traffic controllers went on strike in 1981, he had them all fired. This action broke their union, the Professional Air Traffic Controllers' Union (PATCO), and was consistent with helping the supply side (the airline industry) rather than the demand side (the unionized air traffic controllers). The destruction of PATCO was a major blow to organized labor in the late-twentieth century.

Growth of the Federal Deficit

Reagan's probusiness economic policies had mixed results. By cutting corporate taxes and taxes on wealthy individuals, he cut government revenues. At the same time, he increased spending on armaments. This combination of increased spending and decreased revenues led to a doubling of the national debt from around $900 billion in 1980 to over $2 trillion in 1986. A large debt is a problem because it requires large interest payments. By 1988, the interest on the national debt had reached 14 percent of total annual government expenditures. This huge debt has hindered economic growth to some degree since and has forced future administrations to make difficult decisions in regard to keeping the debt under control.

The Reagan Doctrine

The Reagan Administration supported regimes that were anticommunist, even if they were undemocratic or repressive. This foreign policy came to be known as the Reagan Doctrine. Reagan sent troops to the island of Grenada in 1983 to topple the Marxist leaders of the country. Reagan continued to support the dictatorial regime of the Philippines led by Ferdinand Marcos despite reports of electoral fraud. The regime was finally toppled in 1986, with Corazon Aquino replacing Marcos.

CENTRAL AMERICA AND THE IRAN-CONTRA SCANDAL

As part of the Reagan Doctrine, the Reagan Administration consistently tried to undermine the left-wing Sandinista Government in Nicaragua. The Sandinistas took power in 1979 after toppling the United States–backed dictatorship of Anastasio Samoza. The United States funded and trained an anti-Sandinista military group known as the Contras. Alarmed at reports of human rights abuses by the Contras, Congress passed the Boland Amendment in 1982, to halt U.S. aid to the group.

Congressional action did not deter members of the Reagan administration from funding the Contras. An elaborate scheme was developed by members of the administration to sell weapons to Iran secretly and to use funds from these sales to fund the Contras. In 1986, details of the Iran-Contra affair became public. Ultimately, 14 members of the Reagan Administration were tried for violating U.S. law and 11 were convicted. Among the convicted was Secretary of Defense Caspar Weinberger. Oliver North of the National Security Council, an architect of the program, was initially convicted, but the conviction was overturned on appeal. Reagan himself claimed to not have direct knowledge of the program. Critics labeled him the "Teflon president" because accusations of wrongdoing did not stick to him.

Increased Military Spending

Reagan was determined to challenge the Soviet "evil empire." He initiated several weapons programs, vowing to close what he called a "window of vulnerability"—the ability of Soviet missiles to attack and decimate American missile locations before the United States could adequately respond. He began research on the Strategic Defense Initiative, dubbed "Star Wars" by critics, and initiated the costly MX missile program.

The Election of 1984

Reagan easily won reelection in 1984, defeating former Vice President Walter Mondale. The election of 1984 was significant in two ways. First, it saw the first viable campaign by an African-American candidate. Jesse Jackson garnered over 18 percent of the vote in the Democratic primaries. (In 1972, Shirley Chisholm ran for the Democratic nomination but received less than 3 percent of the vote.) Second, the 1984 election was the first to see a woman on a major party ticket; Mondale chose Geraldine Ferraro to be his running mate.

The Fall of the Soviet Union and the Collapse of Communism

President Reagan is often given credit for precipitating the fall of the Eastern bloc. In 1989, communist governments began to collapse in eastern Europe. It was clear that Soviet leader Mikhail Gorbachev would not try to halt this development as previous Soviet leaders had. The iconic image of this movement was the collapse of the Berlin Wall in November 1989. The wall, separating West Berlin from East Germany, had become a symbol of the rift between the communist bloc countries and the western democratic countries. By 1991, the Soviet Union itself had collapsed, ending communism in Europe. It is true that an accelerated arms race taxed the Soviet economy more than it did the American economy. However, one must also look at the internal dynamics of Soviet society to understand this major development.

The First Female Supreme Court Justice

Reagan appointed the first woman to the Supreme Court, Sandra Day O'Connor (1981–2006).

THE GEORGE H. W. BUSH ADMINISTRATION

Despite the large deficits accumulated during the Reagan years and despite extensive media coverage of the unfolding Iran-Contra affair, Reagan remained popular until the end of his second term. Vice President George H. W. Bush handily defeated Governor Michael Dukakis of Massachusetts in 1988.

The Election of 1988

During the campaign, the Bush team successfully portrayed Dukakis as soft on crime. The most memorable example was an ad featuring Willie Horton, a convicted criminal who committed additional crimes while out on a weeklong furlough. The ad was criticized for inflaming racial antagonisms.

Foreign Affairs During the Bush Administration

Bush's main accomplishments were in the field of foreign affairs. During Bush's presidency, the Berlin Wall came down and the Soviet Union collapsed. After Iraq, under the leadership of Saddam Hussein, invaded neighboring Kuwait in an attempt to gain more control over the region's oil reserves, Bush organized a United Nations military coalition to challenge the move. The Persian Gulf War involved Operation Desert Storm successfully removing Iraqi forces from Kuwait in 1991. During the Persian Gulf War, significant numbers of women served in combat roles for the first time.

"Read My Lips, No New Taxes"

Bush's domestic achievements were more modest. He was criticized for repeatedly telling the American public, "Read my lips, no new taxes" and then, during his presidency, agreeing to raise several taxes.

TIP

A Divided Court
The Supreme Court has been fairly evenly divided between its liberal wing and its conservative wing. Justice David Souter could have solidified a conservative court that would have overturned *Roe* v. *Wade*. Unfortunately for conservatives, Souter joined the liberal wing of the Court despite the fact that he was chosen by a Republican president.

Bush and the Supreme Court

Bush nominated David Souter to the Supreme Court to replace the retiring Thurgood Marshall. Conservatives have since lamented that choice as Souter (1990–2009) consistently voted with the liberal wing of the Court. Bush also nominated Clarence Thomas, an African-American judge, to serve on the Court. Thomas narrowly won confirmation after a grueling nomination hearing in which he was accused of sexual harassment by a former assistant, Anita Hill. The harsh questioning of Hill by members of the Senate Judiciary Committee angered many women. Thomas has remained a steadfast conservative on the Court.

The Savings and Loan Bailout

In the 1980s, the nation's savings and loan (S&L) associations suffered from a spate of irresponsible and risky investments and from a downturn in the housing market.

Their situation was made worse by the deregulation of the industry in 1986. By 1989, over 700 S&Ls had become insolvent. In response to this crisis, Bush signed a bailout bill that extended billions of dollars to the industry.

Subject to Debate

It is difficult to assess the historical legacy of political figures from the recent past. However, with Ronald Reagan's passing away in 2004, his legacy has increasingly been the subject of historical work. Much of that work is highly partisan. On the one side, critics cite Reagan's background in B movies, such as *Bedtime for Bonzo*, and his seeming disinterest in matters of intellect as evidence of incompetency as president. These critics note that Reagan napped during meetings while important policy matters were discussed. He seemed aloof from issues and claimed ignorance of the complicated schemes that comprised the Iran-Contra scandal. Reagan's defenders focus on one of the major events of the Reagan-Bush years—the fall of communism in Europe. Reagan initiated a massive military buildup that the Soviet Union could not keep up with. The Soviets Union's attempt to keep pace broke their bank and led to the opening of the floodgates of change. In much of the recent work on Reagan's legacy, these poles dominate discussion.

Historians of social movements have tried to understand the rise of the New Right. Some historians have drawn comparisons to previous conservative movements—the Red Scare of the 1920s or McCarthyism in the 1950s. Others have connected it to religious movements of the past, such as the Second Great Awakening of the early-nineteenth century. Historians have also looked at the movement in the context of a backlash against the social movements and protest culture of the 1960s. If the legacy of the 1960s is free love, protest, and multiculturalism, the New Right stands for its opposites—conservative approaches to sexuality, respect for authority and discipline, and a unifying patriotism. The persistence of the New Right into the age of President Barack Obama ensures that it will remain a topic of debate.

Practice Multiple-Choice Questions:

Directions: Pick the letter that best answers the following questions.

1. Which of the following actions did President Jimmy Carter take in regard to Panama in 1977?

   (A) He signed treaties with Panama agreeing to transfer control of the Panama Canal and the Canal Zone to Panama.
   (B) He covertly funded Panamanian rebels in the hope of toppling the socialist Panamanian government.
   (C) He ordered Marines to invade Panama and take over rural areas known for growing cocaine.
   (D) He approved funding for a second canal across the isthmus in order to relieve congestion in the first canal.
   (E) He ordered the U.S. Navy to block Soviet ships from using the canal in retaliation for the Soviet invasion of Afghanistan.

2. One major cause of the failure of the savings and loan industry in 1986 was

   (A) the Supreme Court's rescinding of the Federal Deposit Insurance Corporation.
   (B) a series of risky investments that followed the deregulation of the industry.
   (C) close ties to the Exxon corporation in the period leading up to the Exxon *Valdez* oil spill.
   (D) the decline of heavy industry in the United States.
   (E) the arrest of the chairman of the industry on racketeering charges.

3. When President Ronald Reagan uttered the phrase "evil empire," he was referring to

   (A) Nazi Germany and its possessions in Europe.
   (B) a network of gang-related drug dealer kingpins.
   (C) Japan and its possessions in the Pacific.
   (D) the Soviet Union and its allied nations.
   (E) al-Qaeda and its network of terrorist cells.

4. A major result of the Persian Gulf War in 1991 was

   (A) a worsening of tensions with the Soviet Union.
   (B) the toppling of Saddam Hussein.
   (C) a solution to the conflict between Palestinians and Israelis.
   (D) removal of Iraqi troops from Kuwait.
   (E) the occupation of the American embassy in Iraq by radical students.

Practice Free-Response Questions:

1. Analyze the elements of the coalition that comprises the New Right.

2. Assess the legacy of Ronald Reagan with reference to TWO of the following:

   The Iran-Contra Scandal
   The fall of communism
   The deficit rate in the United States in the 1980s
   Illegal drug use in the United States in the 1980s

Answers and Explanations to Multiple-Choice Questions:

1. **(A)** Carter agreed to transfer control of the canal to Panama in 1999. Critics accuse him of giving away the canal, but the decision was perfectly reasonable. Panama got control of the Canal Zone, which runs right through their country, and the United States has access to the canal. At the end of 1999, the United States relinquished control of the Canal Zone, the canal, and approximately 7,000 buildings in the zone.
2. **(B)** In 1986, the government agreed to a massive bailout of the savings and loan industry. Previously, the industry was deregulated. Savings and loan institutions began making very risky investments in a wide variety of ventures. They moved away from their original mission, which was to extend mortgages to people to purchase homes. These risky investments began to backfire, and the government agreed to the bailout.
3. **(D)** The "evil empire" was the Soviet Union. Reagan is lionized among conservatives for his passionate and consistent opposition to communism. He is credited with pushing the Soviet Union to the brink of bankruptcy by initiating a massive arms race.
4. **(D)** The goal of the 1991 Gulf War was to remove Iraqi troops from Kuwait. That goal was successful. President Bush realized how difficult "regime change" would be in Iraq, so he avoided it. His son, President George W. Bush, on the other hand, went further. He ordered the toppling of Saddam Hussein (B) and the installation of a new government. President George W. Bush brought America into a lengthy conflict from which it has had difficulty extricating itself.

America in the Age of Clinton, Bush, and Obama, 1992–Present

CHAPTER 32

TIMELINE	
1992	Election of Bill Clinton
1993	Fighting in Mogadishu, Somalia
	Ratification of the North American Free Trade Agreement
1994	House Republicans issue the Contract With America
	Both houses of Congress shift from Democratic to Republican control
1996	Reelection of Bill Clinton
1998	Impeachment of President Clinton
2000	Election of George W. Bush
2001	Terrorist attacks on the World Trade Center and the Pentagon
2004	Reelection of George W. Bush
2008	Election of Barack Obama

The closing decade of the twentieth century and the opening decade of the twenty-first century have seen an intensification of partisan divisions. The acrimony between the two main parties intensified with the impeachment of President Bill Clinton. The era has also seen the historic election of the first African-American president, Barack Obama.

THE CLINTON ERA, 1993–2001

The Clinton presidency coincided with a period of strong economic growth. President Bill Clinton, the former governor of Arkansas, pushed the Democratic Party toward a more centrist direction. The Clinton years witnessed an increasingly bitter political climate as the Republican Party opposed many of his initiatives and ultimately pushed for his impeachment.

The Election of 1992

Early in the campaign cycle, it appeared that President George H. W. Bush was a shoo-in for reelection. The United States had effectively accomplished its goals in the Gulf War and Bush's approval ratings were high. However, a weak economy in 1992 hurt President Bush. Also, Governor Bill Clinton of Arkansas proved to be a formidable candidate—a candidate younger and more comfortable with the public than Bush. The campaign was complicated by a strong third-party bid for the presidency by Ross Perot. Perot, a billionaire from Texas, largely funded his own campaign and was able to tap into concerns about the size of government and the growth of the federal deficit. Perot ended up receiving nearly 19 percent of the popular vote nationally, probably taking more votes from the Republican candidate Bush than from the Democratic candidate Clinton. Clinton ended up with only 43 percent of the popular vote (compared with Bush's 37 percent) but easily carried the electoral vote.

Clinton and the Soul of the Democratic Party

President Clinton adopted the political stance of the Democratic Leadership Council (DLC). This group was founded in 1985 in the wake of President Ronald Reagan's resounding victory over Democratic challenger Walter Mondale. The founders of the Democratic Leadership Council argued that the Democratic Party should break with traditional liberal positions and move toward a more centrist direction. The group was critical of the close relationship between organized labor and the Democratic Party. Bill Clinton joined the DLC and espoused its approach in the 1992 election. Clinton's break with the traditional liberal positions of the Democratic Party frustrated his Republican opponents, President George H. W. Bush in 1992 and Bob Dole in 1996, by adopting several positions that had previously been associated with the Republican Party.

Stalled Health Care Reform

One of President Clinton's first major domestic policy initiatives was reform of the country's health care system. Clinton put forth the idea of a federal health insurance plan that would provide subsidized insurance to many of the 39 million uncovered Americans and would, according to the plan, bring down health insurance costs for everyone. The president's wife, Hillary Clinton, chaired a task force on the issue. The idea of a federal health insurance plan had been proposed as early as the 1930s. It came to the fore again in the late-twentieth century as health care costs spiraled out of control and more and more people could not afford insurance. The plan was vigorously opposed by the pharmaceutical and insurance industries. It was ultimately shot down by a Republican filibuster in the Senate.

NAFTA (1993)

Clinton broke with organized labor and environmental groups by embracing the North American Free Trade Agreement. NAFTA eliminated all trade barriers and tariffs among the United States, Canada, and Mexico. NAFTA was the subject of much controversy when it was promoted by President Clinton. Free-trade supporters promised global prosperity as more nations participate in the global economy. Opponents worried that nations will no longer be able to implement environmental regulations, ensure workers' rights, or protect fledging industries from foreign competition. Clinton's championing of NAFTA represents a conscious decision by Clinton to try to move the Democratic Party away from its liberal traditions and toward a more centrist approach.

Clinton Moves Right
Clinton frustrated Republicans, especially his opponent in the 1996 election, Bob Dole, by moving toward the right. His embrace of NAFTA and welfare reform stole Republican thunder and assured Clinton's reelection.

The General Agreement on Trade and Tariffs (GAAT) (1994)

The General Agreement of Trade and Tariffs (GATT) is another international trade agreement that has sought to encourage countries to participate in the global economy by reducing barriers to trade. GATT has existed since 1948, but the 1994 agreement was far-reaching in its commitment to free trade. The 1994 GATT agreement called into being the World Trade Organization (WTO), which has served as a global trade referee committed to reducing barriers to trade. The issues of globalization and free trade have inspired vociferous protests, most notably at the 1999 meeting of the World Trade Organization in Seattle.

Globalization and Its Discontents

Clinton's embrace of NAFTA was part of a broader push toward the removal of trade barriers. This push toward free trade is often labeled "globalization." Proponents of globalization argue that the elimination of trade barriers will lower prices of products and stimulate the global economy. However, the movement toward free trade has generated much debate. Labor organizations argue that eliminating trade barriers will lead to the loss of American manufacturing jobs as jobs gravitate toward countries where the going wages are the lowest. Also, environmentalists worry that free-trade treaties will prevent the participating countries from enacting strong environmental protections. These opponents came together in Seattle, Washington, in November 1999 to protest at a meeting of the World Trade Organization, an international body charged with reducing trade barriers.

Chaos in Somalia

President Clinton deployed U.S. forces to aid a United Nations humanitarian mission in Somalia in 1993. Troubles in Somalia began earlier, in 1991, after the government was toppled and fighting broke out between competing factions. The fighting in Somalia resulted in widespread famine, with over half a million people dying. The United Nations took the initiative to deliver food to Somalia, but much of it was stolen by the warring factions and sold for weapons. In December 1992, President Bush approved the use of United States troops to aid U.N. relief activities. By 1993, these U.S. troops had come under attack, resulting in intense fighting in the capital, Mogadishu. American forces suffered 19 deaths. The mission soon ended.

Democracy in Haiti

President Clinton took the lead in insuring a transition to democracy in Haiti in 1994. After decades of dictatorship, a democratic election brought Jean-Bertrand Aristide to power in 1990. Subsequently, a Haitian army general ousted him. Clinton announced American intentions to use force, if necessary, to return Aristide to power. The United Nations authorized such a move. However, former President Jimmy Carter was dispatched to Haiti to try to negotiate an end to military rule. He was successful, and Aristide returned to power in 1995.

The Militia Movement, Waco, and Oklahoma City

During Clinton's presidency, a small but vocal movement of adamantly antigovernment groups grew in different parts of the country. Some members of this movement were against paying federal taxes, while others were against the existence of federally controlled lands. The impulses behind the movement—paranoia, suspicion of foreigners, anti-Semitism and racism, and a belief in shadowy conspiracies—were not new in American history but became focused during the Clinton years. The movement gave rise to several armed militias, mostly in the Midwest and the West, ready to take action against a "tyrannical" federal government.

The movement gained traction following the federal government's handling of a standoff with a religious cult, the Branch Davidians, in Waco, Texas, in 1993. Federal authorities became concerned about reports of stockpiling illegal weapons as well as child abuse at the group's compound. After a standoff with the group lasting over a month, FBI agents attacked the compound on April 19, 1993. The building caught on fire, resulting in the deaths of 77 members of the group. Antigovernment groups saw this as another example of the federal government overstepping its authority. On the second anniversary of the fire at Waco, in 1995, members of the militia movement exploded a massive truck bomb in front of the federal building in Oklahoma City, Oklahoma, killing 168 people.

The Midterm Elections of 1994 and the Contract with America

The Republican Party made significant gains in both the House of Representatives and the Senate in the midterm elections of 1994. The opposition party traditionally does well in the congressional elections that occur between presidential elections. In this case, the Republican Party gained control of both the House and the Senate. The Republicans had not controlled the House since 1954. House Republicans, led by minority leader Newt Gingrich, had signed and publicly issued the Contract With America six weeks before the 1994 election. It was a call to arms for Republicans and a specific blueprint for legislative action. The document called for action on a number of fronts, such as tougher anticrime measures, tort reform, and welfare reform. Many of the House's initiatives died in the Senate, some were vetoed by President Clinton, some were implemented, and some were reworked by both parties before being implemented. The success of the Republican Party in 1994 put President Clinton on the defensive in regard to his dealings with Congress.

Welfare Reform

In 1996, Bill Clinton adopted one of the planks of the Republican Contract With America by ending welfare as a federal program and shifting its administration to the state level. Clinton's embrace of welfare reform shocked many liberal Democrats. The Democratic Party had pushed for federal entitlement programs since the New Deal of President Roosevelt in the 1930s. Clinton perceived that many Americans were growing weary of programs that cost taxpayers money and did not seem to lessen poverty. Some Americans argued that welfare fostered a sense of dependency among recipients of welfare payments and stifled individual initiative. The reform required welfare recipients to begin work after two years—a stipulation known as "workfare."

Intervention in the Former Yugoslavia

The Clinton Administration, like previous Democratic administrations, set out broad domestic reform goals but became enmeshed in foreign policy matters. Clinton became increasingly concerned about violence is the former Yugoslavia. Under communism, Yugoslavia had been a patchwork of different ethnicities. After communism fell in 1989, the country split into several smaller nations. Ethnic violence developed as Serbian forces attempted to gain control of areas of Bosnia with large Serbian populations. In the process, Serbian forces initiated a campaign to remove Bosnians, by force if necessary, from these areas. This ethnic-cleansing campaign resulted in atrocities against the civilian population and became a focus of concern in the media and among foreign countries. The United States and other countries decided to take action as reports of Serbian brutality became known. North American Treaty Organization (NATO) forces, led by the United States, initiated air strikes against Serbian targets in 1994. President Clinton brought leaders from Bosnia, Serbia, and Croatia together in 1995 in Dayton, Ohio. A peace treaty, known as the Dayton Agreement, was signed, and 60,000 NATO troops were dispatched to enforce it.

The United States again became concerned about violence in the region in 1998 when reports emerged of Serbian attacks against ethnic Albanians in the Serbian province of Kosovo. President Clinton approved the use of U.S. forces, under NATO auspices, to engage in a bombing campaign against Serbia in 1999.

Reelection in 1996

Clinton won reelection in 1996, despite the gains of the Republicans just two years earlier in the midterm elections. Clinton continued to frustrate Republicans by stealing their thunder on traditional Republican issues, such as crime and welfare. His opponent was Senator Bob Dole. The economy remained strong as the election approached. Some Americans were concerned with Dole's age, 73, while others found him cold and even bitter. Clinton won handily, but the Republicans still maintained control of both houses of Congress.

Scandals and Impeachment

President Clinton was dogged by accusations of scandal throughout his administration. During his first term, Kenneth Starr was appointed as an independent council to investigate the Clintons' participation in a failed and fraudulent real estate project in Arkansas called the Whitewater Development Corporation that dated back to 1978, when Bill Clinton was governor. Starr pursued the Whitewater case relentlessly but never tied the Clintons to the fraud.

President Clinton, however, was not able to avoid implication in a more salacious scandal. Clinton was publicly accused of having a sexual affair with a White House intern named Monica Lewinsky. Clinton denied the accusations publicly and also before a federal grand jury. When Clinton was later forced to admit the affair, Congressional Republicans felt they had evidence of impeachable crimes—lying to a grand jury and obstructing justice. Clinton was impeached by the House of Representatives in 1998. Clinton was found "not guilty" by the Senate (two-thirds are needed for conviction). The entire incident reflected the tense relationship between the two major political parties. Clinton emerged from the affair largely unscathed. Many Americans disapproved of his personal misconduct but resented the attempt by Republicans to remove him from office.

TIP 

Impeachment
Impeachment is not synonymous with removal from office. Impeachment is the act of bringing charges against the president (or other federal officials). It is parallel to indictment in the criminal court system. After impeachment by the House, the Senate conducts a trial, based on the charges listed in the articles of impeachment. If found guilty of these charges, the president is removed from office.

Clinton and the Conflict in the Middle East

Toward the end of his second term, Clinton put a great deal of effort in attempting to broker a peace agreement between Israel and the Palestinians. Since the founding of Israel in 1948, tensions have existed in the Middle East. The Arab nations refused to recognize Israel's right to exist. Four wars occurred between Israel and its neighbors between 1948 and 1973. Since the Six-Day War in 1967, Israel has occupied lands adjacent to where large numbers of Palestinians live. These lands currently include the West Bank, the Gaza Strip, and eastern Jerusalem. (Israeli forces withdrew from the Gaza Strip in 2005.) Palestinians have insisted that these lands should comprise a Palestinian state. Israel has resisted agreeing to the formation of a Palestinian state as long as Palestinians launch attacks on Israel. The continued growth of Jewish settlements in the West Bank complicates the situation. In 2000, President Bill Clinton invited Palestinian leader Yasser Arafat and Israeli Prime Minister Ehud Barak to Camp David. The goal was to work out a final status settlement to the Israeli-Palestinian conflict. The discussions at Camp David in 2000 did not resolve the conflict, which still remains unresolved.

THE PRESIDENCY OF GEORGE W. BUSH (2001–2009)

George W. Bush is the son of the forty-first president, George H. W. Bush. Before running for president, George W. Bush was governor of Texas and had little national exposure. Bush, a Republican, won the presidency in 2000 amid electoral controversy. He ushered the country through the aftermath of one of the most tumultuous events on American soil since the Civil War—the terrorist attacks in 2001. By the end of his second term, public approval of his presidency was at an historic low, hampering the chances of the Republicans to hold on to the White House.

The Election of 2000

The 2000 election for president was one of the most contentious in American history. The voting in Florida was split almost evenly between the Democratic candidate, Vice President Al Gore, and Republican candidate, Governor George W. Bush. This should not have been a problem beyond Florida. However, based on the electoral votes of the other 49 states, neither candidate had 270 electoral votes, the number needed to be declared the winner. After several weeks of legal wrangling in Florida, the U.S. Supreme Court reversed an order by the Florida Supreme Court to do a hand recount of several counties in Florida. The decision by the U.S. Supreme Court in *Bush* v. *Gore* ended the dispute, with Bush slightly ahead of Gore in Florida, securing the presidency for Bush.

Terrorist Attacks Against the United States

The terrorist attacks on the United States in 2001 had a profound impact on domestic politics and foreign policy. On the morning of September 11, 2001, 19 terrorists working with the al-Qaeda network hijacked four domestic airplanes. The idea was to turn the airplanes into missiles that would destroy symbols of American power. One plane was flown into the Pentagon, inflicting heavy damage. One plane crashed in a field after the hijackers were overtaken by passengers. The other two airplanes did the most damage, crashing into the two towers of the World Trade Center in New York City. The damage inflicted on each building weakened the structures of each so that both buildings collapsed within two hours. Approximately 3,000 people died in the four incidents, the vast majority of the deaths occurring at the World Trade Center.

War with Iraq

The terrorist attacks of 2001 were soon followed by President Bush initiating military action on two fronts—Iraq and Afghanistan. Operation Iraqi Freedom, begun in 2003, was the attempt by the United States to remove Saddam Hussein from office and create a less belligerent and more democratic government in Iraq. President Bush insisted that Hussein was developing weapons of mass destruction that could be used against the United States and its allies. U.S. forces failed to find evidence of such weapons. The administration also suggested that there was a connection between Hussein and the terrorist attacks of 2001. No evidence of such a link has been uncovered, and the administration moved away from that rationale. This operation proved to be more difficult and costly than Operation Desert Storm (1991). Defeating the Iraqi army and removing Saddam Hussein from office was relatively easy. After these goals were accomplished, President Bush declared "mission accomplished" in May 2003. However, creating stability in Iraq proved to be an elusive goal for the Bush administration. Attacks by insurgents continued, both against U.S. forces and between different factions within Iraq. Operation Iraqi

Freedom hurt President Bush's approval ratings in the United States and created tension between the United States and some of the European nations.

War in Afghanistan

The United States also initiated military actions in Afghanistan in 2001, less than a month after the September 11 terrorist attacks. American forces overthrew the Taliban, the government that had given refuge to al-Qaeda. The United States hoped to find the leader of al-Qaeda, Osama bin Laden, who was still at large at the end of President Bush's presidency.

The Patriot Act

The Patriot Act was passed in 2001, six weeks after the September 11 terrorist attacks. It greatly expanded the government's authority in the fight against terrorism. Some critics have said that it impinges on people's civil liberties.

Department of Homeland Security

The creation of the Department of Homeland Security was a result of the September 11, 2001 terrorist attacks. It was created in 2003, absorbing the Immigration and Naturalization Service. It is a cabinet-level department, with the responsibility of protecting the United States from terrorist attacks and natural disasters.

The Bush Doctrine

President Bush shifted American foreign policy away from its traditional reliance on deterrence and containment. Bush put forth a more aggressive approach in the fall of 2002 that called for preemptive strikes against nations perceived as threats to the United States. In a speech at West Point, Bush identified an "axis of evil" consisting of Iraq, Iran, and North Korea. This reliance on preemptive warfare is known as the Bush Doctrine.

Tactics in the War on Terrorism

In 2004, the release of photographs of United States Army personnel humiliating and apparently abusing prisoners at the Abu Ghraib prison in Iraq cast light on new tactics used by the United States in its handling of prisoners in the aftermath of the 2001 terrorist attacks. Army personnel at detention centers in Iraq, Afghanistan, and Guantanamo Bay, Cuba, were given permission to use "enhanced-interrogation techniques." Critics said that these techniques, which include waterboarding, amount to torture. The government also began to hold suspects at these facilities indefinitely, denying them due process rights. The Supreme Court, in *Hamdan* v. *Rumsfeld* (2006), ruled that the Bush Administration could not hold detainees indefinitely without due process and without the protection of the Geneva Accords.

Withdrawal from the International Community

The Bush administration had worked with a coalition of nations in the invasion of Iraq, but it distrusted many of the multilateral entities in which the United States had previously participated. Bush withdrew the United States from the Kyoto Protocol, an international agreement on environmental goals. Also, the administration violated international guidelines about the treatment of military prisoners. Bush withdrew from the Anti-Ballistic Missile Treaty, in effect since 1972, in late 2001 so that the United States could develop a space-based missile defense system. In 2002, the United States withdrew from the treaty creating the U.N.'s International Criminal Court, which went into effect later that year.

No Child Left Behind

The No Child Left Behind Act was signed into law in 2002 by President George W. Bush. As a program designed to reform public education, the law extended the reach of the federal government into education—traditionally a state responsibility. The law mandated that states set learning standards, that students attain "proficiency" in reading and math by 2014, and that teachers be "highly qualified" in the subject area. The law allowed students to transfer to other schools if they were attending a school that fell short of meeting new guidelines. The law also allowed the state to take over schools and school districts that did not meet new guidelines. The program was criticized by many states for its lack of funding to help schools reach these new goals. Also, many educators questioned the increased reliance on standardized exams in judging schools and school districts.

Reelection in 2004

Bush won another very close election in 2004, defeating Senator John Kerry. Early in 2004, Bush's presidency seemed to be in trouble. Poll number showed a low approval rate, as many Americans questioned Bush's handling of the ongoing war in Iraq. Kerry was critical of the Iraq War and noted repeatedly the lack of any evidence of weapons of mass destruction in Iraq. The campaign was marked by relentlessly negative advertising. Some of the most negative campaigning originated with a group called Swift Boat Veterans for Truth. The group accused Kerry of falsifying his war record, including his four months as a commander of a Swift Boat in Vietnam. The accusations proved to be baseless, but they put the Kerry campaign on the defensive. The election was very close. This time, the result hinged on the result of voting in Ohio. When Ohio announced on the day after the voting that Bush carried the state, Kerry conceded the election.

Hurricane Katrina

The Bush Administration suffered a major blow in the aftermath of Hurricane Katrina. In August 2005, the massive hurricane devastated the Gulf Coast area and destroyed much of New Orleans. The hurricane led to over a thousand deaths and severe damage in large areas of Alabama, Mississippi, and Louisiana. President

Bush was slow to acknowledge the extent of the disaster, and the Federal Emergency Management Agency (FEMA) was slow to take action. For days, dire reports with grim images came out of New Orleans, with little sign of federal assistance. Bush's pronouncement that the head of FEMA, Michael Brown, was doing a "heck of a job" seemed to be further evidence of his inability to grasp the gravity of the situation.

THE ELECTION OF PRESIDENT BARACK OBAMA

The election of 2008 resulted in a profound milestone in American history—the election of the first African American to the presidency. Such an event was virtually unthinkable a generation earlier. As late as the 1960s, Jim Crow segregation was still the law of the land throughout the South and informal, de facto segregation existed throughout the nation. The civil rights movement challenged and altered many of these practices, but racist attitudes persisted among large segments of the population.

Obama's victory was the result of a series of factors. First, his campaign successfully held off a strong challenge to the Democratic nomination by Senator Hillary Clinton. Clinton's bid for the nomination, if successful, could have resulted in a different historic milestone—the first female president in the United States. The Obama campaign was able to harness the power of the Internet as well as the candidate's abundant charisma to build a large base. Clinton subsequently threw her support behind the Obama campaign in the general election. She was later named secretary of state.

In the general election, the Democratic Party was aided by an unpopular sitting Republican president, George W. Bush, and by an unfocused campaign by Republican Senator John McCain. The McCain campaign failed to articulate a consistent message. McCain's selection of the relatively unknown candidate Sarah Palin for vice president failed to propel the campaign forward. Palin energized the more conservative elements of the Republican Party but failed to broaden the party's appeal.

The Obama campaign was able to cement support in traditionally "blue" (Democratic) states and successfully challenged McCain in Republican-leaning states such as North Carolina, Virginia, and Indiana. Obama garnered 53 percent of the popular vote and won 365 electoral votes to McCain's 173.

Obama Confronts a Weak Economy

President Obama took office during a major downturn in economic activity. Unemployment reached 10 percent in 2009. Obama initiated several actions to address the economic crisis. He pushed for major economic stimulus packages designed to create jobs on the local level.

Obama and the Supreme Court

Obama nominated the first Latina to the Supreme Court, Justice Sonia Sotomayor, to replace Justice David H. Souter, who retired. Sotomayor was subsequently approved by the Senate in 2009.

Reforming Health Care

Like President Clinton, President Obama chose health care reform as one of his first major domestic initiatives. The issues that motivated Clinton in 1993—spiraling health care costs and large numbers of uninsured Americans—had become more pronounced in the ensuing years. Proposals for creating a public option in regard to health insurance generated enthusiasm among many Democrats but fierce opposition from the pharmaceutical and insurance industries and from the Republican Party. Many Republicans likened such a proposal to socialism. In 2009, both houses of Congress passed versions of health care reform. In early 2010, a special election to fill the late Senator Edward Kennedy's seat was won by a Republican, ending the Democrats' 60-seat filibuster-proof majority in the Senate. Democrats were able to pass a watered-down version of healthcare reform, the Patient Protection and Affordable Care Act, in March 2010.

Obama's Foreign Policy

President Obama has taken a variety of steps in regard to the Muslim world. Soon after coming into office, Obama made a major speech in Cairo, Egypt, pledging to mend relations with the Muslim world. He has committed additional forces to Afghanistan while beginning a withdrawal of troops from Iraq. In 2011, Obama spoke favorably of the changes brought about by the Arab Spring protests in the Middle East and North Africa. He committed United States forces, working with European allies, to challenge forces loyal to Libyan leader Muammar Qaddafi. By October 2011, Qaddafi was killed and an interim government was formed. During the 2008 campaign, Obama repeatedly pledged to commit United States forces to finding and killing Osama Bin Laden. That pledge was fulfilled in the spring of 2011.

The Tea Party Movement and the Reaction to the Election of President Obama

The election of Barack Obama to the presidency has generated a vocal opposition movement known as the Tea Party, harkening back to the American colonists' action against perceived British tyranny. To some extent the movement is a creation of the media—heavily promoted by the Fox News channel. To some extent it represents a grassroots sense of discontent with big government. However, the movement often exhibits hyperbolic language, predicting the onset of "tyranny," "fascism," and "communism."

Subject to Debate

It is very difficult to debate the legacy of the very recent past. One topic that historians have begun to wrestle with is the origins of the toxic partisan atmosphere in Washington, D.C. Some historians look to the impeachment process against President Clinton as a turning point in recent political history. The Republican-initiated inquest went beyond the usual jockeying between parties and made compromise between the parties increasingly difficult. Historians also note the unusual closeness of the two major parties in recent elections and in opinion polls. Both parties always feel like victory is in reach and seek to press any advantage they can to win points with the electorate. Future historians will have to put the election of the nation's first African-American president in a larger context.

Practice Multiple-Choice Questions:

Directions: Pick the letter that best answers the following questions.

1. The Dayton Agreement, negotiated by President Bill Clinton in 1995, was an attempt to end hostilities in
   (A) Bosnia.
   (B) Somalia.
   (C) Israel
   (D) Northern Ireland.
   (E) Vietnam.

2. In the aftermath of Hurricane Katrina in 2005,
   (A) the city of New Orleans was declared uninhabitable and has remained vacant ever since.
   (B) the Army Corps of Engineers won praise for predicting the impact of the hurricane on New Orleans and taking effective steps to minimize the effect of the storm.
   (C) a coalition of European nations initiated a massive economic package for the rebuilding of New Orleans.
   (D) the George W. Bush administration was perceived by many as out of touch and incapable of taking decisive action.
   (E) massive rioting in New Orleans led to the National Guard intervening to put down the rebellion.

3. The No Child Left Behind program, put into law in 2002 by President George W. Bush,
   (A) authorized local authorities to take aggressive steps against sex offenders, including notifying the public of the presence of convicted sex offenders living in the community.
   (B) made the adoption of children easier by removing restrictions that had been applied to gay couples and to single people.
   (C) extended the reach of the federal government into education by establishing a set of standards that local school districts were to achieve.
   (D) provided emergency aid to Asian nations to address the problem of poverty and hunger among children.
   (E) created a program to help child soldiers in Africa escape their captors and become reintegrated into civilian society.

4. The Bush Doctrine, set forth by President George W. Bush in 2002,
   (A) moved the United States away from its traditional reliance on containment and deterrence and toward a more aggressive preemptive approach to foreign affairs.
   (B) affirmed that the United States would extend foreign aid only to nations that demonstrated improvements in human rights.
   (C) approved the use of torture and other enhanced-interrogation techniques in dealing with suspected terrorists.
   (D) asserted the right of the United States to intervene in the affairs of Latin-American nations if essential American economic interests were threatened.
   (E) put forth a comprehensive plan to eliminate nuclear weapons from the arsenals of the world.

Practice Free-Response Questions:

1. Assess the response of the United States to the terrorist attacks of September 2001.

2. Analyze attempts by the United States to help achieve a comprehensive peace between Israel and its neighbors between 1976 and 2001.

Answers and Explanations to Multiple-Choice Questions:

1. **(A)** By 1995, the situation in Bosnia was becoming a bloodbath as Serbians engaged in ethnic cleansing in Bosnia. The United States and other countries took action. After Clinton brought leaders from Bosnia, Serbia, and Croatia together in 1995 in Ohio, 60,000 NATO troops were dispatched to enforce a peace treaty.

2. **(D)** Bush's handling of the aftermath of Hurricane Katrina hurt his standing among many Americans. He seemed out of touch with the devastation in New Orleans. It took several days for the administration to recognize the enormity of the situation. Bush complimented the director of the Federal Emergency Management Agency Michael Brown by saying, "Heck of a job, Brownie." Brown later resigned from FEMA because of his handling of the Katrina disaster.

3. **(C)** No Child Left Behind is a federal law designed to change education on the local level. Its critics have charged that it relies too heavily on standardized testing. Many districts have had difficulty complying with No Child Left Behind guidelines because of lack of funding.

4. **(A)** The key word in the Bush Doctrine is preemptive. Bush attacked Iraq (2003) in a preemptive strike against Saddam Hussein. He asserted that Hussein was stockpiling weapons of mass destruction. After the attack, no such weapons were found.

Answer Sheet

PRACTICE TEST 1

1 Ⓐ Ⓑ Ⓒ Ⓓ Ⓔ	21 Ⓐ Ⓑ Ⓒ Ⓓ Ⓔ	41 Ⓐ Ⓑ Ⓒ Ⓓ Ⓔ	61 Ⓐ Ⓑ Ⓒ Ⓓ Ⓔ
2 Ⓐ Ⓑ Ⓒ Ⓓ Ⓔ	22 Ⓐ Ⓑ Ⓒ Ⓓ Ⓔ	42 Ⓐ Ⓑ Ⓒ Ⓓ Ⓔ	62 Ⓐ Ⓑ Ⓒ Ⓓ Ⓔ
3 Ⓐ Ⓑ Ⓒ Ⓓ Ⓔ	23 Ⓐ Ⓑ Ⓒ Ⓓ Ⓔ	43 Ⓐ Ⓑ Ⓒ Ⓓ Ⓔ	63 Ⓐ Ⓑ Ⓒ Ⓓ Ⓔ
4 Ⓐ Ⓑ Ⓒ Ⓓ Ⓔ	24 Ⓐ Ⓑ Ⓒ Ⓓ Ⓔ	44 Ⓐ Ⓑ Ⓒ Ⓓ Ⓔ	64 Ⓐ Ⓑ Ⓒ Ⓓ Ⓔ
5 Ⓐ Ⓑ Ⓒ Ⓓ Ⓔ	25 Ⓐ Ⓑ Ⓒ Ⓓ Ⓔ	45 Ⓐ Ⓑ Ⓒ Ⓓ Ⓔ	65 Ⓐ Ⓑ Ⓒ Ⓓ Ⓔ
6 Ⓐ Ⓑ Ⓒ Ⓓ Ⓔ	26 Ⓐ Ⓑ Ⓒ Ⓓ Ⓔ	46 Ⓐ Ⓑ Ⓒ Ⓓ Ⓔ	66 Ⓐ Ⓑ Ⓒ Ⓓ Ⓔ
7 Ⓐ Ⓑ Ⓒ Ⓓ Ⓔ	27 Ⓐ Ⓑ Ⓒ Ⓓ Ⓔ	47 Ⓐ Ⓑ Ⓒ Ⓓ Ⓔ	67 Ⓐ Ⓑ Ⓒ Ⓓ Ⓔ
8 Ⓐ Ⓑ Ⓒ Ⓓ Ⓔ	28 Ⓐ Ⓑ Ⓒ Ⓓ Ⓔ	48 Ⓐ Ⓑ Ⓒ Ⓓ Ⓔ	68 Ⓐ Ⓑ Ⓒ Ⓓ Ⓔ
9 Ⓐ Ⓑ Ⓒ Ⓓ Ⓔ	29 Ⓐ Ⓑ Ⓒ Ⓓ Ⓔ	49 Ⓐ Ⓑ Ⓒ Ⓓ Ⓔ	69 Ⓐ Ⓑ Ⓒ Ⓓ Ⓔ
10 Ⓐ Ⓑ Ⓒ Ⓓ Ⓔ	30 Ⓐ Ⓑ Ⓒ Ⓓ Ⓔ	50 Ⓐ Ⓑ Ⓒ Ⓓ Ⓔ	70 Ⓐ Ⓑ Ⓒ Ⓓ Ⓔ
11 Ⓐ Ⓑ Ⓒ Ⓓ Ⓔ	31 Ⓐ Ⓑ Ⓒ Ⓓ Ⓔ	51 Ⓐ Ⓑ Ⓒ Ⓓ Ⓔ	71 Ⓐ Ⓑ Ⓒ Ⓓ Ⓔ
12 Ⓐ Ⓑ Ⓒ Ⓓ Ⓔ	32 Ⓐ Ⓑ Ⓒ Ⓓ Ⓔ	52 Ⓐ Ⓑ Ⓒ Ⓓ Ⓔ	72 Ⓐ Ⓑ Ⓒ Ⓓ Ⓔ
13 Ⓐ Ⓑ Ⓒ Ⓓ Ⓔ	33 Ⓐ Ⓑ Ⓒ Ⓓ Ⓔ	53 Ⓐ Ⓑ Ⓒ Ⓓ Ⓔ	73 Ⓐ Ⓑ Ⓒ Ⓓ Ⓔ
14 Ⓐ Ⓑ Ⓒ Ⓓ Ⓔ	34 Ⓐ Ⓑ Ⓒ Ⓓ Ⓔ	54 Ⓐ Ⓑ Ⓒ Ⓓ Ⓔ	74 Ⓐ Ⓑ Ⓒ Ⓓ Ⓔ
15 Ⓐ Ⓑ Ⓒ Ⓓ Ⓔ	35 Ⓐ Ⓑ Ⓒ Ⓓ Ⓔ	55 Ⓐ Ⓑ Ⓒ Ⓓ Ⓔ	75 Ⓐ Ⓑ Ⓒ Ⓓ Ⓔ
16 Ⓐ Ⓑ Ⓒ Ⓓ Ⓔ	36 Ⓐ Ⓑ Ⓒ Ⓓ Ⓔ	56 Ⓐ Ⓑ Ⓒ Ⓓ Ⓔ	76 Ⓐ Ⓑ Ⓒ Ⓓ Ⓔ
17 Ⓐ Ⓑ Ⓒ Ⓓ Ⓔ	37 Ⓐ Ⓑ Ⓒ Ⓓ Ⓔ	57 Ⓐ Ⓑ Ⓒ Ⓓ Ⓔ	77 Ⓐ Ⓑ Ⓒ Ⓓ Ⓔ
18 Ⓐ Ⓑ Ⓒ Ⓓ Ⓔ	38 Ⓐ Ⓑ Ⓒ Ⓓ Ⓔ	58 Ⓐ Ⓑ Ⓒ Ⓓ Ⓔ	78 Ⓐ Ⓑ Ⓒ Ⓓ Ⓔ
19 Ⓐ Ⓑ Ⓒ Ⓓ Ⓔ	39 Ⓐ Ⓑ Ⓒ Ⓓ Ⓔ	59 Ⓐ Ⓑ Ⓒ Ⓓ Ⓔ	79 Ⓐ Ⓑ Ⓒ Ⓓ Ⓔ
20 Ⓐ Ⓑ Ⓒ Ⓓ Ⓔ	40 Ⓐ Ⓑ Ⓒ Ⓓ Ⓔ	60 Ⓐ Ⓑ Ⓒ Ⓓ Ⓔ	80 Ⓐ Ⓑ Ⓒ Ⓓ Ⓔ

Practice Test 1

SECTION 1
MULTIPLE-CHOICE QUESTIONS

TIME—55 MINUTES

NUMBER OF QUESTIONS—80

Directions: Each of the following questions or statements below has five possible answers. For each question, select the best response.

1. The colony of New Amsterdam could best be characterized as

 (A) a Puritan godly community.
 (B) a Quaker city of brotherly love.
 (C) a refuge for Catholics.
 (D) an island for debtors and criminals.
 (E) a commercial outpost.

2. Unlike British colonies of the Caribbean or the Chesapeake region, seventeenth-century New England colonies did not fit well into British mercantilist plans because the region

 (A) was primarily inhabited by Puritans who devoted more time to prayer and religious instruction and less time to economic activities.
 (B) became a center for anti-British actions that made enforcement of trade laws impossible.
 (C) did not produce sufficient quantities of valuable raw materials needed by Great Britain.
 (D) lacked natural harbors needed to facilitate international trade.
 (E) failed to attract sufficient numbers of settlers to perform agricultural work.

3. "If we might be suffered to be altogether independent of Great Britain, could we have any claim to the protection of that government, of which we are no longer a part? Without this protection, should we not become the prey of one of the other powers of Europe, such as should first seize upon us?"

   The above quotation reflects the thinking of

   (A) the Reverend John Winthrop in his sermon *A Model of Christian Charity* delivered aboard the *Arbella* (1630).
   (B) Patrick Henry in the series of resolutions passed by the House of Burgesses known as the Virginia Resolves (1765).
   (C) Governor Thomas Hutchinson in a speech to the Massachusetts House of Representatives (1773).
   (D) Thomas Paine in the pamphlet *Common Sense* (1776).
   (E) General George Washington, addressing the Second Continental Congress (1777).

4. An important concern of the participants in Shays's Rebellion (1786–1787) was

   (A) heavy taxes imposed on agricultural lands and designed to reduce wartime debt.
   (B) inflationary currency policies caused by the printing of paper currency.
   (C) high import tariffs that reduced foreign demand for American agricultural products.
   (D) the government's refusal to take action against Native-American groups in the western part of the state.
   (E) the elimination of Massachusetts's homesteading program, which allowed farmers to acquire additional lands at no cost.

5. The Supreme Court's power to examine and strike down legislation it deems unconstitutional was

   (A) clearly spelled out in Article III of the Constitution.
   (B) embraced by Thomas Jefferson and other members of the Democratic-Republican Party.
   (C) revoked by an executive order issued by President Andrew Jackson.
   (D) established by the Supreme Court's decision in *Marbury* v. *Madison.*
   (E) established by Chief Justice Roger Taney in the Dred Scott decision.

6. The election of James Polk to the presidency in 1844 was significant in that it signaled
   (A) the success of the free-labor political ideology in the electoral realm.
   (B) a shift from free-trade policies to the implementation of steep protective import tariffs.
   (C) the beginning of a long period of isolationism in regard to European conflicts.
   (D) a rejection of Jacksonian populism and the reemergence of the old New England political dynasties.
   (E) an embrace of expansionistic policies that pushed the boundaries of the United States to the Pacific Ocean.

7. The Republican Party's position on slavery in 1860 was
   (A) the immediate abolition of slavery.
   (B) to leave the question of slavery up to each state or territory.
   (C) to oppose the expansion of slavery into new territories.
   (D) to ignore the issue.
   (E) that slavery was a positive good.

8. During the late 1800s, supporters of social Darwinism would most likely have advocated
   (A) government ownership of major banks and railroad companies.
   (B) a social welfare safety net to help people get through difficult economic times.
   (C) full political equality between African Americans and whites.
   (D) a laissez-faire approach to the economy.
   (E) the teaching of the theory of evolution in high school biology classes.

9. Which of the following accurately describes Arkansas Governor Orval Faubus's response to the Little Rock School Board's decision to integrate Central High School in September 1957?
   (A) Faubus went to Central High School on the first day of school in September 1957 to personally welcome the nine African-American students who were chosen to attend the school.
   (B) Faubus said publicly the issue was a local matter, but privately he organized meetings between opponents and proponents of integration in hopes or working out a compromise.
   (C) Faubus defied the Supreme Court as well as the local school board by calling out the Arkansas National Guard to prevent the nine African-American students from entering Central High School on the first day of school in September 1957.
   (D) Faubus resigned in August 1957 in protest of the imposition of federal mandates on local school policies.
   (E) Faubus closed down Central High School before it opened in September 1957 to prevent the integration plans from going into effect.

10. The colony of Carolina was unique among the British North-American colonies in that it was founded by

(A) French Huguenots fleeing persecution at the hands of the Catholic majority.
(B) religious dissenters who believed that ministers were corrupt and power hungry.
(C) small-scale farmers who tried to establish a democratic, egalitarian community.
(D) wealthy planters from Barbados who tried to duplicate that colony's slave economy.
(E) freed African Americans who had fled from Virginia.

11. When American colonists protested the Stamp Act (1765) and other taxes by asserting "No taxation without representation," the British government

(A) put forth the theory that all English subjects, including colonists in North America, were virtually represented by the members of Parliament.
(B) invoked the divine right of kings, which permitted the monarch to create laws without the consent of the people.
(C) extended the right of nullification to colonial assemblies, allowing them to strike down objectionable legislation.
(D) argued that 100 percent of the revenues raised from the taxes stayed in the colonies to pay administrative costs.
(E) acquiesced and transferred taxation powers to the Continental Congress and to the various colonial assemblies.

12. The Shawnee leader Tecumseh responded to encroachments by white Americans into the Ohio River Valley by

(A) signing the Treaty of Greenville, ceding vast areas of the Ohio Territory to the United States Government.
(B) organizing a long march of members of twelve different Native-American nations to the Columbia River valley in the Pacific Northwest.
(C) reviving traditional religious practices and forming a pan-Indian confederation to resist United States troops.
(D) pushing for Native-American assimilation, through schools, newspapers, land ownership patterns, and government structure, in the hope of gaining acceptance from white Americans.
(E) calling for a protest march in Washington, D.C., of over 25,000 Native Americans from over twenty different nations.

13. During a debate between Illinois senate candidates Democrat Stephen Douglas and Republican Abraham Lincoln in Freeport, Illinois, how did Douglas respond to Lincoln's assertion that the Dred Scott decision rendered the concept of popular sovereignty null and void?

    (A) Douglas said he would push for a constitutional amendment that would recognize the legitimacy of the concept of popular sovereignty and supersede the Dred Scott decision.
    (B) Douglas refused to discuss the issue of slavery, asserting that such discussions undermined national unity.
    (C) Douglas argued that the Dred Scott decision did not impose slavery on free states and territories. The decision allowed only for slaves to be brought into these areas, not for slavery to be practiced there.
    (D) Douglas acknowledged that the Dred Scott decision made it impossible for Congress to legislate against slavery but it did not prevent the president from ending slavery by executive order.
    (E) Douglas argued that popular sovereignty was alive and well. Although slavery could not be outlawed by a territory, he insisted that slavery could not actually be practiced unless territorial legislatures passed legislation protecting it.

14. The Emancipation Proclamation was important because it

    (A) immediately freed all the slaves in both Union and Confederate territory.
    (B) convinced the Confederacy to give up fighting and rejoin the United States.
    (C) persuaded Canada to join the war effort on the Union side.
    (D) turned the Civil War into a war for the liberation of the slaves.
    (E) quieted resentment among Irish-American immigrants.

15. President Theodore Roosevelt pushed for legislation such as the Elkins Act (1903) and the Hepburn Act (1906) in order to

    (A) provide the Interstate Commerce Commission with greater power to regulate the railroad industry effectively.
    (B) empower the Food and Drug Administration to regulate the sanitary conditions of factories.
    (C) challenge the corrupt practices that were endemic to the municipal political system.
    (D) extend the policing practices of the United States military into Central America and the Caribbean basin.
    (E) give federal prosecutors the authority to challenge racial discrimination on the state level.

16. The term "new immigrants," used in the late-nineteenth and early-twentieth centuries, refers primarily to

    (A) African-American migrants from the rural South.
    (B) Irish refugees from the potato blight.
    (C) eastern and southern European immigrants.
    (D) exiles leaving the United States.
    (E) political refugees from sub-Saharan African.

17. The Espionage and Sedition Acts (1917–1918) and the Japanese relocation (1943) are similar in that both demonstrate that

    (A) freedom of speech is absolute and inviolable in the United States.
    (B) domestic spying networks have been successful in undermining American military success.
    (C) the Supreme Court often checks the power of the president.
    (D) immigration patterns change over time.
    (E) the government sometimes restricts civil liberties during times of war.

18. The passage of the Eighteenth Amendment to the Constitution, banning the production, sale, and consumption of alcoholic beverages, was aided by all of the following EXCEPT

    (A) the concerns of women during the Great Depression that men were spending too much of their unemployment checks on alcohol.
    (B) intense anti-German sentiment during World War I that targeted the perceived control of American breweries by German Americans.
    (C) strong nativist sentiment in the United States that identified excessive alcohol consumption with immigrant populations.
    (D) a tenacious anti-alcohol movement with deep roots in the nineteenth century.
    (E) the progressive movement's momentum in pushing the federal government to enact legislation that reformed various aspects of American life.

19. President John F. Kennedy's actions in regard to the Freedom Rides in May 1961 demonstrate that

    (A) Democratic administrations in the 1960s, dependent on electoral support from white southerners, refused to take a stand on civil rights issues.
    (B) Kennedy was willing to ignore Supreme Court guidance in his quest to bring racial equality to the South.
    (C) the president was leery of intervening in southern civil rights battles but would take action if violent opposition seemed to leave him no other choice.
    (D) the White House would provide guidance and material aid to those who sought to limit the influence of the civil rights movement.
    (E) the Republican-dominated Congress could prevent President Kennedy from taking action to end the Jim Crow system in the South.

20. In the 1610s and 1620s, the Virginia Company encouraged people to settle in colonial Virginia by

    (A) granting each settler a headright of fifty acres of land for himself and additional plots for each servant he brought over.
    (B) giving each new settler ten slaves trained in performing agricultural work.
    (C) providing ministers and church facilities to each town in Virginia to allay potential settlers' fears of a godless frontier.
    (D) planning a diverse economy of farming, small-scale manufacturing, processing, and trade to attract a variety of potential settlers.
    (E) brokering peace treaties with the Powhatan People of eastern Virginia to ensure safety and security for new English arrivals.

21. Many Antifederalists would not support the Constitution unless the framers of the Constitution

    (A) added a list of rights of the people.
    (B) allowed for the direct election of senators.
    (C) strengthened the powers of the federal government.
    (D) added a strong system of checks and balances.
    (E) guaranteed that the practice of slavery would be protected.

22. President Monroe articulated the Monroe Doctrine in his 1823 address to Congress in order to

    (A) encourage Great Britain to help the fledgling states of Latin America.
    (B) prevent the United States from becoming involved in Latin American affairs.
    (C) block the spread of communism in Central and South America.
    (D) announce the American intention to expand all the way to the Pacific Ocean.
    (E) warn European nations against further colonial ventures in the Western Hemisphere.

23. Personal Liberty Laws were passed by several states in the 1850s in order to

    (A) protect free African Americans and fugitive slaves from the Fugitive Slave Law.
    (B) allow for non-Protestants to practice their religion without interference from authorities.
    (C) permit women to serve on juries and to testify in court.
    (D) grant apprentices basic rights while they are living with their master.
    (E) extend citizenship rights to Native Americans.

24. Which of the following most accurately describes the outcome of the nullification crisis of 1832–1833?

    (A) President Andrew Jackson won a clear victory in his assertion of federal authority. South Carolina backed down and accepted the high tariff rates adopted by Congress in 1828.
    (B) The outcome could best be described as a compromise. The federal government issued the Force Bill authorizing the use of military force against South Carolina, but it also lowered tariff rates to about half of the 1828 rates.
    (C) South Carolina embarrassed President Jackson by its blatant disregard of federal law. Jackson had neither the will nor the means to challenge South Carolina's assertion of power.
    (D) The outcome of the crisis strengthened the Supreme Court, which issued a censure motion against both President Andrew Jackson and the legislature of South Carolina for putting petty grievances ahead of national unity.
    (E) The crisis greatly weakened the Democratic Party—the party of both President Andrew Jackson and the South Carolina nullifiers. The Whigs and the Republicans rose to prominence in the wake of the crisis.

25. Which of the following is an important result of increased agricultural mechanization in the late 1800s?

    (A) Farmers saw their standard of living rise as production and commodity prices increased.
    (B) Cancer rates increased with excessive use of chemical fertilizers and pesticides.
    (C) Farmers experienced debt as commodity prices fell due to overproduction and a tight money supply.
    (D) The slave system saw a revival as southern plantation owners sought to capitalize on new inventions.
    (E) America was able to supply surplus agricultural produce to the famine-stricken nations of central Africa.

26. During his tenure in the White House, President Theodore Roosevelt's agenda included

    (A) civil rights for African Americans.
    (B) measures to conserve natural resources.
    (C) the adoption of a socialist agenda.
    (D) American isolationism from world affairs.
    (E) United States intervention in World War I.

27. D. W. Griffith's film *Birth of a Nation* has generated controversy over the years since its production in 1915 because of its

    (A) sympathetic treatment of British forces and their loyalist allies during the American Revolution.
    (B) contention that the founding fathers were atheist freethinkers.
    (C) demeaning portrayal of African Americans in the South during the Reconstruction period.
    (D) explicit portrayal of adult sexuality during the Victorian era.
    (E) critical portrayal of the Pilgrims as narrow-minded bigots.

28. Critics of Dr. Benjamin Spock's book, *Common Sense Book of Baby and Child Care* (1946), contend that the book

    (A) focused too much on instilling love of God and country, reflecting the priorities of the Cold War more than on common sense.
    (B) reinforced gender roles with its emphasis on encouraging aggressive behavior in boys and passive behavior in girls.
    (C) ushered in the era of overmedicated children by encouraging parents to rely on a variety of prescription drugs designed to target depression, inattentiveness, shyness, hyperactivity, and other disorders.
    (D) lacked the rigors of university-based studies; its recommendations were based more on anecdotal evidence than on conclusive research.
    (E) eroded a sense of discipline and respect among baby boomers, which contributed to the disorder and permissiveness of the late 1960s and early 1970s.

29. High gasoline prices and long lines at gas pumps in the 1970s were the result of

    (A) the Iran-Contra scandal.
    (B) an oil spill in the Gulf of Mexico.
    (C) the Arab oil embargo.
    (D) the shift from leaded to unleaded gasoline.
    (E) the breakup of the Standard Oil Trust.

30. The victory by Spanish forces led by Hernando Cortez over the Mexica (Aztec) people can be attributed to all of the following reasons EXCEPT which one?

    (A) The Spanish army that arrived in the new world greatly outnumbered the Mexican army.
    (B) Diseases, such as smallpox, greatly weakened the Mexica people.
    (C) The Spaniards had superior weaponry, including full body armor, horses, and guns.
    (D) The Mexica were reluctant to launch an assault against the Spaniards because they initially believed that Cortez was a god.
    (E) The Spaniards were able to exploit divisions between the Mexica ruling elite and tribal groups within the Mexican empire.

31. The first five years after the founding of Jamestown (1607) was mainly characterized by
    (A) warfare with Dutch mercenaries from New Amsterdam.
    (B) economic prosperity.
    (C) constant fear of a Spanish invasion.
    (D) major technological advancement.
    (E) starvation, disease, and frequent Indian raids.

32. Which statement best describes relations between the colonists and the British government in the decade following the French and Indian War?
    (A) The British began to respect American culture.
    (B) The colonists began to question British authority.
    (C) The British began to treat the Americans as equals.
    (D) The colonists became more dependent on Britain.
    (E) The colonies thrived under the British policy of salutary neglect.

33. The Virginia Plan, put forth at the Constitutional Convention at Philadelphia in 1787, broke with the political assumptions implicit in the Articles of Confederation by asserting that
    (A) representation in Congress should be equal for each state.
    (B) political parties were not a threat to national unity; rather, they were an effective means for expressing political differences.
    (C) the federal government should be the instrument of the people, not of the various states.
    (D) the executive branch should assume primary powers in governance; the legislative and judiciary should perform supporting functions.
    (E) citizenship rights belonged to any individual born on United States soil.

34. The Rush-Bagot Treaty, signed by representatives of the United States and Great Britain in 1817, was significant in that it
    (A) resolved disputed land claims in regard to the Oregon Territory and paved the way for the orderly settlement of the Pacific Northwest.
    (B) formally ended the British practice of the impressment of American sailors and increased trade between the two nations.
    (C) settled war reparation claims of each side from the War of 1812 and initiated the special relationship between the two countries.
    (D) avoided dealing with many of the issues that led to the War of 1812 and kept relations between the United States and Great Britain tense until the United States entered World War I.
    (E) demilitarized the border between the United States and Canada along the Great Lakes and Lake Champlain and also helped improve relations between the United States and Great Britain.

35. The Homestead Act and the Morrill Land-Grant Colleges Act are similar in that both
    (A) were passed over the veto of President Andrew Johnson.
    (B) gained passage during the Civil War when the Republican Party controlled Congress and did not have to deal with opposition from the Democratic Party.
    (C) were labeled socialist measures by the Republican Party, inconsistent with American values.
    (D) were part of Henry Clay's American System of economic reforms.
    (E) were heavily promoted by the Populist Party.

36. During the 1880s and 1890s, the Supreme Court issued a number of decisions to protect the interests of big business. Many of these specific decisions were based on the legal principle that held that
    (A) Congress's power to regulate interstate trade, as spelled out in Article I of the Constitution, applied only to the actual movement of goods across state lines, not the overall activities of corporations.
    (B) the products produced by a particular corporate entity were expressions of that corporation; the production of these products, therefore, was protected by the freedom of expression clause of the First Amendment.
    (C) to regulate corporate activities entailed depriving corporations of their profits; according to the Fifth Amendment, Congress could take these profits only if it offered the affected corporation just compensation.
    (D) corporations were defined as individuals and regulating their activities constituted depriving individuals of their property without due process; this violated Fourteenth Amendment protections.
    (E) the regulation of corporate activities is not explicitly permitted in the Constitution; further, the "necessary and proper" language of the elastic clause did not apply to these activities.

37. In their sociological study of American life in a small city, *Middletown* (1929), the authors Robert and Helen Lynd noted a "cultural lag" among the subjects of their study. By "cultural lag," the authors were referring to
    (A) the time it took for the products of popular culture—movies, songs, magazines, books—to make their way from New York City to the hinterlands of America.
    (B) the inability of recent immigrants to assimilate into the cultural mores of mainstream America.
    (C) a sense of mystification and powerlessness felt by ordinary Americans in the face of an increasingly complex and technologically advanced social order.
    (D) a generational rift among Americans in which younger Americans failed to understand and appreciate the cultural products of their parents' generation.
    (E) the frustrations felt by small-town American men in regard to the insolence and independence of their "flapper" wives.

A BIGGER JOB THAN HE THOUGHT FOR.
UNCLE SAM—Behave, You Fool! Durn Me, If I Ain't Most Sorry I Undertook to Rescue You.

38. The 1899 cartoon shown above makes the point that

(A) insurgents in Cuba were being manipulated by Spain into resisting the presence of American troops.
(B) native Hawaiians behaved in a childlike manner when the Hawaiian Islands were annexed by the United States.
(C) the United States misread the reaction of the Filipino people when it acquired the Philippines following the Spanish-American War.
(D) the task of completing the Panama Canal was more time consuming and more costly than the United States had originally anticipated.
(E) Chinese diplomats were excessively and unnecessarily hostile to the American "open door" policy.

39. Congressional approval of the Tonkin Gulf Resolution in August 1964 was significant in that it

(A) reflected a deeply divided Congress in regard to the direction of United States foreign policy in Southeast Asia.
(B) strengthened President Lyndon Johnson's election bid by weakening Republican candidate Barry Goldwater's charge that Johnson was soft on communism.
(C) ushered in the policy of Vietnamization of the Vietnam War—a gradual withdrawal of American troops and their replacement by Vietnamese troops.
(D) stands as the only instance in American history is which military actions were initiated without a formal declaration of war.
(E) led to the division of Vietnam into North Vietnam and South Vietnam along the 17th parallel.

40. "For this end, we must be knit together, in this work, as one man. We must entertain each other in brotherly affection. We must be willing to abridge ourselves of our superfluities, for the supply of others' necessities. We must uphold a familiar commerce together in all meekness, gentleness, patience and liberality. We must delight in each other; make others' conditions our own; rejoice together, mourn together, labor and suffer together, always having before our eyes our commission and community in the work, as members of the same body."

    The above passage is from a speech by

    (A) James Oglethorpe.
    (B) John Smith.
    (C) Peter Stuyvesant.
    (D) John Winthrop.
    (E) Edmund Andros.

41. Which of the following was <u>not</u> a cause of Bacon's Rebellion in 1676?

    (A) The belief that the government was not doing enough to control Native Americans on the frontier.
    (B) Land ownership patterns that favored wealthy planters at the expense of poor farmers.
    (C) The lack of representation of poor people in the House of Burgesses.
    (D) The belief that the king was denying the colonists basic democratic rights.
    (E) A tax structure that unfairly burdened the lower orders.

42. An important result of the Land Ordinance of 1785, which applied to lands acquired by the United States north of the Ohio River and east of the Mississippi River, was that

    (A) most of the land was purchased by speculators who then sold the best parcels at a profit to actual settlers.
    (B) thousands of landless families were able to settle in the Ohio River Valley because the act allowed homesteaders to acquire 40 acres in exchange for agreeing to farm the land for at least seven years.
    (C) the question of slavery was left to votes of each territory as they applied for statehood, putting off into the future an extremely contentious question.
    (D) provisions were made to let Native Americans reside where they already lived; settlement by whites was permissible only on vacant lands.
    (E) the ordinance was coupled with an agreement from Spain that settlers in these lands would be allowed unfettered access to the Mississippi River, including through the port of New Orleans.

43. In the system of checks and balances established in the Constitution, which of the following is <u>not</u> an example of a governmental check?

    (A) Congress overriding President Andrew Johnson's vetoes of the Reconstruction Acts of 1867.
    (B) President Nixon nominating William H. Rehnquist to the Supreme Court (1971).
    (C) The Supreme Court declaring laws banning the burning of the American flag unconstitutional (1989).
    (D) The House of Representatives voting to impeach President Clinton (1989).
    (E) President George W. Bush declaring a state of emergency in Louisiana following Hurricane Katrina in 2003.

44. The Missouri Compromise (1820) was reached after the Senate rejected amendments to Missouri's petition for statehood put forth by Representative James Tallmadge of New York. The Tallmadge amendments would have

    (A) divided up the Louisiana Purchase territory into free and slave sections along the line of latitude at 36°30'.
    (B) immediately outlawed slavery in Missouri and emancipated ten thousand slaves already residing there.
    (C) opened Missouri to slavery based on the principle of popular sovereignty—the residents of Missouri would vote on whether or not to allow slavery.
    (D) mandated that whenever new states enter the union, they do so in groups of two—one free and one slave.
    (E) implemented gradual emancipation in Missouri—any new slaves born in Missouri would be freed at age 25 and no new slaves could be imported into the state.

45. Which of the following is true of alcohol consumption in the United States between 1800 and 1850?

    (A) Alcohol consumption went down dramatically after most states passed dry laws, banning the consumption, sale, or production of alcoholic beverages.
    (B) Alcohol consumption remained steady for men but increased for women with the popularity of alcohol-based "cure-all" medications.
    (C) Alcohol consumption steadily decreased as pure drinking water, brought to homes by municipally built water systems, became more readily available.
    (D) Alcohol consumption remained steady but was not an issue of public interest because most drinking took place in private homes, not in pubs and taverns.
    (E) Alcohol consumption increased markedly as urbanization, immigration, and a growing labor force all contributed to a male-oriented drinking culture.

46. Which of the following describes the impact of the assassination of President James Garfield in 1881?

    (A) Congress passed the Secret Service Act (1882) in order to provide the president with protection at all times.
    (B) The Department of Justice began a red scare that lasted throughout the 1880s, rounding up suspected anarchists and radicals.
    (C) The Constitution was amended to provide for an orderly and clear process of succession to the presidency in case of death or debilitation.
    (D) Congress passed the Pendleton Act (1883), creating a merit-based civil service in the aftermath of the revelation that the assassin had unsuccessfully sought a federal appointment.
    (E) The Republican Party successfully used the incident in the 1884 election, implying that the Democratic Party encouraged the type of lawlessness that resulted in Garfield's death.

47. Henry Ford's financial success can be attributed to all of the following EXCEPT

    (A) retaining skilled European craftsmen and mechanics at his factories to insure quality.
    (B) reducing the price of a Model T from $850 to $300.
    (C) reducing attrition in his workforce by paying many workers five dollars per day.
    (D) using an assembly line to produce an automobile every 93 minutes.
    (E) creating efficient work processes, based on the ideas of Frederick Winslow Taylor.

48. The passage of the Civil Rights Act of 1964 indicated the

    (A) failure of the nonviolent civil disobedience movement.
    (B) desire of the Republican Party to attract African-American voters.
    (C) success of the movement to end de jure segregation.
    (D) fulfillment of the principle of separate but equal.
    (E) betrayal of African Americans by the Democratic Party.

49. Sir Edmund Andros gained many enemies in colonial New England by

    (A) marrying a Wampanoag woman and living in a Native-American community.
    (B) ruthlessly suppressing Bacon's Rebellion.
    (C) preaching a form of Protestantism that cast doubt on some fundamental Puritan beliefs.
    (D) governing the Dominion of New England in an authoritarian, rigid manner.
    (E) forming a secret alliance with the French during the French and Indian War.

50. The 1954 cartoon shown above makes the point that

(A) Senator Joseph McCarthy and President Dwight D. Eisenhower successfully worked in tandem in the 1950s to stanch the spread of communism in the United States.
(B) Senator Joseph McCarthy went too far when he accused President Dwight D. Eisenhower of sympathizing with the communist movement.
(C) Senator Joseph McCarthy had the foresight to guard America's borders from communist aggression, but President Dwight D. Eisenhower failed to perceive threats to national security.
(D) President Dwight D. Eisenhower violated the principle of separation of powers by attempting to influence the activities of the legislative branch of government.
(E) President Dwight D. Eisenhower's criticisms of Senator Joseph McCarthy's anticommunist crusade were weak and ineffective.

51. Which of the following describes an important impact of the religious revivals of the 1720s to the 1740s, known as the Great Awakening?
    (A) Great Awakening ministers convinced colonial legislatures to grant the Episcopalian Church special status as the one established church of colonial America.
    (B) The Great Awakening led to competition among several Protestant denominations and led to growth of smaller denominations, such as the Baptists and Methodists.
    (C) The Great Awakening emphasized a form of energetic, "muscular" Christianity, which led to a drop in church membership by women.
    (D) The Great Awakening revival meetings, with their insistent demands of spiritual conformity, turned people off to organized religion and led to a decrease in church membership.
    (E) Great Awakening ministers, insisting that all people, including Native Americans, were created in God's image, convinced colonial legislatures to negotiate fair treaties with Native-American tribes within their territory.

52. The Proclamation Act (1763) and the Currency Act (1764) were similar in that they both were
    (A) attempts by British authorities to bring the thirteen colonies under closer administrative supervision.
    (B) designed to punish New England for a variety of crowd actions taken against British officials.
    (C) aimed at reviving the economy of the thirteen colonies following the Panic of 1762.
    (D) enacted directly by King George III, without the consent or approval of Parliament.
    (E) meant to extend basic rights of Englishmen to colonial subjects in the New World.

53. The United States's decision to declare war on Great Britain in 1812 was
    (A) strongly endorsed by the Federalist Party, which sought to expand the powers of the federal government, and condemned by the Republican Party, which had moved to reduce the size of the American military.
    (B) based on the United States's long-standing treaty with France, which was at war with Great Britain.
    (C) intended to break Great Britain's boycott of American cotton, which had been implemented during the American Revolution and was never lifted.
    (D) popular with congressmen from the South and the West but was opposed by congressmen from New England and from some of the Middle Atlantic states.
    (E) made in response to Great Britain's refusal to negotiate in good faith a solution to competing claims to the Oregon Territory.

54. One of the most important achievements of the reform movements of pre–Civil War America was that they
    (A) established full legal and political rights for women.
    (B) forced Congress to resolve the issue of slavery.
    (C) established the idea that people could organize to improve society.
    (D) eradicated childhood polio.
    (E) brokered a long-term peace settlement between Native Americans and the government.

55. During the Gilded Age (1870–1900), wages for industrial workers remained relatively stagnant despite a growing economy and an expanding demand for workers. Historians attribute this phenomenon to the fact that
    (A) the cost of living remained low, leading workers to acquiesce to modest wages.
    (B) the first labor unions had yet to emerge; it was not until after the turn of the twentieth century that workers began to organize unions.
    (C) the constant influx of large numbers of immigrant workers pushed average wages downward.
    (D) low tariffs encouraged the importation of foreign goods into the United States, which ate into the profits of American companies.
    (E) a red scare during this period instilled a sense of fear into American workers and encouraged them to make do rather than demand higher wages.

56. The tenures of Mayor Tom L. Johnson of Cleveland (1901–1909) and Governor Robert La Follette of Wisconsin (1901–1905) demonstrate the
    (A) ability of African-American candidates to gain public office in the North, even during the age of Jim Crow discrimination.
    (B) persistence of corrupt political machines on the local and state level in the early-twentieth century.
    (C) success of the anti-immigrant nativist movement in the era of massive immigration to American cities.
    (D) divisions within the Democratic Party between proagrarian southerners and proindustry northerners.
    (E) furtherance of the agenda of the progressive movement onto the local and state levels.

57. Which of the following is <u>not</u> an example of the policy of isolationism?
    (A) Passage of the Emergency Quota Act (1921)
    (B) Passage of the Smoot-Hawley Tariff Act (1930)
    (C) Senate rejection of the Treaty of Versailles (1920)
    (D) Passage of the Lend-Lease Act (1941)
    (E) Passage of the Neutrality Act (1935)

58. The formation of the States' Rights Democrat Party, commonly known as the Dixiecrats, in 1948 reflected opposition to

    (A) reforms in immigration policy allowing more immigrants from Latin America into the United States.
    (B) the enactment of federal guidelines mandating that gay couples be allowed to adopt children.
    (C) the Democratic Party's adoption of a platform plank supporting civil rights for African Americans.
    (D) increased funding for northern manufacturing at the expense of southern agriculture.
    (E) the ratification of the Equal Rights Amendment by over twenty states.

59. President George H. W. Bush initiated the Persian Gulf War in 1991 in order to

    (A) find and destroy members of the al-Qaeda terrorist network.
    (B) remove Saddam Hussein from the leadership of Iraq.
    (C) end the Iraqi occupation of Kuwait.
    (D) defend Israel from attacks by the Hezbollah organization.
    (E) prevent abuses by the Iraqi government of the Kurdish ethnic minority.

60. Which of the following was true of the southern colonies of Virginia, Maryland, North Carolina, South Carolina, and Georgia during the period from 1700 to 1770?

    (A) The population of these colonies grew rapidly so that by 1770, the region had more than twice as many residents as either the middle colonies or the New England Colonies.
    (B) These colonies developed a diverse agricultural economy, with a focus on production for local consumption.
    (C) Woman in the colonial South achieved a greater degree of political equality than in the middle colonies or in New England; by 1770, most colonies allowed women to vote in local elections and to serve on juries.
    (D) By 1770, following the development of the cotton gin, cotton had become "king" throughout the South.
    (E) A revolutionary sentiment had developed in the southern colonies so that by 1770, these colonies were ready to declare independence, well before the middle or New England Colonies were.

61. The Alien and Sedition Acts (1798) were, according to critics, designed to

    (A) provide rifles to the Iroquois Federation in a secret arms-for-hostages deal.
    (B) eliminate the constitutional system of checks and balances.
    (C) provide covert assistance to the Jacobin Party in revolutionary France.
    (D) stifle criticism of government policies by the Democratic-Republicans.
    (E) enrich the treasury of the Federalist Party as midterm elections approached.

62. Decisions of the Supreme Court under the leadership of Chief Justice John Marshall (1801–1835) tended to

    (A) discourage the development of industry and commerce in the United States.
    (B) expand civil liberties for those accused of crimes.
    (C) weaken the Constitution.
    (D) promote the power of the federal government over the power of state governments.
    (E) strengthen the institution of slavery.

63. Henry George's book *Progress and Poverty* (1879) and Edward Bellamy's novel *Looking Backward, 2000–1887* (1888) are similar in that both

    (A) proposed that the government can best encourage economic growth by adopting a laissez-faire approach.
    (B) were important texts in the burgeoning approach to philosophical problems known as pragmatism.
    (C) encouraged the United States to limit immigration from southern and eastern Europe before Anglo-Saxon Americans committed "race suicide."
    (D) encouraged white northerners and southerners to put their differences away and unite on a shared platform of Jim Crow segregation and white supremacy.
    (E) critiqued the inequalities of the Gilded Age and offered radical alternatives to industrial capitalism.

64. The 1893 Chicago's World's Fair, formally known as the World's Columbian Exhibition, was significant in that

    (A) the neoclassical buildings and formal design of the fair's main concourse, known as the White City, influenced urban planning and architecture for the next two decades.
    (B) new technological wonders—radio and television—that would become prominent in the twentieth century were demonstrated to the public for the first time.
    (C) organizers of the fair consciously challenged prevailing racial mores by welcoming African-American fairgoers and insisting that all facilities be open to all races.
    (D) pavilions devoted to the recent American acquisitions of Puerto Rico and the Philippines were created to justify American imperialist ventures.
    (E) it coincided with the completion of the first transcontinental railroad, allowing passengers from either coast to arrive in Chicago by railroad for the first time.

65. During the Gilded Age of the second half of the nineteenth century, the American Federation of Labor (AFL) differed from the Knights of Labor in that

    (A) the AFL was stronger in the industrial North while the Knights were stronger in the agrarian South.
    (B) the AFL was anticapitalist while the Knights were procapitalist.
    (C) the AFL appealed to African-American workers while the Knights appealed to white workers.
    (D) the AFL folded due to internal divisions while the Knights expanded its membership.
    (E) the AFL was primarily a union of skilled craftsmen, while the Knights organized workers of all skill levels.

66. What is the main point of the 1898 cartoon shown above?

    (A) A war had developed between the sexes over women's voting rights.
    (B) War should be avoided at all costs because of its adverse impact on children.
    (C) America should avoid becoming an imperialist power because it would lead to constant warfare.
    (D) America should limit immigration in order to avoid a war between native-born Americans and immigrants.
    (E) Powerful newspaper publishers were pushing America toward war with exaggerated, sensationalist reporting.

67. The Niagara Movement is significant in American history because it led to the formation of

(A) the National Organization for Women and the birth of the modern women's liberation movement.
(B) Greenpeace and the birth of the environmental movement.
(C) Students for a Democratic Society and the birth of the New Left.
(D) the National Association for the Advancement of Colored People and birth of the twentieth-century civil rights movement.
(E) the Moral Majority and the birth of the New Right.

68. The labor unrest immediately following World War I, including the Seattle general strike in February 1919 and the Boston police strike in the fall of 1919, led in part to

(A) President Warren G. Harding pushing for legislation recognizing the right of workers to organize unions.
(B) new labor contracts in key industries that allowed workers to retain higher wartime wages throughout the 1920s.
(C) the defeat of the probusiness Republican Party at the polls in presidential elections throughout the 1920s.
(D) the federal government initiating a red scare against radicals, labor organizers, and suspected subversives.
(E) Eugene V. Debs rejecting the tactics and goals of the labor movement and founding the Socialist Party of America.

69. An important reason that President Richard Nixon was able to normalize relations with the Communist Government of China in 1972 was that he

(A) had the support of prominent corporate executives who were eager to import consumer goods from China, despite its Communist government.
(B) knew that any treaties worked out between the United States and China would be approved by the Democratically controlled Senate.
(C) did not have to worry about political fallout because he knew that he would have to resign soon anyway because of revelations in regard to the Watergate scandal.
(D) had developed a special relationship with Chinese leader Mao Zedong because Nixon had learned Mandarin when stationed in China for two years during World War II.
(E) had established solid anticommunist credentials throughout his political career and did not have to worry about being accused of being "soft on communism."

70. By 1700, Puritan New England experienced

(A) an increase in religious fervor but a decrease in overall population.
(B) success in spreading the Puritan ethos to colonies throughout British North America.
(C) economic success but a decrease in religious piety.
(D) bitter failure as New England became known for licentious behavior and shoddy work habits.
(E) a series of devastating military defeats at the hands of Native Americans.

71. When John Peter Zenger, publisher of the *New York Weekly Journal*, was tried for seditious libel in 1739, his lawyer Andrew Hamilton argued that

(A) British libel laws did not apply to publications that originated in the thirteen colonies.
(B) the newspaper in question had indeed published libelous articles about the royal governor, but Zenger was unaware of their insertion in the paper.
(C) the printed charges against the authorities were true and, therefore, did not constitute libel.
(D) the trial was unlawful because it was carried out by a British judge without a jury; Hamilton asserted that only a trial of one's peers may issue a guilty verdict.
(E) though several articles in the newspaper contained false, and even insulting, charges against royal authorities, such words should be protected from censorship.

72. The Tea Act, implemented by the British Parliament in 1773, was significant because it

(A) brought many women into the arena of popular protest; the Daughters of Liberty played a prominent role in organizing boycotts of British tea.
(B) engendered an alliance between colonists and Native Americans, both of whom suffered from changes in British trade laws.
(C) ushered in a period of détente in regard to relations between the thirteen colonies and the British government.
(D) constituted the first direct tax on the colonists, leading to calls by prominent colonial leaders of "no taxation without representation!"
(E) doubled the price of British tea in the colonies, putting a basic staple beyond the reach of ordinary colonists.

73. Historians often refer to the period of 1780 to 1789 as the critical period in American history because

(A) the government allowed uncensored criticism of the president and of Congress.
(B) the United States faced a series of crises that threatened its very existence.
(C) women and African Americans played a critical role in establishing policies for the newly formed United States.
(D) these years saw the decline and defeat of most Native-American tribes east of the Mississippi Rivers.
(E) art and literary criticism thrived in New England journals.

74. Alexander Hamilton's economic program and Henry Clay's American system were similar in that both asserted that

(A) Congress should fund railroad expansion in order to promote trade between the different regions of the county.
(B) the United States should implement high tariffs on imported goods to promote American manufacturing.
(C) the government should encourage each state to issue additional currency in order to promote economic activity.
(D) Congress should abolish slavery to make more workers available for manufacturing and commercial activities.
(E) the United States should focus its development on agricultural products to export to Europe.

75. An important impact of the decision in the Supreme Court case of *Dred Scott* v. *Sanford* was that

(A) violence broke out in Kansas as antislavery settlers came to believe that the decision precluded their ability to outlaw slavery in the Kansas Territory.
(B) Congress moved to limit the Supreme Court's reach by declaring the power of judicial review to be only advisory rather than binding.
(C) a great migration of escaped African-American slaves fled the United States and made their way to Canada.
(D) the Republican Party was strengthened as more people came to believe that a hostile slave power had gotten control of the levers of power.
(E) President James Buchanan chose to ignore the repercussions of the decision by declaring, "Roger Taney issued this decision. Let him try to enforce it!"

76. In the late 1800s, the Populist Party supported all of the following positions EXCEPT
    (A) an increase in the supply of currency.
    (B) government regulation of the railroads.
    (C) the direct election of senators.
    (D) a graduated income tax.
    (E) an end to Jim Crow laws in the South.

77. The Supreme Court decision in *Plessy* v. *Ferguson* (1896) declared that
    (A) segregation of the races was acceptable under the principle of "separate but equal."
    (B) the government could restrict speech that presents a "clear and present danger."
    (C) states must periodically redraw the boundaries of legislative districts based on the principle of "one person, one vote."
    (D) African Americans were not entitled to citizenship rights in the United States because they were considered "beings of an inferior order."
    (E) the American government did not have to extend Constitutional rights to the residents of United States colonies because "the Constitution does not necessarily follow the flag."

78. Which of the following describes an important reason the Senate did not approve the Treaty of Versailles in 1919?
    (A) Senator Henry Cabot Lodge, chairman of the Foreign Relations Committee, opposed the treaty for not being sufficiently punitive toward Germany.
    (B) President Wilson urged Senate Democrats to oppose a set of reservations put forward by moderate Republican Senators. Without these moderate reservationists, the treaty lacked a sufficient number of "yes" votes.
    (C) The Senate refused to bring the treaty to the floor for a vote until Germany released American prisoners of war.
    (D) Senate Democrats opposed the treaty because the section creating the League of Nations failed to provide the League with military powers to enforce its edicts.
    (E) The treaty failed to garner a sufficient number of progressive Republicans because it lacked any provisions to provide humanitarian aid to war-torn Europe.

79. During the 1920s, a major problem facing American farmers was
    - (A) overproduction of agricultural products.
    - (B) low tariff rates on imported agricultural products.
    - (C) a blight on the potato crop.
    - (D) a lack of available farm workers.
    - (E) chemical runoff from the use of chemical pesticides.

80. During the 1950s and 1960s, the Urban Renewal Program
    - (A) eliminated poverty in American urban centers.
    - (B) used the power of eminent domain to bulldoze "blighted" sections of cities.
    - (C) provided aid to help rebuild the cities of war-torn Europe.
    - (D) extended microloans to small businesses to weather difficult economic times.
    - (E) helped rural Vietnamese refugees relocate to cities.

STOP

END OF SECTION I

SECTION II

Part A

(SUGGESTED WRITING TIME—45 MINUTES)
PERCENT OF SECTION II SCORE—45

Directions: Write a coherent essay that incorporates your analysis of Documents A–G *and* your knowledge of the period in the question. To earn a high score, cite key information from the documents and use your knowledge of the period.

1. Workers and farmers responded to the economic downturn following the Panic of 1893 in a variety of ways.

   To what degree were workers and farmers successful in advancing their interests in the aftermath of the Panic of 1893? What accounts for their level of success?

   Use the documents and your knowledge of the years 1893–1903 in your answer.

Document A

Source: Lyrics to "Marching with Coxey," by Willie Wildwave, 1894.

We are marching to the Capital, three hundred thousand strong
With live petitions in our boots to urge our cause along,
And when we kick our congressmen, they'll feel there's something wrong. As we go marching with Coxey.

Chorus
Hurrah! Hurrah for the unemployed' appeal!
Hurrah! Hurrah for the marching commonweal!
Drive the lobbies from the senate,
Stop the trust and combine the steal,
For we are marching with Coxey.

We are not tramps nor vagabonds that's shirking honest toil,
But miners, clerks, skilled artisans, and tillers of the soil
Now forced to beg our brother worms to give us leave to toil,
While we are marching with Coxey

Document B

Source: "Coxey Abandoned by Congress," *New York World*, May 2, 1894.

The Coxey farce ended rather dismally yesterday, when its leaders were [chased down and arrested] by the police, while the rank and file, that had made a pathetically comical march through the streets of Washington, stood outside and waited with a vague and inarticulate notion that something was about to happen. "Gen." Coxey has had his first collision with the law, with the only result possible and which he might have foreseen. In the mean while the Republican senators and Congressmen are strangely silent at this refusal to grant a "hearing" to American citizens who had travelled to the capital to inform Congress what kind of legislation they wanted. The McKinleyites should not repudiate their offspring.

Document C

Source: Senator William Peffer (Populist Party, Kansas), *Congressional Record*, July 10, 1894.

Without going into all the details, I will state by way of preface that the Pullman company established what most people in this world believed to be an ideal community, in which all the citizens should have equal right, in which none should have special privileges. The object was to build a community where the best modern scientific principles of hygiene, drainage, sewerage, grading, lighting, watering, and every other convenience should abound.

But while the company was doing that, while the world was looking on applauding, the company, like every other corporation of which I have ever known anything, held all the power, all the reins within their own grasp. . . . When pay day came around, the charges that were set up against the residents of the town of Pullman for their lots and for their conveniences were deducted from their pay. . . . Among these charges were rents and stated dues for the purchase of property.

After a while hard times began to pinch the company as it did everybody else, and it began to reduce the pay of the men. The men submitted patiently. Another reduction came and the men again submitted, asking only, however, that their rent charges should be reduced, to correspond to the amount of reduction in their wages. . . .

All these things were denied to them.

Document D

Source: Eugene V. Debs, *The Nation*, July 5, 1894.

The struggle with the Pullman Company has developed into a contest between the producing classes and the money power in this country. We stand upon the ground that the workingmen are entitled to a just proportion of the proceeds of their labor. This the Pullman Company denied them.

Document E

Source: Cartoon in *Harper's Weekly*, July 14, 1894.

Document F

"A Man Without a Soul," *The Coming Nation*, June 27, 1896.

The burning question of today is, shall we fuse with the democrats? Shall all the reform elements of this country drop every other reform issue, except free coinage of gold and silver, join hands with the free silver democrats and fight the common enemy—plutocratic republicanism?

If the democrats would do half of the "fusing," I for one would say yes. But do the democrats offer the reformers one single concession? I fail to see it as yet.

. . . We forced them into making free coinage the issue; shall we then drop all other reform issues and run to meet them with open arms? Shall the outraged girl, who forces her seducer to marry her at the point of a revolver, drop her mother, sisters and brothers at his command, in order to make the marriage perfect and happy?

. . . No, my brother; the democratic party can not swallow me down unless it swallows all the populist reform issues. There are too many horrors fresh in my memory—too many scenes of poverty and want, at which a democratic administration turned a deaf ear.

Document G

Source: Cartoon in *Harper's Weekly*, September 5, 1896.

SECTION II

Part B and Part C

(SUGGESTED TOTAL PLANNING AND WRITING TIME—70 MINUTES)
PERCENT OF SECTION II SCORE—55

Part B

Directions: Select ONE question to write about. You should spend about 5 minutes planning and 30 minutes writing your answer. Support your views with pertinent facts, and present your case clearly.

2. Analyze the motivation and expectations of Americans who remained loyal to Great Britain during the American Revolution. What did these Americans hope to gain by remaining loyal to the crown? Please confine your answer to the period 1775–1800.

3. To what extent was President Andrew Jackson deserving of the label "King Andrew?" Please confine your answer to the period 1829–1837.

Part C

Directions: Select ONE question to write about. You should spend about 5 minutes planning and 30 minutes writing your answer. Support your views with pertinent facts, and present your case clearly.

4. Analyze the response of the United States to TWO of the following Cold War developments between 1945 and 1960.

   The Soviet testing of its first nuclear bomb
   The Berlin blockade
   The election of Mohammed Mossadegh as prime minister of Iran
   The launching of *Sputnik*

5. Analyze the tensions that developed within the civil rights movement in the 1960s over tactics and goals. To what extent were these tensions alleviated?

STOP

END OF EXAM

Answer Key
PRACTICE TEST 1

Multiple-Choice Questions

1.	**E**	21.	**A**	41.	**D**	61.	**D**
2.	**C**	22.	**E**	42.	**A**	62.	**D**
3.	**C**	23.	**A**	43.	**E**	63.	**E**
4.	**A**	24.	**B**	44.	**E**	64.	**A**
5.	**D**	25.	**C**	45.	**E**	65.	**E**
6.	**E**	26.	**B**	46.	**D**	66.	**E**
7.	**C**	27.	**C**	47.	**A**	67.	**D**
8.	**D**	28.	**E**	48.	**C**	68.	**D**
9.	**C**	29.	**C**	49.	**D**	69.	**E**
10.	**D**	30.	**A**	50.	**E**	70.	**C**
11.	**A**	31.	**E**	51.	**B**	71.	**C**
12.	**C**	32.	**B**	52.	**A**	72.	**A**
13.	**E**	33.	**C**	53.	**D**	73.	**B**
14.	**D**	34.	**E**	54.	**C**	74.	**B**
15.	**A**	35.	**B**	55.	**C**	75.	**D**
16.	**C**	36.	**D**	56.	**E**	76.	**E**
17.	**E**	37.	**C**	57.	**D**	77.	**A**
18.	**A**	38.	**C**	58.	**C**	78.	**B**
19.	**C**	39.	**B**	59.	**C**	79.	**A**
20.	**A**	40.	**D**	60.	**A**	80.	**B**

PRACTICE TEST 1: ANSWER EXPLANATIONS

1. **(E)** New Amsterdam was founded by the Dutch West India Company as a trading and commercial outpost. The founders of the colony did not have religious motives. Choice A describes Massachusetts; choice B describes Philadelphia; and choice C describes Maryland. Georgia comes closest to the description in choice D—James Oglethorpe wanted to create a refuge for British debtors and the poor. Great Britain sent many of its criminals to the colony of Australia.

2. **(C)** The economic theory of mercantilism asserts that colonies should produce valuable raw materials for the mother country. At first in the seventeenth century, New England was not producing a valuable staple crop for export to Great Britain. The climate allowed for the cultivation of crops for local consumption but not for large amounts of tobacco or sugar. The Puritans did devote a great deal of time to prayer, however, they were also known for their intense work ethic (A). New England did not become a center of anti-British activity (B) until much later, after the French and Indian War in the 1760s and 1770s. New England has several excellent harbors, including Boston, Newport, and New Haven (D). New England attracted a steady stream of migrants from Great Britain in the seventeenth century (E). The Great Migration of 1620–1640 was the high point of Puritan migration to New England.

3. **(C)** The reference in the quotation to being "independent of Great Britain" suggests that the quotation is from the 1770s—a period of time when tensions between the thirteen North American colonies and Great Britain had reached a boiling point. The Boston Massacre occurred in 1770, the Boston Tea Party in 1773, and violence at Lexington and Concord, Massachusetts, in 1775. As tensions increased throughout the decade, the question of independence from Great Britain became more prominent in public discourse, dividing rebels and loyalists. The quotation reflects a loyalist sentiment, with its discussion of the benefits of maintaining ties with Great Britain. John Winthrop's sermon (A) occurred well before the crisis of the 1770s. Patrick Henry (B) and Thomas Paine (D) were both fiery critics of Great Britain and were leaders of the rebel, or patriot, movement. George Washington was a critic of British policies as early as the late 1760s. By 1777, independence had been declared and General Washington was the commander-in-chief of the Continental Army. In contrast, Thomas Hutchinson, the royal governor of the Massachusetts colony from 1771–1774, remained a loyalist until he was exiled to Great Britain in 1774.

4. **(A)** In many ways, Shays's Rebellion was a catalyst for the convening of the Constitutional Convention (1787). This revolt of Massachusetts farmers who felt cheated by the state's economic policies was eventually put down by state armed forces. Farmers protested the heavy taxes placed on their land. These taxes, which had to be paid in hard currency, were part of the legislature's plan to pay off debts incurred during the Revolutionary War. Failure to pay

these taxes could result in the confiscation of one's property. These farmers also argued that the currency supply was too limited, the opposite of choice B. The rebellion did not deal with tariff rates (C) or with policies in regard to Native Americans (D). Later, the United States encouraged homesteading (E) with the passage of the Homestead Act (1862). This was not an issue in the eighteenth century.

5. **(D)** The Supreme Court established its power of judicial review with the decision in *Marbury* v. *Madison* (1803). In many ways, this is the Court's most important decision. The details of the decision have to do with the seating of judges that had been appointed in the last days of the John Adams administration. More importantly, the decision established the Supreme Court's power to review laws and determine if they are consistent with the Constitution. Laws declared unconstitutional by the Court are immediately disallowed. This power of judicial review has been the main function of the Supreme Court since then and has been instrumental in maintaining balance between the three branches of the government.

6. **(E)** The election of James Polk in 1844 signaled a shift toward a more aggressive expansionist policy by the United States. In the decade before Polk's election, political leaders approached the issue of westward expansion with caution. When Texas became independent of Mexico in 1836, American political leaders avoided taking action on Texas annexation into the United States. Whig leaders were especially reluctant to reopen sectional conflict. This changed with the election of the Democrat James Polk. Although he avoided war with Great Britain over the Oregon Territory (a compromise was worked out), he pursued war with Mexico in part to expand American land holdings. Following the Mexican War (1848), the United States purchased the vast Mexican Cession territory from Mexico for $15 million. The free-labor political ideology (A) is more closely associated with Abraham Lincoln and the Republican Party of the 1850s. Protective tariffs (B) were embraced by the Federalists in the 1790s and later by the Whigs in the 1850s and the Republicans in the 1860s. The Democratic Party, with its deep roots among southern planters in the antebellum period, tended to oppose protective tariffs. A shift toward isolationism (C) occurred in the aftermath of World War I, with the election of the Republican presidents of the 1920s. Polk, in many ways, represented a resurgence of Jacksonian populism, not a rejection of it (E).

7. **(C)** The position of the Republican Party from its inception was opposition to the expansion of slavery into the new territories of the United States. It did not challenge slavery where it already existed. The Republican Party was not an abolitionist party (A). Under President Lincoln's guidance, the party moved toward an abolitionist position as the Civil War progressed. The idea of leaving the question of slavery up to each state or territory, known as popular sovereignty (B), is associated with the Stephen Douglas faction of the Democratic Party in the 1850s. Although the issue of slavery was difficult to ignore in 1860 (D), the Constitutional Union Party attempted to do just that by emphasizing compromise and sectional unity.

8. **(D)** Social Darwinism was an attempt to apply Charles Darwin's ideas about the natural world to social relations. Social Darwinism was popularized in the United States by William Graham Sumner. Sumner was attracted to Darwin's ideas about competition and survival of the fittest. He argued against any attempt at government intervention into the economic and social spheres. Interference, he argued, would hinder the evolution of the human species. The inequalities of wealth that characterized the late 1800s were part of the process of survival of the fittest. Choice A describes socialism; choice B might describe New Deal Democrats; choice C describes a main goal of the civil rights movement; and choice E refers to the Scopes trial (1925).

9. **(C)** By 1957, many politically moderate southern towns and cities had begun to quietly comply with the directives of the Supreme Court in regard to desegregating public schools. These directives were contained in the decision in *Brown* v. *Board of Education of Topeka* (1954) and in a subsequent decision known as *Brown II* (1955) in which the Court instructed communities to act "with all deliberate speed." Little Rock, Arkansas, was poised to follow suit. The school board had devised a plan to allow nine African-American students to enter Central High School at the beginning of the school year in 1957. However, Arkansas Governor Orville Faubus called out the National Guard to block the nine students from entering the school. This open defiance of both federal mandates and local decisions shocked many moderates and galvanized antisegregationist forces throughout the South. Finally, President Dwight D. Eisenhower felt compelled to intervene. He sent federal troops to Little Rock to insure that the African-American students were admitted to Central High School and were protected from violence.

10. **(D)** The founders of Carolina were white plantation owners who had lived in Barbados. All the other colonies were established by people coming directly from Great Britain. In many ways, early Carolina resembled the colony of Barbados. Both colonies were marked by large plantations, brutal work, and many more slaves than masters. Many French Huguenots (A)—French Protestants persecuted by the Catholic authorities—made their way to the various colonies of British North America as well as Dutch New Amsterdam. The New England colonies of Rhode Island and Connecticut were founded by Puritans who ran afoul of the rigid governing style of Massachusetts governor John Winthrop, but the founders of Carolina did not have a similar religious motivation (B). Choice C might describe the Quakers of Pennsylvania. None of the thirteen British colonies were founded by freed African Americans (E).

11. **(A)** In response to the colonial chant "No taxation without representation," Great Britain put forth the theory of "virtual representation." This theory held that members of Parliament represented the entire British Empire. The colonists therefore were virtually represented by the members of Parliament. Needless to say, the rebellious colonists did not find the theory persuasive. The theory of the divine right of kings (B) is associated with royal absolutism. England abandoned royal absolutism after the Glorious Revolution

(1688–1699). The theory of nullification (C) was put forth later in the Virginia and Kentucky Resolutions in the 1790s and during the tariff crisis of the 1830s. Neither choices D or E were true of the British Government in regard to the American colonies.

12. **(C)** Tecumseh was an important Native-American leader who organized an intertribal defense of lands of the Great Lakes region in the 1800s and 1810s. He incorporated the spiritual teachings of his brother, Tenskwatawa, who advocated a return to traditional tribal ways. Tecumseh and his alliance worked with Great Britain during the War of 1812. He was killed by American forces at the Battle of the Thames (1813). The Treaty of Greenville (A) was signed in 1796 by representatives of several Ohio River Valley nations and by representatives of the United States. It followed the Battle of Fallen Timbers. Choice D describes some of the elements of the Dawes Act (1887).

13. **(E)** This question refers to Stephen Douglas's Freeport Doctrine, enunciated at a debate with Abraham Lincoln during the 1858 campaign for one of Illinois's Senate seats. Lincoln insisted that Douglas could not assert the legitimacy of both the Dred Scott decision and the doctrine of popular sovereignty. Popular sovereignty left the slavery question up to the residents of a particular territory. This concept of letting residents of a territory vote on the issue of slavery was the central to the Kansas-Nebraska Act (1854). In the Dred Scott decision, however, the Supreme Court asserted that slavery could not legally be excluded from the western territories. Douglas argued that the two principles do not have to be mutually exclusive. Although slavery could not be outlawed in a territory, it needed the support of local legislation to thrive. If a state chose not to pass such laws, then slavery, in effect, could not be practiced.

14. **(D)** The Emancipation Proclamation did not immediately free any slaves. It was aimed at rebel-held territory where United States authority was nonexistent. It did not apply to slave states that remained loyal to the Union, nor did it apply to those rebel states that had been occupied by Union forces. Some have criticized Lincoln for freeing slaves in areas where he had no power and not freeing slaves in areas where he did have power. However, the Emancipation Proclamation was important because it made clear that the Civil War had become a war to liberate the slaves. People on both sides realized that if the United States defeated the Confederacy, then slavery would come to an end. It certainly did not quiet Irish-American immigrants (E); their anger at being drafted into a war to liberate slaves led to the New York City draft riot (1863).

15. **(A)** The Elkins Act (1903) strengthened the Interstate Commerce Commission (ICC) by fining railroad companies that offered rebates. Large trusts and corporations often demanded rebates, getting around the rates established by the ICC for freight transportation. The Hepburn Act (1906) gave the ICC the power to set maximum railroad rates. Both were part of President Theodore Roosevelt's progressive agenda to rein in the railroad

industry. Choice B refers to the Food and Drug Act (1906), also known as the Wiley Act. Progressive reformers on the local level used a variety of strategies to challenge the power of corrupt political machines (C). Many municipalities adopted the commission form of government, also known as the Galveston Plan, to replace corrupt powerful mayors. President Roosevelt did assert the policing powers of the United States in regard to Central America and the Caribbean basin (D), but that was not the purpose of the two acts. Roosevelt, and most progressive leaders, did not actively challenge racial discrimination (E).

16. **(C)** A large wave of "new immigrants" from southern and eastern Europe arrived in the United States between 1880 and 1920. The "old immigrants" tended to be from northern and western Europe. The perception was that the old immigrants—mostly Protestant and often English speaking—could better assimilate into the United States. In response to the new immigration, there was a powerful nativist movement, which was eventually successful in restricting immigration in the 1920s. Choice A describes the Great Migration of the 1910s and 1920s; choice B took place in the 1840s and 1850s.

17. **(E)** There are several examples of the government restricting civil liberties during time of war. The Espionage and Sedition Acts made it a crime to criticize the World War I war effort publicly. During World War II, the government severely restricted the civil liberties of all Japanese Americans living on the West Coast by forcing their removal to camps in the interior of the United States. One could also cite the Espionage and Sedition Acts during the Quasi-War with France (1798–1800), the suspension of habeas corpus during the Civil War (1861–1865), and the Patriot Act during the war on terrorism (2001–the present) as examples of restrictions of civil liberties during time of war. The Sedition Act clearly demonstrates that freedom of speech is not inviolable (A). There is little evidence that domestic spying has ever undermined American military success (B). The Supreme Court often does check the power of the president (C) but not in the two cases cited. Immigration patterns have changed over time (E), but that is not reflected in the two cases cited.

18. **(A)** All of the factors in the question contributed to the passage of Prohibition except for choice A. The Eighteenth Amendment, banning the sale, manufacture, and consumption of alcoholic beverages, was ratified in 1919, well before the Great Depression which began in 1929. Prohibition ended in the midst of the Great Depression in 1933. However, women activists were important in the passage of the Eighteenth Amendment.

19. **(C)** Both the Eisenhower and the Kennedy Administrations walked a fine line in regard to the civil rights movement. Neither wanted to risk losing white southern votes by actively supporting civil rights activities. On the other hand, both found it increasingly difficult to skirt the issue. President Eisenhower was forced to intervene in the crisis in Little Rock, Arkansas, which revolved around the issue of segregation in the public schools. Governor Orville Faubus's overt flaunting of federal authority troubled

Eisenhower, who eventually sent in federal troops. In 1961 and 1962, repeated violent attacks by white southerners on nonviolent civil rights activists pushed the Kennedy Administration to become more involved. One of the more horrific incidents involved the Freedom Rides in May 1961. The Freedom Riders were civil rights activists who were attempting to test the Supreme Court's ban on segregation in interstate bus travel. The first bus left from Washington, D.C., in May 1961. It was attacked by a mob and subsequently firebombed in Alabama. The riders were attacked again by mobs in Montgomery and Birmingham. With local officials refusing to protect the riders, President Kennedy threatened to commit federal troops. In the end, Kennedy pressured the governors of Alabama and Mississippi to protect the riders in exchange for not sending federal troops.

20. **(A)** The Virginia Company encouraged settlers to come to Virginia by use of the head-right system. The colonial government granted each arrival a fifty-acre piece of land plus an additional fifty acres for each servant he brought over. A wealthy aristocrat with several servants could come to Virginia and immediately be set up with a substantial plantation. This encouraged more people to come, or to be brought, to Virginia. Choice B is incorrect because slavery was not yet a major source of labor in the early 1600s. It became the major source of labor after Bacon's Rebellion (1676). The settlers of Virginia were not especially devout (C); the promise of churches and ministers would not be a major draw. Virginia focused on tobacco, not on developing a diverse economy (D). The settlers of Virginia did not broker peace treaties with the Powhatan People (E). The early decades of settlement were marked by intense violence between the settlers and the Native Americans.

21. **(A)** The Antifederalists were the opponents of the proposed Constitution. They were given this unflattering nickname by the supporters of the document. The Antifederalists were worried about the additional powers that the national government would have with the Constitution. They had vivid memories of living under the distant and arbitrary rule of the British crown. They did not want another distant and arbitrary power ruling over them. Therefore, many Antifederalists made it clear that they would not vote to ratify the Constitution unless the framers of the document promised to quickly add a list of rights of the people. The framers agreed, and the Constitution was ratified. Soon after, the Bill of Rights was ratified (1791), guaranteeing basic rights to the people.

22. **(E)** The main purpose of the Monroe Doctrine (1823) was to limit European influence in the Western Hemisphere. President Monroe was alarmed at threats by the Holy Alliance of Russia, Prussia, and Austria to restore Spain's lost American colonies. He also opposed a decree by the Russian Czar that claimed all the Pacific Northwest above the 51st parallel. Though both problems worked themselves out, Monroe issued a statement warning European nations to keep their hands off the Americas. The United States did not have the military might to enforce this pronouncement at the time, but it was an important statement of intent. Choice C reflects the logic of the domino theory; choice D reflects the goal of manifest destiny.

23. **(A)** A strong federal Fugitive Slave Law was part of the assortment of measures that are collectively known as the Compromise of 1850. The Fugitive Slave Law was the most onerous one from the point of view of many northerners. Previously, the majority of northerners could ignore the brutality of the slave system. Following 1850, though, slave catchers brought the realities of the slave system to the streets of northern cities. In response, many northern states passed personal liberty laws, offering protection to fugitives. Many whites and free African Americans in northern cities even formed vigilance committees to prevent the slave catchers from carrying out their orders. The other choices reflect issues involving personal liberties but not the personal liberty laws of the 1850s.

24. **(B)** The nullification crisis of 1832–1833 began with the Tariff Act of 1828, which revised tariff rates on a variety of imports. The act, known by its critics as the Tariff of Abominations, dramatically raised tariff rates on many items and led to a general reduction in trade between the United States and Europe. This decline in trade hit South Carolina's cotton plantations especially hard. By 1832, John C. Calhoun and other South Carolina political leaders asserted the right of states to nullify federal legislation. Under the theory of nullification, a state could declare an objectionable law null and void within that state. Jackson, a defender of states' rights, was nonetheless alarmed at this blatant flaunting of federal authority. He pushed for passage of the Force Bill, which authorized military force against South Carolina for committing treason. At the same time, Congress revised tariff rates, providing relief for South Carolina. The Force Bill and the new tariff rates, passed by Congress on the same day, amounted to a face-saving compromise.

25. **(C)** The problem of overproduction and falling prices demonstrates a basic rule of economics. With all other factors being equal, dramatically increasing supply will push down prices. It was difficult for an impoverished farmer in the late 1800s to grasp this concept. It seemed like common sense to use new equipment to produce larger yields. Yet, when all the farmers do this, prices for farm products fall. With falling commodity prices, farmers found it difficult to pay off loans. These problems led farmers to band together in the populist movement in the 1880s and 1890s. Choice B seems to be an occurrence of the last 50 to 75 years. Choice D describes the impact of the cotton gin in the early-nineteenth century. Choice E did occur but in the period since the 1970s.

26. **(B)** Theodore Roosevelt was an avid outdoorsman and an advocate for conservation. He set aside millions of acres as protected areas. These include six national parks. Roosevelt, like most progressives of the early-twentieth century, largely ignored the plight of African Americans (A). Few, if any, mainstream successful politicians could be labeled as socialist (C). Roosevelt pursued an active, aggressive foreign policy, especially in regard to the Americas; he was not an isolationist (D). He was president before World War I (E).

27. **(C)** *Birth of a Nation* (1915) is considered to be a groundbreaking film artistically. Griffith pioneered many cinematic techniques that became cen-

tral to moviemaking. However, the movie portrays African Americans in a racist and demeaning manner. The film reflects the old Southern myth of Reconstruction—that Northern whites and Southern blacks crippled the South, until outraged white Southerners, led by the Ku Klux Klan, saved the day.

28. **(E)** Benjamin Spock provided guidance to the millions of parents of baby boom children. The book was a huge success. Spock encouraged parents to treat their children as individuals. His approach emphasized flexibility and affection over discipline. Earlier approaches to child rearing, for example, discouraged parents from picking up crying babies. Such "coddling" was seen as "spoiling" children. Spock's lenient attitude revolutionized parenting. Conservatives blamed Spock for the student radicalism of the 1960s. They argued that if the students of the 1960s had been raised with more discipline, they would not have been so rebellious.

29. **(C)** The Arab oil embargo of 1973 severely impacted American society. All of a sudden, gasoline prices shot up and consumers had to wait in line at gas pumps. It was somewhat of a wake-up call to Americans. However, when the oil started flowing freely again into the United States, Americans went back to their large cars, trucks, and sports utility vehicles. The OPEC Arab nations instituted the embargo to show disapproval of American support for Israel during the 1973 Yom Kippur War. The Iran-Contra scandal (A) occurred during the Reagan Administration in the 1980s. Choice B had an impact on the supply of petroleum, but it occurred later (2010). Choice D occurred in the 1970s but did not affect supply. Choice E occurred much earlier (1911).

30. **(A)** Cortez was able to use all the factors listed to his advantage except for choice A. It would have been virtually impossible for the Spanish to have brought over enough men to outnumber native Mexican forces. Choice E proved to be very important. The tribal groups brought into the Mexican Empire were often mistreated and subject to heavy taxation and human sacrifices. They were more than ready to challenge their authoritarian Mexican rulers.

31. **(E)** The first settlers to Jamestown arrived in 1607. Their first five years were very difficult, marked by starvation, disease, Indian raids, and widespread death. They were ill prepared for the rigors of building a community in the New World. They planned to find riches, plunder those riches, and return wealthy. They were not prepared to farm and build a community. In contrast, the New England Puritans arrived with a plan of staying for the long term. They were skilled in farming and building cohesive towns. The New Englanders tended to come over in family units, while the Jamestown settlers tended to be single men. New Amsterdam was not settled until the 1620s (A). Many Virginians would eventually enjoy economic prosperity (B), but that took at least a generation and the successful cultivation of tobacco. The Spanish monitored British moves in the New World (C), but they did not see the Jamestown settlers as an immediate threat.

32. **(B)** After the French and Indian War (1754–1763), the British instituted a series of measures that angered many colonists and led them to challenge British authority. Most objectionable were a series of revenue or tax acts that the British imposed in part to defray the costs of the war. The British believed their victory in the French and Indian War had been especially beneficial to the colonists. In return, the British reasoned it was fair for the colonists to shoulder some of the costs of the war and of continued protection. The Stamp Act (1765), which imposed a tax on the paper used for various documents in the colonies, provoked the most intense opposition. The conflicts of this period culminated in the colonies declaring independence from Great Britain (1776).

33. **(C)** Under the Articles of Confederation, each state was represented in Congress by one vote. Congress was, therefore, an instrument of the various states. At the Constitutional Convention (1787), leading delegates began to question this approach. These delegates argued that the federal government was an instrument of the people, and therefore the size of state delegations should be pegged to population. This approach was especially popular with delegates from the larger states. These delegates put forth the Virginia Plan, which would have created a bicameral population-based legislature. The small states, concerned that their voices would be drowned out in a population-based legislature, countered with the New Jersey Plan, which called for a one-house legislature with each state getting one vote (similar to the existing congress under the Articles of Confederation). After much wrangling, the delegates agreed on the Connecticut Compromise, also known as the Great Compromise, which created the basic structure of Congress as it now exists—a House of Representatives in which representation is determined by the population of each state and a Senate in which each state gets two members.

34. **(E)** The Rush-Bagot Treaty, signed by both the United States and Great Britain in 1817 and ratified by the United States in 1818, signaled an improvement of relations between the two countries just two years after the conclusion of the War of 1812. The border between the United States and Canada has largely been demilitarized since the treaty. Since the terrorist attacks of 2001, the United States has armed some ships that patrol the Great Lakes. The United States and Great Britain did resolve a dispute over the border of the Oregon Territory (A), but that occurred in 1846 with the signing of the Oregon Treaty. The issue of impressment was one of the main causes of the War of 1812 (B). The Treaty of Ghent (1815), which concluded the War of 1812, did not mention impressment but the practice ended with the war. Both nations suffered damages during the War of 1812, but there were no stipulations for reparations (C). In contrast to choice D, the treaty addressed an important issue and improved relations between the two nations.

35. **(B)** The passage of the Homestead Act and the Morrill Land-Grant Colleges Act (both in 1862 during the Civil War) was dramatically aided by the absence of southern Democratic legislators. The two acts furthered the Republican Party's vision for the United States. The Homestead Act encouraged western settlement by offering free land to people who were willing to settle out West.

The Morrill Act provided federal land to states for the purpose of establishing state agricultural colleges. Small-scale farms and education were central to the Republican free-labor ideal. The acts were signed by President Lincoln, three years before Andrew Johnson assumed the presidency (A). The acts were promoted by the Republican Party (C). The Republican Party of the Cold War era might have labeled the creation of state colleges as socialistic. Henry Clay's American System was promoted by the Whig Party earlier in the century, in the 1820s and 1830s (D). The Populist Party (E) was created in 1891, nearly thirty years after the acts in question were passed.

36. **(D)** During the late 1800s, the Supreme Court consistently interpreted the Constitution in ways that benefited big business. In *United States* v. *E. C. Knight Company* (1895), for example, the Court dealt a blow to the Sherman Antitrust Act by making a distinction between trade (which would be subject to the act) and manufacturing (which would not). In 1886, the Court limited the ability of federal and state authorities to regulate corporate activities by declaring corporations "persons." This reasoning was contained in the case of *Santa Clara County* v. *Southern Pacific Railroad.* The Court reasoned that corporate "persons" were entitled to the same rights as individuals, including the due process rights contained in the Fourteenth Amendment. This reasoning opened the way for the Court to strike down regulations that appeared to deprive corporations of their "property" without due process.

37. **(C)** Robert and Helen Lynd wrote an influential sociological study, *Middletown: A Study in Modern American Culture,* in 1929. The small city they studied was actually Muncie, Indiana. The book is important because it notes some of the rapid changes that were occurring in American life in the 1920s, and it captures the responses of ordinary Americans to these changes. Americans were, according to the Lynds, finding themselves increasingly disoriented in modern society. The Lynds contrasted the harried society of the 1920s with the more harmonious society of the 1890s. The authors noted a "cultural lag" between modernity and tradition in their study.

38. **(C)** The 1899 cartoon makes the point that the United States misread the situation in the Philippines following the Spanish-American War (1898). Under the provisions of the Treaty of Paris (1898), the United States assumed several of Spain's possessions following the war, including the Philippines, Guam, and Puerto Rico. The United States stated that it would grant the Philippines independence sometime in the future. For the time being, it held on to the Philippines. Many Filipinos were deeply disappointed in this outcome, hoping to attain independence as Cuba had following the war. A resistance movement developed in the Philippines. A bloody three-year war, known as the Philippine-American War, ensued. Filipino forces were led by Emilio Aguinaldo. The war cost the American forces 4,000 lives. Over 20,000 Filipinos died in the conflict, and estimates of 100,000 to 600,000 civilians. In the cartoon, the Uncle Sam character seems to have just come to the realization that the Filipino people would actively resist American control. The infantilization of the Filipino people in the image can be read on two levels. It serves as a visual pun, comparing Uncle Sam to a parent coming

to the realization that a baby is more work than he or she thought. Also, it reflects racist attitudes toward the Filipino people.

39. **(B)** The Gulf of Tonkin Resolution had repercussions domestically as well as internationally. It led to the United States becoming heavily involved in the Vietnam War. Congress gave President Johnson a blank check with the Tonkin Gulf Resolution to pursue military goals in the region. The resolution followed an incident in the Gulf of Tonkin, off the coast of Vietnam. Two United States ships, on espionage missions, were fired upon by North Vietnam. Controversy surrounded the event; critics wanted to know why the United States was staging actions so close to the coast of North Vietnam. Also, it is not clear whether or not a second attack even occurred. Nonetheless, Congress saw the incident as an aggressive act and gave President Johnson a free hand in Vietnam. The resolution also reverberated domestically. The resolution was passed just as the race for the presidency was heating up. By taking military action against a communist country, Johnson was countering the charges of the Republicans that the Democrats were soft on communism. Congress was not divided in regard to the resolution (A); it passed overwhelmingly in both houses. The policy of Vietnamization is associated with President Richard Nixon. The Gulf of Tonkin Resolution is one of several instances, including the Korean War, in American history in which military actions were initiated without a formal declaration of war (D). Vietnam was divided along the 17th parallel at the Geneva Conference held in 1954 (E).

40. **(D)** The quotation is by John Winthrop, one of the founders (1630) and first governor of the Massachusetts Bay Colony. The quotation is from his famous 1630 sermon, "A Model of Christian Charity," which was delivered to his fellow Puritans while still on board the *Arbella*. The quotation reflects the goals of the venture—solidarity, community, and shared sacrifice, all a godly mission. This speech also contains the famous injunction by Winthrop that "we must consider that we shall be as a city upon a hill. The eyes of all people are upon us." James Oglethorpe (A) was the founder of the Georgia Colony; John Smith (B) was one of the founders of the Jamestown Colony (1607); Peter Stuyvesant (C) was the last Dutch governor of New Amsterdam (1647–1674); and Edmund Andros was the royal governor of the Dominion of New England (1686–1689).

41. **(D)** All of the grievances listed were important to the Baconites except for choice D. The backcountry farmers who were the backbone of the rebellion (1676) were angry with the local elites of Virginia, not with the King of Great Britain. Later, in the 1760s and 1770s, colonists expressed a great deal of anger at the King. The rebellion was significant because it led to the shift from indentured servitude to slavery as the primary labor source for the colonies. The elites of Virginia did not want to have more disgruntled poor white farmers in the colony; they thought African slaves would be easier to control.

42. **(A)** The Land Ordinance of 1785, passed during the Articles of Confederation period, allowed for the sale of lands in the old Northwest. The price of the land began at $1 per acre, with more desirable land going for higher prices.

Land had to be purchased in plots of 640 acres and had to be paid for in hard currency. Thus, the price of land was beyond the reach of most Americans. Most of the land was initially purchased by speculators, who then divided the plots and sold them to future residents. The government under the Articles of Confederation (1781–1789) did not have many successes, but dealing with the lands of the old Northwest was one of them. Choice B alludes to the 1862 Homestead Act. Under the Land Ordinance, land was sold, not given away. The Land Ordinance did not specifically mention slavery (C). Slavery was outlawed by the Articles of Confederation Congress in the Northwest Ordinance of 1787. The land ordinances of the 1780s did not recognize the rights of Native Americans who inhabited the land (D). For the next two decades, white settlers and Native Americans would battle over control of the land north of the Ohio River. The Articles of Confederation Government did not reach an agreement with Spain over control of the Mississippi River (E); this would remain a contentious issue until the beginning of the nineteenth century.

43. **(E)** Checks and balances is a central component to the governing structure of the United States. The framers of the Constitution were very conscious of the problems of a government with limitless powers. After living under the British monarchy, they came to believe that a powerful government without checks was dangerous to liberty. Therefore, they created a governmental system with three branches, each with the ability to check the powers of the other two. The goal was to keep the three branches in balance. All the choices illustrate one branch of the government taking action in relation to another branch, except choice E, which illustrates a unilateral action.

44. **(E)** Missouri's application for statehood in 1819 set off a bitter debate in Congress about the expansion of slavery. Initially, Representative James Tallmadge of New York proposed an amendment that would have implemented gradual emancipation in Missouri. The Tallmadge Amendment won support in the House but was left off of the Senate resolution on Missouri statehood. Finally, the two houses reached a compromise that admitted Maine as a free state, Missouri as a slave state, and drew a line through the Louisiana Purchase territory (renamed, at that point, the Missouri Territory) separating free from slave territory. Everything north of the 36°30' line of longitude would be free (except for Missouri). Everything south of it would allow slavery.

45. **(E)** Alcohol consumption increased in the first half of the nineteenth century. Historians attribute this increase to both the increased availability of alcohol as well as to increased demand. Urbanization brought more men into the culture of pubs and taverns. Also, changes in the nature of work contributed to increased alcohol consumption. Previously, apprentices might drink moderately under the watchful eye of their masters. The early 1800s saw the decline of the apprentice system and the rise of a wage labor force. These wage laborers would often gather after work hours to drink in taverns and pubs. This increased alcohol consumption came to be seen as a major problem by reformers. The temperance movement became a powerful force

in nineteenth-century politics (D). Maine became the first of several "dry" states, but that was not until 1851 (A). Municipal water did not reach houses until the last decades of the nineteenth century (C).

46. **(D)** President Garfield was assassinated in 1881 by Charles Guiteau, a disappointed and deranged office seeker. The assassination led to an attack on the spoils system of handing out government jobs to friends, allies, and supporters. In the wake of the assassination, reformers enacted the Pendleton Act in 1883, which replaced the spoils system with a professional civil service that allots government jobs on the basis of a competitive exam. This system still covers most of the bureaucratic jobs in the federal government. The Secret Service was created by President Lincoln in 1865 (A). The red scare occurred in the late 1910s and early 1920s (B). The succession process is covered in Article II of the Constitution (C). The assassination had political reverberations, but the Republicans did not imply that the Democrats inspired it (E).

47. **(A)** Henry Ford revolutionized production in the United States. He took all of the actions listed in the choices except for choice A. Ford was attempting to shift production away from highly paid craft workers. The idea was to de-skill the production process so that unskilled, low-wage workers could be inserted into the process.

48. **(C)** The passage of the Civil Rights Act (1964) was a major victory for the civil rights movement. It made segregation in public facilities and accommodations illegal, ending legal (or de jure) segregation. De jure segregation is often contrasted with de facto segregation—social patterns that are not mandates by law. The civil rights movement was successful in ending de jure segregation, but de facto segregation has proven to be remarkably tenacious.

49. **(D)** Andros was the much-hated governor of the Dominion of New England. In 1686, following the brutal King Philips War between New England colonists and Native Americans, royal officials revoked the charters of all the colonies north of Maryland and formed one massive colony called the Dominion of New England. This new colony was ruled directly by Andros, a royal appointee. The governance of New England was no longer based on Puritan beliefs and values. It was a devastating blow to the Puritan movement. Marrying into a Native-American community would have raised the ire of Puritan New Englanders, but Andros did not do that (A). The suppression of Bacon's Rebellion (1676) was ordered by Virginia governor William Berkeley (B). Several ministers during the Great Awakening in the eighteenth century questioned some of the tenets of Puritanism (C). Andros lived before the French and Indian War (1755–1763) occurred (E).

50. **(E)** The cartoon is suggesting that President Dwight Eisenhower did not take a strong enough stand in opposition to the tactics of Senator Joseph McCarthy. McCarthyism is the name given to the extreme anticommunist movement in the early 1950s. Senator Joseph McCarthy became the central figure in this movement. In 1950 he announced that he had a list of "known communists" who had infiltrated the State Department. This and similar

claims, mostly baseless, created a name for McCarthy and set the stage for a host of measures to halt this perceived threat. Congress established committees to investigate Communist Party infiltration in different sectors of society. Finally McCarthy went too far, accusing members of the military establishment of being communists. The Senate voted to censure him in 1954, thus ending the worst excesses of what many people referred to as a witch hunt. Eisenhower walked a fine line in regard to McCarthy. On the one hand, he found McCarthy's tactics reprehensible. He once said of McCarthy, "I just won't get down in the gutter with that man." However, he also welcomed the benefits that McCarthyism brought to the Republican Party. The cartoon notes Eisenhower's reluctance to challenge McCarthy publicly.

51. **(B)** The Great Awakening was a revival of religious sentiment during the 1720s to the 1740s. The revival was spurred on by ministers who had grown alarmed at the decline in church membership by the early years of the eighteenth century. New England ministers noted the decline in the Puritan zeal that had animated the settlers of the region generations earlier. Charismatic ministers attempted to bring a more emotional, and less cerebral, approach to religion. In Massachusetts, the Puritan minister Jonathan Edwards delivered his famous sermon, "Sinners in the Hands of an Angry God," to a mesmerized audience. The most well-known Great Awakening preacher was George Whitefield. A core message of the movement was that anyone could be saved and that people could make choices in their lives that would affect their afterlife. In this, the movement was both egalitarian and democratic. The movement did not lead to an increase in Congregationalist (Puritan) churches in New England, but it did lead to competition and growth among other sects, including Baptists and Methodists.

52. **(A)** The Proclamation Act (1763) and the Currency Act (1764) were both intended to bring the thirteen colonies under closer administrative supervision. Both acts were passed in the wake of the French and Indian War. The Proclamation Act forbade colonists from settling beyond the Appalachian Mountains. The British Government did not want to provoke additional warfare with Native Americans in the region. The act angered colonists who were eager to settle in this region now that the French had been removed. The Currency Act prohibited the colonies from issuing additional paper money. The colonies had issued paper money during the French and Indian War to finance war-related expenses. Eventually, this money ended up in the hands of London merchants as payments for goods. These merchants complained to royal authorities because this colonial money was often devalued. Both acts reflected a greater desire by the British Government to govern the thirteen colonies more closely. They reflected a clear ending to the salutary neglect approach.

53. **(D)** The decision to declare war on Great Britain in 1812 divided many Americans. The war received its strongest support from congressmen in the West and the South. These congressmen, known as War Hawks, believed that the British were aiding and abetting Native Americans on the frontier

of American settlement. The war was especially unpopular with congressmen from New England and the Mid-Atlantic states who feared that war with Great Britain would bring a great reduction to trade. The war was opposed by the Federalist Party (A), which was strongest in New England. The United States had rescinded its treaty with France much earlier, in 1793 (B). Great Britain had not imposed a boycott on American cotton following the American Revolution. Trade between the two nations resumed after the war (C). Tensions over the competing claims occurred later in the nineteenth century and were settled in 1846 (E).

54. **(C)** Reform movements in antebellum America established the idea that people could band together and effect changes in society. This was a very democratic notion that has motivated Americans ever since to band together around particular issues. Antebellum reformers dealt with issues such as alcohol abuse, mistreatment of the criminally "insane," public education, slavery, and women's rights. Women did not gain full political rights (A) until the ratification of the Nineteenth Amendment (1920) extended the vote to women. The issue of slavery (B) was not resolved until the conclusion of the Civil War (1865). A vaccine for polio (D) was developed in the 1950s; new cases are very rare in the United States.

55. **(C)** A massive wave of immigrants came to the United States starting around 1870. The reasons for this "new immigration" included cheaper steamship travel, a variety of local conditions in home countries, and the demand for industrial workers in the United States. Many of these new immigrants were from southern and eastern Europe. The large number of immigrants to the United States contributed to a downward push on wages for industrial workers during the Gilded Age, despite the remarkable growth of the economy. Workers did not acquiesce to low wages (A)—they fought for higher wages in a series of pitched workplace battles in the last decades of the nineteenth century. Unions had emerged before the Civil War (B). The Knights of Labor and the American Federation of Labor both gained many members during the Gilded Age. Tariff rates did not cut into the profits of American manufacturers during the Gilded Age (D). Red scares occurred in the years immediately after World War I and in the 1950s (E).

56. **(E)** Mayor Tom L. Johnson and Governor Robert LaFollette were progressive public officials who initiated extensive reforms. Johnson was an advocate of Henry George's single tax plan, as outlined in George's *Progress and Poverty.* He fought for fair taxation policies, home rule, and greater democracy through the introduction of the initiative, referendum, and recall. His fight for public ownership of utilities led observers to label his approach as gas and water socialism. Governor Robert "Fightin' Bob" La Follette was also a senator from Wisconsin (1906–1925). He ran for president in 1924 on the Progressive Party ticket and garnered 17% of the national popular vote. He was a popular crusader against the power of corporations and trusts over the political process.

57. **(D)** All of the choices reflect isolationist sentiments except for the Lend-Lease Act. The act reflected a desire by the United States to be more involved in World War II, not less involved. The Lend-Lease Act was signed into law in March 1941, a year and a half after the beginning of World War II but eight months before the United States entered the conflict. President Franklin D. Roosevelt and many Americans were increasingly distressed about the war and the early successes of the Axis Powers. The act supplied Great Britain, the Soviet Union, France, China, and other Allied Forces with war supplies throughout the war. Passage of the act marked a clear departure away from United States neutrality and toward active involvement in the war. The Japanese attack on Pearl Harbor, Hawaii, in December 1941 ended debate about United States intervention. The Emergency Quota Act (A) dramatically limited immigration into the United States. The Smoot-Hawley Tariff Act (B) steeply raised tariffs on imported goods. The Senate rejection of the Treaty of Versailles (C) kept the United States out of the League of Nations. The passage of the Neutrality Act (E) imposed an embargo on trading war materials with nations at war. The act was opposed by the Roosevelt Administration, which argued that the act limited its ability to aid allies.

58. **(C)** Many southern Democrats were so angry that the party had adopted a pro-civil rights plank in its platform that they bolted from the party and formed the Dixiecrat Party in 1948. The party, which existed for only one year, ran Strom Thurmond for president. Thurmond did quite well in the South, winning South Carolina, Louisiana, Alabama, and Mississippi. Nationally, Thurmond won about 2.5 percent of the vote.

59. **(C)** The Persian Gulf War was a response to the Iraqi occupation of Kuwait. In 1990, Iraqi leader Saddam Hussein sent the Iraqi military into Kuwait to occupy that country. The goal of Operation Desert Storm was to remove Iraqi forces from Kuwait. The operation was successful. Hussein was quickly forced to withdraw his troops. The United States suffered relatively few casualties. Choice A describes the United States war in Afghanistan (2001–present); choice B refers to the Iraq War initiated by President George W. Bush (2003–present). Choices D and E have not been rationales for U.S. military actions.

60. **(A)** The southern colonies thrived during the eighteenth century, attracting large numbers of settlers. Wealthy planters in the region also brought hundreds of thousands of slaves into the region to work on the variety of staple crops in the region. The region focused on staple agricultural crops for export (such as rice, indigo, and tobacco), not a diverse agricultural economy for local consumption (B). Women were not allowed to vote in the South (C) nor in the other British colonies. The cotton gin was not invented until 1793; cotton did not become "king" in the South until the nineteenth century (D). Most colonists, even opponents of British policies, were not prepared to declare independence from Great Britain in 1770 (E).

61. **(D)** The Alien and Sedition Acts (1798) were four bills signed by the Federalist president, John Adams. Although he presented them as wartime security measures, they were clearly designed to silence criticism by Jefferson's Democratic-Republican Party. The Alien Acts allowed for deportation of "dangerous" noncitizens. The Sedition Act made "malicious" criticisms of government officials a crime. The Naturalization Act made it more difficult for immigrants to become citizens.

62. **(D)** Marshall Court decisions consistently expanded the scope and powers of the federal government at the expense of the state governments. *McCulloch* v. *Maryland* (1819), for example, prohibited Maryland from taxing the Bank of the United States and declared federal power superior to state power. *Gibbons* v. *Ogden* invalidated a monopoly on ferry transportation between New York and New Jersey that had been issued by New York and asserted that only the federal government could regulate interstate trade.

63. **(E)** George and Bellamy both presented sharp critques of the inequalities of the Gilded Age, and both writers offered radical alternatives to the prevailing state of affairs. George, in his book *Progress and Poverty*, was critical of the persistence of poverty in a nation experiencing unprecedented technological and industrial progress. He criticized the vast resources, especially land, controlled by the wealthy elite. He argued for a single tax on land values, which he believed would create a more equitable society. Bellamy's *Looking Backward, 2000–1887* (1888) imagined a man falling asleep in 1887 and waking in 2000 to find a socialist utopia in which the inequities and poverty of the Gilded Age had been eliminated. Neither writer advocated a laissez-faire, or hands-off, approach to the economy by the government (A). Neither were considered founders of pragmatism (B); William James and John Dewey were prominent pragmatists. Neither argued for limits on immigration; choice C reflects the racist thinking of the historian and anthropologist Madison Grant. Neither writer was in the forefront of the civil rights struggles (D).

64. **(A)** The 1893 Chicago's World's Fair became a showcase for neoclassical architecture and planning. The plazas and white, colonnaded buildings heavily influenced urban design for the next two decades. The White City was planned by Daniel Burnham and Frederick Law Olmstead.

65. **(E)** The main difference between the American Federation of Labor (AFL) and the Knights of Labor is that the AFL drew its membership from the "aristocracy of labor"—skilled craftsman—while the Knights tried to appeal to workers of all skill levels. The advantage of the AFL strategy was that skilled workers had a great deal of leverage in their workplaces. The advantages of the Knights strategy was that there were increasingly more unskilled workers.

66. **(E)** The cartoon depicts Joseph Pulitzer and William Randolph Hearst, two prominent newspaper publishers in the late-nineteenth century. Large-circulation papers, such as Pulitzer's *New York World* and Hearst's *New York Journal*, gained readership through exaggerated, sensationalistic coverage of events. This yellow journalism played a role in pushing public opinion toward support for the Spanish-American War (1898).

67. **(D)** The Niagara Movement grew out of a meeting of civil rights activists on the Canadian side of Niagara Falls. The name also alludes to the "mighty current" of the falls. The movement, led by W. E. B. DuBois, was more confrontational than the accommodationist politics of Booker T. Washington. The Niagara Movement did not last, but members of the movement founded the NAACP in 1911. Choice C describes the Port Huron conference (1962).

68. **(D)** The Red Scare of the late 1910s and early 1920s was the crusade against suspected communists, anarchists, and other radicals. The effects of the Red Scare were seen in one of the most famous trials of the decade—the trial of two Italian anarchists, Nicola Sacco and Bartolomeo Vanzetti, for robbery and murder. The Palmer Raids were unwarranted raids into the homes of suspected radicals. The Red Scare of the 1920s should not be confused with the anticommunist crusade of the 1950s, spearheaded by Senator Joseph McCarthy (alluded to in choice E).

69. **(E)** *Détente* is the French word for loosening and refers to an easing of tensions in the Cold War and a warming of relations between the United States and both the Soviet Union and China. The policy was carried out by President Nixon. In 1972, Nixon became the first United States president to visit Communist China. Later that year, he held meetings with Soviet leaders in Moscow.

70. **(C)** New England was doing very well by 1700, but the fire of the Puritan mission was dimming. The trajectory of New England history in the seventeenth century illustrated one of the central problems of Puritanism. Puritanism asserted that all of us have a calling in life—our life's work as determined by God. Puritans were determined to carry out their calling—as God determined it—with a great deal of zeal and determination. Hard work and seriousness of purpose often leads to material success, which is what happened in the towns and cities of colonial New England. Material success, however, often pulled one away from serious devotion to faith. Many New Englanders were pulled away from God by the draw of material objects.

71. **(C)** The Zenger trial helped establish the concept of freedom of the press in America. In 1735, a newspaper publisher named John Peter Zenger was tried for printing material critical of the king. He was ultimately found not guilty on the grounds that what Zenger printed was essentially true.

72. **(A)** The Tea Act was significant because it brought many women into the public arena. Women organized boycotts of British tea in protest. Formed earlier, the Daughters of Liberty played a central role in the boycott movement. In 1773, the British passed the Tea Act, which eliminated British tariffs from tea sold in the colonies by the British East India Company. This act actually lowered tea prices in Boston (E), but it angered many colonists who accused the British of doing special favors for a large British company. In addition to boycotting British tea, some colonists responded by dumping cases of tea into Boston harbor. The British responded to the Boston Tea Party by imposing a series of punitive measures known as the Coercive

Acts (1774). The first direct British tax on the colonies (D) is considered the Stamp Act (1765).

73. **(B)** During the critical period of 1780 to 1789, the United States faced some severe crises, which it was feared at the time could threaten the existence of the fledgling nation. The country was unable to retire its substantial war debt, making lenders leery of lending additional money. In addition, the United States faced humiliations in regard to foreign relations. For instance, the British had not evacuated forts in the western part of the United States following the signing of the Treaty of Paris (1783). The British continued to provide the Shawnees, the Miamis, and the Delawares with weapons. Finally, Shays's Rebellion (1786–1787) worried many Americans about the future of the country. The rebellion involved farmers in western Massachusetts who challenged state taxation and currency policies. The rebellion was put down after several months by state militia. The problems encountered by the United States during the critical period led some political leaders to propose scrapping the Articles of Confederation and creating the Constitution.

74. **(B)** Hamilton and Clay had similar ideas in regard to the role of the government in the economy. Both supported tariffs on imported goods to promote manufacturing. Both also promoted the idea of a national bank to act as a stabilizing force on the nation's economy. Railroad lines would not become viable until after Hamilton's lifetime (A). Neither Hamilton nor Clay encouraged states to issue their own currency (C). Both stressed the importance of an integrated, national economy. Hamilton was anti-slavery; Clay was critical of the institution of slavery, but he was also a slave-holder and was critical of the abolitionist movement (D). Hamilton stressed manufacturing in his vision of the future American economy; Clay pushed for a mixed economy, with regional specialization (E).

75. **(D)** Dred Scott was owned by a doctor serving in the United States Army. Scott, his wife, and their owner lived for a time in the state of Illinois and in the Wisconsin Territories, areas in which slavery had been banned by the Northwest Ordinance. Scot sued to obtain his freedom on the grounds that he had lived in territories where slavery was banned. The Supreme Court ruled against him and went further, declaring that no African American, not even free men and women, were entitled to citizenship in the United States because they were, according to the Court, "beings of an inferior order." The case alarmed African American and many white northerners.

76. **(E)** The Populist Party did not make ending Jim Crow segregation laws central to its agenda. Although some populists did try to forge an alliance with black southern sharecroppers, other populists wanted nothing to do with blacks. In many ways, the movement reflected prevailing racist attitudes. The Populist Party did embrace all the other positions listed in the question.

77. **(A)** The Plessy decision gave the Supreme Court's seal of approval for segregation. The decision upheld a Louisiana law that had established racial segregation practices. Segregation laws, also known as Jim Crow laws, segre-

gated public facilities, such as railroad cars, public bathrooms, and schools. These laws relegated African Americans to second-class status in the South. The Court accepted segregation as constitutional as long as the facilities for both whites and African Americans were of equal quality. It was generally the case that the facilities for African Americans were substandard. However, this "separate but equal" rule was the law of the land until the Supreme Court found segregated schools inherently unfair in the *Brown* v. *the Board of Education* decision (1954). Choice B refers to the Schenck decision (1919); choice C to the decisions in *Baker* v. *Carr* (1962) and *Reynolds* v. *Simms* (1964); choice D to the Dred Scott decision; and choice E to the Insular cases.

78. **(B)** An important reason that the Treaty of Versailles failed in the Senate was that President Wilson refused to compromise with the "reservationists." The treaty stipulated that the nations who signed it would be participants in the new League of Nations, so Senate rejection of the treaty also meant rejection of United States membership in the league. The League of Nations was dear to President Wilson. He included the concept in his Fourteen Points program for the post-war world and campaigned vigorously for it in Europe and the United States. But some senators wanted to isolate the United States from world affairs and opposed membership in the league out of fear that it might obligate the United States to participate in future wars. Reservationists were moderate Republicans who would have voted for the treaty if the Senate added some reservations, or conditions. Wilson refused to compromise with them and the treaty failed.

79. **(A)** Overproduction of agricultural products was a major problem for farmers in the 1920s. Farmers had put more acres under cultivation during World War I to meet increased demand for agricultural goods. By the 1920s, Europe was back on its feet, yet American farmers did not cut back on production. Mechanization and expansion left the farmers of the 1920s in a cycle of debt, overproduction, and falling commodity prices. In addition, increased tariff rates and an isolationist foreign policy further reduced the international market for American agricultural goods.

80. **(B)** Despite its name, the Urban Renewal program did not revitalize cities. It allowed cities to target working-class neighborhoods, declare them "blighted," remove all the residents (using the government's power of eminent domain), and raze the buildings. Often nothing was built in place of the demolished neighborhood. In many cases, federal housing projects were built, but these became rife with crime and poverty to a greater degree than the older "blighted" neighborhood. In some cases, middle- and upper-class housing and amenities replaced the working-class neighborhood that had been leveled. Choice C describes the Marshall Plan (1947).

TEST SCORE WORKSHEET

To estimate what score you would earn on the actual AP exam, follow these steps.

Section I: Multiple Choice

Total correct (out of 80) __________

Number correct × 1.125 __________ (Do not round)
Raw Score

Section II: Free Response*

Question 1 ________ × 4.5 = __________
(out of 9)

Question 2 or 3 ________ × 2.75 = __________
(out of 9)

Question 4 or 5 ________ × 2.75 = __________
(out of 9)

____
Total

Final Score

__________ + __________ = __________
Multiple-Choice Score *Free-Response Score* *Final Score (rounded)*

Score Conversion Chart

Raw Score	AP Grade**
111–180	5
91–110	4
76–90	3
57–75	2
0–56	1

*Do your best to assign an appropriate score for each essay or ask your teacher to do so. But remember that the score you assign yourself may not be the same score you would earn on the actual AP exam.

**The raw score corresponding to each grade varies from year to year. The chart above is an approximation of the score you would earn on the actual AP exam.

GENERAL RUBRIC FOR ALL FREE-RESPONSE QUESTIONS

The guidelines below describe the general expectations for each ranking level and is a good summary of what you need to do to write a good essay.

Top ranked essay: 8–9

1. Has a well constructed thesis that deals specifically with what the question asks
2. Effectively uses evidence to support the thesis
3. Uses English clearly and is well organized
4. Analyzes the information used, choosing relevant points
5. Minor errors are acceptable

Next level essay: 5–7

1. Contains a thesis that is relevant to the question
2. In a question with several parts, may concentrate on one or two parts and cover the other(s) in less depth; analysis may be weak in sections
3. Uses evidence to support thesis
4. Errors in language do not affect understanding of the essay; organization can be followed
5. Errors do not affect the total impact of the essay

Next level essay: 2–4

1. Presents a confusing, inadequate, or badly developed thesis
2. Weak analysis, general coverage, or simplistic explanation; may cover only part of the question
3. Contains general, often inaccurate evidence, or evidence that is irrelevant to the question
4. Organization is poor
5. Major errors are included

Next level essay: 0–1

1. Contains no thesis or an irrelevant one
2. Fails to show understanding of the question; lacks analysis
3. Evidence is lacking, poorly presented, or irrelevant
4. Organization is not clear and interferes with understanding the presentation

Answer Sheet

PRACTICE TEST 2

1	A B C D E		21	A B C D E		41	A B C D E		61	A B C D E	
2	A B C D E		22	A B C D E		42	A B C D E		62	A B C D E	
3	A B C D E		23	A B C D E		43	A B C D E		63	A B C D E	
4	A B C D E		24	A B C D E		44	A B C D E		64	A B C D E	
5	A B C D E		25	A B C D E		45	A B C D E		65	A B C D E	
6	A B C D E		26	A B C D E		46	A B C D E		66	A B C D E	
7	A B C D E		27	A B C D E		47	A B C D E		67	A B C D E	
8	A B C D E		28	A B C D E		48	A B C D E		68	A B C D E	
9	A B C D E		29	A B C D E		49	A B C D E		69	A B C D E	
10	A B C D E		30	A B C D E		50	A B C D E		70	A B C D E	
11	A B C D E		31	A B C D E		51	A B C D E		71	A B C D E	
12	A B C D E		32	A B C D E		52	A B C D E		72	A B C D E	
13	A B C D E		33	A B C D E		53	A B C D E		73	A B C D E	
14	A B C D E		34	A B C D E		54	A B C D E		74	A B C D E	
15	A B C D E		35	A B C D E		55	A B C D E		75	A B C D E	
16	A B C D E		36	A B C D E		56	A B C D E		76	A B C D E	
17	A B C D E		37	A B C D E		57	A B C D E		77	A B C D E	
18	A B C D E		38	A B C D E		58	A B C D E		78	A B C D E	
19	A B C D E		39	A B C D E		59	A B C D E		79	A B C D E	
20	A B C D E		40	A B C D E		60	A B C D E		80	A B C D E	

Practice Test 2

SECTION 1
MULTIPLE-CHOICE QUESTIONS

TIME—55 MINUTES
NUMBER OF QUESTIONS—80

Directions: Each of the following questions or statements below has five possible answers. For each question, select the best response.

1. Which of the following is not one of the guiding principles of mercantilism?

   (A) Colonies should supply raw materials to the mother country.
   (B) Nations should try to maintain a favorable balance of trade.
   (C) The mother country should regulate the trade of its colonies.
   (D) All countries in the world are in a competition for more gold and silver.
   (E) The mother country should usher its colonies toward economic independence.

2. The assault by the Powhatan Tribe on the Virginia Colony in 1722 was significant in that it led to

   (A) a royal investigation into the affairs of the Virginia Colony that resulted in King James revoking the Virginia Company's charter.
   (B) the defeat and departure of the Virginia settlers; only in the 1660s did a new group of settlers create a permanent settlement along the Chesapeake Bay.
   (C) negotiations between the Virginia Company and the Powhatan Confederation that resulted in a land- and power-sharing agreement between the two groups.
   (D) the removal of John Smith from his leadership position and the selection of John Rolfe to lead the Virginia colony.
   (E) an alliance between the English and the Dutch to wage war against the various Algonquian Tribes between the colonies of Virginia and New Amsterdam.

3. After the French and Indian War, British Prime Minister George Grenville instituted a number of measures that were intended to

   (A) reduce the substantial debt that Great Britain had incurred in fighting the war.
   (B) gradually usher the thirteen American colonies toward independence.
   (C) punish Native-American tribes for supporting the French in the war.
   (D) defeat the rebellious thirteen colonies militarily.
   (E) unite the thirteen colonies and Canada under one administrative unit.

4. Shays's Rebellion was a manifestation of resentment among

   (A) Boston workers over British mercantilist policies and laws.
   (B) western Massachusetts farmers over high taxes and hard currency.
   (C) slaves in South Carolina over harsh and arbitrary treatment.
   (D) merchants in New York over price and wage guidelines.
   (E) backcountry Virginians over the presence of Native Americans on the frontier.

5. The novel *Uncle Tom's Cabin* by Harriet Beecher Stowe

   (A) had the effect of intensifying antislavery sentiment among northerners.
   (B) was largely ignored when it was written but has in the twentieth century, come to be seen as one of the classics of American literature.
   (C) was barred from distribution in the North because moderate Republicans feared the novel would drive a wedge between the North and the South.
   (D) was welcomed by southerners because it finally showed slave owners as kindhearted men.
   (E) was the first published narrative written by an escaped slave.

6. Which of the following is <u>not</u> considered a cause of the Panic of 1873 and the economic depression that followed?

   (A) The Coinage Act of 1873 "demonetized" silver, setting the United States on a gold standard and depressing the price of silver.
   (B) An economic crisis beginning in the Austro-Hungarian Empire in 1871 impacted the economics of the rest of Europe and North America by 1873.
   (C) Jay Cooke and Company, a major American banking firm, declared bankruptcy in 1873 after its credit had become virtually worthless.
   (D) Rapid overexpansion of the nation's railroad network led to a decline of railroad companies' stock prices, which had been unrealistically inflated by excessive speculation.
   (E) The agricultural sector suffered a major decline in the 1860s and 1870s when European growers mechanized production but the United States continued to rely instead on labor-intensive methods.

7. Which of the following was an important political development that resulted from American involvement in World War I?
   (A) The Progressive Movement reached its high-water mark in the 1920s as Americans attempted to apply the democratizing impulse of the war to domestic concerns.
   (B) The Republican Party suffered major defeats at the polls in the midterm elections of 1918 as the country rallied behind President Wilson and the Democratic Party.
   (C) Congress passed important civil rights legislation in the early 1920s as the nation demonstrated its appreciation of African Americans for their participation in the war.
   (D) The patriotic fervor that emanated from the war effort contributed to an anti-German impulse and a broader anti-immigrant sentiment among many Americans.
   (E) The movement for greater political equality among women suffered a setback as a more masculine wartime popular culture pushed the concerns of women into the background.

8. Francis Townsend played a significant role in the 1930s by
   (A) pushing for President Franklin D. Roosevelt to initiate a program to provide pensions for retired people.
   (B) promoting the Share The Wealth campaign.
   (C) initiating impeachment hearings against President Franklin D. Roosevelt.
   (D) arguing against American intervention in foreign conflicts.
   (E) serving as President Franklin D. Roosevelt's secretary of labor.

9. The creation of the House Un-American Activities Committee and the Senate Internal Security Subcommittee could best be described as
   (A) Democratic Party initiatives to challenge Republican control of Congress.
   (B) Cold War era responses to the domestic communist movement.
   (C) attempts to silence opposition to United States involvement in World War I.
   (D) congressional checks on corrupt practices by senators and representatives.
   (E) actions taken to stem the flow of illegal immigrants into the United States.

10. The Glorious Revolution (1688) in Great Britain had an important impact on colonial America in that it led to the
   (A) ending of the Dominion of New England.
   (B) establishment of the policy of salutary neglect.
   (C) enactment of the Coercive Acts.
   (D) chartering of the colony of Maryland as a refuge for Catholics.
   (E) beginning of the French and Indian War.

11. Which statement was confirmed by the results of the Battle of Saratoga?
    (A) British forces could dominate the southern colonies, but it would be difficult for them to control the northern colonies.
    (B) The colonists could win major battles only if they had help from France.
    (C) The colonists were most successful militarily when they copied the tactics of the British.
    (D) The British might be able to take major cities, but it would be very difficult for them to control the countryside.
    (E) The colonists needed the help of Native-American allies to win the American Revolution.

12. Which of the following documents laid out a plan for the unsettled areas of the United States to become states with the same rights and privileges as the original thirteen states?
    (C) Proclamation of 1763
    (A) Articles of Confederation (1781)
    (B) Treaty of Paris of 1783
    (D) Northwest Ordinance (1787)
    (E) Tenth Amendment to the Constitution (1791)

13. The completion of the Erie Canal in 1825 was important because it
    (A) eliminated the need for ships to travel around the tip of South America by connecting the Atlantic and Pacific Oceans.
    (B) lowered the price of shipping cotton to Europe by connecting the interior of the Carolinas with the Atlantic Ocean.
    (C) provided irrigation to the cotton fields of Texas by redirecting water from the Rio Grande.
    (D) promoted industrial development in Philadelphia by connecting the Schuylkill and Delaware Rivers.
    (E) aided midwestern farmers by connecting the Great Lakes region with the eastern seaboard.

14. In 1836, when Texas gained its independence from Mexico, President Andrew Jackson was reluctant to push for annexation of the territory because he feared
    (A) a war between the United States and Mexico.
    (B) the influx of immigrants from Mexico into the United States.
    (C) the worsening of sectional tensions over incorporating an additional slave territory.
    (D) additional military conflicts with the Native Americans of Texas.
    (E) a shift in power in the United States from the northern states to the southern states.

15. A riot in New York City in 1863 demonstrated many New Yorkers' dislike of

    (A) recent Irish immigrants.
    (B) wage cuts and dangerous conditions at the workplace.
    (C) the United States Army's practice of quartering soldiers in people's homes.
    (D) incidents of police brutality.
    (E) the Civil War draft law.

16. What is the main point of the 1896 cartoon shown above?

    (A) The different regions of the country were working together to create a thriving national economy.
    (B) Farm animals were being mercilessly exploited with growth-enhancing drugs.
    (C) The demands of the Grangers and the Populist Movement were unreasonable and excessively radical.
    (D) Eastern banking and financial interests were exploiting the hard work of western farmers.
    (E) Unsustainable agricultural practices were depleting the topsoil of the Midwest.

17. A central conclusion of both Lincoln Steffens's 1904 book *The Shame of the Cities* and the 1901 report of the five-man state commission that investigated the aftermath of the Galveston, Texas, flood was that

    (A) municipal governance was often hindered by nepotism, corruption, and inefficiencies.
    (B) federal and state regulations prevented cities from addressing important issues.
    (C) racial prejudice and discrimination on the local level often resulted in dangerous conditions for African-American neighborhoods.
    (D) comprehensive urban planning needed to address environmental concerns.
    (E) criminal gangs in major American cities were a major problem that police forces avoided confronting.

18. "We are glad to fight for the ultimate peace of the world and the liberation of its peoples, for the rights of nations great and small and the privilege of men everywhere to choose their way of life. . . . The world must be made safe for democracy. We have no selfish ends to serve."

    The above quotation was said by

    (A) President William McKinley on the eve of the Spanish-American War.
    (B) President Woodrow Wilson on the eve of United States intervention in World War I.
    (C) President Franklin D. Roosevelt on the eve of United States intervention in World War II.
    (D) President Harry S. Truman on the eve of the Korean War.
    (E) President Lyndon Johnson on the eve of the Vietnam War.

19. The agenda of the New Right included all of the following EXCEPT

    (A) increasing taxes to fund the Social Security system.
    (B) expanding weapons programs such as the B1 bomber and the MX missile.
    (C) opposing affirmative action in hiring and college admissions.
    (D) carrying out a war on drugs.
    (E) injecting religious values into public policies.

20. Which of the following is the most accurate description of the Puritan critique of the Anglican Church?

(A) The Anglican Church had become corrupt. Its ministers were using Church funds for their own personal advantage.
(B) The Anglican Church was too demanding of its members. It should have been easier to be a Church member.
(C) The Anglican Church—even though it split from the Catholic Church—still kept many aspects of Catholicism. It should rid itself of these "Catholic" practices.
(D) The Anglican Church was wrong in allowing pictures and statues of God, Jesus, and Mary to exist. These pictures were treated by Church members as idols or false gods.
(E) The Anglican Church rejected the centrality of Jesus in its services and replaced him with the King of England.

21. Bacon's Rebellion (1676), which occurred in the backcountry of Virginia, was significant because it

(A) eliminated Catholic refugees from the colony of Virginia.
(B) led to the formation of the colony of West Virginia.
(C) convinced Virginia plantation owners to turn to African slaves as their primary labor source.
(D) quickly spread to other colonies and led Great Britain to establish the Dominion of New England.
(E) ended with a massacre of over two thousand Powhatan people.

22. After the American Revolution, which of the following was a problem the United States faced with foreign nations?

(A) Mexico refused to recognize the independence of the United States and sent a battalion to the border of Texas.
(B) France demanded that the United States pay over $10 million for the military aid the U.S. had received from France during the American Revolution.
(C) England refused to leave forts in the western part of the United States until the United States honored debts and gave Loyalists back their property.
(D) China threatened to attack the United States because the U.S. began buying its tea from Dutch-held Indonesia instead of China.
(E) Haiti threatened to organize raids into the southern states in order to foment a rebellion among the enslaved population.

23. The initial purpose for taking a census of the population every ten years, as called for in the Constitution, was to

   (A) assess the level of success of public health measures.
   (B) apportion seats in the House of Representatives fairly.
   (C) set income brackets for the federal income tax.
   (D) allocate funding for federal housing projects.
   (E) adjust state borders to accommodate population shifts.

24. Which of the following significant changes occurred in trans-Atlantic shipping in the 1810s?

   (A) Ships began to specialize in carrying just one commodity, in contrast to eighteenth-century ships that carried a variety of products and materials.
   (B) Shipping increased dramatically as the United States eliminated import duties and the major European economies reciprocated by eliminating duties on American products.
   (C) Shipping companies began to publish and stick to departure schedules, whereas previously ships would simply wait in port until sufficient quantities of goods were loaded to justify departure.
   (D) Slave labor was banned from use on trans-Atlantic crews in 1819, thus increasing the demand for immigrant labor to fill the crews.
   (E) The United States Navy began to provide escort ships to large freight carriers in order to protect them from assaults by the Barbary Pirates.

25. Which of the following is <u>not</u> considered an important factor in the rise of nativist sentiment in the United States in the 1840s and 1850s?

   (A) Mill owners grew increasingly critical of open immigration because unskilled immigrant labor undermined quality and efficiency in textile production.
   (B) Prominent Whig politicians were critical of the wave of immigrants into the country because these newcomers voted overwhelmingly for the Democratic Party.
   (C) Many Americans, noting the desperate conditions in immigrant communities, came to the conclusion that European governments were exporting their "undesirables" to the United States.
   (D) Nativists worried that the influx of Celts from Southern Ireland would pollute the Anglo-Saxon stock that predominated in the United States.
   (E) Temperance reformers were convinced that working-class immigrants from Ireland and Germany contributed to a marked increase in public and excessive alcohol consumption.

26. Which of the following accurately describes the approach toward Native Americans embodied in President Ulysses S. Grant's Peace Policy (1869)?

    (A) Native Americans would be allowed to live in their ancestral homes and pursue traditional religious and cultural practices.
    (B) Native Americans would be immediately granted United States citizenship and be encouraged to live in towns and cities alongside white Americans.
    (C) Native Americans would be exempt from most aspects of the United States legal code; they would be encouraged to develop their own legal code under which they would live.
    (D) Native-American tribes would be offered restitution for the land that was acquired by white Americans from the arrival of the first English settlers until 1865, whether the land was outright taken or whether it was transferred through treaties of dubious legality.
    (E) Native Americans would be provided with resources on reservations and agents from religious orders who would educate and "civilize" them; those who chose not to live on these reservations would be subject to removal by the army.

OUR RELIGIOUS LANDLORDS AND THEIR ROOKERY TENANTS.

27. The 1895 cartoon above makes the point that

    (A) the Catholic Church routinely ignores the plight of the most indigent urban residents.
    (B) the key to financial success is righteous living and regular attendance at church.
    (C) slumlords express piety on Sunday mornings but ignore the suffering of their tenants the rest of the week.
    (D) landlords and political bosses work together to prevent the passage of effective housing legislation.
    (E) Protestant denominations made no effort to provide charity to Catholic immigrants.

28. Public art works created under the auspices of the Works Progress Administration tended to

    (A) focus on flattering portraits of President Roosevelt and other high-ranking members of his administration.
    (B) be seen primarily by wealthy patrons who visited art galleries and museums.
    (C) present images of beautiful landscapes to distract people from the realities of life during the Great Depression.
    (D) employ surrealist and Dada styles.
    (E) show the lives of ordinary people and workers in a dignified and ennobling manner.

29. The Hollywood 10 was

    (A) a coalition of Hollywood production companies that publicly pledged not to hire any artists who had been blacklisted.
    (B) the leaders of the Communist Party in California who were arrested under the 1940 Smith Act.
    (C) a group of German directors and writers who were ordered to leave the United States because of their supposed sympathies for the Nazi Party.
    (D) a group of directors and writers who refused to cooperate with congressional investigations into domestic communism.
    (E) ten leading production companies in Hollywood that agreed to initiate a class-action lawsuit against television networks for showing their films without paying royalties.

30. The Mayflower Compact and the Virginia House of Burgesses are similar in that they both

    (A) established a clear separation between church and state.
    (B) banned the practice of slavery.
    (C) endorsed the idea of declaring independence from Great Britain.
    (D) embodied the principle of representative government.
    (E) restricted colonial trade.

31. "I suppose the newspapers must be wrong when they say that Mr. [John] Adams had taken up his abode [in Paris] with Dr. [Benjamin] Franklin. I am at a loss to judge how he will act in the negotiation. He hates Franklin, he hates Jay, he hates the French, he hates the English. To whom will he adhere?"

Excerpt from a letter by Thomas Jefferson
to James Madison, Feb 14, 1783

The purpose of John Adams's visit to Paris, referred to in the letter by Thomas Jefferson above, was to

(A) encourage France to recognize the United States and to provide the U.S. with assistance in its war for independence.
(B) negotiate a peace treaty to conclude the American war for independence.
(C) urge France to cease and desist from interfering with American shipping.
(D) demand that Great Britain end the practice of impressment of American sailors.
(E) broker an end to hostilities between revolutionary France and Great Britain.

32. The outcome of the Whiskey Rebellion in 1794 demonstrated that
(A) important issues between the North and the South were not yet resolved.
(B) states could nullify decisions of the federal government.
(C) the federal government had the power and the will to put down rebellions quickly.
(D) federal troops could control urban populations but rural populations would be very difficult to control.
(E) George Washington was a more decisive general than president.

33. Which of the following accurately describes government responses to the Panic of 1819?

(A) The federal government and state governments passed stay laws, delaying foreclosure proceedings and providing additional time for farmers to repay debts.
(B) The federal government greatly reduced tariff rates to lower the prices of imported goods.
(C) State and municipal governments provided funds to settlement houses such as Hull House in Chicago and Henry Street Settlement in New York City.
(D) The federal government began a series of public works programs to provide jobs to the unemployed.
(E) President James Monroe refused to acknowledge the depths of the crisis, creating a political opening for the newly formed Whig Party in the 1820 elections.

34. During the 1820s and 1830s, the terms "graduation" and "preemption" were used in regard to
    (A) implementing a policy for the gradual abolition of slavery.
    (B) reducing the price of western lands to encourage settlement.
    (C) retiring war debts incurred during the War of 1812.
    (D) settling a dispute with Great Britain over claims to the Oregon Territory.
    (E) extending citizenship rights to recent immigrants.

35. In 1856, northerners criticized the brutality of southern society after
    (A) an attempted assassination attempt on Abraham Lincoln.
    (B) a South Carolina congressman beat Massachusetts Senator Charles Sumner with a cane in the Senate chamber.
    (C) six free African Americans were lynched in North Carolina for supposedly smiling at a white woman.
    (D) Frederick Douglass was beaten, almost to death, by a mob of proslavery men on the streets of Charleston, South Carolina.
    (E) the publication of a pamphlet by George Fitzhugh, defending the practice of whipping slaves.

36. The Platt Amendment and the Open Door Policy are similar in that they both
    (A) pushed the Progressive agenda into new areas.
    (B) were welcomed by American anti-imperialists who believed in self-determination for all people.
    (C) led to war with European powers.
    (D) expanded the role of the United States in foreign nations.
    (E) encouraged immigration into the United States.

37. One of the primary reasons for creating the Federal Reserve Bank in 1913 was to
    (A) provide short-term loans to developing nations.
    (B) centralize financial power in one city—New York.
    (C) create a mechanism to regulate the amount of money in circulation.
    (D) nationalize the majority of privately owned banks in the United States.
    (E) increase the ratio of silver to gold in circulation.

38. Which of the following describes an important outcome of American involvement in the Korean War?

(A) The war, which began in the summer of 1950, gave a boost to the standing of President Harry S. Truman and the Democratic Party, which scored significant gains in the 1950 midterm elections.
(B) The war vaulted Senator Joseph McCarthy's anticommunist crusade from a curious sideshow to a major popular movement.
(C) The war led the Senate to grow frustrated with the United Nations for foot-dragging in regard to the conflict; the Senate suspended payments to the organization for five years.
(D) The war brought the Soviet Union and the United States to the negotiating table as both nations worked tirelessly to prevent the war from degenerating into World War III.
(E) The war gave rise to a vociferous antiwar movement that addressed a variety of social and political concerns in the 1950s and 1960s.

39. The violence that occurred in Selma, Alabama, on Bloody Sunday in March 1965 was caused by

(A) a mob of white of people inspired by the call for massive resistance to civil rights initiatives.
(B) federal troops who attacked a group of Cherokees who were demonstrating on the anniversary of the Trail of Tears (1838).
(C) tensions within the civil rights movement between the older generation of church-based activists and the younger generation of students in the Black Power movement.
(D) a bomb planted by the Weather Underground at the University of Alabama physics department building to protest links between the university and the military.
(E) Alabama state troopers who were attempting to disperse the Selma to Montgomery march for voting rights.

40. Which of the following was true of college education in colonial America in the first half of the eighteenth-century?

(A) Tuition rates for colleges were extremely high, assuring that college education in America was more exclusive than it was in Great Britain.
(B) College campuses were hotbeds of anti-British revolutionary sentiment and enlightenment philosophy; British authorities periodically closed down Yale and Harvard.
(C) College education was restricted to the New England region; no colleges opened up outside of New England until the 1830s.
(D) Though early colleges were founded to train ministers to serve the towns of colonial America, by the eighteenth century colleges had developed broader liberal arts curricula.
(E) Competitions had developed at Yale, Harvard, Princeton, and Kings College (Columbia) in American-style football, distinct from British antecedents.

41. Which of the following was an important outcome of the XYZ Affair of 1798?

(A) It divided the Democratic-Republican Party and the Federalist Party in regard to revolutionary France. The Democratic Republicans came to support it, and the Federalists came to oppose it.
(B) The United States grew closer to the French Government; this drift toward France paved the way for the War of 1812 between the United States and Great Britain.
(C) President John Adams authorized American ships to seize armed French vessels, leading to a two-year Quasi-War with France.
(D) Federalists in Congress agreed to rescind the controversial Alien and Sedition Acts in the name of national unity.
(E) American negotiators immediately cut off negotiations with France over the purchase of the Louisiana Territory; the issue would not be revived for another five years.

42. "[The Constitution] contains an enumeration of powers expressly granted by the people to the government. It has been said, that these powers ought to be construed strictly. But why ought they to be so construed? Is there one sentence in the constitution which gives countenance to this rule? In the last of the enumerated powers, that which grants, expressly, the means for carrying all others into execution, Congress is authorized 'to make all laws which shall be necessary and proper' for the purpose. . . . What do gentlemen mean, by a strict construction? If they contend only against that enlarged construction, which would extend words beyond their natural and obvious import, we might question the application of the term, but should not controvert the principle."

The above statement was made by

(A) Patrick Henry
(B) Thomas Jefferson
(C) John Marshall
(D) John C. Calhoun
(E) Andrew Jackson

43. In 1828, three times as many people voted as had voted in 1824. What is the best explanation for this?

(A) Between 1824 and 1828, more states joined the union.
(B) In 1826, the Supreme Court ruled that freed African Americans had the right to vote.
(C) In 1824, there was only one political party. In 1828, there were two.
(D) After 1824, many states reduced or eliminated property qualifications for voting.
(E) In 1827, the Nineteenth Amendment to the Constitution was ratified, extending voting rights to women.

44. The acquisition of territory from Mexico as a result of the Mexican War (1846–1848) was significant in that it

(A) settled conflicts between Native Americans and the United States Government.
(B) led to a series of events known as Bleeding Kansas.
(C) provided the United States with territory to build the Panama Canal.
(D) led to the demise of the New England-based Federalist Party.
(E) generated controversy when California applied for admission as a free state.

45. An important effect that Irish immigration had on the American economy in the 1850s was

(A) bringing new skills to the American workplace.
(B) opening up trade between the United States and Ireland.
(C) improving relations between Catholics and Protestants as Irish and native-born workers worked side by side.
(D) providing additional income tax revenues to a depleted treasury.
(E) driving down wages for native-born workers.

46. The 1892 labor strikes of miners at Coeur d'Alene, Idaho, and steelworkers at Andrew Carnegie's plant in Homestead, Pennsylvania, are similar in that both

(A) involved pitched, violent battles between strikers and company agents that left over two dozen dead and hundreds injured.
(B) helped legitimize the "bread and butter" unionism approach of the American Federation of Labor.
(C) were ended by federal mediators after both sides agreed to binding arbitration to resolve their conflicts.
(D) demonstrated the importance of interracial coalitions in achieving victory on the picket line.
(E) involved skilled workers challenging the introduction of mass-production techniques.

47. Which of the following is true of the debates around American imperialism that developed in the wake of the Spanish-American War (1898)?

(A) Most southern Democrats condemned the acquisition of the Philippines, arguing that Asians were innately "inferior" to whites and could not be assimilated into the American system.
(B) The progressive movement was opposed to American imperialism on the grounds that the peoples of Latin America and Asia should be given the same rights of self-determination that Americans had fought for in the Revolutionary War.
(C) The anti-imperialist movement was successful in the 1900 presidential election, helping William McKinley defeat Williams Jennings Bryan.
(D) Even though the United States acquired the Philippines, anti-imperialist sentiment pushed the United States to grant self-determination to Cuba and Puerto Rico.
(E) The American Federation of Labor came out in favor of imperialism, arguing that workers abroad would benefit more from American labor practices than they had been faring under native regimes.

48. President William Howard Taft's support for the Payne-Aldrich Tariff Act and his dismissal of Gifford Pinchot as chief of the Forest Service indicated that Taft was

(A) ready to make difficult choices in order to reduce the swollen federal deficit.
(B) not committed to the progressive agenda that his predecessor, President Theodore Roosevelt, had been.
(C) courting southern and western agricultural interests at the expense of northern and eastern manufacturing interests.
(D) prepared to put party loyalties aside in the pursuit of efficient, clean government.
(E) strongly influenced by muckraking journalists in regard to developing his domestic agenda.

49. "The main element of any United States policy toward the Soviet Union must be a long-term, patient but firm and vigilant containment of Russian expansive tendencies. . . . Soviet pressure against the free institutions of the Western world is something that can be contained by the adroit and vigilant application of counterforce at a series of constantly shifting geographical and political points, corresponding to the shifts and maneuvers of Soviet policy, but which cannot be charmed or talked out of existence."

    The quotation above is from

    (A) the "Fourteen Points" speech by President Woodrow Wilson.
    (B) the third inaugural address of President Franklin D. Roosevelt.
    (C) "The Sources of Soviet Conduct," by X, a pseudonym for diplomat George F. Kennan.
    (D) a memo to President Dwight D. Eisenhower by Secretary of State John Foster Dulles.
    (E) congressional testimony of General Douglas MacArthur.

50. When Oliver Cromwell took power in England following the English Civil War,

    (A) Puritans were forced to practice their religion in secret.
    (B) Puritan migration to the New World nearly stopped.
    (C) Spain was able to regain its position of world supremacy.
    (D) Protestantism was finally able to take root in England.
    (E) the thirteen American colonies declared their independence.

51. Which of the following ideas was contained in the original draft of the Declaration of Independence but was removed from the final draft?

    (A) Women and men should be treaty equally under the law.
    (B) Only the wealthy and powerful should be allowed to vote for president.
    (C) The slave trade was an evil that denied people their humanity.
    (D) The king of England should be allowed to rule over the United States but only as a figurehead (without any real powers).
    (E) Native Americans and white people should live in peace and harmony.

52. The controversy over Secretary of the Treasury Alexander Hamilton's 1790 proposal for the federal government to assume state debts that dated from the Revolutionary War period demonstrates that

(A) sectional interests between North and South were evident from the very early years of the United States.
(B) there were differing opinions within the Washington administration about how the elastic clause should be interpreted.
(C) Hamilton consistently put the interests of the individual states above the interests of the United States.
(D) the Democratic Republicans were ready to challenge Federalist initiatives from the onset of the Washington administration.
(E) Hamilton was more interested in giving the economy a quick jolt than he was in maintaining the long-term stability of the economy.

53. The Virginia and Kentucky Resolutions of 1796 and South Carolina's reaction to the Tariff Acts of 1828 and 1832 both reflected the principle that

(A) moneyed interests should not be permitted to dominate the political process.
(B) controversial questions should be settled by popular sovereignty.
(C) the United States should remain isolated from other countries.
(D) states should have the right to nullify federal legislation.
(E) one should put national unity above partisan political differences.

54. In the 1830s, the government of Mexico grew increasingly uneasy when large numbers of United States residents immigrated to the Mexican state of Texas because

(A) the Mexican Government discovered a spying ring among the immigrants.
(B) the immigrants refused to accept the ancient belief system of the Aztec (Mexica) people.
(C) the immigrants brought the illegal practice of slavery with them to Mexico.
(D) the immigrants formed an alliance with hostile Native-American groups in an attempt to overthrow the Mexican government.
(E) the Mexican Government suspected that the immigrants were polygamous Mormons.

55. The Ostend Manifesto (1854) reflected the hope of many southern politicians that the United States would

(A) declare slavery to be a national institution, legal throughout the entire country.
(B) issue a ban on all abolitionist literature as seditious and dangerous.
(C) allow slavery to expand to all the territories acquired from Mexico following the Mexican War.
(D) purchase Cuba from Spain and make it an additional slave state.
(E) rescind the three-fifths compromise and count each slave as a full person in the census.

56. The War Industries Board, the Committee on Public Information, and the Espionage and Sedition Acts are similar in that they all

(A) were attempts to silence opposition to World War I.
(B) reflect the expanded power of the federal government during World War I.
(C) failed to achieve their stated goals.
(D) were welcomed by organized labor.
(E) were Progressive Era measures that were abandoned when World War I began.

57. The Nye Committee investigations (1934–1936) into the excessive profits made by war industries during World War I were significant in that they

(A) amounted to a setback for Franklin D. Roosevelt's goals for expanding the funding of government relief programs.
(B) were declared unconstitutional by the Supreme Court because the legislative branch was seen as interfering with the president's powers as commander-in-chief of the armed forces.
(C) added fuel to the arguments of isolationists who wanted the United States to avoid intervening in the deteriorating world situation in the 1930s.
(D) led to the resignation of Secretary of War George Henry Dern and a reshuffling of top personnel at the War Department.
(E) resulted in President Franklin D. Roosevelt nationalizing key arms manufacturing firms to take the profit motive away from war production.

58. Following publication of *The Grapes of Wrath* (1939) by John Steinbeck, which depicted the lives of farmers who migrated from Oklahoma to California during the Great Depression,

(A) California passed legislation prohibiting additional migrant farmers from entering the state and establishing checkpoints along California's borders with Oregon, Nevada, and Arizona.
(B) sustained rainfalls in 1939 and 1940 in the dust bowl region ended the agricultural crisis and led to a reverse migration from California to Oklahoma and Texas.
(C) Steinbeck was investigated by the House Un-American Activities Committee because of the radical implications of the novel.
(D) the Farm Security Administration allocated additional funds for the relocation of dust bowl refugees and helped establish temporary camps to house them.
(E) the novel was ignored by the public as its publication coincided with the beginning of World War II; the novel was republished to popular acclaim only in the 1960s.

59. The decision by the United States to carry out the Berlin Airlift demonstrated America's

(A) strategy for halting Nazi atrocities.
(B) support for Turkish refugees in Germany.
(C) policy of isolationism.
(D) commitment to challenge Soviet aggression.
(E) shift from protectionism to free trade.

60. The Puritans, who based their faith on the teachings of John Calvin, believed that salvation

(A) could be achieved through proper behavior—going to church, confessing one's sins, and paying alms.
(B) could be achieved only by publicly demonstrating a deep inner faith in God.
(C) was impossible for human beings because of our flawed, sinful character.
(D) was predetermined by God, not by the actions of humans.
(E) could be achieved by a majority vote of church elders.

61. "Tis really astonishing that the same people, who have just emerged from a long and cruel war in defense of liberty, should now agree to fix an elective despotism upon themselves and their posterity."

Richard Henry Lee, 1788

In the quotation above, Lee was expressing

(A) apprehension over the lawlessness of the participants of Shays's Rebellion in Massachusetts.
(B) opposition to the antislavery clause of the Northwest Ordinance.
(C) support for the Virginia and Kentucky Resolutions.
(D) indignation at the Alien and Sedition Acts.
(E) criticism of those who supported ratification of the Constitution.

62. When the Democratic-Republican Party was first organized in the 1790s, it

(A) favored expanding the powers of the federal government.
(B) thought that America would be successful by developing industry and commerce.
(C) thought that the rich and the educated should have a permanent place in the government.
(D) called for the immediate abolition of slavery
(E) opposed the formation of a national bank.

63. In the 1800s, the newer religious groups that grew during the Second Great Awakening differed from Puritanism in that they

(A) renounced the abolition movement.
(B) allowed women to become ministers.
(C) permitted interracial marriage.
(D) did not allow pictures of Jesus in their churches.
(E) rejected the doctrine of predestination.

64. The impetus behind the founding of the Whig Party in 1833 was to

(A) challenge the policies of President Andrew Jackson.
(B) protect the institution of slavery.
(C) oppose the internal improvements proposed by Henry Clay.
(D) encourage territorial expansion to fulfill America's manifest destiny.
(E) exterminate the Native Americans of the Great Lakes region.

65. "The [Democrats] are given to 'bushwhacking.' After having their errors and misstatements continually thrust in their faces, they pay no heed, but go on howling about Seward and the 'irrepressible conflict.' That is 'bushwhacking.' So with John Brown and Harpers Ferry. They charge it upon the Republican Party and ignominiously fail in all attempts to substantiate the charge. Yet they go on with their bushwhacking, the pack in full cry after John Brown."

Abraham Lincoln, 1859

In the quotation above, Abraham Lincoln is attempting to

(A) find common ground between Democrats and Republicans so as to prevent southern secession and possible war.
(B) challenge the logic of Senator Stephen Douglas's Freeport Doctrine.
(C) distance the Republican Party from the more extreme abolitionist elements in the North.
(D) resurrect the image of John Brown from those who would denigrate his memory.
(E) rebut false claims that he was a slaveholder and a secret apologist for slavery.

66. Poll taxes and literacy tests in the post-Reconstruction South seem to be most clearly a violation of the

(A) First Amendment.
(B) Eighth Amendment.
(C) Thirteenth Amendment.
(D) Fifteenth Amendment.
(E) Nineteenth Amendment.

67. When *Atlanta Constitution* editor Henry W. Grady and others called for a "new South" in the 1880s and 1890s, they were advocating that the South

(A) enter an era of interracial democracy, based on civil and voting rights for African Americans.
(B) revive the pre–Civil War traditions of chivalry, honor, and deference.
(C) remain essentially agrarian but that it diversify its output or crops to reduce dependence on "king cotton."
(D) move beyond the animosities of the Civil War and forge a "blue-gray" alliance with its former foes.
(E) develop commercial and industrial sectors that would allow the South to compete with the North successfully.

68. The 1933 political cartoon shown above makes the point that

    (A) the New Deal's proposals for open immigration would threaten American democracy.
    (B) the New Deal would be ineffective in addressing the problems of the Great Depression.
    (C) the Supreme Court acted in a tyrannical way in declaring certain New Deal measures unconstitutional.
    (D) New Deal programs would usher in unconstitutional restrictions on American freedoms and liberties.
    (E) members of President Roosevelt's cabinet were foreign agents who would undermine American efforts in World War II.

69. In arguing that segregated schools were unconstitutional in the case of *Brown* v. *Board of Education of Topeka*, Thurgood Marshall

    (A) demonstrated that African-American schools received less money per student than white schools.
    (B) insisted that the government live up to the principle of separate but equal.
    (C) showed that segregated schooling was psychologically damaging to African-American children.
    (D) relied on the principle of states' rights to justify Jim Crow laws.
    (E) argued that African Americans deserved reparations for mistreatment during the period when slavery was legal.

70. Which of the following statements represents a position in regard to slavery that most of the delegates at the Constitutional Convention (1787) could come to agreement on?

(A) Slavery was inconsistent with democratic principles and should be immediately abolished.
(B) Slaves would be counted in the census but only as a portion of their actual population.
(C) Slavery could exist in the southern states but would be abolished in the northern states.
(D) Slaves that escaped from a slave state and crossed into a free state would be considered free people.
(E) Slavery would be banned from any additional territories the United States might acquire.

71. The Alien and Sedition Acts (1898) enjoyed widespread public support, despite opposition from Democratic-Republican leaders, because in part

(A) the concept of freedom of expression was not yet universally appreciated by Americans; it was assumed that governments would regulate speech.
(B) President John Adams was extremely popular; any opposition to him was seen as treasonous.
(C) Irish immigration was changing the composition of many American cities; many Americans wondered if the United States could retain its Anglo-Saxon heritage without limiting immigration.
(D) federal authorities had uncovered and thwarted a plot by disgruntled North Carolina farmers to assassinate President John Adams; desperate times, it seemed, called for desperate measures.
(E) large numbers of Americans had become intensely critical of the revolutionary French government in the wake of the XYZ Affair; restricting the ability of French immigrants to participate in American politics seemed reasonable.

72. The term "cult of domesticity" was a critical term coined in the 1820s to describe the

(A) rural utopian communities established by the transcendental movement.
(B) unwillingness of the United States to play a more active role on the international stage.
(C) rigid guidelines established for "homebound" mentally ill patients.
(D) popularity of animal husbandry in rural New England.
(E) "proper" role women were expected to play in pre–Civil War America.

73. Which of the following statements represents a difference between the Democrats and the Whigs as the second two-party system took shape with the election of 1840?
    (A) The Whigs were primarily a northern party, and the Democrats were primarily a southern party.
    (B) The Whigs tended to favor federal measures, such as protective tariffs and internal improvements, while the Democrats favored limiting the reach of the federal government.
    (C) The Whigs supported territorial expansion toward the Pacific Ocean, while the Democrats feared that such expansion would ignite a sectional rift over slavery.
    (D) The Whigs were critical of the role of the church in public affairs, while the Democrats attempted to harness the energy of the Second Great Awakening to implement moral reforms.
    (E) The Whigs supported open immigration in order to increase the supply of laborers needed for industrialization; the Democrats feared the influence of Catholic immigrants on the American electorate.

74. As a result of the Compromise of 1850,
    (A) a stronger federal fugitive slave law was enacted.
    (B) California entered the Union as a slave state.
    (C) Texas entered the Union as a slave state.
    (D) popular sovereignty on the slavery question was granted to Kansas and Nebraska.
    (E) a line was drawn through the Louisiana Territory delineating slave and free territories.

75. Read the telegraph exchange between artist Frederick Remington and publisher William Randolph Hearst. Then answer the question that follows.

    Remington: "Everything is quiet. There is no trouble here. There will be no war."

    Hearst: "You furnish the pictures and I'll furnish the war."

    At the time of the time of the exchange, Remington was

    (A) at Fort Sumter in 1860.
    (B) in the Black Hills of South Dakota in 1876.
    (C) in Cuba in 1898.
    (D) in rural France in 1917.
    (E) in Tokyo in 1941.

76. The Clayton Antitrust Act (1914) differed from the earlier Sherman Antitrust Act (1890) in that the Clayton Act

(A) contained no enforcement mechanization; it relied on voluntary industry-wide compliance.
(B) narrowed the definition of anticompetitive behavior so as to allow for price discrimination and interlocking directories.
(C) broadened the definition of illegal monopolistic practices so as to include vertical integration as well as horizontal monopolization.
(D) prohibited the formation of trusts but allowed for cooperation among munitions manufacturers during times of war.
(E) contained provisions exempting labor and agricultural organizations from antitrust prosecution.

77. The Agricultural Adjustment Act (1933) attempted to solve the farm crisis by

(A) transferring ownership of farms from independent farmers to state-run collective farms.
(B) helping farmers relocate to urban centers.
(C) purchasing excess produce and paying farmers not to grow certain crops.
(D) helping farmers with increased mechanization and chemical fertilizers.
(E) preventing farm imports from Europe into the United States.

78. In the United States just before and during World War II, converting factories from civilian production to war production resulted in

(A) economic expansion and growth.
(B) massive layoffs and an economic depression.
(C) a surplus of consumer goods in the marketplace.
(D) a slump in agricultural production.
(E) a balanced federal budget.

79. Which of the following would not be considered an important factor in the rise of suburbia after World War II?

(A) The building of new highways
(B) Passage of the G.I. Bill
(C) The construction of new train lines
(D) New building techniques used to lower the cost of suburban housing
(E) Loans from the Federal Housing Administration

80. "For too long, we have lived with the 'Vietnam Syndrome.' Much of that syndrome has been created by the North Vietnamese aggressors. . . . Over and over they told us for nearly 10 years that we were the aggressors bent on imperialistic conquests. They had a plan. It was to win in the field of propaganda here in America what they could not win on the field of battle in Vietnam. As the years dragged on, we were told that peace would come if we would simply stop interfering and go home. It is time we recognized that ours was, in truth, a noble cause. A small country newly free from colonial rule sought our help in establishing self-rule and the means of self-defense against a totalitarian neighbor bent on conquest. We dishonor the memory of 50,000 young Americans who died in that cause when we give way to feelings of guilt as if we were doing something shameful. . . . "

Ronald Reagan, August 18, 1980

When Ronald Reagan refers to the "Vietnam syndrome" in the speech excerpted above, he is referring to the

(A) lingering health issues that veterans brought home with them from Vietnam.
(B) tendency of additional countries in Southeast Asia to adopt communist systems.
(C) disrespectful treatment that Vietnam veterans received when they returned to the United States.
(D) reluctance of the Jimmy Carter administration to engage in full-scale military engagements in the aftermath of the contentious Vietnam War.
(E) waves of immigrants from Southeast Asia who came to the United States in the wake of the Vietnam war.

STOP

END OF SECTION I

SECTION II

Part A

(SUGGESTED WRITING TIME—45 MINUTES)
PERCENT OF SECTION II SCORE—45

Directions: Write a coherent essay that incorporates your analysis of Documents A–G *and* your knowledge of the period in the question. To earn a high score, cite key information from the documents and use your knowledge of the period.

1. Americans took differing positions on the Mexican War in 1848. Before, during, and after the war, many Americans voiced support, while many expressed opposition.

   Assess the motivations of supporters and opponents of the Mexican War.

   Use the documents and your knowledge of the years 1840–1860 in your answer.

Document A

Source: President James K. Polk, "War Message to the House and Senate," May 11, 1846.

The existing state of the relations between the United States and Mexico renders it proper that I should bring the subject to the consideration of Congress. . . . The strong desire to establish peace with Mexico on liberal and honorable terms, and the readiness of this government to regulate and adjust our boundary, and other causes of difference with that power, on such fair and equitable principles as would lead to permanent relation of the most friendly nature, induced me in September last to seek the reopening of diplomatic relations between the two countries. . . . The Mexican government not only refused. . . . but, after a long continued series of menaces, have at last invaded our territory, and shed the blood of our fellow-citizens on our own soil. . . .

In my message at the commencement of the present session, I informed you that, upon the earnest appeal both of the congress and convention of Texas, I had ordered an efficient military force to take a position "between the Nueces and the Del Norte." This had become necessary, to meet a threatened invasion of Texas by the Mexican forces, for which extensive military preparations had been made. . . . The Congress of Texas, by its act of December 19, 1836, had declared the Rio del Norte to be the boundary of that republic. Its jurisdiction had been extended and exercised beyond the Nueces . . . it is now included within one of our congressional districts. Our own Congress had . . . by the act approved December 31, 1845, recognized the country beyond the Nueces as a part of our territory, by including it within our own revenue system. . . . It became, therefore, of urgent necessity to provide for the defense of that portion of our country. . . .

The cup of forbearance has been exhausted, even before the recent information from the frontier of the Del Norte. But now, after reiterated menaces, Mexico has passed the boundary of the United States, has invaded our territory, and shed American blood upon American soil. She has proclaimed that hostilities have commenced, and that the two nations are now at war.

As war exists, and, notwithstanding all our efforts to avoid it, exists by the act of Mexico herself, we are called upon by every consideration of duty and patriotism to vindicate with decision and honor, the rights, and the interests of our country. . . . I invoke the prompt action of Congress to recognize the existence of war. . . .

Document B

Source: Representative Abraham Lincoln, Speech to the House of Representatives, January 12, 1848.

.... The President, in his first war message of May, 1846, declares that the soil was ours on which hostilities were commenced by Mexico, and he repeats that declaration almost in the same language in each successive annual message, thus showing that he deems that point a highly essential one. In the importance of that point I entirely agree with the President. To my judgment it is the very point upon which he should be justified, or condemned....

...The President sent the army into the midst of a settlement of Mexican people who had never submitted, by consent or by force, to the authority of Texas or of the United States, and ... thereby the first blood of the war was shed...

... Let the President answer the [questions] I proposed, ... Let him answer fully, fairly, and candidly. Let him answer with facts and not with arguments. Let him remember he sits where Washington sat, and so remembering, let him answer as Washington would answer. As a nation should not, and the Almighty will not, be evaded, so let him attempt no evasion—no equivocation. And, if, so answering, he can show that the soil was ours where the first blood of war was shed—that it was not within an inhabited country, or, if within such, that the inhabitants had submitted themselves to the civil authority of Texas or of the United States, ... then I am with him.... But if he can not or will not do this, ... then I shall be fully convinced of what I more than suspect already—that he is deeply conscious of being in the wrong; that he feels the blood of this war, like the blood of Abel, is crying to Heaven against him ... and trusting to escape scrutiny by fixing the public gaze upon the exceeding brightness of military glory, that attractive rainbow that rises in showers of blood—that serpent's eye that charms to destroy, ... he now finds himself he knows not where....

As I have before said, he knows not where he is. He is a bewildered, confounded, and miserably perplexed man. God grant he may be able to show there is not something about his conscience more painful than all his mental perplexity.

Document C

Source: Senator Thomas Hart Benton, *Congressional Globe*, May 28, 1846.

Since the dispersion of man upon earth, I know of no human event, past or present, which promises a greater, a more beneficent change upon earth than the arrival of the van of the Caucasian race (the Celtic-Anglo-Saxon division) upon the border of the sea which washes the shore of eastern Asia.... It would seem that the White race alone received the divine command, to subdue and replenish the earth! ... For a long time, it was confined to the border of the new field... and even fourscore years ago the philosophic Burke was considered a rash man because he said the English colonists would top the Alleghenies, and descend into the valley of the Mississippi, and occupy without parchment if the Crown refused to make grants of land.

What was considered a rash declaration eighty years ago, is old history, in our young country, at this day.... The van of the Caucasian race now top the Rocky Mountains, and spread down to the shores of the Pacific. In a few years a great population will grow up there, luminous with the accumulated lights of European and American civilization. . . . The Red race has disappeared from the Atlantic coast: the tribes that resisted civilization, met extinction. This is a cause of lamentation with many. For my part, I cannot murmur at what seems to be the effect of divine law. I cannot repine that this Capitol has replaced the wigwam—this Christian people, replaced the savages—white matrons, the red squaws—and that such men as Washington, Franklin, and Jefferson, have taken the place of Powhatan, Opechonecanough, and other red men, howsoever respectable they may have been as savages. . . . Civilization, or extinction, has been the fate of all people who have found themselves in the track of the advancing Whites, and civilization, always the preference of the Whites, has been pressed as an object, while extinction has followed as a consequence of its resistance.

Document D

Source: Cartoon, *Punch Magazine*, 1847.

THE LAND OF LIBERTY.
RECOMMENDED TO THE CONSIDERATION OF "BROTHER JONATHAN."

Document E

Source: Frederick Douglass, Speech in Boston, June 8, 1848

You know as well as I do, that Faneuil Hall has resounded with echoing applause of a denunciation of the Mexican war, as a murderous war—as a war against the free states—as a war against freedom, against the Negro, and against the interests of workingmen of this country—and as a means of extending that great evil and damning curse, negro slavery. Why may not the oppressed say, when an oppressor is dead, either by disease or by the hand of the foeman on the battle-field, that there is one the less of his oppressors left on earth? For my part, I would not care if, to-morrow, I should hear of the death of every man who engaged in that bloody war in Mexico, and that every man had met the fate he went there to perpetrate upon unoffending Mexicans.

Document F

Source: Henry David Thoreau, Excerpt from his Essay "On the Duty of Civil Disobedience," 1846.

I HEARTILY accept the motto,—"that government is best which governs least;" and I should like to see it acted up to more rapidly and systematically. . . . The government itself, which is the only the mode which the people have chosen to execute their will is . . . . liable to be abused and perverted before the people can act through it. Witness the present Mexican war, the work of comparatively a few individuals using the standing government as their tool; for, in the outset, the people would not have consented to this measure. . . .

. . . . Law never made men a whit more just; and, by means of their respect for it, even the well-disposed are daily made the agents of injustice. A common and natural result of an undue respect for law is, that you may see a file of soldiers, colonel, captain, corporal, privates, power-monkeys, and all, marching in admirable order over hill and dale to wars, against their wills, ay, against their common sense and consciences, which makes it very steep marching indeed, and produces a palpitation of the heart. . . .

There are thousands who are in opinion opposed to slavery and to the war, who yet effect do nothing to put an end to them; who, esteeming themselves children of Washington and Franklin, sit down with their hands in their pockets, and say that they know not what to do, and do nothing; . . . They hesitate, and they regret, and sometimes they petition; but they do nothing in earnest and with effect. They will wait, well disposed, for others to remedy the evil, that they may no longer have it to regret. . . . There are nine hundred and ninety-nine patrons of virtue to one virtuous man. . . .

Document G

Source: Lyrics, "Santy Anno" (sung by soldiers and sailors in the Mexican War).

When Zacharias Taylor gained the day,
Heave away, Santy Anno;
He made poor Santy run away,
All on the plains of Mexico.

So heave her up and away we'll go,
Heave away, Santy Anno;
Heave her up and away we'll go,
All on the plains of Mexico.

General Scott and Taylor, too,
Heave away, Santy Anno;
Have made poor Santy meet his Waterloo
All on the plains of Mexico

Santy Anno was a good old man,
Heave away, Santy Anno;
Till he got into war with your Uncle Sam
All on the plains of Mexico

SECTION II

Part B and Part C

(SUGGESTED TOTAL PLANNING AND WRITING TIME—70 MINUTES)
PERCENT OF SECTION II SCORE—55

Part B

Directions: Select ONE question to write about. You should spend about 5 minutes planning and 30 minutes writing your answer. Support your views with pertinent facts, and present your case clearly.

2. How did events in England shape colonial development in English North America in the seventeenth century?

3. Explain the causes *and* consequences of TWO of the following population movements in the United States during the period 1820–1860.

   The settlement of Texas
   The Mormon exodus to Utah
   The movement of the forty-niners to California
   The movement of free-soilers to Kansas

Part C

Directions: Select ONE question to write about. You should spend about 5 minutes planning and 30 minutes writing your answer. Support your views with pertinent facts, and present your case clearly.

4. Discuss the impact of TWO of the following books on American history (1950–1970).

   Baby and Child Care by Dr. Benjamin Spock
   Silent Spring by Rachel Carson
   The Feminine Mystique by Betty Friedan

5. Analyze the social, political, and economic factors between 1960 and 1980 that explain the rise of the New Right.

STOP

END OF EXAM

Answer Key
PRACTICE TEST 2

Multiple-Choice Questions

1.	**E**	21.	**C**	41.	**C**	61.	**E**
2.	**A**	22.	**C**	42.	**C**	62.	**E**
3.	**A**	23.	**B**	43.	**D**	63.	**E**
4.	**B**	24.	**C**	44.	**E**	64.	**A**
5.	**A**	25.	**A**	45.	**E**	65.	**C**
6.	**E**	26.	**E**	46.	**A**	66.	**D**
7.	**D**	27.	**C**	47.	**A**	67.	**E**
8.	**A**	28.	**E**	48.	**B**	68.	**D**
9.	**B**	29.	**D**	49.	**C**	69.	**C**
10.	**A**	30.	**D**	50.	**B**	70.	**B**
11.	**D**	31.	**B**	51.	**C**	71.	**E**
12.	**D**	32.	**C**	52.	**A**	72.	**E**
13.	**E**	33.	**A**	53.	**D**	73.	**B**
14.	**C**	34.	**B**	54.	**C**	74.	**A**
15.	**E**	35.	**B**	55.	**D**	75.	**C**
16.	**D**	36.	**D**	56.	**B**	76.	**E**
17.	**A**	37.	**C**	57.	**C**	77.	**C**
18.	**B**	38.	**B**	58.	**D**	78.	**A**
19.	**A**	39.	**E**	59.	**D**	79.	**C**
20.	**C**	40.	**D**	60.	**D**	80.	**D**

PRACTICE TEST 2: ANSWER EXPLANATIONS

1. **(E)** Mercantilism is an economic and political system based on a series of assumptions about the world. These assumptions include the idea that there is a limited amount of wealth in the world and that governments must try to maximize their country's share of the wealth (D). This is not a system of free trade and laissez-faire capitalism. This is a system in which the government regulates and guides economic activity (C). One of the important ways a nation can maximize its wealth is to obtain colonies. These colonies are to supply the mother country with raw materials (A). If the mother country can get inexpensive raw materials from within its empire, then it can process and manufacture goods to sell on the global market. In this way, the mother country will maintain a favorable balance of trade (B). It is not in the mother country's interest to usher its colonies toward independence.

2. **(A)** King James was concerned about the mismanagement of the colony's finances and was worried about the effect that the recently formed representative assembly, the House of Burgesses, would have on his authority. James wanted to exert more political and economic control over Virginia, hoping to ensure personal profit for himself. Colonists did not suffer a defeat at the hands of native Americans significant enough to force them to leave (B). Negotiations between the colonists and local tribes were regularly beneficial to the colonists (C). Both John Smith and John Rolfe had voluntarily returned to England by 1622 (D), Smith in order to recover from injuries suffered in a gunpowder accident and Rolfe to accompany his Native wife, Pocahontas, and their newborn baby. The Dutch did not ally with the English to attack Algonquian Tribes (E).

3. **(A)** After the French and Indian War (1754–1763), Great Britain was in serious debt after nearly fifty years of constant warfare. Grenville instituted measures to help reduce this debt. One measure was the Stamp Act (1765), which imposed a tax on the paper used for various documents in the colonies, provoked the most intense opposition. This tax was solely a revenue-raising measure as opposed to earlier taxes that were designed to regulate trade. Many colonists asserted that only representatives elected by them could enact taxes on the colonies. "No taxation without representation" became their rallying cry. The Stamp Act itself was rescinded, but a series of additional British taxes were to come. .

4. **(B)** Shays's Rebellion was a major rebellion by western Massachusetts farmers against a series of policies implemented by the state legislature. The legislature was dominated by moneyed interests, and its policies reflected those interests. Taxes were high in order for Massachusetts to pay off its war debt to wealthy creditors. Farmers were losing their farms to banks. Led by Daniel Shays, farmers struck back—employing the lessons and tactics they learned as revolutionaries fighting the British. The rebellion lasted months and struck fear into the moneyed classes in Massachusetts and beyond. The event is an important catalyst for the Constitutional Convention. Choice A describes

events such as the Boston Tea Party (1773). Choice C describes events such as the Stono Rebellion (1739). Choice E describes Bacon's Rebellion (1676).

5. **(A)** *Uncle Tom's Cabin* (1852) is often considered one of the causes of the Civil War because it intensified antislavery opinion in the North and angered defenders of slavery in the South. The novel depicted the cruelty of the slave system, especially of the vicious slave owner, Simon Legree. Stowe's novel is not considered great art. It is written in a melodramatic manner, and the depictions of African Americans are stereotyped and demeaning. However, its impact on American history cannot be minimized. The novel was written by a white woman, not an escaped slave (E). One of the first published narratives written by a former slave is *The Interesting Narrative of the Life of Olaudah Equiano* (1789).

6. **(E)** After the Civil War, the United States had outlawed slavery and enacted programs such as the Homestead Act and Morrill Land Grant Act, both passed in 1862, to encourage western settlement and agricultural and technological advancement. The United States moved away from the labor-intensive system of plantation slavery and toward mechanized agriculture. This enticed residents of eastern cities, former slaves, and immigrants from Europe to the west with the promise of free land under the Homestead Act of 1862. The other choices were all factors in the Panic of 1873 to varying degrees. Political wrangling over the gold standard and bimetallism would continue to be a major issue in the last quarter of the nineteenth century (A). The rampant growth of railroads, aided by government support in the form of free land grants to railroad companies, and economic speculation by Jay Cooke and others contributed to the collapse of many lending institutions (B and C). Increasing trade ties to Europe had a growing effect on the American economy after the Civil War (E).

7. **(D)** American politics during and after World War I were marked by strong nationalist sentiments, as noted by powerful anti-German propaganda during the war and fears of anarchists and communists after the war. Anti-German feelings contributed to such changes as renaming food items like sauerkraut to "liberty cabbage" and sometimes even led to outright violence against people of German heritage. The postwar "Red Scare" capitalized on fears of communist revolution and long-standing fears of the influence of immigrants. Choice A places the greatest influence of the Progressives about ten years later than the movement's actual peak under the presidency of Theodore Roosevelt. President Wilson and the Democratic Party saw political losses in the election of 1918 mainly because of his broken promise to maintain American neutrality in the war (B). With both the implicit and explicit support of President Wilson, African Americans were further marginalized in both politics and society (C), including Wilson's executive action to segregate federal employment and the resurgence of the Ku Klux Klan and persistent racism in both the North and the South. Women saw greater acceptance and recognition because of their wartime contributions, culminating in the ratification of the Nineteenth Amendment in 1920, granting suffrage to women.

8. **(A)** Dr. Francis Townsend campaigned doggedly for a program to provide pensions for the elderly. President Franklin D. Roosevelt addressed this concern by creating the Social Security system in 1935. Social Security remains one of the most important legacies of the New Deal. Choice B refers to Huey P. Long; choice D might refer to Charles Lindbergh. Choice E refers to Frances Perkins, the first woman appointed to a cabinet post.

9. **(B)** The two committees mentioned in the question were congressional committees, charged with investigating domestic communism. This period of anticommunist fear is often called the McCarthy period, named after Senator Joseph McCarthy, the leading figure in the movement. Senator Joseph McCarthy became the central figure in this movement. In 1950, he announced that he had a list of "known communists" who had infiltrated the State Department. This and similar claims, mostly baseless, created a name for McCarthy. Congress especially targeted the entertainment industry, fearing that communists would subtly get their message out through television and movies. Leading members of the party were arrested under the antiespionage Smith Act. Loyalty oaths became commonplace for public-sector employees. Choice C refers to the Espionage and Sedition Acts (1917).

10. **(A)** The Glorious Revolution led to checks on royal power. Protestant members of parliament became concerned when the Catholic king, James II, had a son, who would inherit the throne and create a dynasty of Catholic kings. These Protestants had hopes that the daughter of James II, Mary, would ascend the throne because she and her husband, William, were Protestant. These parliamentarians took matters into their own hands; they joined with allies to topple James II and install William and Mary as monarchs. This had the effect of elevating the stature and power of Parliament. The bold flouting of authority had an impact on the colonies; New Englanders deposed the hated governor Edmund Andros of the Dominion of New England. Soon, individual colonial charters were reinstated.

11. **(D)** The Battle of Saratoga was a turning point in the American Revolution. It demonstrated that the British would have a great deal of difficulty controlling the vast North American countryside. It also demonstrated to France that the Continental Army was a formidable force. France joined the colonists in the war soon after (making choice B incorrect). Great Britain won many significant battles in the North (A); it held on to New York City throughout the war. The colonists were most successful when they used unorthodox, guerilla tactics (C).

12. **(D)** The Northwest Ordinance laid out a plan for the territorial growth of the United States. It stipulated that when a territory reached 60,000 free inhabitants, it would be eligible for statehood. The law was passed during the Articles of Confederation period (1781–1788). Dealing with the land of the Northwest Territory was one of the major successes of this period. This method for creating new states continued to be used after the articles were replaced by the Constitution in 1789.

13. **(E)** The Erie Canal (1825) connected the Great Lakes region, including the cities of Cleveland, Detroit, and Chicago, to New York City and to the Atlantic Ocean. The canal begins at the Hudson River and goes west to Lake Erie. Before the canal, it was incredibly difficult to move goods within the United States. The cost of moving a ton of freight from Buffalo to New York City went from $100 to $5 with the development of the Erie Canal. Choice A refers to the Panama Canal.

14. **(C)** In 1836 Texans fought for and won independence from Mexico, becoming the Lone Star Republic. Many Texans were eager for their Lone Star Republic to join the United States. Jackson and subsequent presidents were reluctant to exacerbate section tensions by admitting an additional slave state. The issue was put off until the election of the expansionist President Polk in 1844. Even before he took office, the outgoing President Tyler saw Polk's victory as a mandate for Texas annexation and pushed Texas annexation through Congress. Texas joined the United States as the fifteenth slave state in 1844.

15. **(E)** The 1863 riot was carried out mostly by Irish immigrants. The initial cause of the anger was the new draft law passed by Congress. It had a stipulation that one could pay a $300 commutation fee to avoid serving. The draft law led many working-class men to reason that the Civil War was a rich man's war but a poor man's fight. In New York City, angry crowds gathered. They initially targeted government offices, but the events soon took an ugly turn. The rioters turned on the city's African-American population. Many African Americans were beaten and lynched. The death toll was about 120.

16. **(D)** The Populist Movement of the late-nineteenth century was concerned that the combined forces of banks and business interests in the East were exploiting the rights of farmers and the working class. The Populists felt that government policies enabled that exploitation to continue. Populist politicians argued that the foundation of American success was in its workers and farmers and that the wealth enjoyed by the so-called robber barons would not exist without the labor of those farmers and workers. Choice C is incorrect because it stipulates that the cartoon is opposed to the Populists and the preceding Granger movement, but the cartoon is in support of the farmers. The cartoon makes reference to class division, not unity (A), and does not refer to the details of agricultural practices (B and E).

17. **(A)** Progressive Lincoln Steffens focused on the political corruption found in Philadelphia and other American cities. He detailed the fraud and cronyism of the political machines that had dominated urban politics in the last half of the nineteenth century, and into the twentieth century. The devastating hurricane that hit Galveston, Texas, in 1900 led to a reorganization of the city's government in an attempt to eliminate inefficiency, which was a major goal of the Progressive Movement. One of the complaints of the Progressive Movement was that there were too few regulations governing municipal politics (B). Although it was true that African-American residential areas were generally worse off than white neighborhoods, their well-being was

not a significant concern of the Progressive Movement (C). The Galveston Commission ended up creating a safer city through urban planning. However, Steffens was not concerned with that aspect of city life (D). Neither Steffens nor the Galveston Commission focused on criminal activity. Steffens reserved his main criticisms for the fraud and corruption of political machines.

18. **(B)** The quotation is from Wilson's address to Congress asking for a Declaration of War against Germany. Wilson's idealism—the desire to make the world "safe for democracy"—is one of several reasons for U.S. involvement in World War I. The United States also had economic reasons for entering the war, such as extensive trade with Great Britain. In the other choices, the presidents and the wars are all correctly matched. However, the speech was given on the eve of World War I.

19. **(A)** All of the items in the choices are elements of the New Right agenda except increasing taxes for Social Security. The New Right had been gestating since the 1960s but really became a powerful force with the election of President Ronald Reagan in 1980. It continued to remain strong with the election of the more conservative George W. Bush in 2000. The agenda touches on social, political, and economic issues.

20. **(C)** Puritans were disappointed that the Anglican Church (the Church of England) had made only a partial reformation. It broke away from the Catholic Church, under the guidance of King Henry VIII, in the 1530s. However, Henry was not interested in implementing the theological agenda of the more radical Protestant reformers, such as Martin Luther or John Calvin. Puritanism developed in Great Britain in the 1600s to urge a more thorough reformation. Kings James I and Charles I did not appreciate the challenges to their religious authority and made life uncomfortable for the Puritans. Hence, many Puritans left Great Britain and made their way to New England.

21. **(C)** Bacon's Rebellion was an important event in colonial history because it convinced the planter elite that having an underclass of discontented poor whites in the hinterland could be dangerous. Poor whites, many of them former indentured servants, had migrated into the hills and backcountry of Virginia to scratch out a living. They became increasingly angry at unfair taxation policies, raids from Native Americans, and a lack of voice in the House of Burgesses. Nathaniel Bacon, a wealthy planter himself, organized this discontent into a violent uprising. In its aftermath, the planter class increasingly turned to African slavery as their primary source of labor. Subsequently, the planter elite and the backcountry farmers could find common ground on the issue of racial hierarchy; both classes could see themselves as part of the "superior" race. The rebellion was about the Indian question, but it was aimed at the planter elite, not at native peoples (E).

22. **(C)** After the American Revolution, Great Britain refused to abandon its forts in the West until the United States dealt fairly with loyalists. The United States had other problems with foreign nations, most notably with Spain over control of the Mississippi River. However, the other choices were not

problems of the United States following the revolution. The United States had problems with Mexico over the Texas border (A) much later (1848). The other events did not occur.

23. **(B)** The makeup of the House of Representatives was initially based on one representative for every 30,000 people. This required knowing how many people lived in each state. The census occurs every ten years. The three-fifths compromise at the Constitutional Convention called for counting each slave as three-fifths of a person. Over time, the population of the nation grew dramatically. The ratio of constituents per representative grew; by 1910, it was over 200,000 constituents per representative. Still, the total number of representatives in the House kept growing as well. It was capped at 435 in 1911. Each member now represents, on average, approximately 650,000 people.

24. **(C)** Led by the Black Ball Line in New York City, shipping companies reformed their policies to establish fixed departure schedules in an attempt to maximize profits. These set schedules forced manufacturers and merchants to adhere more to the desires of the shippers, modifying their own schedules of production. Transatlantic ships continued to carry diverse cargo in the nineteenth century, unchanged from the practices of the eighteenth century (A). Choice B is incorrect because the United States maintained import duties throughout the nineteenth century as its main source of government revenue. Immigrant labor on ships was significantly more common than slave labor (D). American disputes with the Barbary Pirates would not be resolved until 1815. However, naval involvement took the form of sea battles against the pirates, not escort duty (E).

25. **(A)** Mill owners were extremely willing to hire immigrant workers because the unskilled immigrants worked for much lower pay than nonimmigrants. Mill owners advocated open immigration policies as a means to increase the profitability of their factories. All of the other choices were found in the arguments used by mid- and nineteenth-century nativists. The decline of the Whigs came in part because the Democrats expressly courted the favor of the growing immigrant population (B). The poverty of many European immigrants was a concern of nativists, who were sometimes apt to see a conspiracy of Europeans to encourage their lower classes to move to America (C). Cultural prejudices against the Scots, Irish, and Germans were displayed in both politics and in social reform efforts such as the temperance movement (D and E).

26. **(E)** President Grant's Peace Policy towards Native Americans was, in many ways, a precursor of the Dawes Act of 1882, which made assimilation of native peoples into American culture a principle of national policy. Grant was looking for ways to ensure that native tribes would not be violent toward the increasing number of American settlers moving west following the Civil War. He hoped that making reservation life more attractive to the tribes by providing resources would ease tensions, but his paternalistic policy did not achieve this goal. Allowing native tribes to live in their ancestral homes was out of the question for the United States Government since that would require reverting

to a precolonial territorial status, thereby ending the existence of the United States (A). Native Americans were not granted citizenship until the Indian Citizenship Act of 1924 (B). The purpose of Grant's policy was to bring the native peoples under the supervision of the United States government, not allow for more tribal autonomy (C). Similar to choice A, choice D was out of the question because the restitution that would be required would be too exorbitant for the government and the American people to consider.

27. **(C)** The professed religiosity of urban landlords did not seem to match their treatment of tenants. Landlords claimed to adhere to the moral standards of mainstream Christianity but then refused to listen to the concerns of their tenants regarding the squalid living conditions found in the tenements. The Catholic Church was neither a major landlord in the cities nor apt to ignore the urban poor (A). The Protestant churches were willing to provide aid to the poor, no matter their religious denomination (E).

28. **(E)** Art produced by the Works Progress Administration (WPA) often showed ordinary people, especially workers, in an ennobling manner—not demeaning or condescending. These art works could be found in post offices, relief offices, schools, and elsewhere. The main goal of the WPA was to provide work for people. A secondary goal was to get art to the people, not restrict it to stuffy museums (making choice B incorrect).

29. **(D)** The Hollywood 10 was a group of directors and writers who refused to cooperate with McCarthyism. Both the Senate and the House had committees investigating supposed communist infiltration in various walks of American life. Congress especially targeted the entertainment industry, fearing that communists would subtly get their message out through television and movies. In 1947, the Hollywood 10 was summoned to testify in Washington. They refused, citing their First Amendment rights to freedom of speech and assembly. These ten and others who refused to cooperate were blacklisted in the 1950s, unable to find work in Hollywood.

30. **(D)** Both the Mayflower Compact and the Virginia House of Burgesses represented steps toward representative government. The Mayflower Compact was a document written and signed by the Pilgrims onboard the *Mayflower* before it touched land at Plymouth, Massachusetts, in 1620. The King had granted the Pilgrims land farther south in Virginia. To give themselves a sense of legitimacy in an area in which they had no legal status, the Pilgrims agreed in this document to set up a government and obey its laws. The House of Burgesses was created by the Virginia Company in 1619. The company saw the need for some sort of body to govern the inhabitants of the colony and created this representative assembly. Choice A describes Roger Williams's motivation for founding Rhode Island. Choice C describes the Declaration of Independence. Choice E describes mercantilist policies.

31. **(B)** Jefferson's worries about the irascible Adams were well-founded. Adams had a tendency to rub his peers the wrong way, and Jefferson worried that negotiations to end the war with Great Britain would be affected by Adams's often unpredictable temperament. Choice A is incorrect because a delegation

of Americans, including Franklin and Adams, had negotiated an alliance with France in 1778. The strained relationship between the United States and France did not start until after the French Revolution began in 1789 and reached its zenith during the presidency of John Adams from 1797–1801 (C). British impressments of American sailors was a major contributing cause of the War of 1812 between the two nations (D). The conflict alluded to in (E) did not occur until 1793.

32. **(C)** President Washington was determined not to have a repeat of Shays's Rebellion (1786–1787). The Whiskey Rebellion occurred in 1794, but its origins were several years earlier. In 1791, Secretary of State Alexander Hamilton proposed a broad, ambitious financial program to establish the United States on sound financial ground. To pay off war debts, Hamilton proposed enacting new taxes, including a controversial tax on whiskey. This tax hit grain farmers especially hard. A group of grain farmers from western Pennsylvania felt that they could not shoulder this substantial tax. In 1794, farmers took action. Fifty men gathered and marched to the home of the local tax collector. From there, the gathering swelled to 7,000 men who marched to Pittsburgh. At this point, the federal government took action. Washington nationalized nearly 13,000 militiamen into the army and marched them himself to Pennsylvania to suppress the rebellion and ensure that the laws of the land were followed. Washington's response established federal authority and made clear that a strong national government would not tolerate unlawful challenges to its authority.

33. **(A)** The Land Act of 1820 and the Relief Act of 1821 reformed federal policy regarding the sale of land in the western territories and states in an effort to ease the debt burden on farmers. For example, the Relief Act allowed settlers to return land to the government in return for a credit on their debt. There were proposals both to raise and to lower tariff rates during the economic crisis (B), but President James Monroe opted to maintain a stable policy. Settlement houses, which were rarely supported by government funding, did not arise until the late 1880s in the United States (C). President Monroe rejected a proposal for a government-run public works program, believing that a constitutional amendment was needed to implement the plan (D). The Whig Party did not come into existence until the 1830s when the party was formed in opposition to what it considered to be the tyranny of President Andrew Jackson (E).

34. **(B)** As American settlement pushed the western frontier beyond the Mississippi River, the question of how to determine land use and the sale of federally administered land was in flux. Two solutions eventually put into law by Congress were preemption and graduation. Preemption allowed squatters who had settled on land yet to be surveyed to purchase the land prior to a public sale. Graduation refers to reducing the price of land based on how long the land had been for sale. Together, these two policies kept land costs low and encouraged settlement of the American West. Although there were several proposals for gradual abolition of slavery (A), preemption does not match up with those proposals. The debt incurred fighting the War of 1812

(C) was paid off through the combination of the mildly protectionist Tariff of 1816 and the general economic growth at the beginning of the Era of Good Feelings. The claims of the United States and Great Britain over the Oregon Territory were resolved by a series of treaties signed between 1818 and 1871 (D). The citizenship rights of immigrants in the 1820s and 1830s were subject to the same five-year waiting period enacted by Congress in 1802 and would not be altered until 1847 (E).

35. **(B)** The beating of Senator Charles Sumner on the floor of the Senate shocked many northerners. Senator Charles Sumner had just given a pointed antislavery speech in which he singled out Senator Andrew P. Butler of South Carolina. Butler's nephew, a South Carolina representative named Preston Brooks, heard about the speech. Brooks went over to Sumner's desk in the Senate chamber and beat him repeatedly with a heavy cane, nearly killing him. Southerners made Brooks a hero. Lincoln was assassinated (A) but later (1865). The other events did not occur.

36. **(D)** Both the Platt Amendment and the Open Door Policy expanded America's role in foreign nations. The United States forced Cuba to insert the Platt Amendment into their constitution following the Spanish-American War (1898). The amendment allowed the United States to intervene in Cuban affairs militarily if it saw fit. Americans troops intervened in Cuba three times between 1902 and 1920. The Open Door Policy was put forth by President McKinley's Secretary of State John Hay in 1900 in order to open up China to American trade. In the 1890s, the major European powers had established spheres of influence in China. These nations each declared that they had exclusive trading privileges in their sphere of influence. The United States asserted that all of China should be open to trade with all nations. The European nations begrudgingly accepted this concept. Neither move embodied progressive goals (A) nor were they welcomed by anti-imperialists (B).

37. **(C)** The Federal Reserve Bank (the Fed) regulates the amount of money in circulation. The Fed regulates the money supply either to encourage or to discourage economic activity. The Fed might want more money in circulation if the economy is sluggish and unemployment is rising. Conversely, it might want less money in circulation if economic activity is so intense that it threatens to create inflation. The Fed has a number of tools at its disposal to regulate the currency supply. The most well-known mechanism is raising or lowering the interest rates at which the Fed loans money to other banks. Other banks follow suit, raising or lowering the interest rates at which they loan money to the public. Choice A describes the World Bank or the International Monetary Fund (both created in 1944). The creation of the Fed did the opposite of choice B—it decentralized financial power by established Fed branches throughout the country. Choice D never happened in the United States—it entails a shift to socialism.

38. **(B)** The combination of North Korean communism and the involvement of the new Communist government in China fueled America's fear of domestic communism. Senator Joseph McCarthy of Wisconsin was quick to exploit those fears by claiming to have knowledge of communists within the United

States government, claims that led to highly publicized Senate hearings on the issue. McCarthy's claims were eventually discredited. He was censured by the Senate, losing the support of most Americans along the way. The Korean War coupled with the effects of an economic downturn diminished the popularity of both President Truman and the Democratic Party, allowing the Republicans to make electoral gains in 1950 (A). The Senate continued to fund United States involvement in both the United Nations and the ostensibly U.N.-led Korean conflict (C). The United States and Soviet Union did not have any major negotiations during the Korean War and would not meet openly about peace until the 1970s (D). An organized and vociferous antiwar movement did not come about until the middle part of the 1960s when American involvement in Vietnam began to escalate under President Lyndon Johnson.

39. **(E)** The march was organized by the Dallas County Voters League and the Student Nonviolent Coordinating Committee. Marchers were met with fierce opposition by law enforcement at the Edmund Pettus Bridge in Selma. The attack by police on the marchers was captured on network television and served to increase support for the civil rights movement in many parts of the country. There were two subsequent marches. The last march made the entire journey to Montgomery because several thousand soldiers and federal law enforcement officials escorted the marchers. The march was specifically intended to protest the lack of voting rights for blacks and had nothing to do with Native Americans (B) or tensions between the nonviolent and Black Power factions of the civil rights movement (C). The Weather Underground was well known for advocating violence in protest against the United States government, mostly for its involvement in the Vietnam War, not for the civil rights policies of individual states (D).

40. **(D)** Many colonial colleges, including the College of William & Mary, Harvard, Yale, and most other Ivy League schools, were originally intended to educate the young men of their immediate area as clergy in a particular religious sect. This mission changed with the growing nation. By the early part of the 1800s, most of the colleges had expanded their curricula to include programs in the classical liberal arts. In the midnineeenth century, newer colleges arose that focused on agriculture, engineering, and the sciences. Tuition for these colonial colleges was not usually exorbitant and was not often even paid by the student but by a prominent sponsor of that student (A). There were many institutions of higher learning outside of New England prior to the 1830s, the most prominent of which was the College of William & Mary in Williamsburg, Virginia, founded in 1693 (C). College football did not develop until the middle part of the 1800s, with the first official game being played between Rutgers and Princeton in 1869 (E).

41. **(C)** In the XYZ Affair, French officials demanded payment from an American delegation before the Americans would be permitted an audience with the French Foreign Minister Talleyrand. President John Adams deemed the demand to be an affront to the honor of the United States. He moved to make American relations with France more hostile, including authoriz-

ing the U.S. Navy to fire upon French warships in the Atlantic Ocean. The Democratic Republicans and Federalists were divided for nearly a decade over what the American policy toward the government of revolutionary France should be. However, the XYZ Affair temporarily closed that divide (A) and caused United States policy to move away from, not toward, France (B). Another response of the Federalists and President Adams was to enact the Alien and Sedition Acts to curtail activities by any suspected French agents in America (D). Spain was in possession of the Louisiana Territory in 1798, not France (E).

42. **(C)** The source of the quote is Chief Justice John Marshall's decision in the landmark case *Gibbons* v. *Ogden* (1824), a ruling concerning the commerce clause of Article I of the Constitution. Marshall's ruling confirmed that Congress had broad powers to regulate commerce "among the several States" because Congress, in the same article of the Constitution, was granted the power to make all laws "necessary and proper" to carry out its enumerated powers. The other important political leaders listed here were all opposed to extending the powers of Congress.

43. **(D)** In the 1820s, many states eliminated property qualifications for voting. This meant that voting was no longer restricted to just the propertied class. The number of people voting rose dramatically.

44. **(E)** The acquisition of the Mexican Session heightened sectional tensions when California, part of the Mexican Cession, applied for statehood in 1850. A large percentage of the 300,000 people who migrated to California came in 1849, thus their nickname "forty-niners." By 1850, California had enough people to form a state. Californians wrote up a constitution to submit to Congress in which slavery would be illegal. Southern senators objected to the admission of an additional free state. Senate negotiators worked out a series of measures that became known as the Compromise of 1850. The most important elements of the compromise were the admittance of California as a free state, which pleased northern politicians, and a more stringent Fugitive Slave Law, which pleased southern politicians. Choice B was caused by the Kansas-Nebraska Act (1854).

45. **(E)** Irish immigrants tended to push down wages for American workers. Many of the Irish immigrants left Ireland during the worst years of the potato famine (late 1840s and 1850s). They had nothing and were ready to take any job offered at any pay. They tended to be unskilled rural people (A). Relations between Catholic and Protestants worsened during this period (C).

46. **(A)** As workers banded together in the late 1800s to demand better working conditions and fair pay, large corporations and their owners resisted the workers' efforts with violence. The corporations hired independent agents, including the Pinkerton Detective Agency, and received help from local and federal authorities to suppress the striking workers. It would not be until the early 1900s that organized labor received some support from government entities in the form of mediation and arbitration (C). Neither strike was organized by the AFL (B). Since most unions were closed, racially segregated

shops, there was not any real racial unity on the picket lines (D). Miners and steelworkers were unskilled and were seeking to improve working conditions, not an end to mechanized production (E).

47. **(A)** Southern Democrats were critical of the imperialistic tendencies of Republicans, especially because of the apparent hypocrisy of the Republicans—proponents of political and civil rights in the South but opponents of those same rights for conquered people in the new American empire. Southern Democrats felt that their position in opposition to imperialism was more consistent because they felt that anyone considered to be innately inferior would be incapable of political participation. Progressives such as President Theodore Roosevelt were often quite eager to extend the ideals of American democracy abroad (B). The election of 1900 was indeed won by William McKinley. However, McKinley was the imperialist and his opponent William Jennings Bryan was the anti-imperialist (C). Although Cuba was granted self-government in the years after the Spanish-American War, Puerto Rico remains a territory of the United States (D). The American Federation of Labor (E) was, as its name suggests, focused on improving the conditions of American workers.

48. **(B)** As Theodore Roosevelt's chosen successor, William Howard Taft was expected to continue the progressive policies of Roosevelt. Instead, Taft broke from the precedent set by his predecessor and began to roll back much of Roosevelt's agenda, including firing Roosevelt's friend and advisor on conservation issues, Gifford Pinchot. Taft's actions were not designed to reduce the federal deficit (A) or pursue government efficiency (D). Rather, their purpose was to gain the support of business interests (C). He ignored the complaints of muckrakers (E).

49. **(C)** George Kennan's containment strategy, issued in 1947, was adopted by the United States with the hope that by applying political and economic pressure combined with selective military force, the Soviet Union would not be able to expand its influence at the expense of American interests. One of the first tests of this strategy came in the Korean War of 1950–1953. Kennan's memo predated the presidency of Dwight Eisenhower (D). Franklin Roosevelt's third inaugural address focused on rallying Americans to victory in World War II, not defeating communism (B). President Wilson's Fourteen Points were created to address problems after World War I (A). General Douglas MacArthur's most famous testimony before Congress came during the Korean War, in which he argued for more battlefield autonomy for commanders and expressed agreement with Kennan's already-established containment strategy (E).

50. **(B)** The ascension of Oliver Cromwell to power in England led the Puritan movement to stay put in England rather than venture to New England. In fact, some New England Puritans made their way back to England when Cromwell took over. Cromwell himself was a Puritan. So his brief reign as the Lord Protector of England (1653–1658) was an event celebrated by Puritans.

51. **(C)** The original draft of the Declaration of Independence contained a section condemning the slave trade and blaming the king for imposing it on the colonies. Of course, many colonists participated in the slave trade on their own and with great enthusiasm. Even if the statement was somewhat inaccurate, it did reflect pointed criticism of the slave trade. Many southern delegates to the Second Continental Congress refused to sign the Declaration if that language remained, so Jefferson agreed to remove it.

52. **(A)** When Hamilton issued his Report on Public Credit in 1790, it was met with an uproar in many southern states because of the proposal for the federal government to assume the war debts of the individual states. The southern states, which had little remaining debt, felt that this plan favored the northern states and would force the southern states to pay debts that they had not incurred. The sectional rift was calmed by a compromise between Hamilton and James Madison that allowed the assumption plan to proceed and placed the new federal capital in the South. The elastic clause (B) was not an issue yet, although Hamilton and his Federalist Party would soon find opposition to their plans to broaden the scope of federal powers (C) from Democratic Republicans like Jefferson and Madison (D). A major part of Hamilton's plan was to ensure the long-term stability of the national economy by encouraging investment in a national bank by wealthy Americans and by maintaining a sustainable national debt in order to entice foreign loans (E).

53. **(D)** Both events revolve around the question of nullification. Nullification is the theory that a state could declare an objectionable law null and void within that state. In actuality, only the Supreme Court can strike down a federal law if it finds the law to be inconsistent with the Constitution. In the Virginia and Kentucky Resolutions, Thomas Jefferson and James Madison asserted the state power of nullification after President John Adams signed the Alien and Sedition Acts into law (1798). In 1832, Jackson's Vice President John C. Calhoun led a group of South Carolina politicians to assert that the Tariff Act of 1828 should be nullified. Jackson was alarmed at this flaunting of federal authority and challenged the move. A face-saving compromise was arranged.

54. **(C)** American immigrants to the Mexican state of Texas brought the system of slavery with them. They moved to Texas to buy inexpensive land on which to grow cotton. Mexico had previously made slavery illegal. This blatant violation of Mexican law angered the Mexican Government and led to clashes that resulted in Texas winning its independence (1836). Later in 1845, Texas was annexed by the United States.

55. **(D)** The Ostend Manifesto grew out of a meeting of several diplomats in Ostend, Belgium (1854), calling for the United States to buy Cuba from Spain. If Spain refused to sell, the document asserted, the United States would be "justified in wrestling" it from Spain. The manifesto reflects the desires of southern politicians who wanted to extend their slave empire. Events around the Kansas-Nebraska Act (1854) derailed the whole plan.

56. **(B)** The three World War I–era agencies and acts reflect the growing power of the federal government during the war. In many ways, this growth of fed-

eral power was just what the progressive movement had hoped for. It championed the idea of an active government that would address a wide variety of societal needs. Only the Espionage and Sedition Acts were attempts to silence opposition to the war (A). The progressives were disappointed when the government abandoned this approach after the war.

57. **(C)** The Nye Committee made a connection between the profits of war industries and banking during World War I and the reasons President Wilson and Congress declared war on Germany. Another key element in support of an isolationist policy that arose from the Nye Committee was the value of the loans made to European nations prior to World War I, with an inordinate amount going to Great Britain and France as compared with what went to Germany. The implication was that the United States entered the war to protect its commercial ties to Britain, not to secure democracy. Shortly after the Nye Committee started hearings, Congress passed a series of Neutrality Acts at the urging of those holding isolationist sentiments. Roosevelt's New Deal measures to provide government aid to struggling Americans were not at issue in the Nye Committee hearings (A). The committee's recommendations were not acted upon by the Supreme Court (B), nor did the hearings result in a shakeup of the War Department (D) or President Roosevelt nationalizing arms manufacturing (E).

58. **(D)** The increased awareness of the plight of migrant farmworkers brought about by John Steinbeck's novel spurred the Farm Security Administration to provide more resources for economic relief and for relocation expenses that were part of the hardship suffered by the Dust Bowl refugees. California, the destination of many of these refugees, did not and could not constitutionally close its borders (A) to the migrants. Although the sustained drought that contributed to the Dust Bowl ended, it was not enough to entice the "Okies" to return to the Midwest. Virtually all of them remained in California (B). Steinbeck was vilified for having socialist or even communist beliefs after the publication of *The Grapes of Wrath* but never testified (C) before the House Un-American Activities Committee. However, he did speak out against the committee's treatment of his friend, playwright Arthur Miller. *The Grapes of Wrath* was a sensation upon its release and has remained a cultural touchstone in America ever since (E). The novel was cited by the Nobel Committee as a chief reason its author was given the Nobel Prize in Literature in 1962.

59. **(D)** The Berlin Airlift demonstrated United States resolve to challenge Soviet aggression. In 1948, the United States decided to challenge the Soviet blockade of West Berlin. West Berlin was part of West Germany (an American ally), but it was completely within the territory of East Germany (a Soviet ally). In 1948, the Soviet Union blockaded food and other supplies from entering West Berlin. The goal was for the Soviet Union to take over West Berlin and make it part of East Germany. The United States did not stand by idly when it learned of the Berlin blockade. President Truman decided to send thousands of planes, filled with supplies, into West Berlin in an action known as the Berlin Airlift. This action is not part of isolationism (C); it is very much an interventionist act.

60. **(D)** Calvinists, such as the Puritans, held that salvation was determined by God. This view is called predestination. Puritans specifically argued against the idea that salvation could be achieved through proper behavior (A). Martin Luther, another founder of the Protestant Reformation, argued that salvation could be achieved through an inner faith in God (B). Puritan thinking held that only a small percentage of humanity is predestined for salvation, but it did not believe that salvation was impossible (C). Puritans did not believe that salvation was in the hands of man (E).

61. **(E)** Richard Henry Lee and his anti-Federalist colleagues argued against the ratification of the Constitution because they felt that the document granted too much power to a central government, which was in opposition to the entire purpose of the Revolutionary War. Gaining independence from what was considered to be the tyrannical monarchy of Great Britain would be worthless if the Constitution enshrined another powerful government, according to Henry. Shays's Rebellion (A) took place in 1786, highlighting the vulnerability of the United States under the Articles of Confederation, and was a leading reason for the creation of the Constitutional Convention. The Northwest Ordinance (B) was one of the successes of Congress as it operated under the Articles of Confederation. The Virginia and Kentucky Resolutions (C) were a response to the Alien and Sedition Acts of 1798 (D), proposing that individual states could nullify acts of Congress that the states considered to be unconstitutional.

62. **(E)** The Democratic-Republican Party was opposed to the formation of a national bank. The idea of a national bank was put forth by Secretary of the Treasury Alexander Hamilton. Thomas Jefferson and others were suspicious of the idea. They did not want to see so much financial power in so few hands, and they also contended that it was not within the power of Congress to create such a bank. Hamilton countered by citing the elastic clause of the Constitution. The bank controversy was one of several issues that contributed to the formation of the first two political parties—the Democratic-Republicans and the Federalists. The French Revolution was another divisive issue.

63. **(E)** The ministers of the Second Great Awakening rejected the old Calvinist and Puritan idea that salvation was based on predestination. It held that people could try to improve themselves in order to improve their chances of getting into heaven. This was a more democratic notion of salvation and also a more hopeful one. The Second Great Awakening became a huge phenomenon during the first three decades of the 1800s. Temperance was a major issue that grew out of the movement—it involved personal improvement as well as societal improvement. Temperance advocates took a personal pledge to abstain from drinking, and they also advocated for the legal prohibition of alcohol.

64. **(A)** The initial impetus for the founding of the Whig Party (1833) was to oppose the policies of President Andrew Jackson. The Whigs took their name from an antimonarchical party in Great Britain. It fit because the Whigs accused Jackson of acting like a king. The Whigs were especially concerned with Jackson's opposition to the Second Bank of the United States.

The Whigs were not especially proslavery (B) or proexpansion (D). They embraced the internal improvements proposed by Henry Clay (C). Clay himself became a prominent Whig.

65. **(C)** President Lincoln accused the opposition Democratic Party of trying to brand all Republicans as radical abolitionists in an attempt to discredit the Republican Party as a whole, despite a lack of evidence that the Republican Party supported the abolition of slavery. The Republican Party platform only advocated limitations on the spread of slavery, not the outright abolition of the "peculiar institution." Lincoln was aware that there was very little common ground (A) on the issue of slavery. He was in favor of showing that the Democratic position on slavery was one of support for holding humans in bondage. Stephen A. Douglas's "Freeport Doctrine" was a defense of the concept of popular sovereignty. He advocated for local control of the decision over whether or not to allow slavery. Douglas took this position during a series of debates with Lincoln for a Senate seat from Illinois in 1858 (B). Lincoln's rhetoric following John Brown's 1859 raid at Harper's Ferry, Virginia, condemned Brown's actions and argued that Brown's attempts to foment slave rebellions were thoroughly misguided (D). Most of the accusations against Lincoln being a slaveholder have been leveled against him recently and have no historical basis (E).

66. **(D)** Both measures were used to avoid the Fifteenth Amendment. The Fifteenth Amendment (1870) declared that the right to vote shall not be denied on the basis of race. Following the ratification of the Fifteenth Amendment, southern states adopted a variety of measures to prevent African Americans from voting. These measures included instituting poll taxes and literacy tests. Poll taxes required people to pay a tax in order to vote. Literacy tests required people to demonstrate their ability to read before they were allowed to vote. These laws effectively prevented the vast majority of African Americans in the South from voting from the 1800s until passage of the Voting Rights Act in 1965. The First Amendment (A) deals with freedom of expression. The Eighth Amendment (B) bans cruel and unusual punishment. The Thirteenth Amendment (C) outlawed slavery. The Nineteenth Amendment (E) extended voting rights to women.

67. **(E)** Champions of an economic resurgence for the South in the late-nineteenth century hoped to forge alliances with northern investors so that the southern states could become competitive following the abolition of slavery. Advocates for the new South model were often wealthy. They were motivated to maintain that wealth by diversifying the economic base of the South and creating a strong industrial economy, not a resurgent plantation economy (C). Some in the movement pressed for greater racial harmony and an end to the sectional strife that had been the status quo for a century. They believed that northern capitalists would be more likely to invest in the South if the overt racism of southern life became a thing of the past. New South advocates were not concerned with political or civil rights for blacks (A), only industrial growth as a means to wider economic growth. The ideas of regaining southern honor and the antebellum traditions (B) are more associated with the

Lost Cause movement. The new South movement was intended to bolster the southern economy but did not mean to use this to mend fences with the North (D).

68. **(D)** The main point of the cartoon is that President Franklin D. Roosevelt has a secret agenda. The cartoon implies Roosevelt is creating programs to help people, but secretly is attempting to create some sort of dictatorship that would take away people's freedom. The cartoon reflects conservative criticisms of the New Deal. Note that the presence of a Trojan horse in a political cartoon implies that someone has a sinister agenda different from his stated agenda.

69. **(C)** Thurgood Marshall and the NAACP argued that segregation was damaging to African-American schoolchildren. The Supreme Court heard a variety of types of evidence in the case, including studies on the psychological impact of segregation on young people. The Court ruled unanimously that segregation in public schools was unfair and had to end. The Brown decision set in motion a major upheaval in American society. It gave great encouragement to the civil rights movement, which believed that the federal government was in favor of civil rights. Marshall would not have argued that African-American schools received less money than white schools (A); the logic of that argument would be to pressure states to provide additional funding for African-American schools. The NAACP did not want that. It wanted an end to segregated schools.

70. **(B)** The delegates at the Constitutional Convention did not discuss the morality of slavery (A). Their disagreement in regard to slavery grew out of the creation of the House of Representatives. Representation in the House would be based on population. The bigger the state, the more representatives it would have. How would slaves be counted in the census? Southern states wanted slaves counted to increase southern representation in the House. Northerners thought they should not be counted. The compromise counts each slave as three-fifths of a person. Interestingly, the word "slavery" does not appear in the Constitution. The Constitution tacitly accepted the legitimacy of slavery by establishing several rules in regard to slavery. For instance, the Constitution forbade interfering with the importation of "such persons" for 20 years. It mandated that "persons held in service" be returned if they escape to another state, and it included the "Three-Fifths" Compromise.

71. **(E)** The series of laws known as the Alien and Sedition Acts were signed by President John Adams. They were part of a wave of anti-French sentiment that accompanied the notorious XYZ Affair, in which French officials demanded what Adams and the American public perceived as a monetary tribute. Adams was given the authority to jail and deport French immigrants if they were deemed to be a threat to the general order of the United States. Later, Adams authorized the United States Navy to fire on French ships in the Atlantic in what became known as the Quasi-War as a way to protect American shipping. The laws passed Congress and were signed by Adams despite protests that they violated the freedoms of expression (A) guaranteed by the First Amendment, which was ratified in 1791. Adams was not

especially popular before signing the Alien and Sedition Acts and saw his popularity diminish rapidly after enacting the laws (B). However, there were no credible plots to remove him from power through assassination (D). The question of Irish immigration would not become a major part of American political discourse until the middle part of the 1800s (C).

72. **(E)** The cult of domesticity was the term used for the idea that the proper place for women is maintaining the house and caring for children, which prevented them from participating in public life. By using the word "cult," the term expresses a critique of the idea. By the middle of the nineteenth century, some women began to challenge the term, and its meaning. The women's rights convention at Seneca Falls, New York (1848), was an early attempt at challenging prevailing notions of gender.

73. **(B)** The Whig Party formed in opposition to the presidential policies of Andrew Jackson, which the party considered to be tyrannical. The Whigs advocated for the expansion of industrial and commercial enterprises as well as territorial expansion, provided that slavery was not permitted in the territories (C). By passing protective tariffs, the Whigs believed that American business and manufacturing could thrive. They also believed that with increased infrastructure projects such as the National Road, canals, and railroads, a strong and unified national economy would develop. Both parties enjoyed support throughout the country (A). Democrats drew much of their urban support from Catholic immigrants (E). Whigs found support from reformers that had their start in the revivalist Second Great Awakening (D).

74. **(A)** One of the provisions of the Compromise of 1850 was a stronger fugitive slave law. The Constitution stipulates that fugitive slaves are still the property of their owner. Without federal legislation, though, it was sometimes difficult to retrieve fugitive slaves. The act forced northern state officials and individuals to cooperate with southern slave catchers. The implementation of the law angered many northerners and contributed to sectional tensions in the 1850s.

75. **(C)** William Randolph Hearst, publisher of the *New York Journal*, gained prominence in the late-nineteenth century. He increased his readership through exaggerated, sensationalistic coverage of events. This yellow journalism played a role in the Spanish-American War (1898). In the exchange in the question, Hearst is acknowledging his power by indicating that his newspaper could push public opinion and government policy toward a declaration of war against Spain. Hearst's main competitor was Joseph Pulitzer, publisher of the *New York World*.

76. **(E)** Provisions of the Clayton Antitrust Act of 1914 effectively legalized union organizations and peaceful union practices such as boycotts, pickets, and strikes. Later legislation helped strengthen the intent of the Clayton Act, allowing union workers to bargain collectively without fear of prosecution under the price-fixing provisions of the preceding Sherman Antitrust Act. The Federal Trade Commission, established in separate legislation during Woodrow Wilson's presidency, was charged with enforcing (A) the Clayton

Act. The law specifically outlawed the practices in choice B and simply reaffirmed the Sherman Antitrust Act's prohibitions on the monopolistic practices of horizontal integration (C). The only exemptions in the law were the previously mentioned labor exemption and an exemption for agricultural cooperatives, not industrial cooperatives (D).

77. **(C)** A central goal of the Agricultural Adjustment Act (1933) was to reduce the amount of certain crops grown in the United States. This may seem like a counterintuitive idea during the Great Depression. However, there was overproduction of many crops during the 1930s, sending commodity prices down. Farmers barely received enough for their crops to cover the cost of production. By reducing the amount of crops produced, prices would go up and farmers could make a decent living. The act was declared unconstitutional by the Supreme Court in the case of *United States* v. *Butler* (1936).

78. **(A)** War production for World War II brought the United States out of the Great Depression. Almost overnight, unemployment plummeted and people had money in their pocket. During the war, the government tried to prevent inflation from getting out of control. The combination of many people having spending money and the scarcity of consumer goods would normally lead to runaway inflation.

79. **(C)** All of the factors in the question help explain the rise of suburbia after World War II except choice C, the construction of new train lines. New train lines were constructed from the 1830s well into the twentieth century, but very few new train lines were built after World War II. After the war, the automobile and highway construction (A) became far more important. Some suburbs are built on train lines but not usually lines built after World War II. The G.I. Bill (B) provided low-interest loans to returning veterans and helped families buy homes in the suburbs. New building techniques (D) were introduced by real estate developer William Levitt. The Federal Housing Administration (E) also provided loans to families to purchase suburban homes.

80. **(D)** President Reagan campaigned on bold rhetoric that promised to restore America's greatness in the eyes of the world, a standing that many conservatives believed had been damaged by the withdrawal from Vietnam and the perceived foreign policy accommodations of the Carter administration toward the Soviet Union and religious extremists in Iran. Reagan defiantly challenged the Soviet Union once he was elected. He aggressively reinstituted a form of the Cold War strategy of containment as part of U.S. foreign policy. Reagan's nationalistic language was given a great deal of credit for rebuilding the confidence individual Americans had in their country after a decade of domestic political and economic distress. However, the Reagan administration was accused of abandoning Vietnam veterans by cutting services for medical and mental health through the Veterans Administration hospitals (A and C). Reagan granted asylum to the refugees from Vietnam known as the "boat people," feeling that their ordeals in leaving Vietnam vindicated his views that the foreign policy of previous administrations had given way to totalitarian communism in Southeast Asia (E).

TEST SCORE WORKSHEET

To estimate what score you would earn on the actual AP exam, follow these steps.

Section I: Multiple Choice

Total correct (out of 80) ________

Number correct × 1.125 ________ (Do not round)
Raw Score

Section II: Free Response*

Question 1 ________ × 4.5 = ________
(out of 9)

Question 2 or 3 ________ × 2.75 = ________
(out of 9)

Question 4 or 5 ________ × 2.75 = ________
(out of 9)

____
Total

Final Score

________ + ________ = ________
Multiple-Choice Score *Free-Response Score* *Final Score (rounded)*

Score Conversion Chart

Raw Score	AP Grade**
111–180	5
91–110	4
76–90	3
57–75	2
0–56	1

*Do your best to assign an appropriate score for each essay or ask your teacher to do so. But remember that the score you assign yourself may not be the same score you would earn on the actual AP exam.

**The raw score corresponding to each grade varies from year to year. The chart above is an approximation of the score you would earn on the actual AP exam.

GENERAL RUBRIC FOR ALL FREE-RESPONSE QUESTIONS

The guidelines below describe the general expectations for each ranking level and is a good summary of what you need to do to write a good essay.

Top ranked essay: 8–9
1. Has a well constructed thesis that deals specifically with what the question asks
2. Effectively uses evidence to support the thesis
3. Uses English clearly and is well organized
4. Analyzes the information used, choosing relevant points
5. Minor errors are acceptable

Next level essay: 5–7
1. Contains a thesis that is relevant to the question
2. In a question with several parts, may concentrate on one or two parts and cover the other(s) in less depth; analysis may be weak in sections
3. Uses evidence to support thesis
4. Errors in language do not affect understanding of the essay; organization can be followed
5. Errors do not affect the total impact of the essay

Next level essay: 2–4
1. Presents a confusing, inadequate, or badly developed thesis
2. Weak analysis, general coverage, or simplistic explanation; may cover only part of the question
3. Contains general, often inaccurate evidence, or evidence that is irrelevant to the question
4. Organization is poor
5. Major errors are included

Next level essay: 0–1
1. Contains no thesis or an irrelevant one
2. Fails to show understanding of the question; lacks analysis
3. Evidence is lacking, poorly presented, or irrelevant
4. Organization is not clear and interferes with understanding the presentation

Index

THE FOLLOWING DOCUMENTATION APPLIES IF YOU PURCHASED

AP United States History **with CD-ROM.**

How to Use the CD-ROM

The software is not installed on your computer; it runs directly from the CD-ROM. Barron's CD-ROM includes an "autorun" feature that automatically launches the application when the CD is inserted into the CD-ROM drive. In the unlikely event that the autorun feature is disabled, follow the manual launching instructions below.

Windows®

1. Click on the Start button and choose "My Computer."
2. Double-click on the CD-ROM drive, which will be named **AP_US_History.exe**.
3. Double-click **AP_US_History.exe** to launch the program.

Mac®

1. Double-click the CD-ROM icon.
2. Double-click the **AP_US_History** icon to start the program.

SYSTEM REQUIREMENTS

(Flash Player 10.2 is recommended)

Microsoft® Windows®
Processor: Intel Pentium 4 2.33GHz, Athlon 64 2800+ or faster processor (or equivalent).
Memory: 128MB of RAM.
Graphics Memory: 128MB.
Platforms:
Windows 7, Windows Vista®, Windows XP, Windows Server® 2008, Windows Server 2003.

MAC® OS X
Processor: Intel Core™ Duo 1.33GHz or faster processor.
Memory: 256MB of RAM.
Graphics Memory: 128MB.
Platforms:
Mac OS X 10.6, Mac OS X 10.5, Mac OS X 10.4 (Intel) and higher.

Linux® and Solaris™
Processor: Intel Pentium 4 2.33GHz, AMD Athlon 64 2800+ or faster processor (or equivalent).
Memory: 512MB of RAM.
Graphics Memory: 128MB.
Platforms:
Red Hat® Enterprise Linux (RHEL) 5 or later, openSUSE® 11 or later, Ubuntu 9.10 or later.
Solaris: Solaris™ 10.